HERMES

在古希腊神话中,赫耳墨斯是宙斯和迈亚的儿子,奥林波斯神们的信使,道路与边界之神,睡眠与梦想之神,亡灵的引导者,演说者、商人、小偷、旅者和牧人的保护神……

西方传统 经典与解释
Classici et Commentarii **HERMES**
朗佩特集
The Collected Works
of Laurence Lampert

刘小枫●主编

哲学与哲学之诗
——施特劳斯、柏拉图、尼采

Philosophy and Philosophic Poetry
Strauss, Plato, Nietzsche

[加]朗佩特 Laurence Lampert ｜ 著

刘旭 吴一笛 ｜ 译

彭磊 ｜ 编校

华夏出版社

古典教育基金·"传德"资助项目

"朗佩特集"出版说明

朗佩特(1941—)以尼采研究著称,直到《哲学如何成为苏格拉底式的》(2010／华夏出版社,2015)问世之前,他的著述的书名都没有离开过尼采。《哲学如何成为苏格拉底式的》转向了柏拉图,该书"导言"虽然谈的是贯穿全书的问题,即柏拉图笔下的"苏格拉底是如何成为苏格拉底的",却以谈论尼采收尾。在该书"结语"部分,朗佩特几乎完全在谈尼采。

从尼采的视角来识读柏拉图,可以恰切地理解柏拉图吗?或者说,我们应该凭靠尼采的目光来识读柏拉图吗?朗佩特的要求不难理解,因为今人在思想上越长越矮,我们要理解古代高人,就得凭靠离我们较近的长得高的近人。不仅如此,这个长得高的近人还得有一个大抱负:致力于理解自身的文明思想传统及其面临的危机。否则,柏拉图与我们有何相干?

朗佩特在早年的《尼采与现时代》一书中已经提出:尼采开创了一部新的西方哲学史——这意味着他开创了一种理解西方古代甚至历代哲人的眼光。朗佩特宣称,他的柏拉图研究属于尼采所开创的新哲学史的"开端部分"。他提出的问题是:"柏拉图何以是一位尼采意义上的真正哲人?"这个问题让人吃惊,因为尼采的眼光成了衡量古人柏拉图甚至"真正的哲人"苏格拉底的尺度。尼采的衡量尺度是,伟大的哲人们应该是"命令者和立法者"。然而,这一衡量尺度不恰恰来自柏拉图吗?朗佩特为何要而且公然敢倒过来说?为什么他不问:"尼采何以是一位柏拉图意义上的真正哲人?"

朗佩特宣称,"对于一部尼采式的哲学史来说,施特劳斯几乎是不可或缺的源泉"。这无异于告诉读者,他对尼采的理解来自施特劳斯——这让我们想起朗佩特早年的另一部专著《施特劳斯与尼采》。通过以施特劳斯的方式识读施特劳斯,《施特劳斯与尼采》揭示出施特劳斯与尼采的深隐渊源。朗佩特认识到尼采的双重言辞凭靠的是施特劳斯的眼力,尽管在《施特劳斯与尼采》的最后,朗佩特针对施特劳斯对尼采的批判为尼采做了辩护。

《哲学如何成为苏格拉底式的》出版三年之后,朗佩特在施特劳斯逝世四十周年之际出版了专著《施特劳斯的持久重要性》。这个书名意在强调,施特劳斯让朗佩特懂得,为何"柏拉图的苏格拉底让一位神看起来是一个超越于流变的存在者,一位道德法官",让他得以识读柏拉图《王制》卷十中苏格拉底最后编造的命相神话与荷马的隐秘关联,能够让他"从几乎二千五百年后具有后见之明的位置回望"这样一种教诲。

在柏拉图那里,尼采的所谓"大政治"是"一种为了哲学的政治",即为了真正让哲学施行统治,必须让哲学披上宗教的外衣。苏格拉底－柏拉图都没有料到,他们凭靠显白教诲精心打造的这种"大政治"的结果是:宗教最终僭越了哲学的至高法权,并把自己的僭越当真了。尤其要命的是,宗教僭越哲学的法权在西方思想史上体现为哲学变成了宗教,这意味着哲学的自尽。尼采的使命因此是,如何让哲学和宗教各归其位。

朗佩特算得上是诚实的尼采知音。能够做尼采的知音已经很难,成为知音后还要做到诚实就更难。毕竟,哲人彼此的相似性的确已经丧失了社会存在的基础。朗佩特并不是施特劳斯的亲炙弟子,但确如施特劳斯的亲炙弟子罗森所说,他比诸多施特劳斯的亲炙弟子都更好、更准确地理解了施特劳斯。

最后必须提到,朗佩特还是一位优秀的作家。他的著作虽然无不涉及艰深的哲学问题,却具有晓畅而又浅显的叙述风格——这是他的著作具有诱惑力的原因。从这个意义上讲,朗佩特的真正老师是柏拉图。

刘小枫
古典文明研究工作坊
2021 年 5 月

目 录

编者前言 …………………………………………………… 1

致谢 ………………………………………………………… 1

引言 ………………………………………………………… 1

第一讲　施特劳斯恢复哲学之诗的传统 …………………… 1

第二讲　施特劳斯、尼采与未来的哲学之诗 ……………… 25

第三讲　苏格拉底的哲学之诗 ……………………………… 48

第四讲　苏格拉底成为苏格拉底 …………………………… 69

第五讲　尼采成为尼采 ……………………………………… 92

第六讲　尼采的哲学之诗 …………………………………… 116

Contents

Acknowledgement ·· 143
Preface ·· 145
Lecture 1 Strauss Recovers the Tradition of Philosophic Poetry ·········· 147
Lecture 2 Strauss, Nietzsche and the Philosophic Poetry of the
           Future ·· 171
Lecture 3 Socrates' Philosophic Poetry ································· 194
Lecture 4 Socrates Becomes Socrates ································· 216
Lecture 5 Nietzsche Becomes Nietzsche ······························· 241
Lecture 6 Nietzsche's Philosophic Poetry ····························· 267

编者前言

应刘小枫教授之邀，朗佩特教授于2015年4月在中国人民大学古典文明研究中心做了六场讲座，本书即讲稿的结集。

朗佩特教授是加拿大人，1970年代在美国获得哲学博士学位，其后执教于印第安纳大学－普渡大学印第安纳波利斯分校（Indiana University Purdue University Indianapolis），直至2005年荣休。

朗佩特教授的学术热忱一直围绕着尼采、施特劳斯和柏拉图，专注于细致解读三位大哲人的作品。从1980年代开始，他陆续推出一系列厚重的呕心之作：《尼采的教诲：〈扎拉图斯特拉如是说〉解读一种》（1986）、《尼采与现时代：解读培根、笛卡尔与尼采》（1993）、《施特劳斯与尼采》（1996）、《尼采的使命：〈善恶的彼岸〉绎读》（2001）。为了潜心著述，朗佩特教授提前荣休，年逾古稀之后又写出了《哲学如何成为苏格拉底式的：柏拉图〈普罗塔戈拉〉〈卡尔米德〉以及〈王制〉绎读》（2010）、《施特劳斯的持久重要性》（2013）、《什么是哲人：成为尼采》（2018）。身笔双健的朗佩特教授新近出版了一部探讨苏格拉底如何成为苏格拉底的著作，解读柏拉图的《斐多》《帕默尼德》和《会饮》，与《哲学如何成功苏格拉底式的》构成姊妹篇。

朗佩特教授自称"哲学的劳作者"，却以阐明尼采意义上的"真正的哲人"为己任："真正的哲人是命令者和立法者"（《善恶的彼岸》条211）。依照朗佩特的理解，西方哲学自柏拉图伊始就有一个显白/隐微写作的传统，无论是位于现代开端的培根和笛卡尔，还是位于现代晚期的尼采，都深谙并自觉践行这种传统。施特劳斯重新发现了显白写作的技艺，并将哲人的这一秘密公之于众。朗佩特如思想侦探一样,步步追踪施特劳斯发现显白传统的过程,并破解施特劳斯本人的显白写作。

在施特劳斯的启迪之下,朗佩特指出,哲人必定有哲学与哲学之诗的双重教诲,哲学教诲是隐微的,只针对少数潜在的哲人,哲学之诗的教诲是显白的,针对多数人。更进一步说,哲学是对存在或自然的探究,是对本体论问题的回答,是关乎"最高存在"的真理;哲学之诗则是关于诸神的"高贵的谎言",是一套神学-政治方案,是哲人的立法,哲人借之来施行统治,从而服务于哲学的利益。这一区分实际是说,哲学等于形而上学,政治哲学只是哲学的副产品和侍臣。

同样借助施特劳斯的目光,朗佩特看到了柏拉图和尼采两位哲人在表面的对立之下深刻的一致。对于本体论问题,柏拉图答曰,"存在就是作为爱欲存在,而非其他";尼采答曰,"存在就是作为权力意志存在,而非其他"。两个回答名异实同。既然最高的存在永恒不变,哲人们对它的理解必然是古今同一,不可能相互歧异。哲人是一个族类,分享至高的洞见,且只有获得关于存在的至高洞见,才可谓之哲人。

朗佩特认为,柏拉图对存在的最终洞见体现在第俄提玛关于爱欲的教诲中。爱欲的特征在于自我生产,爱欲的起源是爱欲,爱欲的结果是爱欲,爱欲是永恒与流变之间的一种居间状态。爱欲与"权力意志"一样体现着尼采所说的"生成的至高无上性"。朗佩特以极为抽象的语言解释说:"两者都声称生成是一种涌动、满足和再次涌动。两者都声称,在永远的自我更新活动中,有一种旨在达到一种自我满足的内在导向:它以自我为目的(auto‑telic)。"存在自为自足,不断自我更新,同时又处在与一切存在之物的关系之中:

> 两者都声称,这种导向性的能量——或力量——的表达是关系性的;关系是个体的关系,关系的出现是这类关系领域的一部分,这类关系的整个领域是整体性,是**一切存在之物**。(见本书第114页)

哲学之诗则容易明了得多。哲人视乎自己时代的状况,开出面向所有人的神学－政治教诲。柏拉图面对的是荷马的诸神之死,为了疗治时代的虚无主义症状,他以灵魂不死的神话、理念学说来替代荷马之诗,提供新的道德－宗教－政治体系。柏拉图的这套教诲以"柏拉图主义"的面目进入基督教,成为支配西方千年的学说。尼采面对着基督教－柏拉图主义的上帝之死,他深知宗教的必要性,于是以"永恒复返"的宗教来替代柏拉图的宗教,"永恒复返是对万物的整个自然循环的神化","一种对上帝的非有神论辩护"。所以,柏拉图和尼采的哲学完全契合,他们的哲学之诗却截然背离……

在区分哲学与哲学之诗的前提下,朗佩特在研读柏拉图和尼采时还引入了一种传记的、史学式的视角,来考察"哲人如何成为哲人"这一主题的呈现。朗佩特的这一创见源自他早年研读笛卡尔《谈谈方法》的心得。在朗佩特看来,笛卡尔同样是一位柏拉图式的政治哲人,《谈谈方法》以传记的形式讲述了笛卡尔成为哲人以及政治哲人的过程。循着这一思路,朗佩特细致考辨柏拉图对话的戏剧时间,挖掘出苏格拉底成为哲人的三个阶段(《斐多》-《帕默尼德》-《会饮》),以及苏格拉底随后成为政治哲人的三个阶段(《普罗塔戈拉》-《卡尔米德》-《王制》)。他还追踪尼采的笔记,对勘尼采正式出版的著作,发现了尼采发现和呈现"权力意志"和"永恒复返"两大学说的动态过程。朗佩特由此得到的启示是,哲学先于政治哲学,成为哲人先于成为政治哲人。

施特劳斯帮助朗佩特真正理解了尼采所说的"以前的哲人都知道显白与隐微的区别"(《善恶的彼岸》条30)。但施特劳斯恐怕不会同意朗佩特直接把政治哲学等同于显白的教诲,因为区分显白与隐微是政治哲学的应有之义,政治哲学取代了哲学,而非仅是哲学的侍臣。相较而言,朗佩特比施特劳斯显得更哲学。

这部讲稿浓缩了朗佩特教授40年来沉思什么是哲学的心得,展现了他思想中最精华的部分,且娓娓道来如行云流水。一些话题在他之前的著作中出现过,但他做了精心裁剪和编排。来中国人民大学做讲座那年,他提前飞到北京,在宾馆里写讲稿,唯一一次外出是去爬西山,却因惦念写作而无心欣赏山色。

朗佩特教授特别嘱托,本讲稿以中英文对照的形式出版,不再单行英文版,因为他是为中国读者写的,他的知音在中国。

彭　磊

2020 年 9 月于京

2021 年 5 月改定

朗佩特在中国人民大学讲座现场

致　谢

　　首先,感谢刘小枫教授邀请我来中国,在中国人民大学做讲座。受到邀请十分荣幸,我十分感激刘教授。他的邀请使我有机会反思我在过去40年的研究工作,并总结其中的一些要点。

引 言

我的讲座标题显示了讲座[的内容]。①两次讨论施特劳斯(Leo Strauss),两次讨论柏拉图,最后两次讨论尼采(Friedrich Nietzsche)。然而,六次讲座都关乎哲学和哲学之诗。换种说法,我的讲座将讨论隐微教诲(esotericism)和显白教诲(exotericism),即哲人们践行的写作技艺。

这一技艺允许哲人通过他之所说传达他之所思,即通过显白的部分传达隐微的部分,而不是直接说出或者简单地付诸言辞。这一写作技艺既显明又隐藏:显明的精妙在于,显明的东西指向未显明的、隐藏的东西。隐藏的东西总是最重要的——如果你感兴趣,而且只有你[真正]感兴趣,你自己才能发现它。在发现之后,你会更加珍惜它,因为是你自己发现了它。

所以,哲人的技艺是一种引诱,一种对你的引诱,旨在使你迷上他本人和他的思想。哲人的技艺传达给你的隐微内容,是他赠予你的一份礼物,因你是他的专属读者。这份礼物成为你和他的纽带。为此你心存感激。你会一生感激他和他对你的馈赠。你就这样上钩了。尼采说过,我所有的作品都是鱼钩。

前两讲讨论施特劳斯。施特劳斯重新发现了哲学的写作技艺,写作讨论此技艺,或者说揭露了它,而此前没有任何哲人这样做过。但是,即使施特劳斯使此技艺成为公开话题,他本人却也践行了这种技艺。他忠实于他重新发现的哲学技艺,并仅仅间接地表达他的真实想法。

中间两讲讨论柏拉图,这位古希腊哲人是整个西方哲学传统中哲学

---

① 方括号是译者为顺通讲稿内容所做的补充。此外,本译稿的脚注均为译者所加。

写作的典范。但是,柏拉图的写作又在展示他的典范,哲人苏格拉底。作为柏拉图的老师,苏格拉底平生不立文字,只是[与人]谈话,并在他的谈话中践行了一种技艺,柏拉图由这一技艺发现了一种写作方式。柏拉图的写作赋予苏格拉底的谈话一种更固定的形式,这种形式之后产生了一个完整的哲学传统:西方哲学。从柏拉图以降,西方哲学便有显白和隐微,或者说,有政治哲学和哲学。更明确地说,政治哲学是一个神学-政治方案。我的标题称这个神学-政治方案为哲学之诗(philosophic poetry),这一术语可以回溯至柏拉图本人。对于作为一个整体的西方哲学的历史,尼采曾说,从柏拉图以降,所有神学家和哲人一直在同一条道路上。

直到他,也就是直到尼采。我最后两讲讨论尼采,这位德国哲人意图为哲学另辟道路。尼采开辟的道路虽然不同,但也区分隐微和显白,即哲学和哲学之诗,或者用尼采使用过的词,真理和艺术。

就我来说,我是一位研究哲学的学者,是文本的阅读者和解释者。用尼采漂亮的表达来说,我是哲学的劳作者(philosophic laborer),而尼采则是真正的哲人。作为一个哲学的劳作者,我认为尼采是我们这个时代唯一的哲人。我们必须密切关注这位哲人,因为他从早期希腊人开始来理解整个西方哲学,所以他理解我们的时代有着一种无与伦比的明晰和深刻。我认为,我们只有谨小慎微才能区别出尼采这样的哲人。

第一讲　施特劳斯恢复哲学之诗的传统

先从施特劳斯讲起。这位哲人重新发现了显白教诲/隐微教诲，并且公之于众。西方哲学在一个半世纪中几乎遗忘了这种区分，而施特劳斯选择让它广为人知。

我在讨论施特劳斯的两讲中，将首先处理他对显白教诲的重新发现。我会在讲座中一直用显白教诲这个词来指称哲人们的整个实践。其他人称之为*隐微教诲*，但是施特劳斯本人称之为*显白教诲*，因为它更能在字面上描述哲人的写作：*显白的*。

在讨论施特劳斯对显白教诲的重新发现后，我将会处理施特劳斯的一些追随者仍在争论的问题：施特劳斯自己是否践行了显白论。通过细察他对柏拉图和尼采的讨论，我会表明，他的确践行以及如何践行了显白论。

施特劳斯重新发现显白教诲：与克莱因的通信

施特劳斯在书信里记录了他对显白教诲的重新发现，这些书信是施特劳斯在1938至1939年间写给挚友克莱因（Jacob Klein）的，当时他39到40岁。

这些书信理应为人所知。书信以德语书写，且已译为中文，所以你们可以读到。但是书信至今未被译为英文，施特劳斯的许多讲英语的追随者不知道书信，或者不是很了解。那些未曾读过书信的人读到后会感到震惊，因为施特劳斯在书信里完全坦诚。这些书信和他所有的出版物在坦诚度上截然不同。它们理应为人所知，因为它们是如此坦诚，又如此极端。美国的施特劳斯圈内甚至一直在争论，这些书信究竟是否应该由迈尔（Heinrich Meier）在他编辑的施特劳斯著作集中出版。

这些书信当然是私人性的。施特劳斯写给他的挚友，这位挚友毕生也在研究哲人。但是，施特劳斯一定知道这些书信将来会为人所知，因为他知道他的著作将会为他暴得大名，那些被他吸引的读者也想阅读他写下的一切，包括他的书信。毕竟，施特劳斯自己曾密切关注过柏拉图、马基雅维利和尼采的书信。他本可轻易销毁它们——他本可要求他的挚友焚毁它们。他没有这样做。所以我们必须读它们。

这些书信在迈尔的编本里有44页，我将要做的是以时间顺序阅读1938年1月至1939年10月书信中的选段，然后对选段作出评注。我会完全跳过一些书信，或者只读其他书信的部分内容。如果你读了近乎两年来的书信的所有内容，你会看到施特劳斯在这一时期的大致状况：压力重重，操心家庭，自己失业，以及二战前夕在德国的危险处境。施特劳斯私下写信给他的挚友，表达了他深深的忧虑。但是，甚至这些忧虑也无损书信中主要的情绪和感觉：他感到极度兴奋和喜悦，因为他发现哲人们写下的东西好像只是为他而写，某种程度上也确实是为他而写；他还兴奋地感到，必须向世界宣布［他的发现］，这个世界已经对哲人们真正写下的东西一无所知，因此也就对什么是哲学一无所知。

我择取的这些选段只涉及施特劳斯对显白教诲的重新发现。这些书信以迈蒙尼德（Maimonides）开始。迈蒙尼德作为犹太传统中最重要的哲人，施特劳斯已浸心多年。迈蒙尼德生活在西元纪年的12世纪（公元1135至1204年），比施特劳斯研究他时早700多年。施特劳斯在1928年出版的处女作《斯宾诺莎的宗教批判》（*Spinoza's Critique of Religion*）中说，迈蒙尼德是"一个犹太教信徒"。现在，也就是十年后，施特劳斯这样说：

1938年1月20日

[迈蒙尼德]是真正自由的心灵(mind)①……对他来说,至关重要的问题不是创世或世界永恒(因为他确信世界永恒),而是理想的立法者是否必然是先知。②

迈蒙尼德相信世界的永恒:这是哲学的立场而非圣经的立场,因此也不是一个犹太教信徒的立场。现在,施特劳斯看到迈蒙尼德拒绝圣经的观点,即犹太教的创世观。他的问题已经变成了"理想的立法者必须是先知吗?"。犹太教是一种律法(law)传统,犹太人的立法者是摩西(Moses),他是犹太圣经里最重要的人物。在柏拉图那里,哲人是理想的立法者。所以,施特劳斯现在看到的问题是:哲人-立法者也一定是由上帝派来的吗?也就是说,哲人-立法者一定要被视作由上帝派来的吗?一定要把自己表现为由上帝派来的吗?

这一点非常难以证明,因为他是以注疏的形式讨论这个问题。

对于今天阅读施特劳斯的人来说,这很滑稽:注疏的形式是注疏者的外衣,而且注疏者可以隐藏自己对他所注释内容的看法;他可以显得仅仅是在转述。迈蒙尼德正是这样干的,这使得很难证明他自己的想法是什么。施特劳斯也这样做:他选择以注疏家的身份写作。所以,证明施特劳斯的想法十分困难,因为他像迈蒙尼德一样,选择了注疏的写作形式。

1938年2月16日

你无法想象,迈蒙尼德以怎样无限的精炼和嘲讽处理"宗教"

---

① mind 的译法多样,可译为头脑、心灵、心智等,若与自由连用,译为心灵较为妥当。mind 在尼采那里同样具有特殊的用法,朗佩特在最后两讲论之甚详。

② 引文根据朗佩特的英译文翻译,同时参照中译本:施特劳斯等,《回归古典政治哲学:施特劳斯通信集》,迈尔编,朱雁冰、何鸿藻译,华夏出版社,2006,页265-309。

> ……如果我在几年以后(倘若我还能活到那时的话)引爆这枚炸弹，便会引发一场大战。

施特劳斯完全明白，泄露他在迈蒙尼德那里发现的东西意味着什么：他手里拿着一颗炸弹，一颗将会炸毁整个迈蒙尼德理解传统的炸弹。爆炸将会是毁灭性的，因为迈蒙尼德是犹太教最伟大的教师，是最受人尊崇和极具权威的教师。

> 这便产生了一个有趣的结果：一个纯历史的论断——从其信仰看，迈蒙尼德绝对不是犹太教徒——具有重大的现实意义：哲学与犹太教在原则上的不相容跃然眼前。

迈蒙尼德的读者要得出这个"历史的论断"，就得像施特劳斯一样，像一位史学家，把迈蒙尼德的作品视为显白写作，背后为你隐藏了隐微的含义。你是他的专属读者，因为你和他一样，为此他要教导你被禁止的东西。所以，施特劳斯说，注意到这种写作技艺的历史科学，可以表明迈蒙尼德绝非犹太教徒。要做哲人，就要完全凭靠理性，就必须完全拒绝做犹太教徒，因为犹太教徒凭靠信仰，凭靠写在犹太传统所持有的圣书中的启示，一种直接来自上帝的启示。作为一个犹太人，凭靠的是服从这种启示立下的律法。

施特劳斯一生坚持这个重要的观点：启示与哲学水火不容。启示建立起服从的传统，哲学则试图获得自由心灵(free mind)，且自由心灵只接受理性能够证明的真实东西。

> 迈蒙尼德的技巧中最重要的一点当然是，即便在白痴不去关注的地方，他说的**一切**也都是完全公开的。

你们在这里要小心：几乎每个读者都是那个白痴。白痴是我，也是你。完全公开的意思是，只对那个有这种怀疑精神的自由心灵开放，这种自由心灵知道怎样去寻找几乎所有其他读者都不会去找寻的东西。这是极重要的一点:隐微教诲不是藏在低于或高于表面的某处;它就在表面上,但仍然隐藏着,如果你知道怎么去看,它就藏在稀松平常的观点里。施特劳斯最棒的话之一是这样说的:"蕴涵在事物表面的问题,而且只有蕴涵在事物表面的问题,才是事物的核心。"①

N. 有句格言:当我的拳头里攥着真理,我敢打开它吗?

"N."是指尼采。用"N."[表示尼采]就够了。[通信]双方都知道"N."只能指尼采(我得知中译本译者不知道这个"N."是指尼采,他简单地译成了"某人")。1935 年,也就是[写这封信的]三年前,施特劳斯曾在一封信里说道:在他"22 到 30 岁(1921 至 1929 年)"之间,"尼采控制着和吸引着"他,"以至于我几乎相信从他书中读懂的一切"(1935 年 6 月 23 日与洛维特[Löwith]的通信)。②

我一直以来都未能找到尼采关于"拳头里攥着真理"的准确说法,但是这个想法肯定来自他。他说过三个"真实而致命"的基本问题:"生成的至高无上(the sovereignty of becoming),一切概念、类型和种类的流变性,人与动物之间缺乏一切根本的差异。"③而且,尼采不断面对哲人面对的问题:"我敢打开拳头"里致命的真理吗? 我会在我尼采的讲座中细谈它,不过从一开始就认识到这个"致命的真理"对他而言并非致命,他可以轻松接受致命的真理;他[甚至]为致命真理庆祝,因为他在寻找并且热爱真理。但是尼采知道,真理对共同体是致命的,对共同体的健康所依赖的信仰是致命的。

1938 年 7 月 23 日

我本可为解开了这个谜团而感到一丝自豪。可是,或许我还不

---

① 参见施特劳斯,《关于马基雅维里的思考》,申彤译,译林出版社,2003,页 6。
② 参施特劳斯等,《回归古典政治哲学——施特劳斯通信集》,前揭,页 244。
③ 参见尼采,《不合时宜的沉思》,李秋零译,华东师范大学出版社,页 223。据朗佩特引文略有调整。

够胆——或者我还缺乏 scientia[知识]——抑或两者都有。总之,我有时面对我的解释可能造成的后果感到不寒而栗。后果将是,我这个可怜鬼不得不一勺勺喝下 12 世纪那个邪恶的巫师为我熬制的羹汤。

我引用施特劳斯这句个人性的评论,部分是因为,这句话表明他对自己的处境有清晰的认识:他知道自己在迈蒙尼德那里发现的东西有多么重大。但是我引用这一评论主要是因为,它讲了我在施特劳斯的任何著作中都闻所未闻的内容:质疑自己是否能这样做。他的胆子足够大吗?他能承负这个激进甚至毁灭性的异端看法的压力吗?他缺乏知识或胆量吗?他自问是否在智性(intellect)和意志(will)上强大到足够肩负这样的重担:真正领会历代先哲知道的东西,同时也让其他人知道。

至此为止,施特劳斯激进的发现仅限于迈蒙尼德。在他 1935 年出版的著作《哲学与律法》(*Philosophy and Law*)中,施特劳斯讨论了迈蒙尼德及其先驱,不过迈蒙尼德的先驱们是伊斯兰哲人。这些哲人同样身处一个基于启示和圣经的传统之中,信徒必须服从圣经,放弃自己的智性。但是,伊斯兰哲人们指向他们的先驱希腊人,也就是那些身处服从启示的传统之外的异教思想家。

正是在书信里的这个节点上,施特劳斯转向了那些希腊人。这意味着他与克莱因的通信没有讨论影响迈蒙尼德的伊斯兰哲人们的显白教诲。

1938 年 10 月 15 日

现在,我正在读希罗多德(Herodotus)的书——我敢以天主教徒的名义发誓,他同样是个隐微作家,而且是至为完美的一个。总之,这又发生了。

"天主教徒"是施特劳斯漂亮的小玩笑。施特劳斯转向的第一个希腊人就是"历史学家"希罗多德,而不是所谓的哲人。在德国一所古典人文中学(Gymnasium)读书时,施特劳斯学习希腊语、拉丁语,阅读古典著作,而且他一直在读。但是为何希罗多德是他发现迈蒙尼德后转向的第一个希腊作家,施特劳斯并没有说。

1938 年 10 月 20 日

我真的惊呆了,在这样一种技艺(=能力)面前,我佩服得五体投地。我的幸运之星发现,他的作品的确是我所知道的柏拉图的唯一范本。

施特劳斯俯身于地,就像在某个神面前一样,希罗多德作为显白作家由于精湛的技艺而受到如此尊崇。然而,施特劳斯最属意的并非希罗多德,而是柏拉图——在阅读希罗多德时,他想到的是柏拉图,柏拉图跟随的范本不仅仅是苏格拉底,还有作家希罗多德。

因此,我能表明,最切近我内心的有关柏拉图的认识与那种特有的柏拉图式哲学无关。

这是一个真正的炸弹。他将柏拉图一分为二:"特有的柏拉图式哲学",我们可以称为显白的柏拉图,即柏拉图教授的教诲。这种教诲不同于最切近施特劳斯内心的认识——隐微的柏拉图,施特劳斯不会从柏拉图的研究者那里听到这一说法,因为他们抛弃这一观念已有一个世纪之久。施特劳斯可以展示这种区分——他可以像解读希罗多德的文本那样解读柏拉图的文本。施特劳斯的这颗炸弹可以表明,柏拉图没有信守自己的教诲。施特劳斯所爱的是那个隐藏的柏拉图。

由此我们得到如下基本事实:柏拉图是迈蒙尼德及其伊斯兰先驱的老师——同时也是教导显白教诲的必要性的老师,尽管他不像迈蒙尼德及其伊斯兰先驱那样身处于启示传统之中。

1938 年 11 月 2 日

我发现自己处于一种正在吞噬我的迷狂状态中:希罗多德之后,

现在又是修昔底德!

我收入"迷狂状态"这句是因为下一封信:

1938 年 11 月 29 日
>希罗多德、修昔底德和色诺芬并不是史学家——当然不是——而是显白作品的……作家。

这三位古希腊史家都在显白地写作。这里是施特劳斯在发现显白教诲的书信里第一次提到色诺芬(Xenophon)。

>[色诺芬的《居鲁士的教育》(*The Education of Cyrus*)是]一部完全伟大的高雅讽喻之作,苏格拉底是什么样的人,通过他[色诺芬]对居鲁士讽刺画般的刻画呈现出来。只是通过这种手段,色诺芬才展现了真实的、隐藏的苏格拉底,而他在《回忆苏格拉底》(*Memorabilia*)中展示的则是显见的苏格拉底。所以,色诺芬的苏格拉底形象与柏拉图的苏格拉底形象没有根本上的不同。

施特劳斯推进得很快:就在发现了修昔底德的显白教诲几周后,他已经可以说出色诺芬的写作策略。通过对王者或统治者的讽刺刻画,色诺芬展现了所有人中对自己而言最重要的人即苏格拉底的真面目。大多数人会认为,前者的形象比一个微不足道的哲人更重要:居鲁士是波斯帝国的缔造者,这位统治者建立了整个帝国,他是一位实干家而非静观者。施特劳斯看得透彻:真实的、隐藏的苏格拉底凭靠截然不同的方式也是一种统治者和缔造者。苏格拉底是一位静观者,一位哲人,通过他,一个新型的帝国、一个哲学统治者的帝国应运而生。作为苏格拉底的学生,色诺芬在巧妙的写作中呈现了这一点。

在西方古典文明的传统中,柏拉图作为通往苏格拉底的向导,几乎总是被认为比色诺芬更重要。但是传统上色诺芬被授予很高的地位,与柏拉图比肩而立。然而,在施特劳斯的时代,现代学术在一个多世纪里已经完全摧毁色诺芬作为伟大作家的声誉，原因就是，古典作品的研究者已经完全抛弃了显白解读的传统。施特劳斯最伟大的功绩之一就是恢复了色诺芬——作为哲人的那个真正的色诺芬——的地位。施特劳斯发表的首篇讨论古希腊作家的论文就是关于色诺芬的，时在 1939 年，当时他刚开始发现显白教诲。施特劳斯首部讨论希腊人的著作《论僭政》(On Tyranny)就是在讨论色诺芬的《希耶罗》(Hiero)。施特劳斯还说过，他晚年所作的对色诺芬的两本义疏是其平生最棒的两本著作。

在我刚刚读过的信里还有另一关键点：色诺芬的苏格拉底与柏拉图的苏格拉底"没有根本上"的不同。施特劳斯写下这句话时，其观点和当时所有学者的观点完全相反。这是一个重要的洞见：苏格拉底这位最重要的老师，既可以通过柏拉图又能通过色诺芬来理解，两人都让隐微的苏格拉底变得可见，而且彼此相互阐发，因为两人的苏格拉底没有根本上的不同。

1938 年 12 月 2 日

> 我很好奇，在这位据传与希罗多德交谊甚笃的索福克勒斯(Sophocles)背后，究竟隐藏着什么东西——恐怕同样是哲学，而非城邦和祖先。

我收入这句评论，旨在表明施特劳斯恢复古希腊作家时的视野：索福克勒斯是古代雅典的三大悲剧家之一。施特劳斯本人从未发表过任何文字证明他的推测，但他最杰出的追随者伯纳德特(Seth Benardete)做了这一工作。

1939 年 2 月 16 日

> 我特别喜爱色诺芬，因为他有勇气装扮成白痴，并如此独行千年之久——他是我知道的最高明的把戏手。我认为他在自己的作品中所做的，恰恰是苏格拉底毕生所为之事。在[色诺芬]作品的所有情形中，道德也是纯粹的显白教诲，大约每两个字就有双重含义。

色诺芬敢于装扮成白痴,而且整个现代学界都认为他是个白痴。一个"把戏手"(trickster)是一个骗子,一个镇定自若、胸有成竹的人,他赢得你的信任是为了欺骗你,偷走你的东西。如果色诺芬在做苏格拉底做过的事,那么苏格拉底也是个把戏手,是个骗子。

非常严重——这是关于苏格拉底的终极炸弹。苏格拉底被认为是而且确实是教授道德的最伟大的哲学教师。他是道德教师的英雄模范,但是他所教的道德完全是显白的。施特劳斯证明关于这颗炸弹他是正确的:

> Kalokagathia[美好]在苏格拉底的圈子里是骂人话,如同19世纪的"市侩"(philistine)或"资产者"(burgeois)。

Kalokagathia 是两个希腊语词合成的,用来形容希腊的贤人(gentleman),他们是希腊城邦秩序中城邦生活的中流砥柱。这两个希腊语词是高贵的(noble)和好的(good)。在苏格拉底的"圈子"内,表示贤人的"既高贵且好"有什么含义呢?它是用来贬低和嘲弄的戏谑之词。

但我们不能忘记,与年轻的希腊贤人们交谈的苏格拉底是向他们教授美德的老师,他给予这些年轻的贤人充足的理由,让他们踵继乃父乃祖的美德。施特劳斯的意思是,这一教诲是显白的,并且这种显白掩盖了真正的理解,真正的理解看到了贤人美德的真正根基和局限。两者都很重要:苏格拉底的显白道德教诲是对年轻贤人的美德教育;他对美德的真正理解只会被像他那样的极少数人知晓。苏格拉底关于道德的言辞有两种含义,分别针对他的两类听众。

> sôphrosunê[节制]本质上指表达观点时的自我克制。

sophrosune 是表示节制(moderation)或自制(self-control)的希腊语词,古代四美德之一,其余是勇敢、正义和智慧。施特劳斯发现自制在苏格拉底的圈子内的真正含义是什么呢?讲话时的自制。节制意味着显白教诲,意味着控制和警惕你所说或所写的东西。所以,哲人重新诠释贤人的美德，使之对他和他的同类有不同的意义。哲学的节制部分意味着继续使用古老的道德语词，但以截然不同的方式理解它们。哲人节制的、道德的言辞掩盖他激进的思考。

——总之，这里有一套完整的秘语体系，恰如在迈蒙尼德那里，所以，对我来说又是一场寻找盛宴。

你们要小心"秘语"（secret words）——它们如同指示美德的语词一样平常。它们是隐秘的（secret），仅仅因为它们对思想家有着未明言的、不同的含义。

1939 年 7 月 25 日

毫无疑问，色诺芬的苏格拉底与柏拉图的苏格拉底乃一回事，在两人笔下，这是同一个苏格拉底-奥德修斯（Odysseus），教诲也相同。《回忆苏格拉底》与《王制》（*Republic*）的论题相同：正义与真理，或者说行动的生活与静观的生活之间成问题的关系。

色诺芬的《回忆苏格拉底》和柏拉图的《王制》处理了相同的问题：行动的生活与静观的生活之间成问题的或可疑的关系。只有在施特劳斯出版的作品中，他才详细解释了这个"成问题的关系"。行动的生活基于对共同体认为真实的共同价值或道德德性的忠诚；静观的生活基于求知的热望（passion to know），而且会达到这样的认识：所有人效忠的美德在根本意义上并不真实，而仅仅是必要的。

施特劳斯不需要向克莱因解释这个成问题的关系中的"问题"是什么，因为克莱因早已知晓。这个问题简要来说如下：哲人过着静观的生活，他所知道的东西可能摧毁共同体的根基，而他也是共同体的一部分。如果共同体知道了哲人所思考的东西，有可能会毁灭哲人——共同体会将哲人视作敌人，可能会杀死他，就像雅典人对苏格拉底所做的那样。行动的生活与静观的生活之间成问题的关系引使哲人走向显白教诲。显白教诲既保护共同体免受哲学侵害，又保护哲人免受共同体迫害。显白教诲之所以必要,除了这个成问题的关系外,还有其他原因,我已经提到主要的原因:显白教诲是一种引诱,引诱与哲人同类的青年。

注意施特劳斯在这封信里称苏格拉底为"苏格拉底-奥德修斯"。奥德修斯是荷马(Homer)笔下最有智慧的人。在荷马的《奥德赛》(*Odyssey*)中,智慧的奥德修斯成了哲人。不过,施特劳斯在这里的主要观点是基于奥德修斯诡计多端的名声,他好耍花招,好撒谎,本人却无法被愚弄。我提到这个,是因为奥德修斯会在我的第一场柏拉图讲座中作为苏格拉底的模范出现。

1939 年 10 月 10 日

> [赫西俄德(Hesiod)的《神谱》(*Theogeny*)是]对何谓初始的、非生育的事物这个问题的回答,进而通过这个问题说明奥林匹亚神族,最终启迪[人思考]这个问题和答案的含义,即智慧的含义。初始事物并非众神,而是诸如大地、天空、星辰、海洋这类事物,它们所在的地方明显不同于诸神。

我引用这段主要是因为,它将存在显白教诲的重要事实回溯到古希腊的奠基性诗人:赫西俄德和荷马。他们的诗歌是显白的。赫西俄德的《神谱》是讲诸神诞生的诗歌;《神谱》对每个人都是权威的,但它的写作方式只允许少数人知道"非生育的事物是什么"——那些始终存在的事物,自然的事物,对寻求理解的人来说比诸神更为重要的事物。

认识非生育事物是什么,也就阐明了"奥林匹亚诸神"是什么,也表明关心人类事务的诸神是什么:诸神是像赫西俄德这样的智慧的诗人们的发明。这一启迪还说明了智慧是什么:智慧是关于自然和人的自然的知识,也是关于神是什么的知识。施特劳斯当时在这些书信中写下的发现将会是萦绕其一生的重要问题。

> 我深信,荷马的作品并无不同。

施特劳斯从赫西俄德转移到荷马这位最重要的诗人,柏拉图称荷马为"全希腊的教师"。施特劳斯认为荷马的作品与赫西俄德"并无不同",但他没有在书信或出版的著作中阐发这一洞见。然而伯纳德特却踵继其志:《弓与琴》(*The Bow and the Lyre*)解读荷马《奥德赛》,论证了希腊的奠基诗人也是希腊的奠基哲人。

1939 年 10 月 25 日

> 现在,我大体上已经理解了[柏拉图的]《会饮》(*Symposium*):它是关于阿尔喀比亚德(Alcibiades)亵渎秘仪(mysteries)的"真实"启发,并非阿尔喀比亚德而是苏格拉底泄露了秘仪的秘密。这是下述著名事实的一个例子:苏格拉底的实际"指控者"是柏拉图。

这是我将提到的施特劳斯写给克莱因的最后一封信,引用这封信是因为它单单挑出柏拉图的《会饮》。二十年后,在 1959 年芝加哥大学的课堂上,施特劳斯说明了他为何会因《会饮》揭示了秘仪的真正秘密而视之为柏拉图最重要的对话。我会在我的第二场柏拉图讲座中谈论这点,因为《会饮》中发生的情形至关重要。现在,我想只提到书信中的一点。苏格拉底"泄露了"秘仪的秘密。泄露意味着说的过多,说了你本不应该说的。"秘仪"是雅典宗教的核心,雅典人通过特殊的秘密程序和仪式入教。一旦入教,新入教者严格禁止透露仪式的内容——它们是秘仪,要保密。但是苏格拉底在《会饮》中泄露的秘仪是有关哲学和哲人的隐秘真理。在我的第二场柏拉图讲座中,我将表明,这些真理对于苏格拉底成为苏格拉底至关重要。

我以此结束对施特劳斯与克莱因通信的引述。在这些书信中,施特劳斯讲述了他对哲学的显白教诲的发现和复原。施特劳斯与克莱因的通信与他所有的出版物都不一样,因为他在这些书信中松开了握着炸弹的拳头:首先是迈蒙尼德,然后是苏格拉底、柏拉图和色诺芬。这些书信让施特劳斯其他著作的读者们得以直接认识到,施特劳斯在学习显白写作的那几个月里学到了什么。同时,这些书信有助于解决有关施特劳斯真正观点的诸多争论。

但是,施特劳斯在做出了这些书信记录的发现之后,他如何引爆了他手中握有的关于哲学传统的所有这些炸弹呢?他很快形成了一种呈现他的发现的策略,这一策略在某种程度上确保炸弹不会立即和明显引爆。他的策略本身是间接的。我们可以说,施特劳斯的炸弹带有长长的导线,这根长线会点亮你这个读者的内心,在你内心燃烧,并且慢慢引导你,借由你自己发现他真正要说的话,这个炸弹会为你引爆,但只是在你长久的努力之后。施特劳斯的策略教会你阅读,同时也教导你哲学作家那里真正有什么。

所以,施特劳斯形成了自己的显白写作的方式,它比传统的写作方式更加公开,而且它最终会建立一个阅读传统,这一传统将使哲人们的隐微理解更广为人知。他余生大部分时间都在写作讨论这一传统中的伟大哲人们,而且做得很成功,他的著作以及他的读者群体遍布全球证明了这一点。

但是,1938年至1939年与克莱因的通信提供了理解施特劳斯的持续重要性的清晰指引。研究这些书信可以锚定我们阅读施特劳斯的方式,帮助我们广泛地阅读哲人们[的著作],并在阅读时持续关注他们著作的双重性质:他们表面的教诲是什么,以及他们引导或诱使读者从表面推断出什么。

在余下关于施特劳斯的讲座中,我将只探讨他对哲学史的研究,并且只探讨他对柏拉图和尼采的研究。这意味着我会忽略施特劳斯致力理解的其他重要话题,包括他分析当今哲学的十分重要的著作,这部著作旨在理解当今哲学为何已经丢弃或遗忘显白传统:显白传统有遭永久丢弃的危险,因为当今的哲学潮流有力地论证了哲学的不可能性,即理解事物的真相的不可能性。

关于施特劳斯对柏拉图和尼采的讨论,我将只探讨两个文本,一个关乎柏拉图,另一个关乎尼采。两个文本处理的都是哲学,并且意图表明哲学产生或孕育了哲学之诗。两个文本都很简短,但是它们取自更长的文本,它们的含义部分取决于它们在那些更长文本中的语境。我将紧盯这些较短的文本的语词,偶尔依仗更大的文本中的语境。我不得不说的内容会表明,施特劳斯留给我们——他的读者——的困难与迈蒙尼德留给他的读者的困难是相同的:如同迈蒙尼德,施特劳斯以注疏的形式探讨哲学和哲学之诗,这会使他自己的观点只有通过推断才变得可见。

我对这些文本的讨论,部分是要表明施特劳斯在显白地写作,但更重要的是为了说明,施特劳斯让我们得以看到柏拉图和尼采写作的显白特征。我首先讨论施特劳斯对柏拉图最重要的论述:《城邦与人》(*The City and Man*)的中心篇章《论柏拉图的〈王制〉》。我在《施特劳斯的持久重要性》(*The Enduring Importance of Leo Strauss*)中详细地讨论了这篇文章。

施特劳斯论柏拉图的《王制》

施特劳斯的文章《论柏拉图的〈王制〉》分为两个部分,由一个小标点符号隔开:第 13 段结尾的破折号。前 13 段讨论如何阅读一篇柏拉图对话,随后出现这个破折号。剩下的部分是对《王制》的解读,总共 65 段,可以视作一个独立又完整的单元。65 个段落的中心段落是第 33 段,①而这个段落处理了中心问题。这一段有 38 句话,位于中心的第 19 和 20 句是两个问句。我会集中讨论这两个问句。我需要对我在这里做的说明两点。

其一:施特劳斯教导说,最伟大的作家们都在中心位置隐藏最重要的问题。他称中心为"最不暴露的位置"(the least exposed place),开头和结尾相比则是最暴露的位置。但是,施特劳斯强调中心反而使中心成了最暴露的位置。施特劳斯本人是否追随那些最伟大的作家,也采用这种写作技巧?当然如此。他的所有著作都显示出这种将最重要的问题置于中心的技巧。

---

① Leo Strauss, *The City and Man*, The University of Chicago Press, 1964, p. 97 – 100.

其二：你不能只看中心。要理解中心，你需要付出，需要费心思看看中心前有什么铺垫，中心后又接续什么。你需要思考这一切意味着什么。我现在要说的是一种欺骗或犯罪。只盯着中心绝对不够，但这正是我将要做的。

施特劳斯的中心段落开始于柏拉图《王制》中的教育，即儿童通过故事和歌曲所受的教育。这是一种通过"诗"进行的教育，"诗"一词极其重要。故事和歌曲通常有关诸神和英雄，这些形象的行为受到儿童们的尊重和模仿。柏拉图强调，正确的故事教导正确的行为，并且让人警惕错误的行为。"为了表明正确的故事，"施特劳斯说，为诸神，"苏格拉底立下了两种法。"苏格拉底提出了一种神学，这一神学部分由关于诸神的虚假故事构成。

注意：施特劳斯悄悄说苏格拉底是一个立法者，而且是为诸神立法。极重要的是，苏格拉底是为诸神立下新法。那些虚假的故事是讲给小孩子的，但施特劳斯说它们也是"讲给好城邦的成年邦民们的"。邦民们从小接受了那些虚假故事，他们成年后依然相信：人在童年接受了什么，他成年后会继续相信和奉行。

苏格拉底掌控《王制》中的对话，正如施特劳斯所说，苏格拉底让对话几乎悄无声息地"从需要关于诸神的高贵谎言转向需要关于诸神的真理"。现在到了我想要读的中心段落的部分。我会读这些句子然后解释它们。

> 对话者由一个隐含的前提开始，即存在诸神或者存在一个神，而且他们知道神是什么。这个困难可以用一个例子说明。

从句子的语法上看并不清楚"这个困难"指的是什么，但我们会清楚地看到："这个困难"就是"知道神是什么"。

> 苏格拉底问阿德曼托斯（Adeimantus），神是否会因为他对古代事物的无知而撒谎或者说假话；阿德曼托斯回答说，这简直荒谬

(382d6 – 8)。但是,阿德曼托斯为何认为荒谬?是因为诸神一定最知道自己的事务,就像蒂迈欧(Timaeus)认为的那样?(《蒂迈欧》40d3 – 41a5)

这两个问题位于施特劳斯中心段落的中心。施特劳斯在他讨论柏拉图《王制》的中心段落的中心放置了这样两个问题,即神是否会因为阿德曼托斯对古代事物的无知而撒谎。

第一个问题:阿德曼托斯对诸神的看法。阿德曼托斯是当晚与苏格拉底交谈最多的两个青年之一。他年轻,高贵且善良,是个地道的贤人,他对诸神的看法应该就是他自幼在雅典所接受的观点,即从荷马和赫西俄德的故事中流传下来的观点。

我必须在这里停下来多说一说阿德曼托斯,因为这对[理解]中心位置的问题至关重要。我们最能了解阿德曼托斯的地方是他之前发表的长篇讲辞,这篇讲辞迫使苏格拉底开始着手处理整部作品的主要问题:为正义辩护,以便劝说阿德曼托斯和其他青年相信正义好过不义,正派或道德好过不道德。在他的长篇讲辞中,阿德曼托斯表现出开始在道德上拒斥哺养他的荷马和赫西俄德关于诸神的故事。青年阿德曼托斯已开始对他幼时接受的有关诸神的神话丧失信心。

简单来说,换我们熟悉的语言来说,青年阿德曼托斯正开始经历一场诸神之死。荷马笔下的诸神,旧的诸神,他唯一知道的诸神,对他而言正在死去,而且他有充分的理由深深动摇:如果诸神像故事里似乎暗示的那样是不道德的,如果诸神可以被收买,如果诸神甚至支持坏人,那么似乎没有充分的理由做正义之人。然而,阿德曼托斯这位正派且高贵的年轻贤人,非常想继续做正派且高贵之人,继续做正义之人,但如果连诸神自己都是不义的,为什么他应该选择那种艰难的生活道路呢?这一点至关重要,因为它有助于看清柏拉图所处的时代。柏拉图小心翼翼地通过阿德曼托斯和他的兄弟格劳孔(Glaucon)的讲辞描绘了那个时代:对受希腊启蒙运动影响的正派青年来说,这是一个诸神死去的时代。

第二个问题：蒂迈欧对诸神的看法。蒂迈欧是位哲人，尽管施特劳斯未在此处提及这点。在柏拉图对话《蒂迈欧》中，苏格拉底聆听这位哲人的高论，他阐发了一整套宇宙论，对作为一个整体的世界做出了解释。哲人蒂迈欧与阿德曼托斯共同出现在施特劳斯中心段落的中心位置，由此揭示出阿德曼托斯之不是：阿德曼托斯既不是哲人，也不是潜在的哲人。他的兴趣在别处，在于从小学习并依旧热爱的诗，在于与一个年轻贤人匹配的正义和正派。

> 确切无疑的是，蒂迈欧区分了明显循环往复的可见的诸神与那些选择显现才会显现的诸神，区分了宇宙诸神与奥林匹亚诸神，而在《王制》的神学中并没有这种区分，在那里只能找到奥林匹亚诸神。

哲人蒂迈欧对诸神作出了区分；他把诸神分为宇宙神和奥林匹亚神两类，前者是像太阳和月亮这样的自然的力量或实体，后者有人格并向人类显现自己。施特劳斯指出此点是想说明下面这点：

> 但这个事实恰恰表明神学的"神话"性质，或者说无法提出和回答"神是什么"或"诸神是谁"这个问题的严重性。

所以，《王制》中关于诸神的讨论存在严重的失败，即无法提出和回答"神是什么"的问题。为了理解这个严重的失败，我要读读别的东西。如果你们读过施特劳斯的《城邦与人》，你们知道它的结尾如何。我现在要读的就是结尾句。所以，我暂时打断这一段来看施特劳斯文章的结尾：

> ……前哲学的……城邦把自身看成从属和服从于神——普通意义上的神——或仰望神。只有从这点出发，我们才易于感受到与哲学相伴而生的至关重要的问题带来的剧烈冲击，尽管哲人们不常挑明这一问题——"神是什么"(quid sit deus)的问题。

注意,在著作的结尾,施特劳斯事实上没有挑明哲人们不常挑明的问题:神是什么?或者神可能是什么?他没有挑明这个问题,而是用拉丁语表达。但是,在他讨论柏拉图《王制》的文章的中心段落,他却挑明了这一问题。他说到,"无法提出和回答'神是什么'或'诸神是谁'的问题"是苏格拉底和阿德曼托斯"严重的失败"。

这是谁的错?是阿德曼托斯的错吗?阿德曼托斯在《王制》中表明自己不是哲人或潜在的哲人。为何阿德曼托斯没有提出这个问题?因为他没有问题。阿德曼托斯知道神是什么。神是荷马和赫西俄德称其所是的东西。阿德曼托斯的问题并非"神是什么?",而是为何诸神不比他们实际所是的那样更正义、更道德、更值得信任。

没有提出这个问题是苏格拉底的错。就像哲人蒂迈欧一样,哲人苏格拉底本应提出和回答"神是什么"的问题。但在提出和回答这个问题后,哲人知道经常挑明这个问题是不智的。因此,苏格拉底没有对阿德曼托斯挑明这个问题。

回到中心段落,施特劳斯自己挑明这个问题后,继续说:

> 苏格拉底的其他发言或许可以使我们弄清苏格拉底的答案,但它们无助于弄清阿德曼托斯的答案,因而无助于判断他和苏格拉底达成的一致有多深。

所以,施特劳斯指向苏格拉底的答案,但并未和盘托出。他留给你来追问,他接下来只讨论了苏格拉底和阿德曼托斯一致同意的内容。追问苏格拉底的答案有许多不同的路径,最容易的一条是追随施特劳斯:他在讨论尼采的文章中指出了两处这样的发言。你们可以查阅这两处来揭晓苏格拉底的答案:《智术师》(*Sophist*) 216b5-6 提到了"一种驳斥的神"(爱利亚异乡人),《泰阿泰德》(*Theaetetus*) 151d1-2 说"他们不知道没有神会恶意对人"。这两处都暗示某些非同寻常的东西:哲人是神;各位将在我的尼采讲座中看到,施特劳斯讨论尼采的文章中的语境恰恰暗示了这种含义。

但对我们来说,施特劳斯讨论《王制》的文章的中心位置的关键点在于:为何苏格拉底没有在《王制》中挑明那个问题或者给出自己的回答?原因是苏格拉底与青年阿德曼托斯的交谈另有目的。苏格拉底无意于提出"神是什么"这个问题,因为他在《王制》中所做的正是施特劳斯说他在做的事:为诸神立法。苏格拉底立法规定神是什么,是为了饱受折磨的阿德曼托斯:这个年轻人认为自己知道神是什么,但他诟病那些他从小就相信的故事中诸神的行为,由此被驱使着不相信或不信任诸神。苏格拉底所做的是修改或校正阿德曼托斯认为自己知道的诸神,以便使诸神更道德,更值得阿德曼托斯尊重和崇敬。

如果我们从施特劳斯的中心段落转到前面一段,我们看到施特劳斯在那里谈到了哲人如何首次被引入《王制》。引入哲人的方式修正了苏格拉底先前对技艺的看法。技艺就是人参与其中的行动和制作,在修正的技艺观中,各技艺之间有一种等级,其中"最高的技艺,指导其他所有技艺的技艺……会被证明是哲学"。所以,施特劳斯在中心段落的前一段引入了哲学指导性的行动。作为一门技艺,一种行动或制作,哲学是最高的或者说指导性的技艺;哲学是统治性的技艺。

柏拉图在《王制》中稍后才引入苏格拉底著名的论点:哲人必须统治。事实上,柏拉图把这句话放在了《王制》的正中心。所以施特劳斯所做的是,将柏拉图的中心论点正好移到他自己的中心之前。同时,我们很容易看出为何施特劳斯这样做:在讨论柏拉图《王制》的文章的中心,施特劳斯表明柏拉图置于《王制》中心的论点实际如何实现。在讨论《王制》的文章的中心,施特劳斯表明哲人苏格拉底实际如何统治:哲人通过为诸神订立新法实行统治;哲人通过统治对诸神的看法来实行统治,而对诸神的看法将统治青年们的心智。如果我们具体看阿德曼托斯的情况,我们可以说哲人通过统治像他这样的青年的心智来实行统治,这些青年会欢迎苏格拉底改造荷马的诸神。阿德曼托斯处在雅典历史上的危机时刻,适值诸神不受信任或受到怀疑,而他代表了这一时期走向成熟的所有高贵青年。

苏格拉底成功地统治阿德曼托斯和其他像他一样的青年的心智,这指向了苏格拉底终极的成功:通过阿德曼托斯和他的同类人,苏格拉底为诸神立的新法会统治未来的一代代男童和女童的心智。他们会在父母的观念中浸淫成长,即使成为城邦的成年邦民也会继续秉持这些观念。哲人苏格拉底如何统治——这是施特劳斯在他讨论《王制》的文章中心所写的内容。

现在,我从这个中心要点转向一般的教训。

历史地看,亦即从希腊的历史背景看《王制》中的这个事件,我们可以说:荷马和赫西俄德作为奠基性的希腊诗人、全希腊的教师,通过他们笔下的诸神和英雄,以诗歌的方式成为哲人王。但是,在柏拉图《王制》的时代,荷马和赫西俄德的诸神陷入危机。当荷马笔下的诸神正在死去,荷马的宗教岌岌可危之时,《王制》中的苏格拉底开始成为哲人王。这是第一场柏拉图讲座的一个主题。

倘若朝后从尼采的视角**历史地**看,我们可以说:苏格拉底成功了。如尼采所说,苏格拉底成了"所谓世界历史的唯一转折点和漩涡"(《悲剧的诞生》15)。这将是尼采讲座的一个主题。

所以,回到施特劳斯讨论柏拉图《王制》的文章,我们可以看到施特劳斯在中心位置表明,苏格拉底把自己的神学-政治方案置于合适的位置。我们再次引用尼采的话:从柏拉图以降,"所有神学家和哲人都在同一条道路上"(《善恶的彼岸》格言191)。

总结一下,我可以说这是我接下来的五次讲座即将涉及的部分内容:哲人柏拉图和哲人尼采的神学-政治方案,我在标题中称之为他们的哲学之诗。但是,显然有某种甚至比哲学之诗更重要的东西,而我的讲座也会涉及。更重要的是藏于神学-政治方案背后的哲学,藏于这些方案背后或孕生这些方案的对存在或自然的理解。

思考哲学自身的方式之一就在于此。在《城邦与人》的末句中,施特劳斯谈到"与哲学相伴而生的至关重要的问题",这个问题即"神是什么?"这个问题与哲学"相伴而生",因为无论哲学何时何地产生,该问题就随之产生。该问题的产生是因为"神是什么?"是本体论(ontological)问题,是关于存在的问题。它问的是,最高的可能的存在是什么?所以,尽管"神是什么?"这个问题有实践的维度,如同在苏格拉底与阿德曼托斯的谈论中有实践的维度一样,但对哲人来说,这个问题本质上是本体论的,是理论性的而非实践性的。该问题是综合的本体论问题内一个具体的本体论问题,综合的问题问的是,"诸存在的存在是什么?"这一问题内的具体问题问的是,"最高的存在是什么?"

所以,余下的讲座的两个主题是柏拉图和尼采的哲学和哲学之诗。我的方法就是一个读者的方法:显白和隐微的区分如何引领我们恰当地理解柏拉图和尼采的哲学和哲学之诗?

我想以有关施特劳斯的一个观点结束这一讲。我关注他讨论《王制》的文章的中心段落的中心句,不是为了证明施特劳斯也显白地写作。他当然显白地写作。实际上,我关注这一中心段落的中心句,是为了表明施特劳斯在中心选择处理什么问题,"神是什么?"不仅是一个本体论问题,也是哲人立法的一部分。我们从施特劳斯对"神是什么?"的重要处理看出,立法规定神是什么在某种程度上来说是哲人统治的一种手段。施特劳斯指出,柏拉图是这样,尼采亦如是。

柏拉图在《王制》末尾的卷十回到了"神是什么?"的问题,其中苏格拉底强行回到诗的话题,解决"哲学与诗古老的争论"(607b)。争论的解决基于智慧者的自然优越性,即哲人自然正当的统治。作为自然的统治者,哲人利用诗。卷十表明,诗最引人注目的一面是哲人关于诸神和灵魂的新教导。苏格拉底在卷十提出的教导接续了他关于诸神和灵魂的立法:他使诸神成为人类行为的道德法官,并使灵魂不朽,灵魂在来世将因在此世的行为而受到赏罚。

讲述西方哲学的漫长故事必定会用很大篇幅讲到,柏拉图式哲人们的这一新教导为启示或基督教开辟了道路,由此引发了多大的灾难。我将会在后续的讲座中更多谈到此点,但我暂时得忽略它,以便用施特劳斯的一个绝妙表达结束此讲。施特劳斯把苏格拉底关于诸神和灵魂的新立法称之为"侍养之诗"(ministerial poetry),①这两个词都很重要。②"诗"是某种制作的东西,是人的发明、人的想象力制作的东西,这是我的标题"哲学之诗"的由来。"诗"的这一用法追根溯源属于柏拉图,我会在柏拉图的讲座中处理这个问题。但施特劳斯通过加上形容词 ministerial 来修饰"诗",从而创造了自己的用法。Ministerial 至为恰当,因为它有双重含义,政治的和社会的含义,而且两种含义都成立。

施特劳斯强调政治的含义:Ministerial 政治上的含义是为统治者或政府服务,例如,财政部部长(minister)服务于执政的政府。柏拉图关于诸神和灵魂的新侍养之诗服务于新王,即哲人王;新的侍养之诗服务于哲学的利益,这就是它存在的根本理由。但是,第一种含义的独特性被施特劳斯未提及的第二种含义所修正和美化。

动词 minister 在英语中有第二层含义,社会的(social)或治疗(therapeutic)的含义,即给予那些需要的人援助或服务。一个人通过减轻病人或伤者的痛苦来照料(ministers)他们。这也是哲学的侍养之诗所做的事情:对于那些像阿德曼托斯那样因为对正义和诸神丧失信念而饱受精神折磨的人,苏格拉底关于道德的诸神和不朽的灵魂的诗给予他们帮助和慰藉。阿德曼托斯代表一整代人,他们将从新的苏格拉底之诗得到照料。

这是为何我在标题中使用"哲学之诗"这个短语的原因:哲学,即想要理解的冲动,它要达到理解;从这种理解中,哲学孕生或诞下了一种诗,这种诗服务于哲学的利益,同时也服务于更大的政治共同体,只有在政治共同体中,哲学才能繁荣。

所以,我的讲座有关"哲学和哲学之诗"。它们有关柏拉图和尼采的哲学,我现在要说并试图在讲座中证明的是,当按照施特劳斯所展示的方式来阅读柏拉图和尼采时,我认为柏拉图和尼采的哲学相互聚合,或拥有

---

① Leo Strauss, *The City and Man*, p. 136.
② [编注]依照朗佩特下面的解释,ministerial 既有服侍、服务之义,又有照料之义,姑且黏合二义译为"侍-养之诗",表示"侍奉哲学"和"养护人的灵魂"两层意思,尽管"侍养"在汉语中侧重于侍候奉养长辈。

相同的精义。我的讲座也有关尼采和柏拉图的哲学之诗,他们的哲学之诗完全相互岔离,或者彼此剑拔弩张,互不相容。二者的岔离有充分的理由,正如二者在哲学本身上的聚合有充分的理由。

我的讲座最后也有关尼采反对柏拉图的哲学之诗的充分理由,以及这些理由为何自然地让我们转向尼采的哲学之诗。

第二讲　施特劳斯、尼采与未来的哲学之诗

在第一讲中，我考察了施特劳斯在致克莱因的信中对显白写作的恢复，然后考察了施特劳斯的一个文本来说明他如何也显白地写作，更重要的是，他如何引领他的读者进入柏拉图的显白之作《王制》的隐微中心。

在今天的讲座中，我会研读施特劳斯的另一个文本来说明他如何也显白地写尼采，而且更重要的是，他如何引领他的读者进入尼采的显白之作《善恶的彼岸》(Beyond Good and Evil) 的隐微中心。今天的讲座将疏解施特劳斯晚年的文章《注意尼采〈善恶的彼岸〉的谋篇》(Note on the Plan of Nietzsche's Beyond Good and Evil) 部分内容。这篇文章从 1972 年 3 月写到 1973 年 2 月，七个月后，施特劳斯于 1973 年 9 月辞世。施特劳斯清楚《柏拉图式政治哲学研究》(Studies on the Platonic Political Philosophy) 将是他的辞世之作，①所以他精心设计，这篇讨论尼采的文章在文集中理应占有特殊的地位。文集大致按照从古至今的时间顺序编排，但是施特劳斯将论尼采的文章置于正中间，而且与紧随其上的《耶路撒冷与雅典》一文构成一对，从而打破了这一顺序。这一结构上的调整意义重大，因为施特劳斯认为居中(centering)是谨慎作家的写作技艺之一，同时他本人不断地以漂亮的方式践行居中的技艺。这也是更加意义重大的主题上的调整：在耶路撒冷与雅典长久的、具有历史决定性意义的冲突之后，尼采出现了。

在发现哲人们的显白教诲之后，施特劳斯毕生的研究是柏拉图式的政治哲学。尼采这位哲人曾影响和吸引 22 岁到 30 岁之间的施特劳斯，

---

① 中译参见施特劳斯，《柏拉图式政治哲学研究》，张缨等译，华夏出版社，2012。

以至于他几乎相信他从尼采书中读懂的一切。即使在而立之年(1929年)停止了单纯被尼采影响和吸引,施特劳斯对尼采的研究仍然不辍。通过将论尼采的文章置于辞世之作的中心而打破时间顺序,施特劳斯似乎悄悄地在说:在柏拉图式政治哲学的研究中,尼采现在占据了中心位置,就在耶路撒冷与雅典之后。

施特劳斯文章的开篇:尼采与柏拉图

在文章开篇,施特劳斯指出《善恶的彼岸》是尼采"最漂亮"的著作,为了阐明这句话的意思,他在第一段转向了柏拉图及其作品。从这一开头开始,施特劳斯就把尼采和柏拉图放在一起。他在文中会一直把他们放在一起,包括文章结尾。

在第三段,施特劳斯指出尼采"把自身呈现为柏拉图的敌对者",他还总结了第二段中对尼采及其最漂亮的著作的讨论,其中再次提及柏拉图:他说在《善恶的彼岸》一书中,尼采"在'形式'上比在其他任何地方更加'柏拉图化'"。尼采在这部著作中展示其思想的方式就是柏拉图化,与柏拉图展现其思想的方式相仿。柏拉图和尼采都是显白的作家,他们通过施特劳斯所称的"形式上、意图上以及缄默技艺上优雅的精妙"来美化他们的思想。显白技艺的关键要素是:形式,意图和缄默技艺。

之后,施特劳斯在第四段立刻转向尼采《善恶的彼岸》的前言,特别转向与柏拉图敌对的尼采:"柏拉图的根本错误在于他发明了纯粹心智(pure mind)和善本身(the good in itself)。"施特劳斯引入柏拉图,是为了抛出一个重要观点,指出柏拉图发明纯粹心智的巧妙:

> 从这一前提出发,我们可以轻易地被引向第俄提玛(Diotima)的结论,即没有人是智慧的,只有神才智慧;人只能寻求智慧或搞哲学,诸神则不用搞哲学。

因此,施特劳斯从尼采反对柏拉图发明纯粹心智和善自身,转向为柏拉图辩护,由柏拉图的一篇对话引入诸神。这篇对话认为人类没有纯粹心智,只有诸神才有。柏拉图很精妙:他的"根本错误"似乎不是关于人的心智,而只是关于诸神的心智的论断——然而这是什么意思?

施特劳斯借由柏拉图的精妙之处为柏拉图辩护,这使他随后从尼采著作的前言跳到结尾:

> 在《善恶的彼岸》的倒数第二个格言,尼采描绘了"心灵的天才"(the genius of the heart)——一个超级苏格拉底,他实际上是狄俄尼索斯(Dionysos)神——尼采在充分的准备后泄露出一个新奇观点:也许尤其在哲人们中间才有的怀疑,即怀疑诸神也搞哲学。

所以是柏拉图理解错了诸神和他们的纯粹心智吗?诸神是否如尼采所泄露的那样也搞哲学?泄露是为了揭开一个秘密,可能是个危险的秘密。如果哲人们尤其怀疑诸神在搞哲学,那智慧的第俄提玛,苏格拉底的老师,在《会饮》中说诸神不搞哲学是怎么回事?

施特劳斯随后做了他作为一个细心的读者很早就学会的事情:把作者笔下的角色、对话中的人物与作者本人区分开来。他把第俄提玛和柏拉图区别开来,以便提出极其值得注意的一点:"柏拉图很可能认为诸神在搞哲学。"(参见《智术师》216b5-6,《泰阿泰德》151d1-2)如果你查阅这两处文献,会发现它们暗示诸神的确在搞哲学——不仅如此,它们还暗示那些搞哲学的诸神就是哲人们自己。

所以施特劳斯暗示,柏拉图所持的观点和他笔下第俄提玛所教的不一样。但对我们来说更重要的是,施特劳斯在其论尼采文章的开篇安排或设计尼采与他显见的敌对者柏拉图之间的对比,这迫使我们思考,柏拉图自己是否真的认为尼采所说的那些是他的"根本错误"。哲人柏拉图曾在自己的思考中犯了这个错误吗?或者哲人柏拉图觉得让他笔下的第俄提玛、苏格拉底的老师教授这个观点是可取的?

通过建立对比,然后仅仅给出两个参考文献,施特劳斯提示有心的读者,柏拉图所思考的正是尼采所思考的,但柏拉图认为通过第俄提玛教授不同的东西是可取的。这暗示,施特劳斯认为尼采和其敌对者柏拉图关于诸神和哲学的思考实际一样,不同之处在于尼采通过引入搞哲学的狄俄尼索斯神泄露了诸神也搞哲学的秘密。

但是,尼采自己暗示"这种新奇观点"完全不新奇,因为它是"也许尤其在哲人们中间才有的怀疑"。尼采可能十分清楚,他引入的这个新奇观点完全不新奇,而是哲人们早就知道的东西,但是它被哲人们掩盖,就像他的敌对者柏拉图让其笔下的第俄提玛教授相反的东西一样。所以尼采的柏拉图化,他的"形式上、意图上以及缄默技艺上优雅的精妙",包括了泄露他对诸神的思考,而他对诸神的思考就是柏拉图对诸神的思考,但柏拉图并未泄露,或者仅向施特劳斯这样的读者泄露。施特劳斯将目光从第俄提玛所教授的东西移向柏拉图的其他文段来发现柏拉图真正的思考。

所以,在论尼采的文章开篇,施特劳斯没有泄露深藏不露的柏拉图的隐秘观点,而是微妙地暗示柏拉图和尼采知道相同的真相,但是柏拉图保守了秘密而尼采则泄露了秘密。通过指向柏拉图的秘密,施特劳斯在考察尼采的柏拉图化的语境下指向柏拉图自身的柏拉图化。通过指向柏拉图的秘密,施特劳斯暗示第俄提玛讲述了一个关于诸神的高贵谎言,这一谎言服务于柏拉图关于哲学的政治目的。施特劳斯可能也暗示,尼采泄露秘密是为了服务于他关于哲学的政治目的。

我在这里摆出结论,这样余下的讲座才能显得合理:柏拉图和尼采出于相同的原因而柏拉图化,即为了哲学的福祉;他们柏拉图化是为哲学服务。他们的差异在于保守和泄露秘密——在有关诸神和哲学的事情上!——这可以追溯到相同的原因:他们各自诠释了他们时代的精神状况,各自教授了时代为了哲学的福祉所要求的东西。

施特劳斯的文章通篇比较尼采和柏拉图,但我们没有时间考虑所有这些情形,我将跳到施特劳斯文章的末尾,那里对比了尼采和柏拉图。议题不再是诸神而是诸美德,道德的关键性问题,尼采著作第二个主要部分的主题之一。具体的议题是美德作为"未来的哲学"的一部分——尼采曾说,《善恶的彼岸》是"未来哲学的序曲"。具体来说,议题是"未来哲人的美德"。施特劳斯说这些美德"不同于柏拉图式的美德",从而引入了柏拉图。在施特劳斯的举例中,两项柏拉图式的美德被两项现代的美德取代。文章最后一句说道:

> 这是阐明[尼采]为何通过自然的 Vornehmheit[高贵性]来描述自然的众多例证之一(格言188)。Die vornehme Natur ersetzt die göttliche Natur[高贵的自然取代神圣的自然]。

这就是结尾。施特劳斯以一句德语结束了他的英文论文。他把他的意思藏在外语中,藏在尼采的语言中。"高贵的自然取代神圣的自然",也就是尼采所教导的自然、高贵的自然取代柏拉图所教导的自然,即自然和超越自然的超自然。施特劳斯是赞成这一取代吗?施特劳斯全文对比尼采和柏拉图,他在结尾是不是隐蔽地支持尼采关于自然的教诲取代柏拉图关于自然的教诲?施特劳斯隐藏起自己的主张。所以我们至少暂时可以让它隐藏。

在本讲的第一部分结束时,我想说说施特劳斯就柏拉图化对比柏拉图和尼采的另一个方面。接近文章的开头,施特劳斯提醒注意尼采赋予其著作的整体结构,其"谋篇"正好分为九章。施特劳斯强调,第1章和第2章有关哲学,第3章关于宗教,"大约123条'格言和插曲'"组成的第4章将前面三章与后续篇章分隔开来。第四章由此把全书分为两个主要部分。关于尼采赋予其著作的这一形式,施特劳斯总结说:"哲学和宗教似乎不可分割。"尼采在形式上的柏拉图化部分在于,把哲学和宗教放在一起,并把它们与道德和政治区分开来;尼采将两个最重要的东西与同样重要的东西区分开来。现在我可以转而说明哲学和宗教如何对尼采而言是不可分割的。

尼采的哲学篇章

《善恶的彼岸》第一章是"论哲人们的偏见":它批评那些偏见是为了

从中解放心灵。第二章"自由心灵"也讨论哲学,阐述了自由心灵可获取的东西,即尼采的自由心灵已经获得的东西。第二章形式上的柏拉图化部分在于,尼采赋予它一个意义深远的中心。

施特劳斯论哲学篇章的第一段的开头是:"尼采在前两章很少谈到宗教。"尼采的确如此:这些篇章关乎哲学。施特劳斯这句话表明,他这里的兴趣点在宗教,即哲学篇章中宗教的存在。施特劳斯最终的兴趣当然是哲学。但是,这是施特劳斯所写的文章,而它的主要兴趣是哲人尼采笔下的宗教,是尼采的神学-政治方案或尼采作为宗教的哲学之诗。施特劳斯的下一句说:

> 我们可以说,尼采只在一条格言中谈及宗教,那条格言碰巧是最短的(格言37)。那条格言是紧前面一条格言的某种推论,在前一条格言中,他以符合其意图的最直接和最清晰的方式阐明了他的基本观点的特殊性质,根据这一观点,生命是权力意志,或从世界内部来看就是权力意志,而非其他。

注意:施特劳斯说"一条格言"关乎宗教,而且那条格言是前一条格言的"某种推论"或结果,前一条格言包含尼采的基本观点。也要注意,施特劳斯暗示尼采"阐明"其"基本观点"的方式并不完全直接和清晰:尼采没有完全公开他的根本观点;他阐明其基本观点的方式有他特殊的意图。但是,施特劳斯的要点在最后:尼采的"基本观点"关涉尼采意义上的生命,尼采意义上的生命就是"世界",是万物的整全。我们可以用尼采所拒斥的哲学用语来说,他的基本观点关涉存在本身。这是一种本体论,一种对作为一个整体的诸存在的性质或特征的论述:"从内部看",即以我们实际永远无法看的方式看,"世界是权力意志,而非其他"。施特劳斯明白:权力意志是尼采对诸存在的存在、自然的自然的命名。

然后,施特劳斯把尼采的本体论与柏拉图的本体论联系起来:

> 权力意志取代了爱欲(eros)——对"善本身"的追求——在柏拉

图思想中占据的地位。

施特劳斯这里把爱欲界定为"善本身",而"善本身"是他之前说尼采所认为的柏拉图的根本错误之一。我认为这表明了施特劳斯的意图:他无意以一种完全直接或清晰的方式阐明尼采的本体论与柏拉图的本体论之间的关系;他使这种关系在某种程度上比实际的情况更加含糊。

施特劳斯在这段中接着处理了在哲学的显白教诲的整部历史背后潜藏的一个问题:哲人们认识到他们发现的真理是危险的,施特劳斯用尼采所用的"致命的"一词描述这种危险。权力意志和爱欲两者都表达一种关于现实的真理——这个真理是致命的。正如伯纳德特在论述柏拉图《会饮》中爱欲的一开始所说:"关于爱欲的真理是恐怖的。"尼采如何处理他认为致命的根本真理?施特劳斯说:

> 尼采的陈述或暗示刻意扑朔迷离(格言40)。通过暗示或声明真理是致命的,他尽其所能地破坏致命真理的力量;他暗示最重要、最包罗万象的真理——关于所有真理的真理——是赐予生命的。

"刻意扑朔迷离":尼采故意含糊,为了暗示一些东西而含糊;"格言40"谈到,对于一切"深刻的"事物来说,面具是必要的。在说"最包罗万象的真理"是致命的时,是在为什么而刻意扑朔迷离?施特劳斯说,这是尼采开始破坏真理的致命力量的方式。这至关重要。包罗万象的真理一开始看上去致命,但实际上是赐予生命的。正确地看,看上去致命的东西是赐予生命的。施特劳斯将会表明,尼采在那只说了一次的段落中正是这样做的:尼采表明看上去致命的如何实际上恰恰相反。这便触及我此讲的重点。

为了得出这一点,施特劳斯处理了尼采在形式上的柏拉图化的另一方面:他赋予自己的一系列格言的结构。施特劳斯让我们注意论自由心灵的这章中心的格言,由此表明尼采精心地编排序列:

> 格言34和35之间的联系是一个特别显著的例子,表明有某种

清晰、尽管有所隐藏的秩序支配着格言的序列;尼采的论证散乱芜杂,这更像是假装的而非真是如此。

看起来散乱芜杂,或者似乎缺少一个明确的计划或目的,实际上明晰或清楚,尽管有所隐藏。明明有一个计划或目的,为何却假装没有?在尼采那里明显和常见但施特劳斯并没有说的是:假装没有计划或目的,这使你能够注意到一个计划,然后去发现这一计划的目的。你发现了它,你就拥有了它:你认识到尼采在教导你。

施特劳斯的下一段如此开头:

> 我们现在可以转向《善恶的彼岸》第 1 至 2 章中的两条格言,可以说,它们是论述宗教的(格言 36 – 37)。

施特劳斯之前说有一个段落论述宗教,但现在他说两个段落论述宗教。他将纠正自己,重提一个段落,但他在这里说两个段落,这让你寻找如此说的理由,而这个理由似乎是宗教格言和前一条格言之间的联系。这个联系反映出格言 34 和 35 的关联,并且非常重要:"格言 36 呈现出支持权力意志学说的论证。"

格言 36 是论证(reasoning),是哲学。格言 37 仅仅是一种推论,因为它紧随论证之后,内容不是论证,而属于宗教。施特劳斯没有重复第 36 节的论证。但他给予格言 36 的论证极高的评价:结合了"同时是极不妥协的智识真诚与最让人着迷的戏谑"。这个论证结合了最严谨的哲学逻辑的严肃与戏谑。第 36 节论证的智识真诚遵照严格的逻辑,推导心灵能够对自身、他者和作为整全的世界知道什么。第 36 节的论证得出如下结论:从内部看,世界或整体将是权力意志而非其他。第 37 节延续了最让人着迷的戏谑,论证在此处激起了尼采"朋友们"的恐惧以及尼采对朋友们不可或缺的帮助。论证和戏谑是在根本问题上进行哲学交流的高峰。

我会在最后一场尼采讲座中探讨这一论证。此时,我想让大家只注意施特劳斯的这一强调,即格言 36 是运用于作为整体的自然的哲学方法。在其哲学篇章中,围绕自然的自然,围绕哲学最终寻求之物,尼采引导读者得出一条全面而理性的结论。施特劳斯讲得甚至比尼采更简略,因为他已经告诉我们,他的文章关心的是《善恶的彼岸》中的宗教。宗教不可能比哲学更重要,但施特劳斯选择关注宗教,即哲学之诗。在论证之后是某种推论或推理。施特劳斯表明,这种推论是论证从听到它的听众那里引出的,从尼采正在训练的自由心灵那里引出的。自由心灵对论证的回应,不是更多的论证,不是哲学,而是对哲学的理性结论深具人性的反应,这正是尼采期待他那些准备最充分、心灵自由的朋友们做出的回应。

我们转向第九段,尼采"根本命题"的"某种推论":

> 在以权力意志学说引诱他的一些读者们(参格言30)之后,尼采让他们提出问题,即是否这一学说并未断言——通俗地说——上帝被驳倒,而魔鬼却没有。

尼采迫使哪些读者提出问题从而引诱他们?施特劳斯接下来引用尼采的答案:"我的朋友们"——尼采引诱他的"朋友们",即自由心灵们,那些通过他对他们的教诲而成为他的朋友的人。但是,他们在这里面临一个严肃的问题。施特劳斯说到"(参格言30)",暗示我们在考虑尼采的读者时应该记着尼采在格言30所做的区分,那是尼采唯一一次明确提及显白和隐微。如果你按施特劳斯所说的做,并且阅读格言30,你会看到,尼采说当哲人的"至高洞见"来到"那些并非为它们而生的那类人"的耳畔时,会听起来愚蠢而且有时像是罪行。尼采在第37节暗示,即便是他潜在的朋友,那些就是为至高洞见而生的一类人,在听到他的论证的至高洞见时,也会像格言30所说的那样,会评判这是疯狂,是大逆不道。尼采说,他的朋友们通俗地谈论上帝和魔鬼。但他的朋友们是自由心灵,他们不信上帝或魔鬼。作为现代的自由心灵,他们不再有一种语言能足够强烈地陈明他们发现尼采的结论是多么大逆不道。所以,他们采用旧语言,也就是某一时刻的通俗用语,并使用这一用语的两个极端,即上帝和魔鬼,来表达他们对尼采罪行的震撼。

在仅仅转述尼采的朋友们所说的话之后,施特劳斯引用尼采本人的话:

> 他回答道:"恰恰相反!恰恰相反,我的朋友们!真该死,什么迫使你们通俗地说话来着?"

尼采在强调,重复"恰恰相反"!但是,他没有解释"相反的"是什么,施特劳斯也没有解释。所以读者不得不自己想清楚。这不难。"上帝被驳倒"的反面是"魔鬼被驳倒"。基督教神学的超验上帝是尼采的朋友们认为的上帝;他们是后基督教的无神论者,他们对上帝的唯一概念是基督教的上帝。如果世界的整全确实就是权力意志而非其他,那么彼岸世界和此世界就没有什么不同。尼采的论证驳斥一个超验的上帝。但基督教的超验上帝已经宣告此世界为黑暗的国度,上帝要从这魔鬼的地盘把我们拯救出来。所以尼采的朋友们一定会想到,"相反的"是,那个被驳倒的上帝就是魔鬼,被驳倒的魔鬼。尼采邀请他的朋友们思考最大的亵渎。当他们按尼采所暗示的做并且思考"相反的"东西,他们自己思索出尼采本人没有说出的最大亵渎。施特劳斯注意到马基雅维利那里的一个相似技巧,并且给出了使用这一技巧的原因:迫使读者成为马基雅维利的共犯,因为读者自己得出了可怕的想法。

尼采"恰恰相反!"的另一半是尼采教授他的基督教-无神论者、心灵自由的朋友们的神学:"魔鬼没有[被驳倒]"的反面,是"上帝没有[被驳倒]"。尼采因此暗示他的权力意志观给上帝留有位置,或者说给诸神留有位置,正如我们将会看到的那样。尼采的朋友们必须拓宽他们对上帝或诸神的思考。

尼采和施特劳斯默默地邀请我们思索两个相反之处,我们在照做之后,来到施特劳斯的翻译:"真该死,什么迫使你们通俗地说话来着?"施特劳斯将尼采的德语 wer[谁]译为 what[什么]:尼采问"谁迫使你们?"这很重要,因为这一问题隐含着答案:尼采的朋友们不信上帝或魔鬼。所以迫使他们"通俗地谈论"上帝和魔鬼的那个谁,一定是死去的上帝自己。这个超验的上帝已死,但未离去。已死的上帝甚至继续为尼采拥有自由心灵的朋友们定义上帝是什么。两千年的古老传统在最近的无神论者那里依然强大——当他们想到"上帝"时,他们只想到那个上帝,已死的上帝,他们仅有的上帝观念依然强大。如果权力意志观没有驳倒上帝,那么尼采的朋友们将不得不开始重新思考神是什么。

所以,格言 36 和 37 中论证和戏谑的结合使施特劳斯能够以此结束这一关键小段:

> 权力意志学说——《善恶的彼岸》的整个学说——在某种意义上是对上帝的辩护。

施特劳斯说,而且五次说到,尼采的本体论,亦即从内部观看的世界观,在为上帝辩护。尼采的本体论引入了思考神性、思考神是什么的新方式。施特劳斯引领读者进入尼采这一引诱的核心。哲人尼采思考过神是什么,他会提供关于诸神的新教诲。这新的教诲不一定是全新的。在文章的开篇,施特劳斯已经暗示尼采和柏拉图可能对神是什么并无异议:"超级苏格拉底",搞哲学的狄俄尼索斯神,可能代表一个对神是什么共有的观点。我们可以将这个问题暂时放下,转而问:

为何尼采会为上帝辩护,为何尼采会让上帝免于责难或者证明上帝合理?即使"上帝"现在意味着与超验上帝完全截然不同的某种东西,为何不干脆做个无神论者?施特劳斯没有直接问这个问题,但他做出了回答:他结束这个段落时说,"(参格言 150 和 295,以及《道德的谱系》前言,条 7)"。

施特劳斯之后提及格言 150 是为了暗示,尼采认为,若没有诸神,就不存在人可以生活的"世界"。尼采似乎同意柏拉图和哲学传统的观点,认为诸神对一个健康的社会秩序是必要的。施特劳斯之前已经引用过"格言 295",表明"超级苏格拉底"事实上是狄俄尼索斯神。施特劳斯的另一个参考文献《道德的谱系》前言,条 7",谈论的是关于"酒神剧'灵魂的命运'"新的纠葛和可能,以及利用这个新的可能的狄俄尼索斯本人——"那个我们所有人里伟大、古老、永恒的谐剧诗人!"遵照这条参考文献,施特劳斯开启了他对宗教篇章的论述,正如尼采以论"迄今灵魂的整个历史"开启他的宗教篇章一样——对尼采而言,在人类灵魂面对新的纠葛和可能的节点上,宗教史或许以一种与超级苏格拉底-狄俄尼索斯相关联的方式提供了一种人类灵魂的历史。

施特劳斯在结束他对《善恶的彼岸》中哲学篇章的论述时,讨论了那些哲学篇章中一条关于宗教的格言。他以尼采的邀请结束他对哲学的处理:尼采邀请他那有哲学倾向的朋友们重新思考神是什么,摆脱圣经的超验来思考神性,思考与根本命题关联的神性,思考权力意志本体论对上帝或诸神的意涵。更具体地说,施特劳斯结束他对哲学的论述时说,哲学论证的最终结论,即世界是权力意志而不是其他,这是对上帝的一种辩护;而且施特劳斯补充了三条参考文献来助你思考一个关于诸神的新观点。或许尼采的哲学能产生一个关于诸神的新观点,一种关于神性的新诗,提供给其世界只可能围绕一个神旋转的人类。在暗示尼采的哲学对宗教的承诺之后,施特劳斯直接转向尼采论宗教的篇章。

尼采的宗教篇章

施特劳斯首先阐明宗教篇章的谋篇:它处理了直到现在的宗教、未来的宗教以及作为一个整体的宗教。施特劳斯详尽讨论了涉及当今和未来宗教的系列格言。尼采在位于第 3 章中心的格言 53 和 54 处理当今的宗教;一个有关当今的无神论,另一个有关当今对灵魂的谋杀(the assassination of the soul)。当代思想拒绝基督教关于上帝与灵魂的这两个核心教诲。下一个格言 55 处理当今的无神论和灵魂-暗杀的后果,认为它们导致了远比基督教糟糕的后果:现代虚无主义,尽管尼采和施特劳斯都没有用虚无主义(nihilism)一词。施特劳斯在另外一个自然段讨论了虚无主义之后的走向。

尼采没打算为了虚无而牺牲上帝,因为在认识到上帝已死的致命真理的同时,他旨在把这一致命真理转换为激发生命的真理,或者毋宁说在致命真理的深处发现其反面。

施特劳斯说"旨在……转换为"——但是他知道这么说不对,这不是尼采所为,然后他纠正了自己:"或者毋宁说"尼采发现反面,发现一个意想不到的事实——没有什么需要被转换;实际上,尼采发现了致命真理的反面。所以这里的举动与施特劳斯先前就尼采的"刻意扑朔迷离"所说的相似:初看上去致命的,实际是"赐予生命的"。然后,施特劳斯转向紧接在有关虚无主义的格言后的格言 56。这是宗教篇章中最重要的格言,唯一一条关于永恒复归的格言,施特劳斯做了复述、引用和评注。

但是,尼采受到"某种谜一般的渴望"的怂恿,曾长久地尝试浸入悲观主义的深处……因此,他掌握了一种比之前任何悲观主义者还要否定世界(world–denying)的思考方式。

这个"谜一般的渴望"只可能是在尼采的探究中驱使他的求知的热望(the passion to know)。尼采浸入悲观主义的深处,由此通达看上去最否定世界的思考方式。这种思考方式视世界为权力意志而非其他——尼采的朋友们对此首先的反应是,骇人地否定世界。

然而,一个走上了这条道路的人或许无意间向相反的理想,向属于未来宗教的理想,睁开了双眼。

这恰恰是尼采所说的话:"向相反的理想睁开了他的双眼。"这个理想是一切存在之物的永恒复返,它如此重要,以致尼采和施特劳斯都称之为理想(ideal)。但是,为何加了那个含糊的"或许"?"或许"可以表示"或许无意间"。施特劳斯的下一句解释了这个或许,而尼采则没有:

无需多言,在其他人那里只是"或许"的情形,在尼采的思想和生命中却是事实。

不,不是"无需多言",而是必须得说,施特劳斯必须得说,因为尼采的一些追随者坚称尼采根本上是在寻找一种新理想,尼采大体上是一个宗教导师,他在寻找一种新理想来应对我们当今虚无主义文化中理想的缺失。通过澄清"或许",施特劳斯说了尼采本人曾经说过的话:他不曾有意发现一种新理想,他发现了新理想,"但实际上却无意如此"。

所以,施特劳斯再次纠正自己,正如他纠正了转换和发现。这两处纠正说明同一件事:尼采是个哲人,不是个宗教思想家。尼采的思想和生命意图一件事:发现真理。尼采不曾意图找到一种新理想;实际上,他找到一种新理想,这是他欲求真理的结果,是他的发现的结果,他发现世界是权力意志而非其他。这个发现的意外结果是他瞥见了一种新理想。这个重要的次序让尼采从哲学转向宗教:他对真理的发现使他睁开眼睛看到了一种新理想;哲学导向哲学之诗。

> 对虚无的崇拜证明是从每一种否定世界到最无限的肯定——对曾经存在和现在存在的一切的永恒肯定——不可或缺的过渡。

深入思考虚无主义的寻求真理者得到意料之外的洞见,那就是这样一个新理想:世界本身无限次地返回至世界本身。施特劳斯在这段继续对这个理想作了一些有趣的评注,而我在这里略过了;然后他引用了这条格言的结尾:

> "而这",尼采这样总结他关于过去和现在存在之物的永恒重复的说明:"不是 circulus vitiosus deus[神恶性循环]吗?"

这个拉丁文短语正如施特劳斯所注意到的那样含混:一个恶性循环造了神?神是个恶性循环?施特劳斯做了两个重要评注。第一,

> [尼采的]无神论并非毫不含混,因为他曾怀疑是否可能存在一

个不以上帝为中心的世界。(格言150)

格言150再次出现,尼采似乎以之作为《善恶的彼岸》的中心格言。施特劳斯指出,该格言表明,万物只有围绕一个神才能成为一个世界;人的世界,生活的世界,文化的世界,亦即一个有意义且重要的地域,只有在神或诸神存在时才可能。尼采的无神论含混是因为他表明诸神是必要的,在社会层面是必要的,对成就一个文化世界而言是必要的。第二,

> 当前格言[格言56]的结论经由它的形式提醒我们想起出现在头两章的神学格言(格言37),在那里,尼采说出这个事实,即权力意志学说在某种意义上是一种对上帝的辩护,即便是对上帝决然的非有神论辩护。

(顺便注意施特劳斯回到了他真正的判断:哲学诸篇章中唯一的神学格言是第37条,其中尼采的友人们错误地回应他的权力意志观,认为上帝被驳倒了但魔鬼没有。)施特劳斯重述格言56的结尾:永恒复返"不是神恶性循环吗?"如果这一点"提醒我们想起"格言37,那我们不得不补充某些东西,我们不得不说尼采在第37条所说的:"恰恰相反!恰恰相反,我的朋友们。"这里的"相反"是,永恒复返不是一个恶性循环,恰恰相反,生命的恶性循环造就了永恒,造就了某种意义上的神。永恒复返是对万物的整个自然循环的神化。永恒复返是一种对上帝的非有神论辩护。

所以,施特劳斯引领他的读者看到,尼采在格言56向他的朋友们展示了对将世界理解为权力意志而非其他的真正回应。权力意志观没有驳倒上帝,反而引向一种新的理想,甚至引向一种新的神性概念。

我在自己1996年的著作《施特劳斯与尼采》(*Leo Strauss and Nietzsche*)中说过,施特劳斯对尼采研究最大的贡献,就是洞见到权力意志与永恒复返的联系,洞见到哲学与宗教的联系。这是一种注疏式的贡献,来自一个极为厉害的读者,他穷其一生研读柏拉图式的政治哲人们。施特

劳斯表明他是尼采想要的读者;他给予《善恶的彼岸》中两个最重要的结论恰当的解释。第一个是哲学的至深洞见:存在就是权力意志而非其他。第二个是哲学对宗教的推论:关于什么是的新观点引向一个新的最高理想,即肯定如其所是的世界,从而引向为神辩护,因为只有神能够使一个世界对人们变得可能。

施特劳斯看到尼采思想的内在一致,正如尼采在《善恶的彼岸》前三章展开的那样。这一内在一致就是尼采最深刻的柏拉图化:也就是说,在尼采那里如同在柏拉图那里一样,哲学在其最深处产生或孕生政治哲学或以神学-政治方案为形式的哲学之诗。尼采最终是由此成为一个柏拉图式的政治哲人,一个成功做到柏拉图所做之事的哲人。首先是对为哲人保留的世界的隐微洞见,这完全是理智之事。然后是一种对所有人的显白教诲,一种建立在人类激情上的教诲,它让单纯的整体变成世界,一个适合人类共同体的可生活的世界。

我的柏拉图讲座会处理柏拉图的这两个问题:柏拉图关于哲学对爱欲的至深洞见的阐述,以及柏拉图对哲学之诗的阐述——柏拉图主义是柏拉图理解其时代的精神状况的后果,并在后来主导了西方哲学。我的尼采讲座会处理尼采的这两个问题:尼采对权力意志作为根本事实的哲学洞见,以及尼采的哲学之诗,后者是对柏拉图的柏拉图主义的理性反对,是尼采对我们时代精神状况理解的结果。

我想引用施特劳斯论述尼采宗教篇章的最后一个论述:

> 尼采的"神学"有一个重要的组成部分,甚至是其中枢,我未曾谈及,也不会谈及,因为我无从进入它。

这语气很强,很激烈——施特劳斯坚决拒绝谈论。我想就此谈谈,但我会等到我的尼采讲座时再谈尼采神学的中枢,也就是他实际重新引入了诸神,在他看来,诸神对造就一个世界是必需的。但现在,为了结束我的施特劳斯讲座,我想转入他在处理尼采的道德和政治篇章时最重要的论点。

尼采关于道德和政治的篇章

施特劳斯已经表明,尼采的哲学产生了一种作为哲学之诗的新的至高理想。但施特劳斯也表明,尼采的哲学产生了一种道德方案,一种与柏拉图主义的善恶根本不同的新的好坏。在这里,我只讨论施特劳斯触及道德和政治的一个论点。该论点出现在施特劳斯论述"我们的美德"一章的结尾,他在那里表明,一种关于人类德性的教诲如何产生于尼采对自然新的理解。施特劳斯强调,哲人尼采意图再次观看"homo natura[自然人]可怕的基本文本",即尼采所称的"永恒的基本文本"。尼采不止观看人性,还基于他所看到的而行动。他的行动所关切的是,在数千年认为人性在某种程度上既次于自然又超于自然的道德思考之后,"人该如何'重新被译入自然'",人如何可能"成为自然的"。

所以我们来到施特劳斯的第 35 段,施特劳斯文章中这一部分最重要的段落。他说道:

……诸自然的一种等级秩序;在这一等级的顶端是补充性的人。

尼采在《善恶的彼岸》中提过到过一次补充性的人(complementary man),施特劳斯提过五次。尼采用这一名称指在人类历史的当下的哲人,既是思考者也是行动者的哲人。施特劳斯关于补充性的人有些值得注意的说法,我不得不略过。但是接下来这句可能是施特劳斯在这篇文章中最引人深思的一句话:

他的至高无上[补充性的人的至高无上]由以下事实得到展现:他解决最高、最困难的问题。

施特劳斯的用语十分小心。他没说旨在解决最高、最困难的问题或者尝试去解决。他说的是解决。那个问题是什么呢?施特劳斯称之为晚期现代的问题,面对这个问题的哲人生活在成熟的现代,此时统治现代的理想自身已成为问题。

关于现代,我不得不说一点,这一点无法在六场讲座中细致展开。现代是基于对自然的科学理解达成对自然的技术征服的时代。革命性的思考和行动方式不是随便发生的;它是那些判定这一方式为必要的哲人们协作的结果——这是西方历史和全球史上最为重要的事件之一。这是西方哲学史上美妙的一章:哲人们打下现代的地基,在我看来其中最为重要的哲人是培根(Francis Bacon)和笛卡尔(René Descartes)。他们判定必须推进一种观念,这一观念导致了施特劳斯这里讨论的问题重重的后果。我会在讲座的结尾就此稍加扩展。

施特劳斯在接下来的两句话中定义了这个问题:

> 正如我们已经观察到的,对尼采而言自然已经成为一个问题,可他离了自然又不行。我们可以说,自然已经成为一个问题是因为这个事实,即人正在征服自然,而且这种征服没有可规定的界限。

按我们通常的理解,征服自然的问题就是现代技术科学努力统治自然的问题:统治自然的尝试可能产生生态灾难。但在这里,施特劳斯紧随尼采对这个问题做了不同的界说。征服自然"没有可规定的界限"的问题是征服人的自然的问题。这一征服是现代德性的直接结果。

施特劳斯如此界说这个问题:

> 作为结果,人们开始想到消除苦难和不平等。

据尼采说,消除苦难和权利平等是现代德性的两个主要特征。正如尼采表明的,它们是基督教德性在现代的世俗版本。它们给尼采提出了根本问题,只是出于一个原因,即施特劳斯指出的原因:

> 然而,苦难和不平等是人之伟大的前提条件。(格言239和257)

最要紧的伟大是最伟大的人的伟大,也就是哲学自身,最高的人类精神得到的洞见,以及只有那种洞见才能看到其必要性的必要的行动。施特劳斯的观点正是尼采的观点:无限制的征服自然可能会带来哲学的终结。

施特劳斯随后转向《扎拉图斯特拉如是说》(*Thus Spoke Zarathustra*),来佐证他之前所说的内容。我不得不略过这一点,因为我没讨论他之前的观点。但对我们来说,阅读这段的结尾就够了。施特劳斯的最后一句是这样说的:

> 自然,自然的永恒,它的存在归因于一种假设,归因于最高的自然的权力意志采取的行动。

施特劳斯的措辞把尼采解决最高、最难问题的做法与哲学史上伟大哲人们相似的做法联系在一起。关键词是假设(postulation)——它意味着假定某个东西为真或声称某个东西是真的。假设某个东西为真,是所有伟大的立法哲人们一直以来所做的事。最高的自然,即创造历史的哲人们,采取的行动就是假设他们认为对他们时代的哲学和人性有益的东西为真。最开始只是一个哲人的立法性假设,却慢慢变成真实,因为社会秩序逐渐接纳了这些假设。哲人们的这些假设其实就是施特劳斯所说的尼采的那个假设:最高的自然的权力意志所采取的行动。

施特劳斯说,尼采的假设行动关乎自然的永恒,即自然的永恒复返。施特劳斯在结尾没说他在开头说过的话:尼采对永恒复返的假设解决了最高、最难的问题,即不知道任何可规定的界限的征服自然的问题。只是,尼采的假设如何解决这一问题?施特劳斯没直说,但文中一直在说的内容的整个基调提供了答案,尼采的答案。永恒复返的学说解决了最高的问题,因为它是一种保存性的(preservative)教导,终极的保守主义,正如施特劳斯略带反讽地说的。

永恒复返根本上不是一种宇宙论主张,不是对世界所存在的方式的一种描述,尽管大多数人可能认为是。实际上,尼采对永恒复返的所有论述都同意,永恒复返是对欲望,对爱者的欲望的一种述说:爱者对如其所是的世界说,对自然而然所是的整体性说,这就是我想要的,而且我无数次如其所是地想要。正是爱者的爱为征服自然,为征服被爱的自然,规定了界限,尽管这说起来也许稀松平常。被爱的自然,首先是被爱的人之自然,将不是通过改造被征服,而是将如其所是地被庆祝。这种听上去稀松平常的解决方案实际很深刻,完全不是浪漫主义的,它实际上基于尼采对人类激情的分析,特别是对复仇激情以及这一激情取得历史至高地位并为我们的善恶观奠定基础的诸种方式的分析。

施特劳斯论尼采的文章差不多以这一论点结束:他说,补充性的人解决了最高最困难的问题。我将这一点视为施特劳斯对尼采最重要的洞见之一。这一洞见所关乎的尼采思想的那个方面,我在自己讨论尼采的一系列著作中做了阐发。从我自己的第一部著作开始,我便提出,尼采的哲学是第一个全面的生态论哲学,这种哲学的道德命令便是尼采的扎拉图斯特拉甫一开始便宣布的:"要对大地真诚!"或"要对大地忠诚!"

施特劳斯的文章差不多以此结束,我的施特劳斯讲座也以此结束。补充性的人解决最高最困难的问题。这让我激动不已。对我来说,没有比这更强烈的对尼采的认可了。尼采解决了晚近现代最高最困难的问题,为征服规定了界限。我在施特劳斯那里发现的所有美妙事物中,再也没有比这更为美妙的了。

我的施特劳斯讲座到此结束,但是施特劳斯将继续出现在我余下的讲座中。在接下来论柏拉图和尼采的讲座中,施特劳斯在哲学史中发现的隐微与显白的区分会呈现为柏拉图和尼采对哲学和哲学之诗的区分。

对于柏拉图,施特劳斯展现了如何用一种新的方式来阅读柏拉图,这种新的方式其实是一种古老的方式,经典的方式。这一阅读方式恢复了真正的柏拉图,也就是施特劳斯所说的"最切近我内心的"柏拉图。我将使用施特劳斯的观点来支撑我关于柏拉图的主要论题,即施特劳斯注意到却未深入探究的主题:苏格拉底如何成为苏格拉底,即苏格拉底如何成为哲人和如何成为政治哲人的双重故事。尼采说,苏格拉底是所谓世界历史的转折点和漩涡。

对于尼采,我将更直接地使用施特劳斯的观点,但我的主要论点是他没有深入探究的:尼采如何成为尼采,即尼采认为他有必要讲述的他如何成为自己的故事。我会使用尼采的自传评论来追溯他的生成,但最主要的是细致考察他的私人笔记,尼采的生成不自觉地展现在他的笔记条目的时间顺序中。

所以,我的柏拉图和尼采讲座既考察古代或古典传统的开端,也考察另一极,即现代传统在我们时代的终结。我将表明,施特劳斯为理解我在自己的第二部著作《尼采与现时代》(*Nietzsche and Modern Times*)①中所称的"因尼采而成为可能的哲学史"的这两极提供了不可或缺的帮助。得到施特劳斯帮助的新历史可以表明,有赖于柏拉图或苏格拉底,哲学采取了一种新转向,而这一转向又结束于尼采清醒地、反柏拉图地转向一条新道路。新哲学史必然要突出柏拉图和尼采这两极之间的过渡点,但我无法在这些讲座中详尽处理。所谓的转折点就是现代世界的奠基,而奠基者是那些完全意识到自己在做什么和为什么这么做的哲人们。在此,我想稍作引申。

现代世界的奠基

西欧的现代世界的奠基是哲学和哲学之诗的大事件,这一大事件依然围绕着我们,正如施特劳斯所说,这波浪潮"至今还承负着我们"。这一欧洲的事件已经成为全球的事件,奠基者们早知道会是如此。这是一个哲学事件,最伟大的哲人们联合击败共同的敌人,确保哲学的统治。施特劳斯表明,马基雅维利是现代哲学首位伟大的奠基者,而且《思索马基雅维利》可能是他最杰出的一部著作。

我不想争论马基雅维利的异常重要性,但对我而言,现代世界的奠基与马基雅维利的两位哲学追随者培根和笛卡尔最紧密相关。两位大师的

---

① 参见朗佩特,《尼采与现时代》,李致远、彭磊、李春长译,华夏出版社,2009。

显白作品导致了科学的和技术的自然观的建立和推进。像他们赞赏的前辈哲人马基雅维利和蒙田（Montaigne）一样，也像向他们学习的后辈哲人霍布斯（Hobbes）和斯宾诺莎（Spinoza）一样，他们与施特劳斯同样称为"黑暗王国"的基督教斗争，并成功地驯服了它。依我之见，培根和笛卡尔用他们的哲学之诗驯服了基督教，他们将基督教的彼世性许诺修正为此世性许诺，即许诺通过一种应用于自然的科学技术在历史终结时实现天堂。他们清醒地将基督教的梦想世俗化，从而逐渐将欧洲的梦想重新聚焦于此世的而非天国的目的；他们由此成功驯服了基督教。作为支配性的宗教，基督教在他们那个时代的战争狂热耗费了欧洲的文艺复兴。他们的哲学奠基带入了对自然和人类目标的现代看法。这是一个复杂又精彩的故事，我曾试图在《尼采与现时代》一书中公正地评判培根和笛卡尔的角色，并表明尼采在修正现代革命的技术层面或为之设置界限的同时，接纳了现代革命的科学层面。

培根和笛卡尔公开的显白教诲依然印刻在我们的时代，一个由征服自然和施特劳斯视之为最高最困难的问题界定的时代：这一问题即，人在征服自然，而这一征服却没有可规定的界限。充分评价尼采为哲学拟就的政治方案，需要详细研究早期现代的哲学奠基，以及这一奠基如何回应宗教对哲学的统治：基督教把柏拉图主义变成现实，从而使宗教对哲学的统治在西方变得可能。

我要对这一伟大的现代转折点再说一点。笛卡尔很长时间所沉思的是，他如何能如他所说的那样以最佳的姿态登台亮相，如何能在反对支配性的宗教、重建哲学的伟大现代斗争中最好地开始扮演自己的角色。他尝试了多种亮相方式，最终选择了他在自己的第一部作品中采用的方式。这部作品出版于他四十岁时，当时他已经是闻名欧洲的数学和科学天才。这部作品以分为六部分的自传开头，为此他称《谈谈方法》（*Discourse on the Method*）是讲述他成为自己的"历史"，并邀请你把它当作一部寓言。在这部寓言式的历史中，笛卡尔展现了他成为哲人以及随之必然成为哲学诗人的过程：他的诗，他对梦想的许可，将推进培根为科学和技术所作的诗。

我从笛卡尔也从尼采那里学到，一位哲人讲述他如何成为自己的故事具有修辞上的裨益。有了尼采和笛卡尔的范例，当柏拉图以不同的方式着重讲述一位哲人成为自己的故事时，我便也密切关注。柏拉图讲述了苏格拉底如何成为苏格拉底的故事，但他选择只让那些研究其对话结构的读者能够读到。尽管省略了现代的哲学开创，我的柏拉图和尼采讲座还是会考察西方哲学伟大传统的起源，以及尼采代表的西方哲学的晚期现代阶段。对于柏拉图和尼采，我都将以他们关于一个哲人如何成为自己的故事作为指引，由之进入他们的哲学和哲学之诗的主要主题。

第三讲　苏格拉底的哲学之诗

比起先前的作家,施特劳斯使哲人写作中显白与隐微的区分更为明晰。柏拉图是这种哲学写作技艺不容置疑的大师:刚开始,你在他的对话中发现的是苏格拉底的显白教导,容易理解;仔细研究35篇对话,你将察觉一系列鲜为人知的结论,而这些结论只有在仔细勘察之后方能看到。柏拉图的写作清楚地表明,苏格拉底是他特有的老师。柏拉图的写作也让他的许多读者把苏格拉底当作他们特有的老师。对于这些忠于苏格拉底的读者,一个问题自然而来:我这般钦佩的老师是如何成为他自己的?只有通过仔细研究对话,柏拉图的答案才能向读者显现。

大多数柏拉图对话清楚显明,苏格拉底和谁说话,以及每篇特殊对话刚好发生的时间和地点。柏拉图常常用地点、时间和听众这些细节回答读者将会产生的疑问:苏格拉底如何成为苏格拉底。我的两次柏拉图讲座都在处理这一主题。

柏拉图从两个不同的方面展示苏格拉底成为苏格拉底:第一,柏拉图展示了哲人苏格拉底如何逐渐理解存在和认知的根本真相;他展现了苏格拉底成长为自然与人的自然的思考者的各个阶段。第二,他展现了哲人苏格拉底如何逐渐理解一位哲人在自己的时代和地点必须做什么。柏拉图展现了苏格拉底如何成长为政治哲人,如何成长为一种神学-政治观的教导者,或出于充分的柏拉图式理由来说,如何成长为我在标题中所称的哲学之诗的教导者。

今天我将着手处理第二个方面,即苏格拉底如何成为他所是的政治哲人。我按照这一顺序,有着充分的柏拉图式理由:柏拉图通过政治哲人苏格拉底,带领他的读者走向哲人苏格拉底;他通过显白或明面的苏格拉底，引领读者走向隐微或隐藏的苏格拉底。

先以施特劳斯为引。在《城邦与人》一书中，施特劳斯论述柏拉图的部分开始于对柏拉图全部 35 篇对话的划分。他将全部对话视为一幅巨大的写作艺术品：每篇对话都从属于全部对话的构造。施特劳斯的划分实际就是柏拉图的划分，遵循柏拉图内置在对话中的区分。35 篇对话有 9 篇是叙述或转述体，也就是说，我们阅读的文本是由某一个人讲述或转述他亲历的整场对话，而且转述者是在对话中向某个或某些听众进行转述。在转述者转述时，我们侧耳倾听。我把这些对话称为转述性对话。其他 26 篇对话是表演性对话，像是戏剧一样，每个角色只讲属于他自己的台词，讲话者在我们面前表演他们的言辞。本次柏拉图讲座将不考虑这 26 篇表演性对话，仅偶尔参引。

柏拉图的 9 篇转述性对话可进一步细分。其中有 6 篇，苏格拉底是转述者。其他 3 篇的转述者另有其人，而且均有名姓。今天我将讨论由苏格拉底转述的 6 篇对话中的 3 篇。这些对话相互关联，首先是因为柏拉图赋予其对话的另一个特征，即戏剧日期。对话发生的时间或年份，是苏格拉底一生中的某个时间，也是苏格拉底的家乡雅典历史中相对应的某个时间。柏拉图所构造的对话都有一个日期，一个可被发现的日期，它经常要求读者去思考"对话发生在什么时候"，并去寻找答案。柏拉图让寻找答案变得可能，同时又使日期看起来至关重要或值得你花功夫思索。

柏拉图的研究者们关心另一种日期：不是柏拉图所安排的苏格拉底一生中的时间，而是柏拉图被假定写作对话的时间。这类时间考订，即所谓的写作日期，不过是一位学者的理论，而我们能够做的就是施特劳斯做过的：全然不顾这种时间考订，只考虑不是一种理论的日期，也就是柏拉图设定的对话日期。

在每一个戏剧日期，苏格拉底处在一定的年纪，雅典也处在其历史的某个时间点。雅典在经济和军事上都是希腊城邦的领头羊，是由其商船和战船维系的帝国的中心。雅典已成为希腊启蒙的引领者，柏拉图经常展现苏格拉底与希腊启蒙的领头人物之间的交谈，这些人来到帝国之都是为了外交事务或是为了招揽学生。施特劳斯极为关注对话的所有细节,但对于戏剧日期的一些非常重要的特征,他要么没有留意,要么没有解释。

就像施特劳斯所说,"内在于事物表面且仅仅内在于事物表面的问题,才是事物的核心"。在一部柏拉图对话中,事物的表面是非常复杂的一系列细节。只有对细节进行细致的研究,才能引领读者抵达事物的核心,获得最为重要的结论。因此,我必须提及对话的大量细节,之后才下结论。今天我讨论的三篇对话是《普罗塔戈拉》《卡尔米德》和《王制》。苏格拉底在这三篇对话中都是转述者。拙著《哲学如何成为苏格拉底式的》(*How Philosophy Become Socratic*)耗费400页的笔墨讨论过这三篇对话,①所以,此处我不得不有所选择。

在《城邦与人》中,施特劳斯首先对《王制》做了这样的观察:"尽管谈话的地点相当清晰地展示在我们眼前,但时间亦即年份却非如此。"②这一看法不对。柏拉图在对话首句就清楚地给出了地点和时间亦即年份。首句如下:

> 昨天,我和阿里斯通的儿子格劳孔一起下抵佩莱乌斯港,向那位女神祈祷;与此同时,我想看看他们怎样举办这个节日,因为他们是头一次举行这样的节日。

柏拉图将《王制》设定在雅典人首次举行"那位女神"的节日的那天。首句内含一个问题:苏格拉底在世时,雅典首次举办了哪位女神的节日?从首句自身看,日期确实有些不确定。不过,在对话稍后的位置,柏拉图让忒拉绪马科斯(Thrasymachus)提到本迪斯节(Bendideia)的宴饮,所以柏拉图告诉读者,那天是本迪斯(Bendis)的节日,本迪斯是一位忒腊克女神,一位外邦神,节日的首次举行是在昨晚雅典的佩莱乌斯港——说昨晚

---

① 参见朗佩特,《哲学如何成为苏格拉底式的》,戴晓光、彭磊等译,华夏出版社,2015。

② Leo Strauss, *The City and Man*, p.62.

是因为苏格拉底今日在雅典转述对话。

柏拉图将《王制》的日期放在首句,同时制造了一点不确定性,不过他在稍后便解决了这一不确定性,从而清楚地凸显戏剧日期。那一天当然是一个著名的日子,一个重大的日子。在那一天,雅典,虔敬的雅典,做了一件当时在世的雅典人从未体验过的新鲜事:将一位外邦神引进这个城邦敬拜的诸神中间。虔敬的雅典一般不会邀请外邦神进入自己敬拜的诸神中间——只有出于巨大的压力,它现在才会这样做。

柏拉图明显想让《王制》的日期为任何关注这个问题的人知晓。而且每位关注日期的雅典人也会准确地知道日期,因为那天是一件相当重要又史无前例的事件。究竟是哪一天?我们距离那一天近乎2500年,准确了解颇为困难。不过,我的学生普莱诺(Christopher Planeaux)积十年之功,一门心思专搞一项工作,最终成为柏拉图对话戏剧日期所有问题的权威,给每篇对话都排定了戏剧日期。普莱诺确定《王制》的日期为公元前429年6月初。

我们对那年夏天的事情了解甚多,因为修昔底德描述了当时发生的事情,这位史家说自己的著作是"永世瑰宝"(1.22)。许多柏拉图对话自身也是永世瑰宝,柏拉图将它们与修昔底德的永世瑰宝联系起来,因而能够确定它们确切的戏剧日期。从修昔底德那里,我们知道公元前429年是雅典和斯巴达战争的第三年。战争的第二年夏天,雅典瘟疫肆虐,修昔底德详细描述了这场恐怖的瘟疫。忒腊克女神本迪斯于公元前429年6月初被引进雅典,部分原因与战事策略相关,但是女神的引进主要是因为她带来了她的男伴,一位治疗之神:雅典期盼深重的瘟疫得到治愈。

柏拉图将《王制》设定在雅典人万分危急的时刻。对话清楚显明,危机还有另一个甚至更重要的方面,即修昔底德描述而柏拉图强调的精神危机,一个社会可能出现的最深的精神危机。所以,《王制》的时间在此异常重要。柏拉图安排《卡尔米德》的戏剧日期时更加凸显了这一时间的重要性。

《卡尔米德》的首句如下:

> 昨天傍晚,我们从波提岱亚回来,离开军营,由于在外很长时间,我就兴冲冲地奔我惯常打发时间的地方而去。

《卡尔米德》的首句同样显明发生的日期,即苏格拉底从波提岱亚(Potidaea)返回之后的那一天。到底是哪一天?柏拉图如法炮制,没有在首句话中直接点明确切的日期,因为雅典军队在波提岱亚待了很久,而身为常规重装步兵的苏格拉底很可能提前一点回来,尽管全军在那里驻留了三年。稍后,苏格拉底向他正在对之转述对话的人讲:

> 就在我们开拔前不久,波提岱亚开仗了,留在这里的人刚听说这回事。

从这一解说,我们得知《卡尔米德》的确切日期:时在苏格拉底回来后的第二天,在苏格拉底回来前,雅典在波提岱亚遭受惨败,全军溃散而还。苏格拉底是首批回来的人,那些聚集在健身场亦即对话发生地的人急切想听到战斗的状况,谁幸存下来,谁战死沙场。与《王制》一样,心有所虑的雅典人应该知晓对话的日期。

对于我们来说,那可是 2500 年以前。但普莱诺同样准确断定了日期,他部分得益于修昔底德:修氏详细叙述了雅典军队在战争的首次战役中的行动,以及雅典人在那场战斗中遭受的惨败。柏拉图的研究者们现在承认,《卡尔米德》的时间设定在公元前 429 年 5 月后期。

《卡尔米德》让苏格拉底说了一些引人注意的事:不仅仅让他远离雅典一段时间(两年半到三年),还引人注意地让他说归来的他不同以往,他从他所称的"扎尔摩克西斯(Zalmoxis)的医生"那里学到了新东西。

我们刚刚看到,柏拉图为饶有兴味的读者所做的事情:他将《卡尔米德》设定在公元前 429 年 5 月后期,而且将日期放在首句并稍后予以显明。他让苏格拉底在《卡尔米德》中说,回来的他不同以往。柏拉图把《王制》设定在公元前 429 年 6 月初,晚于《卡尔米德》一周或两周,并同样将日期放在首句并稍后加以显明。他让《王制》中的苏格拉底以这部巨著赋予的种种精巧展现他关于正义的教导。施特劳斯向读者表明,柏拉图技艺精湛的对话不存在任何偶然:柏拉图赋予《王制》和《卡尔米德》前后接近的时间,这促使好思的读者追问,柏拉图为什么引导我去想,《王制》在时间上为何与《卡尔米德》如此接近?《卡尔米德》会怎样为我理解苏格拉底归来的第二篇对话《王制》做准备,尤其考虑到苏格拉底说回来的他不同以往这一醒目的事实?

一旦将《卡尔米德》与《王制》的戏剧日期连接在一起,并将两篇对话中的苏格拉底视为一个回来的且与以往不同的苏格拉底,那么势必要提出关于回来之前的苏格拉底的问题。有没有柏拉图设定在公元前429年之前的对话?依照戏剧日期而言,《普罗塔戈拉》是诸对话之首。柏拉图让我们很容易看到,《普罗塔戈拉》发生在战争之前,彼时伟大的雅典处在权力与声名的巅峰:这是伯利克勒斯的雅典,古典时代的雅典,雅典卫城宏伟的大理石神殿也在此时建立。柏拉图将《普罗塔戈拉》设定在公元前433年,当时所有神殿中最威严的帕特农神殿装修完成。柏拉图将《普罗塔戈拉》设定在战争爆发前,这场战争持续28年之久,以雅典溃败告终。按照时序,《普罗塔戈拉》是第一篇对话,也即最早的对话。(还有其他一些战前的对话,其中《阿尔喀比亚德》尤其与《普罗塔戈拉》有关联,但此处不予讨论。)

《普罗塔戈拉》是时序上的第一篇对话。柏拉图将其他三篇叙述体对话设定在苏格拉底一生的末尾,一篇是在他受审和离世之际,另两篇是在他死后。这三篇对话即《斐多》《帕默尼德》《会饮》,它们有一个值得注意的事实:它们各自都包含一个部分,其中一篇对话中的这个部分还相当长,这一部分将读者带回苏格拉底更早年的时期,也就是在他公元前433年出现在《普罗塔戈拉》之前的时期。这三篇对话分别展现了一个比公元前433年的苏格拉底更为年轻的苏格拉底;柏拉图对这一更为年轻的苏格拉底进行了三次描述,其最为重要之处在于,它们都展示了一位处于哲学生活转折点的年轻的苏格拉底。这便是柏拉图为大有兴味的读者预留的特殊馈赠:在三篇对话中,柏拉图让读者有机会去思考苏格拉底如何成为他所成为的哲人。这三篇对话显明，苏格拉底在公元前433年之前完成了他的哲学教育，之后所有对话才开始，苏格拉底才在公元前433年的《普罗塔戈拉》中登台亮相。我的另一场柏拉图讲座即围绕这一主题：苏格拉底如何成为苏格拉底（也是我计划撰写的第二本柏拉图著作的主题）。

《普罗塔戈拉》

今天余下的讲座讨论《普罗塔戈拉》《卡尔米德》和《王制》，我从公元前433年《普罗塔戈拉》中的苏格拉底开始。我的问题很简单：发生在战前的《普罗塔戈拉》中的苏格拉底是谁？这一问题之所以重要，是因为在苏格拉底从波提岱亚之围返回后的对话《卡尔米德》中，苏格拉底说他此次回来与以往不同，离开期间学到了一些东西。

柏拉图表明，苏格拉底在《普罗塔戈拉》中有两大目的，这两个目的可被视为隶属于哲学的政治。

其一，苏格拉底安排了一场与年老的普罗塔戈拉的论辩竞赛。普罗塔戈拉是"希腊最智慧的人"，希腊启蒙运动的开创者，声名理当远播希腊各地。时年约36岁的苏格拉底挺身而出，为的是约束和矫正伟大的普罗塔戈拉，普罗塔戈拉当时65岁，生平与人论辩从未败绩。只要仔细研读这篇对话，就会发现，苏格拉底挑战普罗塔戈拉，是因为他认为普罗塔戈拉口无遮拦，陷希腊智慧与希腊哲学于险境。普罗塔戈拉不够谨慎。柏拉图自己必须谨慎处理，以便让哲学的显白实践继续受到遮掩。因此，只有经过仔细研究才能发现，普罗塔戈拉也懂得隐微与显白的区分。普罗塔戈拉尊重这一区分，但苏格拉底隐蔽地向他表明，他的显白论太过张扬，以至于威胁到整个希腊智慧的传统。那么《普罗塔戈拉》中的苏格拉底是谁？苏格拉底是一位启蒙者，他认为启蒙运动的开创者置整个启蒙运动于危险之中，因为其显白论并不充分。年轻的苏格拉底警示年高望重的普罗塔戈拉，他对待真理必须慎之又慎。

其二,柏拉图表明,《普罗塔戈拉》中苏格拉底的第二个目的是吸引并且争取不到 20 岁的阿尔喀比亚德做他的学生。这同样是一个政治目的,因为在所有渴望政治荣誉和伟大的雅典年轻人中,阿尔喀比亚德是最有前景的一位。修昔底德表明,在雅典与斯巴达的战争中,阿尔喀比亚德将成为雅典最大的希望。但是,阿尔喀比亚德被普罗塔戈拉吸引,一如其他富有前景的希腊年轻人。苏格拉底认出阿尔喀比亚德是一位年轻的政治天才,他渴望统治希腊,而且很有可能这么做。苏格拉底的目的是把他争取到自己这边,赢得这位雅典未来的政治领袖,苏格拉底这么做部分是为了挽救希腊的启蒙。苏格拉底的目的不是说服阿尔喀比亚德成为哲人,而是在雅典保留一份友好对待哲学的公共精神。

按照这种方式,即按这种政治的方式理解战前最重要的对话《普罗塔戈拉》,那么就会打开一个有关《卡尔米德》和《王制》的问题。这两部对话都设定在苏格拉底随军离开很久并归来之后,柏拉图将它们结合在一起,构成一位归来的苏格拉底的对话:苏格拉底说他此次回来与以往不同,在离开期间学到了一些重要的东西。这个问题就是:归来的苏格拉底是谁?他与战前即《普罗塔戈拉》中的苏格拉底有何不同?

注意:这些疑问并非产生于对对话的外部考量,而是产生于柏拉图设置在对话表面并迫使读者提出疑问的问题。只有求索对话表面的问题所内含的疑问,才能发现对话的核心。

《卡尔米德》

通过提及荷马,《卡尔米德》回答了它所提出的一些问题。柏拉图同时代的读者都知道荷马,这位希腊文明的奠基诗人受到全希腊人的崇敬,被视为最智慧和最有权威的老师,为热爱学习的年轻人铭记。荷马有两部史诗,《伊利亚特》记述了很多代之前的希腊人与特洛伊人的十年战争,《奥德赛》记叙了奥德修斯战后从特洛伊返回的十年征程。奥德修斯是伊塔卡的王,也是在特洛伊的希腊人中最智慧者。柏拉图在对话中引用或提及荷马数百次,他对这位希腊宗教和希腊智慧的奠基诗人的引用和改写始终值得深究。

柏拉图在《卡尔米德》中四次提到《奥德赛》,而且四次提及都至关重要,因为智慧的荷马在《奥德赛》中展示了智慧的王者奥德修斯离乡20年后的返回。伯纳德特的《弓与琴》论证说,荷马的《奥德赛》表明,奥德修斯的旅程是他一步步学习作为哲学的智慧和作为政治哲学的智慧的历程。伯纳德特让我们得以看到,荷马智慧的王者奥德修斯就是荷马的哲人王。在《奥德赛》中,智慧的王者阔别多年回来,为他的王国拨乱反正。他伪装成乞丐秘密回来,因为他要完成一项重任,不能冒被认出来的风险。在《奥德赛》中,荷马让奥德修斯经过一系列的相认场景来揭示自己,争取必要的同盟以实现目标。

有了这样的背景,我们就可以理解《卡尔米德》表面的一个重要特征:对话中四次提到《奥德赛》,所提到的全都是相认场景:智慧的王者秘密归来,通过揭示自己来选择追随者,让他们明白他必须做的事情,同时获得他们的帮助。柏拉图恰如其分地安排对《奥德赛》的四次提及,使之与《奥德赛》中的次序相应;他让苏格拉底久别归来的对话《卡尔米德》与荷马的《奥德赛》在这一重要方面相对应。那么,《卡尔米德》中久别之后回到雅典的苏格拉底是谁?他是一位归来的新奥德修斯,一位归来的智慧的王者,他公开而又秘密地归来,怀揣着一项政治谋划,身为智慧者的他将借助这一谋划实施统治。

奥德修斯在《奥德赛》中的政治谋划是一项奠基行动,含有两个层面。第一,一种新的政治秩序不再依赖像他自己那样稀有的智慧者去统治:他归来是着眼于在没有智慧的统治者的情况下智慧的统治的继承。第二,创立一套新的关于诸神的教诲:奥德修斯纯政治的奠基需要宗教的奠基,一位智慧的统治者通过变更诸神来辅助智慧的统治的继承。所以,柏拉图邀请读者把他笔下归来的苏格拉底视作苏格拉底/奥德修斯,邀请读者把归来的苏格拉底视作怀揣着一项奠基行动,也就是一项神学-政治方案。

按照柏拉图在《卡尔米德》中的编排，苏格拉底作为医生被引介给卡尔米德，这位医生拥有一种药，能够治愈卡尔米德的疾病，或许是与那场瘟疫有关的疾病。苏格拉底被迫扮演医生的角色，他首先说自己有一种治病的叶子，但是让叶子生效就必须得说某些"咒语"，即有魔力的言辞或行话，而且治疗性的言辞渐渐地取代了叶子。苏格拉底说，他在离开自己的老师时学到了这些咒语，他的老师是扎尔摩克西斯的医生。扎尔摩克西斯是神，他教导治疗身体的同时也必须治疗灵魂，只有用作为"美的言辞"的咒语才能治疗灵魂。苏格拉底补充说，扎尔摩克西斯的医生甚至"能让人不朽"——他们教导说灵魂不朽。

通过引入扎尔摩克西斯，柏拉图指涉希腊史家希罗多德，却未提到他的名字。柏拉图的读者可从希罗多德那里了解到扎尔摩克西斯的更多信息。希罗多德表明，信仰扎尔摩克西斯的人相信自己是不朽的，而且他们的神是唯一的神。希罗多德还补充到，相信这些的革塔人（Getae）是诸族群中最勇敢和最正义的，也唯有他们成功阻击了波斯入侵者——他由此暗示，信仰一神和灵魂不朽使信仰者勇敢、正义，使信仰者有美德。通过提到扎尔摩克西斯进而指涉希罗多德，柏拉图告诉我们更多有关久别回到雅典的苏格拉底的信息。这位新奥德修斯，这位智慧的王者，他归来是要建立新政制，并且要带来关于诸神的新教诲。归来的他学到了能治病的美的言辞，这些言辞教导说，只有一个神，而且灵魂是不朽的——扎尔摩克西斯的医生教给了苏格拉底《王制》的教诲。柏拉图将《卡尔米德》安排在《王制》几周之前，又让《卡尔米德》宣告一种它未加详述的新教诲，这迫使细心的读者断定，苏格拉底在《王制》中关于诸神和灵魂的教诲是一位作为苏格拉底/奥德修斯秘密归来的苏格拉底的新政治谋划。

《卡尔米德》是短篇对话，在我刚刚提到的这些内容之后，对话主要在处理节制（moderation）的主题。苏格拉底与克里提阿斯讨论节制，后者是他随军队离开前最出色的学生。对话暗示，克里提阿斯曾从苏格拉底那里学到一种观点，这种观点最终导致他成为臭名昭著的雅典罪人，雅典内战期间极不节制的智术师和僭主。在《卡尔米德》中，苏格拉底认识到自己已败坏了克里提阿斯——这是他改变自己教诲的另一个强有力的原因。我必须忽略这一重要主题,忽略《卡尔米德》最为突出的主题,因为它将使我们偏离我当前的主要论点。

苏格拉底是一位归来的奥德修斯,对此我最后要说的是:苏格拉底在《卡尔米德》中始终没有教授他声称自己带回的治疗性言辞,全神贯注的读者将会看到《卡尔米德》的这一事实。以这种方式结束《卡尔米德》,并且将之安排在《王制》稍前,柏拉图让这类读者而且只让这类读者得出他为之隐藏的结论:《王制》的教诲是一位久别归来的苏格拉底/奥德修斯的教诲,他旨在基于一种外来的、非荷马的关于诸神和灵魂的教诲建立一种新的政治秩序。

由此,我可以转向《王制》中的苏格拉底,并开始为我今天的讲座"苏格拉底的哲学之诗"正名。我可以开始表明,苏格拉底的哲学之诗如何就是施特劳斯所说的侍养之诗,即服务于哲学,并救助或照料病者和伤者。

《王制》

归来的苏格拉底作为奥德修斯

在《王制》中,柏拉图提到奥德修斯的名字仅两次,一次差不多在开头,一次在结尾。他在别处避免使用奥德修斯的名字,代之以"在特洛伊的最智慧的男人"。在《王制》首次论辩的结尾,苏格拉底说到奥德修斯的名字,并且首次提到荷马。他说:

> 看起来,正义之人已经显现为某类窃贼,我担心你从荷马那里学到了这一点。因为荷马钦慕奥德修斯的外祖父奥托吕库斯,说他"在窃取和发誓方面"超过所有人。(《王制》334a - b)

奥托吕库斯(Autolycus)意即"狼自身",发誓意味着将你的行动与诸神联系起来:这是一种虔敬的行为。奥托吕库斯结合了窃取和虔敬,他给

奥德修斯取名奥德修斯,这象征着智慧的外祖父将他的智慧传给了外孙。苏格拉底补充说:

> 看起来,按照你与荷马的看法,正义……就是某种窃取的技艺,是为了朋友的利益。(《王制》334b)

正与苏格拉底讨论的珀勒马科斯(Polemarchus)当然不是这个意思。如若珀勒马科斯对正义的定义暗含此意,那么他认为一定是自己错了。但苏格拉底确实是这个意思:智慧者的实践智慧是某种窃取的技艺,表面虔敬的智慧者从父亲们那里偷走儿子,使他们追随自己,而这对他们极为有益——老师苏格拉底就是这么对待《王制》中与他交谈的年轻人的。

所以,《王制》开篇就点明奥德修斯带有其外祖父的特征。《王制》仅有的另一次提到奥德修斯的名字是在《王制》末尾神话的结束处。这个著名的神话描画了不朽的灵魂在冥府经受了长时期的奖赏或惩罚后选择来世的场面。众灵魂大多做出了鲁莽愚蠢的选择。最后一个灵魂的选择与众不同:

> 由于偶然,奥德修斯的灵魂抽到最后一个签,上前做选择。回忆起以前的辛劳,它从对荣誉的爱中清醒过来,它来回走了很长时间,寻找只料理自己事情的平民生活,最终它发现这种生活躺在一个被其他灵魂忽略的地方。(《王制》620c)

《王制》的结尾表明,奥德修斯的灵魂选择了苏格拉底的生活,一个只料理自己事情的私人的生活,①即只料理哲学事业以及保护哲学和推进哲学所要求的每件事情。注意:做出这个选择的是奥德修斯的灵魂,不是奥德修斯本人,而是他在某种意义上从赐予他名字的外祖父奥托吕库斯那里得来的灵魂。

---

① private 兼有"平民"和"私人"两层意思。

所以，柏拉图的《王制》从未真正叫出过奥德修斯本人的名字。首先提到的是奥德修斯的一位祖先，奥德修斯之前的一位智者。最后提到的是奥德修斯的后继者，荷马的奥德修斯之后的一位智者，即苏格拉底本人。柏拉图在《王制》中让《卡尔米德》中归来的苏格拉底成为一个思考者，他认识到自身之中具有奥德修斯的灵魂。柏拉图表明，苏格拉底承载并推进古希腊智慧的传统，这一传统发端于智慧的奥德修斯之前，发端于荷马之前，并经过荷马的改进而传递下去，现在传到苏格拉底手里。苏格拉底是荷马的"儿子"，他改进荷马的智慧，又将之传给他身后的"儿子们"。

"改进"（improve）一词也许用得不对。柏拉图在《王制》中似乎在说，苏格拉底修改或调适希腊智慧以适应随时间流逝而被引入希腊的新情况，我们将看到，其中有一种情况最为重要。柏拉图似乎在暗示，一个智慧者知道自己是谁，也知道自己在何处，并认识到他因为自己是谁和在何处而必须做什么。

柏拉图在时间上将《卡尔米德》放在《王制》紧前面，由此他展现给读者两样东西，这就是其中之一。思索两篇对话的安排，读者就会认为，《王制》中苏格拉底的革新或全新教诲来自一位归来的智慧者奥德修斯。

归来的苏格拉底作为扎尔摩克西斯的学生

在《卡尔米德》中，苏格拉底说他此次归来与以往不同，也就是不同于之前的苏格拉底，不同于柏拉图在《普罗塔戈拉》所展现的苏格拉底。《卡尔米德》表明，苏格拉底是作为医生回来，他在离开期间学到一种治疗的技艺。他归来时学到了一些能够治疗生病的灵魂的咒语，他是从一位外邦神的信徒那里学到了这些治病的言辞。

苏格拉底在《卡尔米德》中从未说出他那治病的咒语。几周后，在合适的时机，苏格拉底将一种新的教诲引入雅典。在《王制》中，归来的奥德修斯即苏格拉底教授了他在离开期间学到的咒语。那是个合适的时机，因为在苏格拉底引进他从外邦神扎尔摩克西斯学到的教诲的同时，在佩莱乌斯港的房子外面,在那个晚上,雅典人自己也正在引入外邦神本迪斯。

在《卡尔米德》中,治病的言辞原本要用来治疗卡尔米德的头痛。在《王制》中呢?尽管《王制》发生在遭受了瘟疫的雅典,但它表明雅典患了另一种疾病,比瘟疫更严重也更要命的疾病。

《王制》的主要对话发生在苏格拉底与阿德曼托斯和格劳孔两兄弟之间,紧跟在两兄弟发表长篇大论之后(卷二)。这些长篇大论表明,两位天资不凡的年轻人已受到希腊启蒙的影响,他们了解普罗塔戈拉之类的老师们的教诲,在他们看来,此类教诲摧毁了道德生活即正义生活的理据。他们是真正正派的青年才俊,想过正派的生活,却被普罗塔戈拉及其他人的教诲左右。他们要求苏格拉底向他们证明,正义的生活比不义的生活好。

从他们俩的发言,柏拉图的读者了解到新奥德修斯所回到的雅典陷入的深刻危机:不仅是战争和瘟疫,还有那可能最大的危机,一场精神的和道德的危机,我想我们可称为诸神(荷马的诸神)之死的危机。阿德曼托斯和格劳孔的发言代表了所有正派的雅典年轻人,他们遭逢战争和瘟疫,受到普罗塔戈拉之类的老师带来的启蒙的影响。普罗塔戈拉不充分的显白论未能充分隐藏自己的怀疑论观点,从而导致年轻的一代不信任神。

归来的苏格拉底不同以往,他回到的雅典也不同以往:在雅典,战争、瘟疫和启蒙使对道德和诸神的怀疑演变为文明生活的一场危机,一场最紧急的危机,类似于尼采所称的虚无主义的危机。

柏拉图邀请我们在读《王制》时要想着《卡尔米德》,因为他让两部对话仅仅相隔几周。我们由此了解到,归来的奥德修斯即苏格拉底如何应对特别是正派的年轻人所面临的精神危机,这些年轻人学了像普罗塔戈拉这样太过轻率、有失谨慎的智慧者的一些思想。

在此,柏拉图对《普罗塔戈拉》《卡尔米德》《王制》的时间编排,允许我们对比战争前的政治哲人苏格拉底与回到一个不同以往的雅典的不同以往的政治哲人苏格拉底。通过使这一比较变得可能,柏拉图让他的忠实读者看到苏格拉底成为苏格拉底,在公元前429年大概40岁时成为他之后所是的成熟的政治哲人。苏格拉底的关切依然是他在《普罗塔戈拉》中的关切,即希腊启蒙和雅典青年,但他处理两者的方式都发生了变化。

首先涉及苏格拉底的这一目的:节制希腊启蒙,教导希腊启蒙的开创者普罗塔戈拉及其追随者践行更为有效的显白论。在《王制》中,忒拉绪马霍斯是希腊启蒙的典型代表,作为智术师的第二代领军人物,他比普罗塔戈拉更不收敛或更不节制。他在表达启蒙教师们真实和激进的立场时更加露骨,更不关心给自己的教诲加一层显白论的保护——尽管我们必须记住,《王制》中的忒拉绪马霍斯是在私下里与一小撮人谈论。

施特劳斯完美地表明,《王制》中的苏格拉底花费一番心思才成功争取忒拉绪马霍斯成为他的朋友。大概在对话的中间,苏格拉底甚至说,他和忒拉绪马霍斯刚刚成为朋友,之前也不是敌人——尽管忒拉绪马霍斯在对话开头,为了在年轻人面前压苏格拉底一头,表现得像是苏格拉底的宿敌。苏格拉底在《王制》中的策略性目的在于说服忒拉绪马霍斯相信,他如果采用苏格拉底为哲学设计的策略,就能够最好地服务于自身的利益。作为苏格拉底的朋友,忒拉绪马霍斯就需要采用苏格拉底为哲学设计的节制策略,来与年轻人亦即他未来的主顾谈话。

关于希腊启蒙,《王制》中的苏格拉底学到了一种新策略,这一新策略会赢得受其启蒙的忒拉绪马霍斯的认同,而苏格拉底在战争前的策略未能赢得希腊启蒙的开创者普罗塔戈拉的认同。

其次涉及苏格拉底的另一目的:吸引并指导雅典的年轻人。《王制》表明,苏格拉底已经学到一种公开展示哲学的策略,这种策略能使他对年轻人的教育比他过去对阿尔喀比亚德的教育更成功。苏格拉底在战前就认识到,他对阿尔喀比亚德的教育失败了,柏拉图让我们从《会饮》中阿尔喀比亚德本人那里了解这点。当然,苏格拉底从波提岱亚回来后,与他谈话的年轻人之中没有阿尔喀比亚德。阿尔喀比亚德是一个无与伦比的政治天才,独一无二。但与苏格拉底谈话的是阿德曼托斯和格劳孔,以及珀勒马科斯和其他更加具有政治天赋和抱负的年轻人,他们在雅典这样的民主政制中可以成为卓有影响的领导者。他们是年轻、有血气的贤人,渴望在雅典发挥贤人的作用,成为具有公共精神的政治和军事人物。

柏拉图以这第二种方式展示了苏格拉底在政治哲学方面成为他自己。就此而言,《卡尔米德》是个关键,因为我们在《王制》里听到,《卡尔米德》中归来的奥德修斯实际上是回来施教。我们还听到了《卡尔米德》中所许诺的治疗的咒语,即那些"美的言辞";我们听到了苏格拉底作为扎尔摩克西斯的追随者准备教授的东西。有了柏拉图在《卡尔米德》中为读者所做的准备,我们就能理解《王制》主要教诲的意义,这些教诲有关灵魂,有关关于实在的知识,有关诸神。苏格拉底的新教诲全都是异于希腊传统的反荷马的教诲,它们旨在说服并治愈阿德曼托斯和格劳孔这样的年轻人。我会非常简明扼要地总结一下这三个教诲。

第一,归来的苏格拉底教导一种反荷马式的新灵魂观:

苏格拉底教导阿德曼托斯和格劳孔,灵魂分为三部分,血气部分必须受理性部分的统治。血气部分主导了那些受荷马滋养的希腊人的灵魂,年轻人全都渴望成为像特洛伊最伟大的战士阿喀琉斯(Achilles)一样的人。他们甚或渴望超过阿喀琉斯,因为荷马的典范就是竞争,特洛伊所有的英雄都想在战士的德性上超过其他人。依照苏格拉底关于灵魂的新教诲,血气部分的美德即勇敢,苏格拉底称之为"政治的"勇敢,并将之置于理性部分的统治之下。

在《王制》卷十的论辩中,苏格拉底给他关于灵魂的教诲添加了一种新元素:他向年轻的听众们证明,灵魂是不朽的。这一陌生的、非荷马的灵魂观包含苏格拉底有关冥府(Hades)或来世的非荷马教诲。在荷马那里,冥府就是所有人的魂影在死后下去的地方,阿喀琉斯憎恶这种地方。苏格拉底让冥府成为人们死后灵魂接受赏罚的地方,好人和正义之人得赏,坏人和不义之人受罚。归来的苏格拉底教导灵魂的来世,最清楚不过的是,这一教诲是他离开雅典期间从扎尔摩克西斯的医生那里学到的——或者,如柏拉图所暗示的那样,是从希腊史家希罗多德那里学到的。希罗多德讲述了扎尔摩克西斯的教诲及其有益的效果,还说扎尔摩克西斯的子民最为勇敢也最为正义。

第二,归来的苏格拉底带来一种关于认知和存在(konwing and being)的新教诲:

这就是《王制》中关于理念的著名教诲。关于这个话题,施特劳斯几乎直言不讳。他在其讨论《王制》的文章中说,"对于这一理念学说,没有人曾成功地给出一种令人满意或清晰的解释"。[①] 施特劳斯给出了一种令人满意和清晰的解释:他表明,理念学说是一种显白的教诲,可以轻松地说服非哲人,即那些从小被教育信仰如胜利女神和正义女神等荣耀之神的人。正义女神是独一、自立、不朽的存在,人的一切正义行为的荣耀之因。正义的理念与正义女神相似,它是永恒、不变、荣耀的实在,每一正义的行为均参与其中。苏格拉底努力劝说受智术师影响的雅典年轻人相信正义比不义好,部分就是在劝说他们相信正义拥有永恒、独立的实在,而且能为人知晓。年轻人怀疑荷马的诸神,他们有关神的观念使他们易于接受苏格拉底关于理念的教诲。施特劳斯说,对我们来说,"最一开始",理念学说"根本不可信,甚至还显得虚妄"。[②] 施特劳斯的这一著名说法是为了证明,对于格劳孔来说,理念学说不是一开始就根本不可信,而是事实上很容易相信,因为他从荷马那里了解到神是什么。

施特劳斯让读者容易理解:苏格拉底有关永恒的、超验的理念的教诲,有意识地与它所处的时代联系在一起,那是个荷马的诸神死去的时代。这一教诲是显白的,是哲学之诗,但不是最切近施特劳斯内心的那个柏拉图。(当然,关于苏格拉底对人的知觉和认知或感受和理智的真知灼见,还有更多可学习的内容——但那是完全不同的问题,格劳孔对此不会感兴趣。)

第三,归来的苏格拉底带来一种关于诸神的新教诲,以道德的方式革

---

① 参见 Leo Strauss, *The City and Man*, p.119.
② 参见 Leo Strauss, *The City and Man*, p.119.

新荷马的诸神：

在《城邦与人》中，施特劳斯选择将这一内容置于他对《王制》的论述的中心，对此我已在第一讲讨论过。立法者苏格拉底为诸神奠立了两条新法。其一，诸神仅仅是善的原因。苏格拉底在此明确反对荷马：他引用荷马的说法，荷马说宙斯把好和坏分配给人类。其二，诸神不会改变形状或撒谎。这一观点也与荷马针锋相对，施特劳斯强调，苏格拉底必须与阿德曼托斯论辩，使之摒弃他从荷马那里承继的认为诸神撒谎的观点。苏格拉底教导诸神不会撒谎，实际是教给阿德曼托斯一种谎言，高贵的谎言。我认为这样说之所以合适，是因为苏格拉底对神是什么的看法——由之我们触及一个施特劳斯非常谨慎但还是清楚表明的问题：他表明，柏拉图像尼采一样认为，诸神搞哲学，或说诸神是哲人。后面的讲座将会进一步阐发这一点。

为了让诸神比荷马塑造的更加道德，苏格拉底在《王制》卷十补充了一个关键部分：他让诸神全权负责奖惩死后下到冥府的灵魂。

苏格拉底还教授了一种关于诸神的新观念：通过教授诸理念以及诸理念之理念即善的理念，苏格拉底走向扎尔摩克西斯的一神论。身为基督徒的一神论者们，比如圣奥古斯丁，无疑就是以这种方式阅读柏拉图。尼采和他之前的其他现代哲人们认为，这种向一神论的开放是柏拉图教诲的灾难性后果的重要部分：它打开了基督教成功进入西方的道路。在后续的讲座中，我还会讨论这一大事件。

以上总结了归来的苏格拉底从波提岱亚带来的新教诲。他的新教诲就是他的新哲学之诗，施特劳斯所称的侍养之诗，他的诗服务于哲学，同时还照料阿德曼托斯和格劳孔这样的年轻人的精神需求。苏格拉底在公元前429年夏天引入的这一新教诲，就是他成熟的政治哲学，并一直保留至终点。柏拉图是说苏格拉底生命的终点，即公元前399年，因为柏拉图让苏格拉底在《斐多》中，在临终之际，在生平最后一次论辩中，重复了他三十年前引入的关于理念的教诲；柏拉图还让苏格拉底讲述了新的故事，这些故事教授有关灵魂不死和诸神的观念，与公元前429年苏格拉底从波提岱亚归来后讲述的故事如出一辙。

通过关注施特劳斯说《王制》没有给出的时间和年份,我们学到了很多有助于我们理解《王制》的东西。认识到《卡尔米德》和《王制》中的苏格拉底是于公元前429年暮春和初夏之间回到雅典,我们就能够思考那令人赞叹的场景,柏拉图赋予"所有时代最著名的政治作品"富于诗性之美和妥帖的场景。在那一天,无数雅典人涌回雅典,通宵讲述引进新神的壮观场面;苏格拉底也回到雅典,叙述他在同一个晚上和同一个地方悄悄引进的东西,而且他现在是向在雅典的任何想听的人引进这些东西,因为苏格拉底在雅典转述整个《王制》没有限定听众,无论谁都可以。

雅典人引进本迪斯神没有改变雅典最终的命运。苏格拉底引入的新教诲却成功地改变了哲学在雅典的命运,且最终改变了西方文明的命运。如尼采所说,苏格拉底是"所谓世界历史的漩涡和转折点"。

最后我想讨论柏拉图、荷马和尼采,由此结束本讲。

从波提岱亚归来的苏格拉底带来反荷马的教诲。在《王制》卷十,苏格拉底更为明确、更为彻底地批评了荷马。他的批评旨在打破荷马对年轻人头脑的控制,并帮助自己取代荷马的教诲,伸张他自己的新教诲。以一种戏剧的方式,通过打破荷马的权威影响,苏格拉底杀死荷马并取而代之。

但苏格拉底也崇敬荷马。作为归来的奥德修斯,苏格拉底从荷马那里学到奥德修斯为取得成功而不得不做之事。在苏格拉底从荷马那里学到的东西中,有一项教诲使他获得某种许可,取代荷马或夺取荷马的权威地位,从而杀死荷马。荷马的《奥德赛》强调,归来的奥德修斯必须杀掉妻子佩涅洛佩(Penelope)的108个求婚者。这些求婚者争着与奥德修斯的妻子结婚,因为她的国王丈夫已离家二十年,有理由认为他早就成为孤魂野鬼了。那个成功的求婚者将与奥德修斯的"遗孀"结婚,成为伊塔卡的国王。108个求婚者代表将延续旧的方式的旧秩序:奥德修斯已逝,一位正当的新国王登位。

归来的奥德修斯是王者奥德修斯,是智慧的王者,他知道他必须在政治和宗教上建立新的秩序。在政治方面,他要建立由他的儿子忒勒马科斯(Telemachus)统治的新秩序,忒勒马科斯是一个很好的年轻人,却没有其父罕见的品性,并非一个智慧的统治者。智慧的奥德修斯必须确保建立一个更加民主的秩序,由忒勒马科斯与其同盟——比如忠诚的养猪奴欧迈俄斯(Eumaeus)——统治。但是,新秩序要成功,108个求婚者就必须都得死——只有扫除旧秩序,新秩序才能稳固建立。所以,求婚者当然必须都得死。

不过,新秩序的正当建立不止要求求婚者必须死,还要让他们的死看起来罪有应得;他们必须被判为恶徒,有关他们的记忆只能是他们的邪恶。所以荷马把他们描绘成恶徒,让我们记住他们是邪恶的求婚者,而公正的奥德修斯在雅典娜本人的协助下将他们绳之以正义。荷马做了两千多年后马基雅维利明确宣称必须要做的事。

苏格拉底呢?苏格拉底从荷马那里得知,只有杀死旧秩序,他才能建立新秩序。他还从荷马那里学到,他必须杀死荷马。他也从荷马那里得知,他必须让荷马看起来罪有应得。所以苏格拉底教导我们,荷马应该死去,作为最终的权威应该被取代,因为荷马让宙斯造成人间的恶,而且荷马对理念和灵魂不死的命运一无所知。苏格拉底不仅表面上,而且实际上杀死了荷马,并取代荷马成为最终的权威,用自己的教诲取代荷马的教诲。但苏格拉底暗地里尊崇荷马,把他视作自己的老师,一位正在逝去的权威,他必须让位给继承者,一如奥托吕库斯让位于奥德修斯。

荷马期望被杀死,他教导他必须被将至的智慧者杀死,不管这人是谁,来自哪里,带来什么。将至的智慧者从荷马那里学到:108个求婚者全都必须死,而且荷马也非常清楚,为了让必将来到的新的智慧教诲落地生根,他必须死。

时代变了,诸神死了,政治智慧必须通过教导新神而随时代变化。

对于我而言,再也没有比以下更好的方式来开始尼采:尼采倾尽全力要杀死柏拉图,这位哲人拥有"迄今为止所有哲人所能支配的最大力量"(《善恶的彼岸》格言191)。但是,尼采杀死柏拉图获得了柏拉图的许可,他杀死了在荷马的许可下杀死了荷马的柏拉图,他杀死了显白的柏拉图,因为其教诲最终导致了一场文化浩劫。

但尼采尊崇柏拉图一如柏拉图尊崇荷马。柏拉图始终是他之所是,"古代最美的生长物"(《善恶的彼岸》序言),古代最美的生长物是不朽的,作为隐匿的智慧者,他永远生活在智慧者的地下世界。但是从历史上讲,没有回去的可能,古代自身必须被晚期现代取代,一如它最初被现代取代。柏拉图必须被尼采取代。

第四讲　苏格拉底成为苏格拉底

我的第一场柏拉图讲座处理的对话，我在自己已出版的关于柏拉图的专著中讨论过。今天的柏拉图讲座则有关我还没有写的一部关于柏拉图的专著，我想在完成我讨论尼采的新著后开始撰写。

今天的柏拉图讲座同样集中于三篇对话，三篇叙述的或转述的对话，它们独一无二，因为柏拉图使它们成为仅有的由他人而非苏格拉底转述的对话：《斐多》由斐多（Phaedo）转述，《帕默尼德》由克法洛斯（Cephalus）转述，《会饮》由阿珀罗多罗斯（Apollodoros）转述。此次讲座同样会充分利用柏拉图赋予对话的戏剧日期，也就是设置在谈话中的日期。这三篇对话独一无二，还因为另一个特征：每篇对话开始之后，柏拉图都带着读者回到苏格拉底早年的一个时期，而且其中每一个时期都显得意义重大，因为在其中的每一个时期，苏格拉底都处在哲学生活的不同阶段，都学到了某种促进其哲学理解的关键东西。

作为读者，如果你思考这三个事件，思考三者之间的关系，你就会十分轻松地按照正确的顺序排列三者，你不得不认为，柏拉图有意让你这么做。柏拉图故意将这三个事件分散在三篇不同的对话中，并赋予三篇对话相似的形式，表明它们是仅有的由他人叙述的对话。柏拉图故意营造的复杂所产生的效果就是真正得到你的关注，促使你思考：一定有比这更多的东西，更多要学的东西。柏拉图一定在试图教我一些东西。

柏拉图邀请你看的顺序是时间上的序列，同时也是一个逻辑序列：《斐多》最早，然后是《帕默尼德》，最后是《会饮》。逻辑序列是苏格拉底思想上的进步。首先是《斐多》中苏格拉底作为哲人最早的开端，其中包括苏格拉底完全凭靠自己迈出的一步，希腊哲学新的一步。随后是《帕默尼德》中的一步：伟大的帕默尼德向苏格拉底表明，他的新观点逻辑不充分——不，逻辑上不可能，即便可能，我们也绝不会知道它是可能的。学到关于自己自豪的发明的这一点后，苏格拉底被引向最终的一步，即哲人能够获得的最深刻洞见，那就是他在《会饮》中学到的内容。

这三篇对话在形式上连接在一起，成为仅有的由他人而非苏格拉底转述的对话；在逻辑上连接在一起，展现苏格拉底从其最早的阶段到最终的洞见的变化。通过这三篇对话，柏拉图教导你，教导真正感兴趣、真正在思考的你，苏格拉底如何成为苏格拉底，那位作为柏拉图的典范、被尼采称作"所谓世界历史的漩涡和转折点"的哲人如何成为他自己。换种方式说，柏拉图对显白的苏格拉底的精心呈现，意在引导他最上心的读者走向隐微的苏格拉底。

柏拉图还有意在三篇对话的这一编排中置入了其他东西。一旦你看到苏格拉底学习的独有次序，并按柏拉图设想的时间顺序排列这些步骤，你就会看到，柏拉图让我们有可能以雅典的历史为背景，追溯苏格拉底生命中这些步骤的日期。柏拉图让我们很容易发现实际的日期，其中一个重要事实是，它们全都是在《普罗塔戈拉》之前。也就是说，柏拉图表明，苏格拉底在《普罗塔戈拉》中作为公众教师首次登上舞台之前，苏格拉底作为哲人的个人成长在某种意义上就已经完成了。

认识到下面这些很重要：这些细节不是有关对话的某种理论，没有给文本带来一系列固定的关于文本的观念；它们只是柏拉图置入这些对话却没有过分声张的特征。它们之所以呈现在文本中，只能解释为柏拉图自己的意图。柏拉图将它们放入文本的表面，会留意这些特征的是那些聚精会神的读者，那些旨在学习柏拉图必须教诲的东西的读者，那些已经认识到柏拉图是一位精妙的写作大师——他以苏格拉底的方式教导，即不会说出一切——的读者。

施特劳斯注意到三篇对话的时间设置，认为它们表明苏格拉底正在成为一位哲人。伯纳德特也注意到这一点，他称这三篇对话是"苏格拉底哲学教育的三个阶段"。但是，他们俩都没有将柏拉图编排的三个事件详细地联系起来,因而也没有阐明这些阶段。这就是我在此要做的事情,更详细的内容将出现在我的下一部柏拉图专著中。

还必须提及最后一处复杂的地方:柏拉图在《苏格拉底的申辩》中给出了另一份对青年苏格拉底的叙述。苏格拉底在辩护时说,德尔斐的神告诉他的朋友凯瑞丰(Chaerephon),没有人比苏格拉底更智慧。苏格拉底陈述道,他听到神所说的话之后,便转向践行哲学的道路,至今不辍。苏格拉底向"雅典的男人们",向所有出席审判的同胞公民讲述了这个故事。在他唯一面向整个雅典的公共发言中,在他的辩护词或自我解释中,苏格拉底向他的所有同胞公民们讲述了他如何成为自己的故事。

苏格拉底面向公众的言辞必须解释为政治言辞。他对所有同胞公民们说:这样来看待我,作为哲人我所做的是遵从神而做。这就是说,苏格拉底告诉雅典的男人们,我做我所做的事是遵从你们所有人都知道的最高权威,即德尔斐的神。苏格拉底对自己的公开陈述是一份神话式的对他如何成为自己的真实陈述:通过服从最高权威,他成为自己。但是如何理解最高权威?苏格拉底知道最高权威就是理性,他的同胞公民们知道最高权威是德尔斐的神。柏拉图将另一份对苏格拉底如何成为苏格拉底的陈述分散在《斐多》《帕默尼德》和《会饮》中,等待你去发现,那是对苏格拉底如何成为自己的非神话陈述,是对苏格拉底的推理引导他发现的东西的陈述,是你非常想学习和钻研的陈述。那一陈述也是苏格拉底在《申辩》中告诉每个人他如何成为自己的显白故事的隐微呈现。

考虑到对话中两种不同的陈述,我们兴许会问,德尔斐的事情是苏格拉底人生的转折,在柏拉图让我们能够从作为一个整体的众对话中发现的事件序列中,它发生在什么时候?在我看来,这是对一个神话故事的错误提问——错把神话陈述当作历史陈述。柏拉图将历史陈述分散在这三篇独一无二的对话中。

有了以上准备,我们可以开始今天要说的内容。我将遵照《斐多》《帕默尼德》和《会饮》展示苏格拉底一步步变成自己的逻辑进展。

《斐多》

《斐多》的叙述者是斐多,他是频繁去牢房探望苏格拉底的人当中的一位,并出现在苏格拉底临终的现场:那天,苏格拉底与他的朋友们交谈,然后饮下毒药死去。斐多是向一帮菲利亚(Phlia)(伯罗奔半岛的一个城邦,离雅典很远)的毕达哥拉斯派分子讲述了苏格拉底的临终故事。毕达哥拉斯派是古希腊的哲学学派,他们的学说对苏格拉底有些影响。菲利亚的毕达哥拉斯派对苏格拉底感兴趣。柏拉图也许在暗示,早已存在的毕达哥拉斯学派或许是传扬对苏格拉底的记忆以及苏格拉底教诲的一个可能的途径。

斐多向毕达哥拉斯派叙述了苏格拉底临终之日发生的事情以及他所说的话。那天,苏格拉底要在太阳下山时吞下毒药赴死,他说的最多的是死后灵魂会怎样,而毕达哥拉斯派早就相信灵魂不死。两个毕达哥拉斯派的年轻人也经常去看望苏格拉底,但他们心存疑虑;他们怀疑自己被教导的灵魂不死观念是否真实。所以,那天谈话的大部分内容是,苏格拉底向两位心存怀疑的毕达哥拉斯派年轻人提出论证,以便用论证劝服他们相信,他们的灵魂事实上是不死的。

斐多的叙述最终引向其中一个年轻人刻贝斯(Kebes)提出的最后一个怀疑的理由。苏格拉底在回答之前停顿了一下。他在那天他最后的论证前停顿了,他知道这将是他一生中最后的论证,因为太阳正在西沉,他必须在日落前饮下毒药。他说,他停顿是因为刻贝斯提出的反驳要求他考虑"作为一个整体的关于生成与消亡的原因"。刻贝斯的问题关系到哲学综合性的主题:在自然的整体、生成的整体中起作用的原因。为了讨论生成和消亡的原因这一宏大主题,苏格拉底选择"说说我自己对它们的经验"。之后苏格拉底返回平生中的第一次哲学反思。

所以,柏拉图做了某种醒目的安排:开始一生中最后的论证之前,苏格拉底回顾了自己的第一次哲学经验,以便从头讲述他成为哲人的故事。

苏格拉底说,"我年轻的时候就好奇地欲求那种智慧——他们叫做'探究自然'"。我们在柏拉图那里看到的最年少的苏格拉底,是一位热切渴望理解作为整体的自然的年轻人,也是一位西方哲学传统称为"前苏格拉底哲人"的年轻人。按照苏格拉底在临终之日的叙述,早期希腊的自然哲人们根据自然中运作的自然原因来解释原因,他逐渐看到了这一方式有问题。在探究那些有关原因的问题时,他无从解决这些问题,直到听见一位哲人解释说,自然中的变化由心智(mind)所造成,心智是赋予秩序的原因。按照这种对原因的解释,自然中的每一事物是其所是,是因为心智判定它那样存在最好。所有的生成和消亡,都可以通过目的论得到解释:所发生的一切之所以发生,是因为居于统治地位的心智为其设定了目标或目的。施特劳斯在《色诺芬的苏格拉底言辞》(*Xenophon's Socratic Discourse*)中讨论这一观点时,称之为苏格拉底的目的神论(teleotheology)。施特劳斯发明此词是要表达这样的观点:诸神促使每件事情朝向最好的目的,由此统治世界。①

但苏格拉底在《斐多》中说,当他阅读教授这一目的论的阿纳克萨戈拉(Anaxagoras)的著作时,发现这位老师本人没有使用以上解释模式,没有表明此物或彼物是其所是由于它那样存在最好。阿纳克萨戈拉甚至也凭靠自然原因而非心智。(这也许表明阿纳克萨戈拉使用显白而有益的教诲掩盖了自己隐微的自然主义。)

苏格拉底继续说,自然原因单独不能解释属人事物,比如什么造成他入狱,坐等吞下毒药。这一事实的真实原因不能用他"筋骨"的运动来解释,只能用人的意见来解释:人们和雅典人判定,苏格拉底受死对他们最好;苏格拉底判定,他饮下雅典人说他应该饮下的毒药对自己最好。自然原因不足以解释一切事情,尤其是属人的事情;同样,统辖一切的心智似乎也不是一个充分的解释。什么是作为一个整体的生成与

---

① 参见施特劳斯,《色诺芬的苏格拉底言辞》,杜佳译,华东师范大学出版社,2010,页159–160。

毁灭的原因?

在开始一生中最后的论证之前,苏格拉底说他早年就设计了他自己的道路,并问毕达哥拉斯派的年轻人刻贝斯:"你想让我展示……我为了探索原因而从事的第二次起航吗?""第二次起航"是比喻,来自古希腊航船的经验:无风撑起船帆时,旅行者不得不采用另一个法子,用橹桨划船。苏格拉底把他哲学的"第二次起航"解释为一次转向,即驶离要解释的事物,转向人们用于讨论和思考事物的言辞:也许在言辞中,在逻格斯(logoi)中,他会发现事物的恰当原因。苏格拉底在表述这一向言辞的转向时说:"我试图要向你展示的不过是我已经做成的那种原因的理念(eidos, idea)。"(100b)他说,他自那以后一直谈论的理念就是这样起步的。

他在《斐多》中讨论的理念是美的理念,善的理念,大的理念。基本的想法是:每个美的事物之所以是美的,是因为它分有美本身;美的理念从不变化,但是每个美的事物都会变化;每一美的事物变美,随后就不再美,它们变得分有美,随后就不再分有美。现在不需要深入理解苏格拉底的"理念论"——如施特劳斯所说,"对我们而言,最一开始,理念论完全不可信,甚至还显得虚妄"。① 对我们来说重要的是,年轻的哲人苏格拉底曾执迷于解释自然事物的原因,但是不满意古希腊哲学的前辈们有关作为一个整体的所有生成与毁灭的原因的说法,此时他所转向的是理念。

苏格拉底在临终之日说,他仍然在以这种讨论理念的方式解释原因。现在,他开始人生的最后一次论证,用理念证明灵魂不朽。年轻的刻贝斯发现理念完全具有说服力;通过论证,他认识到自己的灵魂是不死的。现在他可以让苏格拉底死去了,因为苏格拉底治愈了他的疑惑——又多了一条理由献给阿斯克勒皮俄斯(Asclepius)一只公鸡。

苏格拉底做了人生当中最后一次论证,然后饮下毒药,这时他大约70

---

① Leo Strauss, *The City and Man*, p. 119.

岁。当他转向他此后一直在谈论的理念时,他有多少年岁?当他迈出他的哲学生活的第一步——由希腊的自然哲人们开始,之后转向理念——他有多少年岁?他没有说,但是柏拉图让读者在《帕默尼德》中得知了这一点。我们现在来看《帕默尼德》,以便更加清晰地把握苏格拉底成为苏格拉底的第一阶段。

《帕默尼德》

《帕默尼德》叙述的对话设置在雅典哲学史上的一个著名时刻,当时有智识追求的雅典人都会知道的一个时刻:伟大的哲人帕默尼德和芝诺到访雅典。到访发生在公元前450年的一个雅典节日,柏拉图谓之宏大的泛雅典娜节。《帕默尼德》中的一位发言人说,与帕默尼德和芝诺谈话的苏格拉底"非常年轻",但是他已经形成理念的观点,因为他用理念向年迈的哲人帕默尼德及其年轻的追随者芝诺发难,挑战他们并取得大胜。

这意味着,《斐多》所叙述的苏格拉底转向理念早于公元前450年的这场对话。公元前450年,苏格拉底大约19岁。所以,苏格拉底热切地投身自然哲学,之后洞察到自然原因的问题,然后执着于目的论,又认识到目的论在解释原因时的不足,最后转向言辞和理念并以之作为原因,所有这一切发生在他19岁以前或19岁时。由此柏拉图展示了苏格拉底的某种显著特征:他是个哲学奇才,哲学上的天才,不到19岁就通透思考过他之前的整个希腊哲学的历史,并得出他自己解决原因问题的新方案:理念论。

《帕默尼德》的场景

柏拉图设置的场景告诉我们,19岁的苏格拉底与65岁的帕默尼德及其40岁的学生芝诺之间的这场谈话为何会保存下来。对于关心苏格拉底如何成为苏格拉底的人来说,这一场景虽然复杂,但极为重要。

《帕默尼德》的叙述者或转述者名叫克法洛斯（Cephalus）；他是"克拉左美奈人"（men of Clazomenae）中的一位，克拉佐美奈是位于小亚细亚的希腊城邦，这群人乘船跨过爱琴海来到雅典，调查可能记得那场谈话的那个人是否还能记起60年前的谈话——柏拉图将《帕默尼德》的"框架"设定在公元前394年（普莱诺确定的戏剧日期）。克拉左美奈人曾经听说，那个人年轻时被教导记住那天所说的一切，而教导者实际参加了公元前450年的那场谈话，亲耳听到并记住了一切。询问苏格拉底或其他参与过谈话的人为时已晚，因为他们全都过世了。

克拉左美奈人来到雅典，在集市上碰到阿德曼托斯和格劳孔。后两位是《理想国》的主角，克拉左美奈人寻找的正是他们同母异父的兄弟安提丰（Antihphon）。他们一起到安提丰那里，问他能否记起多年前他记住的那场交谈。安提丰的确记得他曾记住的东西，但他不愿费劲从头到尾说一遍。安提丰已经完全丧失兴趣，但是克拉左美奈人说服他无论如何都要回忆一下。

公元前450年的交谈

在交谈的第一阶段，安提丰对克拉左美奈人说，年轻的苏格拉底把他的理念论呈现为他自己的创制；他像一位19岁的哲学革新者那样呈现理念论：信心满满，争强好胜；他急切想证明两位名哲错了，而他，也只有他，解决了他们的大问题，即原因问题。这场交谈完全是一场竞赛，年仅19岁的小伙子知道自己将会胜出。

在场的皮托多洛斯（Pythodorus）确信，遭到如此对待，帕默尼德和芝诺肯定会生气。但他们不但没有生气，反而欣赏苏格拉底所说的东西。也就是说，他们在年轻的苏格拉底身上看到了他们同类人的特质，一种哲人始终追寻的罕见特质。

苏格拉底自信满满地反驳了帕默尼德和芝诺之后，针对苏拉拉底超验的、不变的理念，帕默尼德提出了第一个逻辑困难。苏格拉底没有回应这个困难，因此帕默尼德对他说：

> 好吧,你还年轻,苏格拉底,哲学还没有抓住你,依我看它还是会抓住你……至于现在,由于你的年纪,你还在顾及人们的意见。(130e)

帕默尼德因此暗示年轻的思者苏格拉底,过度的热爱胜利驱使着他,他依旧太在乎"人们的意见",但是帕默尼德相信,苏格拉底前程远大。

苏格拉底以为理念论能使他获胜,但针对理念论的可能性,帕默尼德随后提出更为深刻甚至更为严肃的反驳。苏格拉底没有捍卫超验的理念,借以反驳帕默尼德的论证。帕默尼德的论证没有得到回应,他在结尾时对苏格拉底说:

> 只有一个天性极卓越的人才能认识到,每一事物都有某个类和存在自身;只有一个更加奇妙的人才会发现所有这些,而且有能力教导其他人,让他自身能够清晰并充分地判断它们。(135a–b)

苏格拉底是那个"天性极卓越的人"吗?他能认识到每一事物都有某个类和存在自身吗?帕默尼德正在挑战年轻的苏格拉底。看起来,苏格拉底已经迈出了哲学上根本性的一步,自己认识到事物皆有自然,每一事物属于一个类,一个自然的类:这就是一个事物的"理念"的含义。但在这场唇枪舌剑中,老一代哲人进一步发难:你是那个"更加奇妙的人"吗?你能发现所有这些东西,并且"有能力教导其他人,让他自身能够清晰并充分地判断它们"吗?

好心的老帕默尼德结束发难,告诉年轻的苏格拉底,为什么他有必要推进对理念的思考,而非将他的溃败当作对理念说的驳斥:

> "然而,"帕默尼德说,"苏格拉底,反过来,如果有人在思索所有这些及其他问题后,他**否认**有关于存在的理念,不去区分每个单一事物的某个理念,不论他转向哪里,他什么都理解不了,因为他不承认每一存在具有永远同一的理念。由此,他将完全摧毁对话或辩证法的力量。但是,在我看来,你也充分意识到这一点。"(135b–c)

理解的可能性系于理念。如果事物要能被理解,那么每一事物必须有自己的理念,必须是它所属的类的一例。每一事物必须拥有一种自然。进一步讲,这一自然必须在某种意义上能被认识。哲学要是可能的,事物就必须拥有自然或属于一个类,这些类必须在某种意义上能被认识。苏格拉底,你能否超越你那被反驳的理念论,要看你身上有没有那个类。你属于我们——芝诺和我——所属的那个类吗?你那天纵之才是否到了能够发现并向他人表明哲学可能性的根基的程度?苏格拉底当然知道,帕默尼德的论证已经证明他的理念论不合理性,是错的。但是他能迎接帕默尼德的挑战吗?他和伟大的帕默尼德属于同一类吗?他原本认为能用理念论来反驳帕默尼德,现在却受到了帕默尼德的反驳。

这就是故事的原委。克法洛斯说克拉美佐奈人是"地道的哲人"(126b)。听到这个故事,他们一定会庆幸自己扬帆远航的决定——仅仅为了听年轻的苏格拉底与帕默尼德和芝诺交谈的故事。

场景和谈话的含义

皮托多洛斯在公元前450年的谈话现场,他听到了一切。帕默尼德和芝诺在雅典期间,就住在他家中。作为招待这些大哲人的东道主,他知道他与年轻的苏格拉底一起听到的内容很重要,所以铭记在心。很久以后,为了保存自己听到和记住的内容,他传给了年轻的朋友安提丰,还帮助他记忆。但安提丰对之兴味索然,他不理解为什么非要把这些内容传下来,也不想不辞烦劳记住它们。若没有克拉左美奈人,故事会随着他而湮灭。

阿德曼托斯和格劳孔呢?柏拉图将《帕默尼德》设置在公元前394年,在36年前,在公元前429年的《王制》中,苏格拉底曾教导过这两个年轻人。柏拉图表明,这两个人对年轻的苏格拉底的这个故事不怎么上心:这些年来,他们从未要求自己的兄弟告诉他们年轻的苏格拉底的故事。他们根本不关心这个故事是否会随自己的兄弟失传。

在我看来,这完全正确,也极富教益:阿德曼托斯和格劳孔年轻时曾听到苏格拉底必须教授给他们的东西,那时苏格拉底已学到了他特有的诗,即他特有的显白教诲。这些教诲对他们来说足够了。他们学到了《王制》的全部教诲,苏格拉底公开教授的所有主要教诲,对此他们十分满意。对他们来说,苏格拉底教授的是作为他们正义和正派生活的基础的观点,而他们十分满足地相信这一观点。苏格拉底教他们如何摆脱希腊启蒙造成的怀疑,教给他们认识他们灵魂的自然、理念的恒定不变,以及道德诸神的恒定不变——诸神将在冥府奖赏他们的正义。

克拉左美奈人呢?他们与安提丰、阿德曼托斯和格劳孔有本质的区别:他们必须知道年轻的苏格拉底对帕默尼德和芝诺所说的内容,或从两位大哲人那里学到的内容。他们早就充分地了解过苏格拉底,因此才认为必须听这个有关苏格拉底早期思考的故事。以我在此处所用的语言来说,他们想了解苏格拉底如何成为苏格拉底,苏格拉底如何成为他们钦佩的哲人——他们如此钦佩苏格拉底,哪怕只是风闻有关年轻的苏格拉底的这一故事或许还听得到,他们也愿意越洋而来。

如此设置《帕默尼德》,柏拉图或许是想说:真正渴求聆听苏格拉底年轻时这一重大事件的人只会是少数无名的后来人,他们从外邦越洋而来,仅仅是希望听到年轻的苏格拉底和年老的帕默尼德相互说了些什么。柏拉图似乎在说,他在这部对话中保存的内容仅仅是为了少数兴趣浓厚的人,他们是未来自远方来的无名旅行者,也是潜在的哲人;他们愿意花费时日和精力了解甚至苏格拉底亲密的同伴也不需要知道的事情。

对于哲学传统如何运作,苏格拉底的哲学如何传承,柏拉图的思考似乎是:本质上隐微的苏格拉底深嵌进显白的苏格拉底被保存下来的对话中。这些对话会以教化性的、道德的教诲继续训练阿德曼托斯和格劳孔,而这些教诲将会被等同于哲学,而且他们也会相信这些教诲。但是,还会有少数人像无名的克拉左美奈人一样,被驱使着进一步去探究,被驱使着去探究苏格拉底的言辞以求理解其所隐藏的隐微教诲:他们不会单纯地相信苏格拉底告诉他们的东西,他们会致力于理解苏格拉底暗含的意思,亲自检验并判断其中的隐含之意。

克拉左美奈人学到了苏格拉底在19岁时学到的东西。他们学到,超验、不变的理念,亦即阿德曼托斯和格劳孔所信任的理念学说,是不可能的。这是他们获得的奖赏,因为他们渴求知道年老的帕默尼德对年轻的苏格拉底所说的内容。学到这些后,他们知道他们的旅行必须继续下去,必须进一步跟进苏格拉底的学习。学习什么呢?我们可以假定,柏拉图让这个问题敞开,以便使之按照他所安排的方式得到追寻。

柏拉图是所有这些故事的作者,记录了苏格拉底过往的这一重大事件,该事件是苏格拉底成为苏格拉底过程中的转折点,并迫使苏格拉底放弃把超验的理念作为一种对原因的恰当理解。此外,柏拉图通过他赋予两篇对话的时间顺序揭示了更多信息。很清楚,《帕默尼德》表明,苏格拉底已经迈出《斐多》所展示的哲学上的第一步。《帕默尼德》展示了苏格拉底哲学教育的第二步。但是,通过把《帕默尼德》和《斐多》这样联系起来,柏拉图迫使读者面对一个大问题:在临终之日的最后一次论证中,70岁的苏格拉底教给毕达哥拉斯派年轻人的理念论,恰是50年前他从帕默尼德那里认识到不合理性的观点。而且苏格拉底在临终之日说,作为原因的理念,就是他一直引进的东西。当然,苏格拉底从未忘记帕默尼德对理念论的反驳。那么,尽管他19岁时就知道理念论不合理性,他为什么在临终之际还要教导理念论,为什么他一直在教导理念论?

《斐多》本身默而不宣地表明了缘由:在《斐多》中,苏格拉底反复把他运用理念的最后一次论证称作安全的观点,他的年轻听众可以信赖这一观点;他甚至鼓励他们在任何人提出相反观点的时候喊出这种观点。他们确实信赖,也确实相信理念论,我们可以想象到他们的叫喊。如此相信理念,他们就不会受制于他们在《斐多》中表达的怀疑和恐惧。这对他们足够了,正如《王制》对阿德曼托斯和格劳孔也足够了。他们没有继续质疑苏格拉底的最后论证,而苏格拉底本人表明,即便他生命中的最后一次论证,那一基于理念的论证,也是可以质疑的——事实上已被某人质疑,斐多说,"我没有记住是谁"(103a)。两位年轻人没有质疑而是仅仅相信基于理念的论证,从而证明他们不属于苏格拉底所属的类。他们也许绝不会为了听一个关于苏格拉底起源的故事而远渡重洋。

《斐多》与《帕默尼德》叙述的年轻的苏格拉底相隔 50 年。柏拉图将苏格拉底临终之日与他认识到理念并非对原因的恰切解释的那一天联系起来,以此表明《王制》和《斐多》中的理念论属于政治哲学,是一种安全的观点,能够让哲学在道德上值得信赖,从而得到公开辩护。这是哲学之诗的一部分,是施特劳斯所说的侍养之诗的一部分。但我们仍然要面对苏格拉底 19 岁时遇到的那个严肃的哲学问题,即理解自然,理解原因。带着这一问题,我们可以直接转向《会饮》,也就是苏格拉底哲学教育的第三即最后阶段。

《会饮》

施特劳斯认为《会饮》是柏拉图最重要的对话,出于两点理由。它是唯一一部以赞美一位神(爱若斯神或爱神)为主题的对话,也是唯一一部以对话场合命名的对话:一场酒宴,人们借着酒劲畅言无忌,说一些其他场合或许不会说的话。从以上清晰的两点出发,施特劳斯发现《会饮》的戏剧日期暗示了它的一个隐秘特征:这场对话亵渎了宗教密仪,讲述了一个有关诸神以及诸神知晓什么的秘密,而讲述这些是一种罪行。

伯纳德特同样对《会饮》提供了重要的指引。我不得不就《会饮》说的内容,参照了施特劳斯和伯纳德特,尤其是后者。

在《斐多》中,斐多讲述了他亲历的苏格拉底的临终故事,但在他讲述的故事里面,苏格拉底讲述了自己哲学生活最早的开端。在《帕默尼德》中,两场对过往的回忆带领读者回到苏格拉底 19 岁时进行的一场真实交谈。在《会饮》中,两场对过往的回忆再次带领读者回到所转述的真实交谈,其中苏格拉底再次讲述了他成为他自己的最后阶段,他想要讲述自己年轻时候的一个故事——他知道有一位忠实的追随者正在倾听一切,因为是他邀请这位追随者参加了这次聚会。

《会饮》有一个复杂的年序。开篇时,两组不同的雅典人热衷于打听阿伽通家里举办的酒宴,席间苏格拉底和阿尔喀比亚德以及其他人发表了有关爱若斯神的讲辞。普莱诺表明,对话的框架设定在公元前399年,就在苏格拉底受审判前不久:这就是人们对苏格拉底和阿尔喀比亚德这么感兴趣的原因。

公元前399年为何重要?

首先是因为那是苏格拉底受审的时间。苏格拉底受到的指控,部分缘于雅典人怀疑他败坏了阿尔喀比亚德。许多雅典人认为阿尔喀比亚德有可能甚或多半罪大恶极,因为他被怀疑在公元前416年亵渎宗教密仪。《会饮》证明,苏格拉底是清白的,没有败坏阿尔喀比亚德。两组听众听到《会饮》所转述的对话,就可以判定苏格拉底是无辜的。公元前399年发生在雅典的另一场审判是"安多基德斯(Andokides)的审判",可能在苏格拉底的审判不久前。安多基德斯的审判表明,公元前416年的罪行是一个非常紧迫、广受议论的话题,安多基德斯因牵涉其中而受到审判。像苏格拉底的审判一样,安多基德斯的审判发生在雅典城涤罪(purification)期间,彼时与斯巴达的战争已于公元前404年结束,反对部分由克里提阿斯(Critias)——另一个被认为被苏格拉底败坏的雅典豪杰——领导的三十僭主的内战也已结束。公元前399年是宗教涤罪的狂热时刻,苏格拉底因此沦为这场运动的牺牲品。

公元前399年重要的另一个原因是,苏格拉底在其辩护词中讲了一个著名的故事:德尔斐的神说没有人比他更智慧,这使他转向了他后来一直从事的事情,检验神所说的话,由此来侍奉这位神。如我所说,我们可以把这个故事当成神话式的真实。但在同样设定在公元前399年的《会饮》中,苏格拉底讲述了关于自己的故事,我们听到有关苏格拉底如何成为自己的更深刻的真相——在《会饮》中,我们听到苏格拉底讲述自己智慧的真正起源。

公元前399年的叙述者是阿珀罗多罗斯(Apollodorus),他说他是从阿里斯托德摩斯(Aristodemos)那里听到这个故事,后者受到苏格拉底的邀请才参加了那场宴会。酒宴在东道主阿伽通(Agathon)赢得悲剧竞赛后的第二天晚上进行。作为悲剧竞赛的获胜者,阿伽通受人瞩目;所有雅典人都知道,他获奖的那一年是公元前416年。

公元前416年为何重要?

每个人都知道,亵渎宗教密仪发生在公元前416年,这项泄露雅典宗教的秘密核心的罪行骇人听闻。阿尔喀比亚德被普遍认为犯有这一罪行,他嘲弄并且暴露了最神圣的秘密。研读《会饮》时,读者如果牢记这一揭露秘密的罪行,他就会看到施特劳斯所强调的事情:对不同密仪的亵渎,对于哲人是什么以及哲人能知道什么的密仪的亵渎。有赖于苏格拉底在畅言无忌的酒宴上的发言,我们得以看到柏拉图所曾揭示的哲学最隐秘的真相:柏拉图揭开了苏格拉底作为哲人的存在的秘密,同时揭开了存在自身的秘密。亵渎雅典宗教密仪的罪行违背了雅典的法律。但是,苏格拉底在某种意义上揭示的秘密是关于自然的真正秘密。这一秘密之为秘密,并不依赖某种规定谈论它为违法的习俗。自然的真正秘密总是拒绝被表述,抵制被付诸言辞。赫拉克利特(Heraclitus)说,自然爱隐藏。但《会饮》暗示,在一定程度上或以某种方式,自然的秘密可以被领悟——但《会饮》暗示这一点是通过一种本身就是秘密的方式,以与自然隐藏的方式相一致。

第三件事使得《会饮》的年序变得错综复杂。苏格拉底酒宴上的发言带着他的听众回到他早年的一件事。他叙述,在公元前440年左右,他大概30岁的时候,他学到了某种至关重要的东西。

公元前 440 年为何重要？

苏格拉底所言表明，这一学习一定发生在公元前 450 年之后，即帕默尼德反驳了他关于超验理念的看法之后。苏格拉底在此说他学到的东西，可以看作对帕默尼德的反驳留给他的问题的解决。苏格拉底讲述的公元前 440 年的故事发生在帕默尼德的反驳之后，从而完成了苏格拉底哲学教育的三个阶段。

公元前 440 年的这一完成还告诉我们其他重要信息：在公元前 433 年的《普罗塔戈拉》之前，即在柏拉图展现的苏格拉底的首次公开亮相之前，苏格拉底已完成其哲学教育。前一场讲座讨论的三篇对话设置在公元前 433 年和 429 年，柏拉图在其中展现了苏格拉底的政治哲学教育，因此苏格拉底的哲学教育先于其政治哲学教育。

回到公元前 416 年的宴饮。众人决定以爱若斯神为主题发表讲辞之后，苏格拉底说："我要说，除了爱欲的事情，别的我都不知道。"（177d）这句话对他接下来的讲辞极为重要。爱欲首先被体验为爱或吸引的一种深刻的属人激情，希腊人将之升格为一位神。《会饮》中的讲辞全都用于赞扬爱若斯神，但苏格拉底的讲辞是一位自称有知者的言辞，苏格拉底已是一位大名鼎鼎的哲人，他声称爱欲是自己唯一懂的东西。苏格拉底以宣称无知而出名，但在《会饮》中，他却声称自己知道所有其他人正准备谈论的东西。其他人构成一个非常特殊的群体：他们属于极其雅致的雅典城中最雅致的有知者，是少数特殊的智识人，每人都像一位专家那样发言。他们是柏拉图曾为我们展示的苏格拉底的言辞最为出色的听众。

公元前 416 年的宴饮是一群特殊的人的私人聚会，参加者在某种意义上全都是希腊的启蒙人。他们没有饮酒，而是在宴席上发表有关爱若斯神的讲辞，并让女簧管手退场。现场只有他们，这一小撮启蒙人得以发表私密的讲辞。公元前 416 年，苏格拉底大约 53 岁，已经完全成熟。他第六个或最后一个发言，只是在他讲完之后，阿尔喀比亚德醉醺醺地来到,发表了一通赞扬苏格拉底的话。苏格拉底发表所有讲辞中最高妙的讲辞时,阿尔喀比亚德不在场。

苏格拉底如往常谈话一样开始他的讲辞。他审查并反驳了东道主阿伽通刚刚表达的对爱欲的看法。苏格拉底让阿伽通感到困惑,他承认自己不知道他原以为知道并谈论得如此美妙的东西。也就是说,苏格拉底惠及年轻的阿伽通,向他表明他实际上是无知的,缺乏他误以为自己早就拥有的知识。之后他又给予阿伽通另一大恩惠:他说,一位智慧的老师也曾将他置于同样的状态,经过他自己的连番发问,这位老师引领他走向关于爱欲的真正知识。苏格拉底的讲辞面向每一位在场者,并特别针对一个人,即那位刚刚赢得悲剧竞赛的年轻悲剧作家。苏格拉底向他表明:获奖在其次;他有可能靠自己把握对爱欲的真正理解——他误以为自己已经拥有这种理解——获得这一理解更多要依靠他像苏格拉底曾经那样发问。

苏格拉底告诉阿伽通,他的老师是一位智慧的女人,名叫第俄提玛(Diotima)。她让苏格拉底陷入困惑,于是苏格拉底向她发问,她便教给他有关爱欲的基本教诲。苏格拉底叙述了他与第俄提玛的部分对话。

苏格拉底在公元前440年学到了什么

第俄提玛首先反驳苏格拉底的观点,阿伽通同样持此观点,即认为爱若斯神美、善、智慧。但爱若斯神并不丑、坏、无知。第俄提玛教导苏格拉底说,在美与丑、好与坏、智慧与无知的两极之间存在着一种居间(between)。第俄提玛从居于智慧与无知之间的东西开始论述爱欲,她开始的地方正是哲人一贯开始的地方。她首先把这种居间说成"正确的意见"——这是占据智慧与无知之间的居间的通常方式。哲学也占据这一居间,但占据的方式不同。哲人既不智慧又非无知,他体验到对智慧的激情,他被驱使去补救他在智慧上的缺乏:哲人爱欲地占据居间,渴望拥有他知道自己缺乏的东西。

苏格拉底在《会饮》中的发言始于两极(extremes),正如他在《帕默尼德》中的发言一样,那里的两极是理念和殊相(particulars),或者我们可以说,是纯粹的永恒和纯粹的流变。《会饮》接下来表明,受爱欲驱动的哲学如何能够最好地思考居于永恒和流变的抽象概念之间的实在(reality),富有爱欲的哲人实际就是这样一种实在,是众殊相总体中的一个殊相。哲人能够通过认识自己而逐渐认识[真理]。

之后第俄提玛教导苏格拉底,爱若斯不是神,而是介于神与凡人之间。苏格拉底对爱若斯不是神感到震惊,回过神来后,他问第俄提玛,这样一种居间会是什么,爱若斯拥有什么样的力量。第俄提玛回答,转运(ferrying)的力量,在不朽者和有死者之间中转或运送东西的力量。这一陈述似乎暗示,爱欲的力量就是持续地生产近似于不朽的有死之物。第俄提玛在此似乎处在神话领域,处于一种神学之中,通过这种神学,根本状况或人的根本状况由神话得到呈现,并由神话得到说明。苏格拉底接下来的问题引使第俄提玛提供了一幅极具启发性的关于爱欲的神话图景。谁是爱欲的父亲?谁又是他的母亲?苏格拉底问道。换种说法就是,爱欲的起源是什么?

第俄提玛的回答是一个有关爱若斯出生的神话。这个神话所暗示或指向的只会是那些应被理性思考的事物。神话必须继之以对神话所暗示的东西的思索,而第俄提玛确实接着给出了她的思索。我将泛泛地处理这一神话,然后只讨论第俄提玛思索的一个特征。

按照第俄提玛的神话,在情爱女神阿芙洛狄忒出生的那一天,诸神举办了一场宴会。理智神之子珀洛斯(Poros)或丰盈神(Resource)出席了宴会,珀尼阿(Penia)或贫乏神(Poverty)来到宴会乞讨。丰盈神喝醉躺在宙斯的花园。贫乏神缺乏丰盈,便计谋与丰盈神生个孩子,她躺在丰盈神身旁,怀上了爱若斯神。着眼于贫乏神的计谋、盘算、算计,施特劳斯得出了他关于这一神话或关于《会饮》整体的主要结论。贫乏神能够谋划,这表明她不可能完全无知:她知道自己缺乏什么,她想要获得所缺乏的东西,并付诸行动来得到它。也就是说,贫乏神是丰盈的,不缺乏理智。施特劳斯说,"我断定,爱若斯仅仅与其母相似"——因为爱欲也是丰盈的贫乏。爱若斯与其母拥有相同的基本品质,即丰盈的贫乏。这个神话暗示,爱欲的父母就是爱欲。培根曾就这一点总结说,爱若斯没有父母,这才是最伟大的事情。柏拉图似乎也在说,最伟大的事情就是爱欲没有父母,而且我们能知道爱欲没有父母。爱欲源自爱欲,爱欲产生爱欲。

邓恩(George Dunn)①有个妙词形容这一点:他说爱欲是 auto‑poietic,这一希腊语意为自我制作、自我生产。自我生产的爱欲绝不会完全存在,而总是由于自身的活动而成为存在,又总是由于它的自我消耗——爱欲在表达自身的同时渐渐消逝——而脱离存在。

伯纳德特对爱欲得出相同的论点,还补充了一条对柏拉图神话的有用概括:神话将实际上一的东西分离为二,这种分离展现了一的复杂结构,我们在理解了这一分离之后能够回到一,因为我们现在知道一的内部结构。爱若斯是一,并有一个复杂的结构。用伯纳德特的话说,爱若斯是需要和需要性(意识到需要),爱若斯是"自觉的渴望"。伯纳德特还强调了第二个必不可少的问题:爱欲的深层结构总是消失在它使之可能的具体经验中;使爱欲本质上难以捉摸的正是这总是在消失的东西;爱欲在原则上难以捉摸,因为爱欲的深层结构总是掩藏在它总是消失进的殊相之中。

那么,对那总是掩藏之物的初步结论是:爱若斯是具有一种内在结构的欲望或冲动。第俄提玛的神话表明,爱欲的结构就是将一种指向或推动力置入它之所是之中:因其所是,爱欲是动态的,被指引着超越自身,朝向它作为爱欲所针对的对象。神话因此意味着,这一结论可以像伯纳德特提出的那样得到扩展:因其动态结构之故,爱欲总是处在一种关系中,总是与外在于它的某物相联系,就像贫乏神渴望和丰盈神结合以求生育子嗣。

---

① [编注]George Dunn 是朗佩特的学生和朋友,现执教于美国印第安纳波利斯大学,2015 年曾现场参加朗佩特的讲座。

神话还表明了另一个结论:爱欲总是处在一种关系中,这一动态使爱欲总是时间性的;爱欲总是在时间中伸展,朝向某种未来的拥有。我们可以将这个结论的三个方面归纳如下:神话表明,欲望的内在结构使它总是*动态的、关系性的、时间性的*。

神话将爱若斯与爱若斯的母亲分离开来,并给予两者相同的品质,这意味着,欲望的起源是欲望,欲望的结果是欲望。爱欲往回朝向其源头,向前朝向其结果,爱欲作为欲望总是因自身的性质而被引向实现或满足;爱欲的实现总是逐渐消失,又重新寻找完满。

我还得补充一个有关实现的语词。这意味着走到神话之外,审视第俄提玛讲完神话后论证的要点。第俄提玛论证的第一阶段把爱欲看作对美的欲望,她问爱欲的实现意味着什么,苏格拉底却无法回答。所以第俄提玛接着把爱欲视作对善的欲望,苏格拉底得以能够逐步回答爱欲的实现的问题:最终,对善的欲望实现在善永远属于自己的幸福之中。但是,"永远"的困难使第俄提玛对爱欲的实现做出最后的表述:"在美中孕生。"(206b)"在美中孕生"是《会饮》对爱欲的实现的最终定义。但第俄提玛清楚地显明,这种实现总是在衰退或消失,而爱欲同时总是在更新自己。关于爱欲的起源,我用到邓恩的术语 auto‒poietic [自我生产]。关于爱欲的实现,爱欲的目的或目标,我可以用他的术语 auto‒telic,即爱欲的目标或目的(telos)在进行孕生或生育的它自身之中。所以神话表明,爱欲的起源是爱欲。论证表明,爱欲的目的或实现是爱欲。

综上,我们可以看到,智慧的第俄提玛教给了苏格拉底终极的哲学教诲,这一教诲开始于一位有爱欲的哲人的自我认识,然后延伸至有爱欲的存在的整全。苏格拉底说自己"除了爱欲的事情,别的我都不知道"时,似乎只是谦虚或节制地声称自己拥有的知识,但实际上这一声称超群无比,是所有关于知识的可能声称中最大的声称:他知道一切存在之物的品质或方式。施特劳斯如此陈述这一全面的结论:"我们可以说,爱若斯是生成和毁灭的核心。我们可以说,爱若斯是自然之自然。"

第俄提玛把苏格拉底引向的是存在的整全的可理解性。她将苏格拉底引向一种本体论,一个有关作为整全的诸存在的合乎理性的结论:存在就是作为爱欲而非他物存在。因此,第俄提玛暗示的本体论是一种具有"生成的至高无上"的本体论,用尼采的话说便是,生成在其中拥有爱欲的可理解性。应当惊奇和感激的是,整体性拥有一个可理解的结构,生存于其中的人有能力认识这一结构。

如果我们退后一步,将《会饮》中的这一教诲解释为柏拉图展现的苏格拉底成为苏格拉底的过程的一部分,我们就会看到柏拉图所讲故事的融贯,更准确地说,他将之分散于三篇对话中,从而故意遮掩了这一故事。当我们把三个阶段放在一起时,《会饮》的最后阶段就清楚显现为前两个阶段的完成。柏拉图把第一阶段放在《斐多》中,让苏格拉底在临终之日讲述其哲学探究的开始:他从他之前的希腊哲人们开始的地方开始,追问作为一个整体的关于生成与消亡的原因。苏格拉底在凭靠自己转向言辞或陈述时,其关注的范围并没有仅仅收缩到属人事物上。第二次起航提供给他一条道路,这条道路最先带他抵达超验的理念,并将之作为所有生成和衰败的原因。但柏拉图在《帕默尼德》中的第二阶段表明,19 岁的苏格拉底对原因问题的首次解决不成功,因为帕默尼德证明超验理念在理性上不可能。《会饮》中苏格拉底哲学教育的第三阶段解决了帕默尼德设置的问题,从而解决了原因问题。苏格拉底选择呈现为,他从第俄提玛所学的内容是理解原因的恰当方式:存在居于纯粹的流变与理念的纯粹固定或永久之间;一切存在都拥有爱欲动态的、关系性的、时间性的品质。苏格拉底关于爱欲事物的知识根本上是有关作为一个整体的生成和毁灭的原因的知识。《会饮》完成了柏拉图所讲的苏格拉底成为苏格拉底的故事,因为它表明苏格拉底解决了他由之开始成为自己的原因问题。该方案回答了哲学的终极问题,诸存在之存在或自然之自然的问题。

通向这一知识的道路途经哲人的自我认识,哲人充满爱欲或满怀激情地生活在智慧与无知的居间之中。我们最终可将哲人有爱欲的居间视为指向万物有爱欲的居间性。这一点可以帮助我们理解苏格拉底经常念叩的那句话:认识你自己。这一命令被当作神的命令铭刻在德尔斐神庙,对哲人来说有着特殊意义:通过认识到自己富有爱欲,他至为清晰、切近地瞥见了万物的真相,即所有存在存在的方式与最高的、最理智/精神性的存在存在的方式相似。自我认识和关于人本身的知识就是通向关于诸存在的知识的道路。

现在,我们再次思考柏拉图设置在《会饮》中的年份。它始于公元前399年,恰在苏格拉底受审判前,它带我们回到公元前416年,那时苏格拉底讲述了他在公元前440年学到的终极教诲。公元前416年,雅典宗教的秘仪遭到亵渎,这在雅典是极大的罪行。柏拉图是否在暗示,苏格拉底犯下了罪行,亵渎了真正的秘仪,即哲人们的最高秘密和诸存在之存在的秘密?不,因为柏拉图写作了《会饮》:如果苏格拉底是说出秘密的罪犯,那么柏拉图便是写出秘密的罪犯,是更罪大恶极的罪犯。不,柏拉图通过他复杂的年份设置暗示了一些别的东西:他将发现终极秘密的真相、亵渎宗教秘仪之罪和苏格拉底受审这三个时间串联起来。柏拉图表明,苏格拉底发现了真正的秘密,并以恰切的方式处理这些极难认识又可被认识的秘密。如果我们审判苏格拉底,检验他所说的话,我们也会发现苏格拉底——和柏拉图——以一种恰切的方式来处理真正的秘密,这种方式自身难以认识但可被认识。不像那些亵渎宗教秘仪的罪犯(可能包括阿尔喀比亚德),苏格拉底恰切地处理真正的秘密:他提供了一种把人引入秘密的方式,一种把密切关注他的人引入自然的真正秘密的方式。苏格拉底在轮到自己发言的时候首先反驳阿伽通,或让他陷入困惑,这样做就暗示了这一引入:苏格拉底帮助阿伽通认识到,如果他要知道爱欲是什么,他必须得重新开始。

阿伽通要开始的方式就是苏格拉底开始的方式:向第俄提玛发问。阿伽通能做到这一点吗?他能一步步走过第俄提玛带发问的苏格拉底走过的那些路吗?苏格拉底开始向第俄提玛发问时,大约就是在阿伽通的年纪。只要阿伽通做了这些,只要苏格拉底变成他的第俄提玛,他就能认识苏格拉底认识的东西。他将认识那个东西,因为在某种程度上他凭靠自己学到了它。《会饮》中的苏格拉底没有泄露秘密,而是准备了一个把人引入秘密的门径。苏格拉底是阿伽通得以可能进入秘密的工具,但通过写作《会饮》,柏拉图让苏格拉底能为所有未来的阿伽通所用,为你和我所用。为了把我们引入秘密。

我想以第俄提玛在《会饮》中的最后之言作为我对苏格拉底成为苏格拉底的最后之言。第俄提玛引导苏格拉底到达哲学的最终阶段,获得本体论的洞见:存在就是作为爱欲存在。引导苏格拉底获得这一洞见后,她发表了一篇很长的言辞,这就是她的最后之言。长篇讲辞描述了一架梯子,她沿着阶梯或台阶一直往上爬,直至顶峰。她把发生在顶峰的事情描述为一种观看和一种行动。登上顶峰的人注视或观看完全的美,并且在美的面前孕生或参与到一种制作或创制中。两件事发生在顶峰:一种注视和一种孕生,一种观看和一种制作。我以此结束"苏格拉底成为苏格拉底"的讲座,因为尼采成为尼采的最后阶段也发生了与之十分相似的事情。尼采也将描述一种注视或观看,也将讲到一种孕生或制作,后者是观看的自然结果。在柏拉图和尼采那里,哲学作为观看,通向作为制作的哲学之诗。

施特劳斯理解这些。他在论尼采的文章中说,尼采的"根本命题"是,"生命是权力意志,或从世界内部来看就是权力意志,而非其他"。他接着说,"权力意志取代了爱欲……在柏拉图思想中占据的地位"。施特劳斯表明,在尼采的宗教篇章中,尼采在根本的或本体论问题上的哲学洞见如何通向一种对新的最高理想的孕生、制作或创制。

柏拉图与尼采同属一体:在成为自己的过程中,哲人们成为一家;他们同属一类;他们看到存在,而且他们所看到的当然相似或共通,因为他们看到的是存在。

每位哲人都会由他所看到的存在产生一套教诲。每位哲人产生的教诲各不相同,因为每种教诲必须符合自己的时代,必须以一种有效的方式侍养,而这取决于对时代的真正理解。因为时代在改变,哲人们的教诲也就彼此不同。哲人族柏拉图和尼采的教诲截然不同,他们势同水火。这种情形是必要的:因为要建立新秩序,108位求婚者必须死。

第五讲　尼采成为尼采

最后两讲的主题是尼采,只要有尼采陪伴,我便在家乡故土。我最先从尼采而非施特劳斯那里学到什么是哲人、哲人能知道什么。我学到这些,是在研究《扎拉图斯特拉如是说》尤其是"舞蹈之歌"时。我在那里第一次学到,尼采宣称有一种本体论,一种对诸存在的存在的理解。通过进一步研究尼采的著作,我确证了我首次学到的东西——我的研究始于《扎拉图斯特拉如是说》名为"论自我超越"的章节,其中扎拉图斯特拉向唯一的听者("你们最智慧的人")道说了他在"舞蹈之歌"里的发现。随后,我研究同样指向尼采本体论的施特劳斯,研究柏拉图、培根和笛卡尔,都确证了我从尼采那里学到的东西。此次尼采讲座反映出我受惠于尼采,我与尼采的结盟,以及施特劳斯和柏拉图如何推进了这一结盟。

写作大师柏拉图在编织对话时允许你发现:他自己想让用心的读者关注,让你关注,苏格拉底成为苏格拉底这一主题。先前的柏拉图讲座意在表明,柏拉图极为巧妙地安排他的对话,从而允许你发现苏格拉底成为苏格拉底的两个基本层面:成为哲人和成为哲学诗人。

本次尼采讲座关注尼采成为尼采。在其哲学生活的一个重要节点,尼采把他如何成为自己作为一个主题呈现给读者。也就是说,他看到他不得不解释他如何成为自己,不得不转向自传,并且写到"尼采先生",尽管作为哲人,他天性孤独,是天生的隐士,他的个人思考至为重要。所以,我强调尼采成为自己,实际是遵循尼采本人鼓励读者所做的事情。

尼采在其哲学生活的某个节点才开始公开谈论他如何成为自己。在成熟期完成两部巨著《扎拉图斯特拉如是说》和《善恶的彼岸》后,尼采于1886年下半年为他此前的著作写作新的序言。他意图以这些序言表明,这些著作回顾了他的思考历程,直至他在 1882 年写于《扎拉图斯特拉如是说》前不久的《快乐的科学》中获得成熟的思想。写完这些自传性的前言两年之后,在 1888 年末,当他打算发表新的要著时,他出版了一部完整著作《瞧啊,这人》。这部自传性的著作旨在表明,他已获得权利发表一部决定性的、创造历史的著作,这部著作即将到来,但他从未完成。

另一个事实也指明尼采成为自己的重要性:他认为《扎拉图斯特拉如是说》是他发表过的最重要的著作,撰写此书是为了展现扎拉图斯特拉如何成为扎拉图斯特拉,展现他达致成熟所经历的思想阶段。扎拉图斯特拉成为扎拉图斯特拉是尼采成为尼采的诗化版本。《扎拉图斯特拉如是说》本身是尼采自传的一个版本。

讨论尼采成为尼采之前,我想说一说他与他的哲学前辈们的关系。他非常挑剔并挑出来特别批评的哲学前辈是古代哲人柏拉图和现代哲人卢梭。他认为,这两位哲人对西方哲学和西方文化在他自己时代的状况负有主要责任。在《人性的,太人性的》中,在他本打算作为第二卷和最后一卷结尾的地方,他安排了非常特殊的一节,即"杂乱无章的观点和箴言"中的第 408 节:

> 我也到过地下,像奥德修斯一样,我将会一次又一次地到那里……有四对人,他们没有拒绝我……伊壁鸠鲁和蒙田,歌德和斯宾诺莎,柏拉图和卢梭,帕斯卡尔和叔本华……无论我说什么,决定什么,为自己和他人透彻思考了什么,我的眼睛紧紧盯着这八个人,发现他们也盯着我。

在这一惊人的反思中,尼采表明,这就是他之所是,这就是他之所属:最顶尖的思想家。他在地下拜访了这八位思想家,他们全都死了,却又活着,在他们的著作中活着。尼采描述自己所做的就是荷马的奥德修斯所做的。奥德修斯下降到地下,首先遇到智慧者忒瑞西阿斯(Teiresias)——他从忒瑞西阿斯那里了解到他作为一个智慧的统治者的任务。尼采下降到智慧者的地下世界,这八位特殊的人就是他的忒瑞西阿斯。他们包括柏拉图和卢梭,尼采对二者批评甚严。尼采就这八位所说的是,无论他说什么,决定什么,为自己和其他人透彻思考什么,"我的眼睛紧紧盯着这八个人,发现他们也盯着我"。尼采把这句话置于《人性的,太人性的》结尾,而在该书的开头,他试图为自己的心灵争取完全的自由。说、决定和为自己和其他人透彻思考这三个动词并没有说,他的思考来自他们。他的思考不同于他为自己和其他人的透彻思考(以德语来说,他的 denken[思考]不同于他的 andenken für mich und andere[为自己和其他人的思考])。尼采的思考完全是自己的。尼采致力于自己的思考获得完全的自由,他从伟大思想家和行动者的历史中汲取自己行动的标准,是这些人决定了西方的精神和智识进程。

尼采在伟大思想家的面前生活和行动。他们是他决定自己的作为的标准,他知道他们的作为决定了西方历史。尼采作为他们之中最新的一员生活和行动,他以他们衡量自己,并看着他们衡量他。

尼采自视甚高。他完全有权这么做。他认识自己。

关于尼采及其作品,我想提出的第二个一般性论点是:在他的自传《瞧啊,这人》中,他称他自《善恶的彼岸》以来的所有作品为"鱼钩"。他在书信中解释了他所说的鱼钩:他的作品意图捕捉他真正想要的读者,少数与他"相关联"的读者。他们会受到尼采的吸引,在一所类似于古希腊的哲学学园中进一步接受教导。在写作《人性的,太人性的》的时候(1876—1878 年),他想象着建立这样一所学园。他的理由是,并非什么都能在书中道说,哲学上的训练最好在心灵相通的小型学园中进行。尼采从未建立这样一所学园,所以,这些作品不得不凭靠自身立足。不过,哪怕是作为鱼钩,尼采写这些书就是作为一种培育,为了教导他的读者如何阅读和思考。

尼采视其作品为鱼钩业已表明,显白/隐微的区分呈现其中。《善恶的彼岸》极为清楚地讲到这种区分。在第二章"自由的心灵"中,尼采说,几乎所有人都生活在"简化和伪造"之中,每个人都满足于此,但这一规则存在例外。这一规则的例外想要认识真实。不唯如此,那些例外之中的例外想要准确知道自己的思考如何异于其他每一个人:他们"下去"检查其他人,"进到里面"认识自己。他们在做苏格拉底做过的事情。"自由的心灵"第一部分为读者做了这般准备之后,第30节讲到隐微与显白:

> 我们的至高洞见必须——而且应该!——听起来像蠢话,也可能像犯罪,当它们未经允许便传到了那类注定并非为此而生者的耳中。

我们的至高洞见指例外之中的例外,即哲人的洞见,哲人有认识和认识自己的冲动。如果哲人的洞见传到非哲人的耳中,非哲人将会把哲人看作疯子或罪犯。他们的耳朵不是哲人针对的类型——苏格拉底在《王制》中说过同样的话。尼采接着说,这是古老且众所周知的观点:

> 以前的哲人区分显白和隐微,在印度人、希腊人、波斯人和穆斯林当中……

尼采的朋友、印度哲学专家多伊森(Paul Deussen)将东方哲学引入德国。他回答了尼采有关印度哲学的问题,可能后来又告诉了他中国哲学的情况,但尼采对中国哲学知之甚少。

尼采接着说到,显白与隐微的区别并不意味着什么:它不是外和内的区别,似乎仅仅告诉你或对你耳语一番,你就可以从外走进内。他说,

> 更为关键的是,[显白之法]从下面观看事物,隐微之法从上往下看。

例外中的例外从极高处——从一种你必须努力才能获得的视野往下看。例外中的例外已获得优越的视点,除非你亲自攀爬至他达到的高处,否则你就不能享有这一视点。尽管如此,尼采会讲述他从高处看到的

东西：

> 从灵魂的高处往外看,悲剧自身不再具有悲剧效果,而且把世上的所有悲痛汇聚在一起,谁又敢断定悲剧的景象是否必然引诱且强迫同情,从而使悲痛加倍呢?

尼采从高处所作的讲述仅仅在说,作为例外中的例外,哲人从上往下看待悲剧,感受不到悲剧的通常效果,即同情和恐惧。悲剧还是悲剧;生活没有因从上往下的视角发生转变。悲剧的效果是不同的。

我刚才读的第二部分将悲剧扩展为人类的全部苦难,并且在问:谁敢断定从上往下看的视野必然导致对人类的同情,即导致伟大的现代美德?谁敢?答案一定是例外中的例外,哲人现在敢这么做。尼采拥有优越的视角,从上往下看,所以他面对一个深刻的问题:是否要同情受难的人类,是否要观看人类的悲剧命运,并因此——尽管尼采此处未说——感到有责任给予人类某种救助、拯救或其他什么。这就是隐微/显白的区分这一事实带给尼采的问题——今天的哲人是否愿意炮制一套教诲,去遮盖悲剧和总体的苦难,使之因为存在某类救助而看起来能够承受,就像柏拉图传统中的哲人们迄今还在教导的那样?又或,哲人现在是否认为,是时候对从上往下看待人类的苦难作出新的回应?是否是时候提出一种新教诲,不对苦难撒谎,不是杜撰或认可某种关于存在之目的的喜剧,从而赋予苦难意义?尼采回答说,是的,是时候提出这样一种新教诲了。两年后,1888年的一条笔记通过谴责所有柏拉图式的老师提出了这一结论的一个方面:

> 我们很自豪,再也不用做生命的撒谎者,或造谣者,或诽谤者了。

尼采有意识地终结了显白的高贵谎言的哲学传统。他自豪于不用作撒谎者。我很容易想象,尼采在这里感觉到地下世界的裁判者正盯着他,因为他不再继续柏拉图所谓的"高贵"谎言了。尼采知道,此举极度危险,因为它暴露了他自己称为"真实却致命的"根本真理(生成的至高无上,一切概念、类型、种类的流变,人与动物缺乏主要的区别)。值得再次指出,"致命的"真理对尼采不致命,他认为这些真理对基于对人类存在之目的的信仰的社会才是致命的。

我要强调,尼采自豪于不再是撒谎者,但他确实有一种显白的教诲。在下面的意义上,显白/隐微的区分对尼采和柏拉图含义相同:在尼采那里,真正的哲学同样产生哲学之诗;用尼采的话说,哲学产生艺术(art)。可以赋予在尼采那里哲学产生的诗或艺术一个源自施特劳斯的标签:尼采那里的终极艺术是一种神学-政治教诲——哲学之诗。

以上就是我余下的尼采讲座的主题:尼采是真正的哲人,他与其他伟大的哲人们一起生活在地下世界;哲人尼采延续了显白/隐微的哲学传统,但是是以一种新的方式。

我正在撰写一部有关尼采的著作,讨论尼采如何成为尼采。学界还没有充分讨论尼采如何成为自己,这部分是由于施特劳斯复兴的显白/隐微的区分尚未被应用到尼采身上。我的新著就是要利用这一区分,阐明尼采如何真正成为自己。此次讲座的其余部分,我会概述尼采如何成为自己,并更详细地概述他实际上成为什么了。

尼采 1876 年的转向

在前五部作品(1872—1876 年)中,尼采为叔本华和瓦格纳服务。这些作品是前尼采的作品,尽管其中有很多内容对于真正认识尼采相当重要。1876 年夏,尼采做出决定性的转向,从前五部作品的视野转向自己的哲学道路,一条通向他所谓的自由心灵的道路。解放心灵有一个最重要的目的,即发现真理。通向真理的道路要途经理解心灵如何不自由或怀有"偏见"。在有关解放心灵的一系列作品中的第一部作品中,尼采引用了笛卡尔作为"代前言",① 而且尼采引用的就是笛卡尔对自己转向哲学

---

① 指《人性的,太人性的》1878 年初版的"代前言"。

生活的陈述。尼采1876年的转向可以视为转向哲学生活。

对尼采而言,解放心灵意味着研究人的灵魂:灵魂的冲动和激情如何影响人的理解,或使人的理解怀有偏见？其中一个重要组成部分是认识自己的灵魂,即自我认识。解放心灵同时意味着研究人类文化,从人的开端到希腊人的高等文化(尼采受过这方面的专业训练)的历史:文化如何将偏好和偏见置入人的理解之中？解放心灵还意味着研究哲学的历史,研究伟大的前辈们,审视他们的教诲如何影响了西方文化的特殊视野或偏见;尤其意味着研究康德及其追随者,以便理解感知和认知的功能如何在根本上限制了人的心灵认识世界的能力。

对身处19世纪下半叶欧洲的尼采至关重要的是,解放心灵意味着要动用现代科学的所有资源。自近三个世纪前的启蒙运动开端以来,现代科学一直在推进和宣扬知识,用严格的方法获取和传播知识,并取得了坚实的进步:现代科学取得了可靠的发现,如今成为解放心灵不可或缺的一部分。尼采强烈批评自己所接受的教育,因为这种教育没有给他奠定物理学、化学和人类学的基础。(完成《扎拉图斯特拉如是说》后,尼采打算去大学学习五年的物理学。)

所以,1876年做出决定性的转向后,尼采需要做更多事情,以便获得自由心灵,同时教授自由心灵的理想,以吸引其他天才的心灵参与这项理解的计划。

尼采遵循着通向自由心灵的道路,同时继续发表著作。这些作品中的第一部是1878年的《人性的,太人性的》,副标题为"一本献给自由心灵的书"。1879年,他以同样的标题单独出版了一部作品,不过是作为附录或增补;1880年,他出版《漫游者和他的影子》,此书有着相同的目的。之后,在1881年的《朝霞》中,他那解放心灵的计划首次获得一个聚焦点,并将一直聚焦于此。他将这部书视为一个新的开始,他称之为"反对道德的战斗"。一旦理解了道德的力量及其危险而消极的后果,尼采对道德的研究便扩展为一场反对道德的战争。

完成《朝霞》后,尼采如往常一样,再次开始写一本新笔记,为他的下一本书做准备。他原打算把笔记的条目作为第二部《朝霞》的第 6 到 10 章。① 最后,他发表了这本新著,只有四章,题为《快乐的科学》。在该书第 4 章,尼采讲述了他最初曾在笔记中写到的决定性的突破。我将尼采解放心灵之路上的这一突破视为他迈向成熟的决定性一步。伴随着《快乐的科学》的第 4 章,尼采成为尼采。

1881 年的转向

《快乐的科学》首版于 1882 年夏,尼采在封底放了一则"布告",释放出突破的信号。布告说,

> 尼采的一系列作品随着本书而达到终点,这些作品的共同目标是树立自由心灵的新形象和理想。

随后,他列出了从《人性的,太人性的》到《快乐的科学》的一系列作品。尼采 1876 年的转向的重大计划——树立自由心灵的新形象和理想——到 1882 年告结:他成功地完成了这一计划。也就是说,尼采的自由心灵已达到整个自由心灵的计划试图达到的目标:解放心灵从一开始就旨在获得的根本真理。因此,树立自由心灵的理想不再是他最高的理想。现在,他的作品应该有另外的目的:展现自由心灵能够知道什么,展现自由心灵可以正当地依系于、正当地捆缚于真理——因为自由心灵就是真理。这就是尼采接下来的作品所做的:《扎拉图斯特拉如是说》和《善恶的彼岸》引领读者走进尼采发现的真理。

所以,尼采首次在《快乐的科学》第 4 卷公开的 1881 年的转向,是其生命中决定性的转向。他究竟发现了什么,获得了什么真理,才使这一转向变得可能?这就是两次尼采讲座的主题:尼采的自由心灵发现了什么,他从那之后撰写的作品是为了引入什么。

---

① 《朝霞》现为五章,尼采打算续写《朝霞》,增至十章。

笔记中的新发现

为了展现尼采的发现,最好回到他首次写到这些发现的作品:他在完成《朝霞》后于1881年3月开始写的新笔记。笔记中的条目从1881年春天一直写到秋天。之后他用这些条目组成了《快乐的科学》的大部分内容。《快乐的科学》以尼采想要的形式首次公开呈现了新的发现。尼采从未打算让人阅读他首先写到这些新发现的笔记,笔记是私人的,仅供他自己使用。然而,我们很幸运,尼采的妹妹伊丽莎白(Elizabeth)保存了这部笔记和其他任何写有内容的纸片,并建立尼采档案馆供研究者永久使用,还打算出版这些私人笔记。

在查看1881年的笔记之前,我想泛泛地说说尼采的笔记。尼采的笔记独一无二,因为他出生时视力极差,患有高度的近视。写作《人性的,太人性的》期间(1876—1877年),他的视力变得更为糟糕:眼睛对光越来越敏感,以致每天只能读写一个半小时,这还是在造成剧烈头痛之前。对于一个凭借读写推进思考生活的思想者来说,这是一场灾难。为挽救他赖以为生的东西,尼采设计了一个办法,并照之度过余下的写作生活。他在一封致密友的信中描述了这一办法。

他每天用六到八小时散步。散步过程中,他构思想法、论证和意象,将之组成句子和段落。散步结束后,他回到房间,通常是某栋公寓中租下的一个单间。他在大笔记本上写下构思好的段落,并保存在房间里。除了接近他的写作生活结束时的那些笔记外,其他笔记都井井有条,画线的纸张上几乎每一行都写有沉着的笔迹。笔记的条目并非随意写成,也非急促地记下的零星想法,而是他在散步时早已构思好的,精雕细琢,长短不一。进入将笔记整理成一部作品的阶段,尼采会将这些连贯的段落组织、整合成有条理的主题和章节,编辑和重写、增补和删削条目,直到整理为完整的章节。尤其在他后期的作品中,每章都有开头、中间和结尾,井然有序。

尼采在《朝霞》后开始写作的这本笔记构成了《快乐的科学》的材料。在我看来，这本笔记是尼采所有笔记中最重要的一本。里面的条目表明，尼采发现了其成熟的哲学所具有的最为重要的两个洞见。这正是本次尼采讲座余下部分的主题：有了这两个发现，尼采得以结束他解放心灵的一系列著作，开启标志他成熟期的著作。

1881年的笔记和本体论

1881年的笔记表明，尼采的思想已超越对道德的密切关注。道德流行以自利和利他来区分人的行为。自利的行为服务于自我或那个"我"，利他的行为服务于他者。盛行的道德认为，自利行为极坏，利他行为极好。早在《朝霞》中，尼采便判定，一切的人类行为，包括道德行为，都基于种种在原则上是自利的或为自身服务的冲动或激情。每一个看起来利他的行为实际上实现了一种掩盖的或隐藏的自利冲动。

尼采对人的行为背后的冲动的研究，属于心理学（psychology）或对人的灵魂的研究。① 这是一项对他人行为的研究，但正如自苏格拉底以来的哲人们所强调的那样，这也是对自己灵魂的研究，对自我的研究，从而引向自我认识。尼采持续研究人类，他的自我认识和对他者的认识使他得出结论：种种冲动不仅是自利的，还分享了一个根本的特征，它们在某个方面全都相似。尼采在这本笔记中赋予这个方面不同的名称。听一听他用来描述这一共通的性质的语词吧。下面是我对尼采德文的英文翻译，每个词原本都是复合词，因为德语可以轻易地构成很长的单个词语：

> 沉迷拥有。想要拥有。想要拿住。渴望财产或所有权。想要据为己有。为所有权所驱动。占用的激情。对权力的激情。

这些复合词试图命名冲动自身：沉迷、渴望、想要、激情。它们还试图

---

① psychology 亦可译为"灵魂学"。

命名冲动的对象：拥有、拿住、据为己有、占用、成为我的财产。尼采用这些复合词首先来描述人的行为，试图正确命名他发现所有人类行为共有的特征，即便这些行为看上去并非它被命名的那样。尼采的笔记还常常提到这一共同冲动的另一面：爱。爱是一种占有和占有所渴望的一切对象的激情。

尼采笔记条目的另一个主要特征赋予各种冲动等级秩序，从最低和最普通的冲动再到最高和最罕有的冲动。尼采常用一个词组描述最高的冲动：认知的激情，他将之视为自己最有力量的激情，与其他激情没有本质不同但却是其他激情的顶峰，也就是最理智／精神（geistigste）的激情，位于诸激情等级秩序的顶端。

笔记条目的另一主要特征是，在个体灵魂中，各种冲动彼此不断争斗，争夺至高权，或争夺统治。

这本笔记最重大的进展表明，尼采有关道德及作为基础的种种冲动的思考转入了哲学始终转入的方向：从理解特殊朝向更为全面的理解。这本笔记同时表明，对于那些表示人类灵魂的种种冲动的共同特征的词语，尼采做了可能最全面的应用：这些词语描述了一切人类行为的真相；不止于此，还描述了所有生物全部行为的真相。之后可以做出最为全面的判断：这些词语描述了万物全部行为的真相。

所以，心理学扩展至生物学，再扩展到物理学，即包括自我认识在内的对人类灵魂的认识扩展为对有机体、对所有活物的认识，再扩展为对所有存在和所有行为的认识：在其中每一领域，共同的特性是对起作用的东西的最终解释。正是在这本笔记中，尼采完成了最终的扩展。他没有使用哲学术语本体论，因为他怀疑他所称的"大学哲学"。但是我们可以用这一哲学术语表示最全面的研究，对存在或对诸存在的存在的研究，亦即本体论在希腊语中的字面意思。尼采在1881年的笔记中得出了他的本体论结论，将呈现于万物之中的冲动命名为"沉迷拥有"，德语为 Habsucht，尼采在笔记中最常用此词表示这一冲动。

很重要的是，在一年之中，尼采赋予那个根本现象另一个名称，因为他更好地、不同地、更精细地理解了那个根本现象。他用一个全面的新术语 Wille zur Macht 取代了 Habsucht,用"权力意志"取代了"沉迷拥有"。这一变化缘于尼采继续努力更充分地理解根本的力量。根本的力量不是一种对拥有的欲望,就好像对外部事物的拥有是其驱动力一样。尼采看到,基本的东西是一种对克服的欲望,是一种越过自身、直面抵抗形式的他者并且驱使克服这种抵抗的力量。他者在本质上不是他者,而也是一种对克服的欲望。所以,在万物中起作用的根本事物是一直存在于诸力量领域的力量。尼采认定,最好名之为权力意志,因为权力意志就在于它需要消解自己多余的力量,反对那种本身就是力量的抵制。尼采在《扎拉图斯特拉如是说》以及后面的所有作品都使用了"权力意志"这一名称,但尼采清楚认识到,甚至这一标签也非完全恰当。他称权力意志为"软弱和有限的隐喻"(《善恶的彼岸》格言 22),但在他看来,其他术语都没有接近于命名那一根本现象。

因为我是在讨论尼采成为尼采,所以我想说得清晰一些:我从 1881 年的笔记所表达的本体论跳至他大概在一年之后首次获得的更为充分的本体论洞见和术语。我这么做是为了从一开始就显明,尼采提炼和改进了 1881 年的笔记中的本体论洞见。在扼要查看尼采最终的本体论洞见后,我想跳回 1881 年的笔记,因为在那里,他首次迈出从本体论理解存在本身的步伐。

1881 年的笔记表明,尼采开始全面运用他对人类的诸种冲动的解释原则。笔记同样表明,尼采获得了他的第二个关键发现,正因为这第二个发现,这本笔记广为尼采研究者所知:它记录了尼采对他期待为人所知的永恒复返学说的发现。这就是 1881 年的笔记(写于《朝霞》之后,《快乐的科学》之前)极为重要的原因:它包含尼采最重要的两个思想,借由这两个思想,尼采迈入了哲人的成熟。获得了这两种思想,尼采成为尼采,成为他之所是。

现在,我想考察尼采在写作他的著作时用他在 1881 年的笔记中获得的本体论做了什么?他首先在《快乐的科学》中讲述了这一本体论,此书公开了笔记的所有主要洞见。《快乐的科学》的结构很重要。前三章探讨道德、艺术和科学,与《朝霞》非常相似。尼采似乎在1882年1月写出了前三章。随后他又写出了截然不同的第4章,而且决定以之作为最后一章。第4章与前三章不同,只有一个原因:1882年1月,他决定写一部名为《扎拉图斯特拉如是说》的著作,这本书将更为完整地论述1881年的笔记中的发现,第4章的写作即在此之后。所以,在着手写作他最重要的作品之前,尼采补充了与前三章截然不同的最后一章,完成了《快乐的科学》。最后一章是唯一有标题的一章:拉丁文是 Sanctus Januarius[圣雅努斯],英语是 Saint January。

一月是新年的第一个月。此时,人们回顾过去的一年,向往新的一年;评价自己的生活,为更好的生活发愿。圣雅努斯开启了尼采思想中新的一年;尼采将这一章的第一节题为"致新年",以之作为自己的新年愿望。然后他围绕他的两个新思想组织这一章。第一个最重要的思想是拥有的冲动,他小心翼翼地将之放在中心紧后面,由实际的中心为之充分准备;第二个最重要的思想是永恒复返,他小心翼翼地将之放在结尾。

"圣雅努斯"如何引入尼采的本体论

在最重要的一节之前,尼采漂亮地准备了两节内容。中心前的一节题为"每天的历史",其中问你(单数的亲切称呼),你如何度过你的每一天,像其他人一样吗?像他们每天都关心赞扬或责备或受人崇敬吗?或者你是另一类人,被驱使着检审事物的内里和你自己?通过这个你,尼采挑出他真正的读者,他真正想要的唯一读者。此处,他为你,为与他关联的人设下鱼钩。

接下来就是题为"走出第七孤独"的中心。[①] 在此,"漫游者"已经克

---

① 参见《快乐的科学》,黄明嘉译,华东师范大学出版社,2007,页291。

服每个障碍,他面对着一场始料未及的、最终的危机——他站在一所充满诱惑的花园中,在花园中,漫游者最终可以休息,而且相信自己已经达到目标。但尼采称其为"阿尔弥达的花园"(Armida's garden),只有少数人知道它的文献出处。阿尔弥达的花园是对一位身负使命的男人——故事中伟大的里纳多(Rinaldo)——的诱惑。里纳多受到诱惑,止步于他最终的胜利之前,止步于征服或占领圣城之前。为了实现困难重重的最终征服,你必须挣脱阿尔弥达的花园,奋力争取最终的胜利。一旦你看到中心的这两节挑出你并警醒你提防最后的诱惑,你就知道你不是在臆测,你发现的是尼采为你而设的东西。你没有发明某个理论,实际上是按照你自己的方式发现了中心问题。

在这番精心准备后,尼采推出了"意志与浪潮"一节。这一节以一段对浪潮的诗性描述起头。1881—1882年的冬天,尼采经常观赏意大利热那亚附近的地中海浪潮,他就是在那里写下了"圣雅努斯"。

> 这波浪潮来得多么贪婪,仿佛要得到什么!它以令人恐惧的急切潜入岩壁的深罅之中。好像它想要抢在某人前面,好像那里隐藏着有价值的东西,价值不菲的东西。——这时,慢慢退潮了,但依然白花花一片,兴奋不已。——这波浪潮失落了吗?找到要找的东西了吗?是佯装失落了吗?——可是,另一波浪潮袭近了,比第一波还贪婪,还狂野,它的灵魂显得充满了秘密和夺宝的激情。①

这里描述了整个活动,热烈的冲动迫使自己进入最隐秘之处。它又兴奋地退回,白花花一片。它失落了吗?抑或是佯装的失落?倘若它假装失落,它就找到了要找的东西,实现了自己的目标。它取得的成就发生在谋求隐秘之物的竞赛中,因为下一波浪潮正在奔来。

尼采接着写道:

---

① 据朗佩特英文引文翻译。比较《快乐的科学》,黄明嘉译,华东师范大学出版社,2007,页292。

浪潮就是如此生活——我们,有意志的我们,也是如此生活。

本节标题是"意志与浪潮"。我们是有意志的漫游者,就像那些浪潮一样,那些浪潮是我们之所是的意象。接下来,尼采补充了一个决定或誓言,然后对复数的亲切人称所代表的浪潮自身发言:

——我不想再说了。——你们不相信我吗?你们要冲我发火吗?你们这些漂亮的怪物。你们是担心我泄露你们的整个秘密吗?……因为——好好听着!——我认识你们,知道你们的秘密。我认识你们这一类!——你们和我,我们确实共有一个秘密!

尼采说这些是针对你,针对每天的生活像他一样的非凡读者。只要你也是一个像他那样的漫游者,能够越过阿尔弥达的花园走向最终的收获,你或许就能够获得有意志者与浪潮共享的秘密。

秘密是什么呢?"意志与浪潮"一节没有说,我最后读到的话是这一节最后一句话。尼采没有说出他与浪潮共享的秘密;他没有泄露也没有亵渎自己的秘密和浪潮的秘密。他留待你去探索和发现这一秘密。

尼采说,"我不想再说了"。但在"意志与浪潮"的草稿中,他写下了他决定不公开而予删去的文字。这些文字有助于泄露他与浪潮共享的秘密。查看它们是作弊,可它们的确在这里出现了。尼采描述说,贪婪的浪潮涌进岩壁,潜入隐藏之物,另一波浪潮随之而来,"比第一波还贪婪,显得充满了秘密和夺宝的激情"。恰在此之后,他直接对浪潮说话,我想重复一下他使用的两个德语词:Oh ihr Habsüchtigen, ihr Wissensgierigen。这两个德语词命名了浪潮的秘密,同时也是他的秘密。Habsüchtigen 意为沉迷拥有,指被驱使去占有,被驱使去获取的你们。Wissensgierigen 意为贪求知道的你们。所以尼采对浪潮说,"哦,你们这些沉迷拥有者,你们这些贪求知识者"。他对大海的浪潮说了这些话。

在1881年的笔记中,尼采用沉迷拥有表示呈现于万物或万事之中的品质或性质,表示全面的或普遍的本体论冲动。贪求知道指认知的激情,也就是人的存在方式的最高或至高冲动。所以,这两个词命名了所有存在的冲动和最高存在的冲动。在"意志与浪潮"公开发表的版本中,尼采没有对浪潮说,"哦,你们这些沉迷拥有者,你们这些贪求知识者",而是说,"你们不相信我吗?……你们是担心我泄露你们的整个秘密吗?"公开的版本保守着秘密,但草稿没有。公开的版本留待你去发现你与浪潮共享的秘密:你寻找知识,而浪潮涌进岩壁,试图流经岩壁的每道缝隙和每个角落。发表的版本保守秘密,只将秘密放在刻画浪潮与寻求知识者之相像的诗中。

我们正在思考尼采成为尼采,而他的本体论洞见是他成为自己的关键一步。在此,尼采首次公开言明他获得了有关全面的本体论的结论,洞悉了从大海的浪潮到迫切的探问者等万物共通的隐秘性质。尼采选择以这一美妙的形式首次言明自己已经获得了一个自由的心灵能够获得的最深刻洞见。尼采小心翼翼地将这一洞见置于"圣雅努斯"的中心,这一中心包含中心问题,而中心问题即本体论应该以这种间接的、秘密的方式得到处理。请记住,施特劳斯提请每个人注意中心,因为他强调,一位出色的写作者会把最重要的观点隐藏在中心;施特劳斯使中心变得突出,而在此之前,中心是一部作品最不突出的地方,因为相比于开头和结尾,我们在中心最容易丧失注意力。但是你——当尼采问你如何度过每一天,他实际是在对你言说——你关注中心,因为尼采对你这么说。

1881 年的笔记和永恒复返

现在,我将要讨论尼采第二个最根本的发现以及他选择首次公开这一发现的方式。如果你继续阅读 1881 年的笔记,在尼采首次表述关于沉迷拥有以及相似的本体论术语的本体论结论之后,你几乎会立即看到尼采首次谈论永恒复返的著名条目。尼采在七年后的自传中提到这一条目,并在谈论《扎拉图斯特拉如是说》时最先说到这一条目,甚至提到他将之写在笔记本上。因此,尼采自己使这一条目变得出名。该条目是 1881

年的笔记中第一个标有日期的条目,"1881 年 8 月之始"。日期的标注说明,该条目对尼采很重要。

在这第一个关于永恒复返的条目之后,很多页的条目都涉及这一新思想;包括第一个条目在内的所有这些条目都有一个首要关切:如何引入这一思想。看起来,尼采在散步途中首次产生对永恒复返的思考,而且这个思考到来时势不可挡。但他没有在笔记中写下这一经验自身:第一个条目并非有关势不可挡的思想自身。实际上,第一个条目是一个详细、结构谨严的写作计划,处理如何将这一思想介绍给其他人的问题。

问题在于:在尼采看来,永恒复返是一种新理想,与自他所谓的道德时期(moral period)的开端以来形塑西方文化和所有其他文化的理想截然相反。如何能引入一种新思想?如何引入一种与盛行的理想相反的理想?当一种新理想与我们早已相信的理想如此相反时,有谁会相信或重视甚至严肃看待它呢?

在尼采首次提到永恒复返的笔记中,那项写作计划包含五章,永恒复返仅仅出现在最后一章。写作计划井井有条,内容丰富,阐述了尼采多年思考所得的结论。我们没有时间查看尼采的全部计划,所以我将之压缩为一个词,此词极为重要,尼采在笔记中一直将之与永恒复返关联使用。此词是 incorporation[摄入],德文是 Einverleibung,与英文单词的结构相同。incorporation 的前一部分 in 表示摄入,摄入进身体或机体。incorporate 就是摄入进你的体内,如同摄取食物变成身体、骨骼和血肉的一部分。身体由其摄入的东西形成和维持:身体是摄入的产物。

尼采对生理或身体层面的摄入感兴趣,并将之视为基础。但他对精神层面的摄入更感兴趣,在这一层面起作用的是同一类操作。尼采的德文词 geistig 比 spiritual 更恰切,因为前者包含精神和理智两层意思,当然对尼采而言,理智才最为重要。因此,尼采的前四章表达了他的这一观点:成为一个成熟的人就是始终已经被无法逃避的摄入过程所形塑或打上印记,这一摄入过程造就了我们。一个哲人就是一个竭力解放自己心灵的思考者,他尽可能地将自己的心灵从摄入的观点中释放出来:在他的自由心灵所看到的其他事物中,他的自由心灵看到文化摄入必然的错误,我们在教育和训练中摄入并内化的一切理想和价值都必然错误:这些理想和价值造就了我们。但哲人的自由心灵还看到,文化摄入的错误可以改变。它们能够改变,因为它们全都是教导出来的。所以,教授与已经摄入的那些不同的理想和价值是可能的。

这就是我对尼采计划写的前四章的概括。我的概括旨在表明,尼采意识到引入他的新理想——施特劳斯称之为新的最高价值——将面对的问题。正因为是新理想,所以对于那些已经摄入一种不同的最高价值的人来说,它必然听起来奇怪、陌生和虚假;它将遭受冷遇,因为它反对那已经被深深摄入为一种思考和信仰方式的东西。新的理想要想奏效,必须已经被摄入,必须成为每个人已经知道的一部分,成为一个人从有意识的生活之始就知道的东西。当尼采首次产生对永恒复返的思考时,他知道自己面对着奠基者必须面对的难题,即如何把一种新奇观念引入已经摄入另一种观念的文化中。

现在,跟随笔记,我们从摄入问题转到另一个关于永恒复返的重要问题。尼采第一条论述永恒复返的条目出现在他全面的本体论结论之后。尼采写下他散步时获得的这些思想的先后顺序表明,他首先得出了他的本体论结论,之后他才得出永恒复返的理想。如果你仔细斟酌,这才是这两种思想唯一合理的序列:首先得出对世界之所是、所有存在之所是的全面理解。之后,永恒复返的思想才能出现,因为这种思想对现在已知的世界说:这就是我想要的,我想要这个世界,这个如其所是的世界,我想再次拥有它,我想无数次拥有这个如其所是的世界——因为我想再次拥有如其所是的我的生活。

施特劳斯看出尼采的两个主要思想之间的关联:他称权力意志为"根本事实",称永恒复返为"最高价值"。两者之间的关系就是事实与价值的关系。所以,当然是首先出现事实,然后出现对事实的确证,对事实的肯定。事实与价值的关系就是理解世界与热爱所理解的世界的关系。施特劳斯赋予这一关系恰当的名称:他称之为尼采的"重新堕入柏拉图主义",哲人不能完全避免这一重新堕入。

尼采1881年的笔记通过条目的先后顺序表明了以上这些。笔记表明,哲人尼采最终理解了存在就是作为权力意志存在,而非其他任何东西,之后,仅仅在此之后,尼采瞥见了想要所理解的那个世界无数次存在的新理想。

"圣雅努斯"如何引入永恒复返

现在,我想再次查看《快乐的科学》最后一章"圣雅努斯",以便弄清尼采选择如何首次公开呈现他对永恒复返的发现。他选择公开这一发现的方式与他选择公开他的本体论发现的方式一样富有启发性。他将他的本体论发现作为秘密,放在这一章的中心,刺激你去发现你与浪潮的相似之处。尼采将他的本体论发现隐藏在这一章的中心。但是,他把他的第二个发现,对永恒复返的发现,置于这一章的末尾,使之引人注目,甚至那些迅速翻阅到章末的人也会看到这本书如何收尾。

在"圣雅努斯"的结尾亦即《快乐的科学》的结尾,尼采安排了一系列重要的小节;他以雅努斯/一月的方式作结,这种方式适合新的一年。首先,他用一系列重要的小节总结了他关于道德的主要主题,为结尾做铺垫;然后,在倒数第三节中,他讲到正在终结之事,即旧的一年的核心教诲。在题为"临终时的苏格拉底"一节,他让苏格拉底为最终主导西方文明的教诲负责,这一教诲认为:生命只有受苦,人类需要一位医神把他们从受苦的生活中救赎出来。尼采把苏格拉底的临终遗言——"我欠阿斯克勒庇俄斯一只公鸡"——解释成,对生命来说,结束生命是一种福佑。但现在,随着旧的一年过去,濒死的苏格拉底正在死去,他的理想、他的反生命教诲也在死去。

下一节即倒数第二节许诺新的一年将会带来之物,新的教诲将取代濒死的苏格拉底的教诲。这一节题为"最重的分量",宣布新教诲将会再次给予事物重量,让事物再次变得重要。此节是尼采第一次公开宣布永恒复返。《快乐的科学》倒数第二节首次为新的"一年"引进尼采的新教诲。这一节再次对你说话,让你想象一个恶魔趁你孤独时对你耳语,对你说:你将一次又一次地体验你那如其所是的生活,一成不变,一仍其旧,一如既往。这一节的整个问题是:你会有什么反应?你会因恶魔的危言耸听而咒骂他吗?或者,你会对他说,"你是神,我从未听过如此神圣的事情?"

随后,情景变换,恶魔消失,"这种思想压倒了你"。尼采首次公开宣布自己的思想,并在此转向了他在1881年的笔记中萦绕于心的问题。恶魔突如其来的宣告被可能发生在你身上的情形取代:如果你由于你的一切训练和你曾从父母和师长那里聆听的一切而已经摄入永恒复返的思想,这一情形就会发生在你身上。随着你的成熟,随着你开始思考,你越来越清晰意识到那已经始终呈现在你身上的思想,那时这一思想"会改变你之所是,也许还会碾碎你"。永恒复返思想是一种遴选的思想,是一种分离的思想,取决于你是谁。对一些人而言,永恒复返的思想改变你,提升你,使你欢悦。对另一些人而言,永恒复返的思想碾碎你,压制你,让你绝望。一切取决于你的生命性情,取决于你爱还是恨自己的生命。

在"圣雅努斯"倒数第二节,尼采首次公开宣告永恒复返思想。随后是"圣雅努斯"的最后一节,描绘了一位名为"扎拉图斯特拉"的人离开家乡,走进高山,十年间孤独求索发现了新的教诲,现在准备回返。"圣雅努斯"以此作结,全书也就此告终:这一结尾方式突兀而古怪,没有读者可以理解,每位读者都会觉得奇异和有问题。少数博学的读者也许知道,扎拉图斯特拉是伟大的波斯先知,他教导超验观念和赏善惩恶的来世生活,但即便是他们也好奇,尼采为什么以扎拉图斯特拉的回归结束全书。只有尼采知道他的读者后来才能知道的东西,因为《快乐的科学》最后一节就是他即将要写的《扎拉图斯特拉如是说》一书的第一节,《扎拉图斯特拉如是说》将要描述这位伟大的导师准备回归人性,并最终教授永恒复返。《扎拉图斯特拉如是说》的存在就是为了呈现永恒复返的教诲。

所以，尼采在1881年夏天的笔记中写下的两个重大发现奠定了他接下来的写作生涯。尼采在《快乐的科学》中首次公开处理这两个发现，从中已经可以看到两个发现之间的不同：本体论是隐藏在中心的秘密，永恒复返是结尾宣告的醒目教诲。"圣雅努斯"中呈现两个发现的这一方式，成为尼采在《扎拉图斯特拉如是说》和《善恶的彼岸》中处理它们的模式。"圣雅努斯"设定了理解尼采1881年笔记中的这两个发现的模式。

尼采成熟期的要著如何处理两个重大发现

《扎拉图斯特拉如是说》中，"权力意志"第一次出现，成为占有的冲动这一本体论的新名称。《扎拉图斯特拉如是说》第一部分使用过一次权力意志，以之作为对"大地上最强大的力量"即道德背后的真相的最高洞见。① 只有在第二部分，权力意志才得到解释，而且只为少数且特别的听众：他称为"你们最智慧的人"的那些人。② 仅仅是为这类人，他才把权力意志命名和解释为"真理意志"（will to truth）背后的真相。尼采的解释只可能发生在"舞蹈之歌"之后，因为在那首歌曲之诗中，扎拉图斯特拉放弃自己怀疑式的"狂野智慧"，他原本认为生命或存在深不可测，如今他拥抱自己真正所爱的生命自身，生命自身向他表明她并非深不可测。生命自身向爱她的扎拉图斯特拉表明，她可以被探测，她拥有一种可被理解的品性或方式。随后，扎拉图斯特拉为"你们最智慧的人"提及并论证"权力意志"。论证的结尾，他对他们说，"让我们一起谈论这个吧！"——唯独他们需要与他谈论他最新发现和表达的本体论观点。

扎拉图斯特拉结束对最智慧者的发言时说，"许多房子尚需建造"。

---

① 参见《扎拉图斯特拉如是说》"论一千零一个目标"。
② 参见《扎拉图斯特拉如是说》"论自我超越"。

权力意志是一种真理,它仅仅需要那些有最强烈的认知激情的人知道——他们将与扎拉图斯特拉一道建造还未建造的房子。他们将建构的教诲会给未来的人类提供居所,或被摄入未来的人类之中。永恒复返是新教诲,是针对所有人的教诲,会给未来的人类提供居所。因此,只有在扎拉图斯特拉向最智慧者论证权力意志之后,《扎拉图斯特拉如是说》才让永恒复返出现:一个是针对少数人的洞见,一个是针对所有人的教诲,两者的次序必然如此。

《善恶的彼岸》以同样的方式处理权力意志和永恒复返。在讨论哲学的第一章,尼采说到四次权力意志。权力意志最终推动最高的探究,即哲学;权力意志也推动生物学研究的一切,即所有生物;推动物理学研究的一切,即万物;推动心理学研究的事物,即人的灵魂。在讨论哲学的第一章,尼采没有解释权力意志这一根本真理,正如施特劳斯所说,以上这些主张全都看下来像独断论。在下一章"自由的心灵"中,尼采确实为作为全面的真理的权力意志提供了一项论证,但他的论证仅仅针对他一直在教育的拥有自由心灵的特殊听众。①他们所受教育的最后一步就是这一准备充足的论证,其结论为:世界就是权力意志,而非其他。这一论证只针对他们,我们也已经看到他们如何反应:"上帝被驳倒而魔鬼却没有。"②我将在最后一讲对此详加说明。至于永恒复返,《善恶的彼岸》于宗教章在恰当的位置以恰当方式进行处理,③将之作为面向所有人的公开教诲,脱胎于旧的公开教诲、旧宗教的死亡造成的虚无主义。

所以,我的主要观点是:在1881年的笔记中,尼采成为尼采。尼采在笔记中首次得出了他成熟的哲学的两个主要结论。其一,一种对如其所是的世界的洞见,此类洞见只能吸引那些主导的激情就是认识的激情的人。其二,一种对永恒复返的洞见,永恒复返是那些天性热爱生活和热爱

---

① 参见《善恶的彼岸》第二章"自由的心灵",格言36。
② 参见《善恶的彼岸》第二章"自由的心灵",格言37。
③ 参见《善恶的彼岸》第三章"宗教性的本质",格言56。

属己生活的人的最高理想。第一种洞见属于哲学本身,第二种洞见属于哲学之诗。尼采在1881年笔记中获得的东西决定了他余生的写作,从"圣雅努斯"到《扎拉图斯特拉如是说》和《善恶的彼岸》,再到尼采计划写作,甚至精神崩溃时还在写作的下一部要著。在计划的最后一部著作中,权力意志也是那些热衷思考的人将透彻思考的一种真理,而永恒复返会是一种教诲,在此教诲之中,每个人都能过自己的生活,庆祝自己的生活,庆祝整个生命。

成熟的尼采,成为尼采的尼采,是一位哲人和一位哲学诗人。最后一场讲座中,我将对哲学诗人尼采详加说明。在此,我想在结尾就哲人尼采再多说一点:他与柏拉图的关系。哲人尼采获得了一个终极的本体论洞见,依据这一洞见,存在就是作为权力意志存在,而非其他。哲人柏拉图获得了一个终极的本体论洞见,依据这一洞见,存在就是作为爱欲存在,而非其他。在我看来,这两种洞见是近亲,是表述相似洞见的不同方式。在此,我们到达最高、最艰难之处。在此,语言和思考以及我的思考的局限最为明显,但我想试着总结作为本体论的权力意志与爱欲的亲缘关系。

两者都声称"生成的至高无上"。两者都声称生成是一种涌动、满足和再次涌动。两者都声称,在永远的自我更新活动中,有一种旨在达到一种自我满足的内在导向:它以自我为目的(auto-telic)。两者都声称,这种对能量或力量的消解是对自身的超越,而自身面对着作为一种超越自身的对力量的消解的他者,面对着作为抵抗的他者。两者都声称,这种导向性的能量——或力量——的表达是关系性的;关系是个体的关系,关系的出现是这类关系领域的一部分,这类关系的整个领域是整体性,是一切存在之物。

柏拉图关于爱欲的语言深具魅力,积极肯定,用富有人性的术语表达了上述进程,使之易于招人喜爱。尼采关于权力意志的语言不大吸引人,这与他坚决避免他所谓的"语词的华而不实"或语词的美化相一致,他选择的表达更准确地描述了这一进程,尽管一定仍有欠缺:"作为一个软弱和有限的隐喻——太人性了"(《善恶的彼岸》格言22)。但是,在术语本身上的这些初始差异掩盖了我认为柏拉图和尼采共通的理解的根本相似。

尼采成为尼采与苏格拉底成为苏格拉底的方式相似。真正的哲人们是真正的亲族。

第六讲　尼采的哲学之诗

　　最后一次讲座拟以施特劳斯对恰当方法的表述开始:"蕴涵在事物表面的问题,而且只有蕴涵在事物表面的问题,才是事物的核心。"①施特劳斯密切关注的事物的表面是哲人们的文本的表面。通过写作技艺编织进表面的是事物的核心,创制这一表面的哲人想让你按图索骥进入事物的核心。施特劳斯发现并且想让谨慎的读者发现的事物的核心,就是一位哲人始终想要发现的真理,根本而言就是关于存在或所是之物的真理,本体论的真理。要发现这一真理,我们只有借助于最可靠和最彻底的怀疑方法,这一方法检验单纯的信念,以便发现是否有任何东西能被认识。而施特劳斯表明,遵照好方法,即用注疏的方法学习哲人的写作技艺,我们就能进入哲人柏拉图和尼采真正的核心。核心就是一种本体论:存在就是作为爱欲存在,而非其他;存在就是作为权力意志存在,而非其他。这是我全部讲座的一个要点,它引向第二个要点:真正的哲学产生哲学之诗,一种可以身体力行的教诲。正如第俄提玛在描述顶峰时所说的,哲学的观看导致一种孕生即作诗。

　　由此我到达今天的话题:尼采的哲学之诗。施特劳斯在论尼采的文章中首先考察了尼采的哲学,尽管那篇文章的主题是尼采的宗教。我的第二次讲座考察了施特劳斯关于《善恶的彼岸》最重要的第36条格言的说法,格言36包含书中为权力意志所作的唯一论证。我想再次考察这一论证,以便看清它如何开启向尼采的哲学之诗的转折。

---

　　① 参见施特劳斯,《关于马基雅维里的思考》,前揭,页6。

尼采的哲学之诗:《善恶的彼岸》格言 36

格言 36 紧随"自由的心灵"一章的中心之后。自 1876 年 8 月尼采与瓦格纳以及早期作品中瓦格纳式的视角决裂之后,自由的心灵一直是尼采的首要主题。现在,也就是十年后,"自由的心灵"一章的中心处理了现代自由心灵最终获得的结论,"知识论的怀疑主义",怀疑是否有任何事物能被真正认识的怀疑主义,由康德的认知论强化的怀疑主义。①

尼采认为这种怀疑主义是现代自由心灵达到的最高点,这些心灵的自由部分受到尼采论述自由心灵典范的著作的训练;这些自由心灵代表他唯一可能的听众,是他的"朋友"。在"自由的心灵"一章篇幅较长的中心格言 34 中,尼采旨在提出有关怀疑主义的终结性的问题,即怀疑主义是否事实上是人类理智的最高成就。与较长的这一节相连的是极短的格言 35,其中,尼采提出一个发人深省的问题,有关现代怀疑主义隐藏的动机。格言 35 总体谈到这一问题:

> 哦,伏尔泰!哦,人性!哦,荒唐!有些东西关乎"真理",关乎寻求真理;一旦一个人太人性地务于此事——"他寻求真理只为行善"——我打赌,他一无所获!

法国怀疑论者伏尔泰坚称,"他寻求真理只为行善"(尼采原文中为法语,我将之译为英语)。尼采想说什么?这是在控告伏尔泰似的自由心灵的怀疑主义。在尼采的第一部自由心灵之作《人性的,太人性的》中,伏尔泰曾是位英雄。尼采控告拥有自由心灵的现代怀疑论者对真理的寻求受到致命的限制,因为他们相信,真理和善必须一致;他们首要的欲望是持守现代的善和现代的美德,这就抑制了他们对真理的寻求,使得有关知识的怀疑主义成为一种诱人的退却立场,保护了他们对善的看法。有关

---

① "知识论的怀疑主义",见《善恶的彼岸》第三章"宗教性的本质",格言 54。

知识的怀疑主义为继续信仰现代美德辩护,允许他们不自由的心灵持守权利平等和终结苦难的现代美德。以伏尔泰的经典语言来说,对善的信仰依旧束缚他们不自由的心灵,阻止它们获得真理。把寻求真理当作对它们的善的支撑注定会失败:"我打赌,他一无所获。"

这种可爱、幽默、深刻的控告表明,怀疑主义极易吸引现代的、受启蒙的自由心灵,因为如果你不能知道真理,那么你可以继续信仰善,现代的善。怀疑主义允许将道德置于认识之上。自由心灵的知识论怀疑主义实际是受束缚的心灵的标志,这些心灵是单纯的道德心灵。

所以,位于"自由的心灵"中心的这两个相连的格言旨在刺激和扰乱拥有自由心灵的读者,迫使他质疑自己的心灵是否确实自由。尼采向他唯一可能的听众发难,邀请他们走进困惑,怀疑他们的怀疑,在此之后,尼采随即论证了一个真正的自由心灵能够认识什么。很明显,尼采将他对权力意志的唯一论证精心设置于此,意在警醒认真的读者注意,他即将作出的本体论主张所处的现实的、历史的背景:说出这一主张的时机并不成熟,但是哲人无论如何都得言说,他必须说出他的论证。

尼采没有假定他的论证会有说服力,尽管这一论证完整而有效。作为一个有效的论证,它所做的就是邀请自由心灵考虑他的论证,质疑他们的怀疑主义,承认可能有一种可被认识的根本真理。尼采在此所用的策略与扎拉图斯特拉一样:在为权力意志作的唯一论证的结尾,扎拉图斯特拉对他唯有的听众说,"让我们谈谈这个吧,你们最智慧的人"。尼采两部最重要的作品中这一论证的听众是最精挑细选的听众:《扎拉图斯特拉如是说》中是你们最智慧的人,《善恶的彼岸》中是你们最自由的心灵。两种情形中,只有你们需要关注这一论证。这就是尼采思想的隐微核心,尽管它就写在纸面上。

尼采的论证精微,必须按照他所设计的步骤加以研究。在此,我只是观察论证的核心,观察而已,不解释细节或试图说服你什么。但请记住,施特劳斯赞扬这一论证是"极不妥协的智识真诚"。

论证一开始,尼采强调,科学的方法需要原则的简化,因此,"我们必须做个实验,假设性地将意志的因果关系设想为唯一的因果关系,唯一一类原因"。"必须"是由于科学方法的双重要求,即原则的简化和假设性地得出的结论。因此,"必须冒险假设……只要有力量参与其中,是否一切机械事件就不是意志的力量、意志的作用"。我们无论在何处认识到自然中的原因,我们都必须悬置经典的现代物理学的观点(笛卡尔和牛顿的物理学),这一观点认为,一种因果的机械学在一个机械的世界-整体中起作用。我们必须假设性地把自然中的事件看作意志事件,意志起作用的事件。

然后,尼采转向这一对原因的探究要考察的对象。尼采之前一直是从被给定的东西即人的激情和欲望为起点,那是他十年来探究的主题;在此,他从他为驱动激情和欲望的本能假定的基础为起点:"假定我们成功地把我们全部的本能生活解释为意志的一种基本形式——即我提出的权力意志——的发展或衍生。"自由心灵做尼采所做之事,研究自身和他人,以期理解我们所有行为的根基可能是什么。以认识人的灵魂为起点,我们能像尼采那样解释我们的本能生活,即首先解释成沉迷拥有(Habsucht)的不同形式,尼采后来更深刻地把这一冲动理解为权力意志。假定你能这么做;然后,按照适当的方法,你必须实验性地将你有关人类行为根基的结论扩展到更宽广的领域:"假定所有的有机体功能都可以追溯到这种权力意志。"你必须从对人的行为的解释转向对所有有机体、所有生物以及生物科学研究的每一事物的作用的解释。需要实验性地证明的未言明的前提是,人类与其他生物没有本质区别。

最后,假定你成功地将权力意志的假设应用于整个生物领域:

> 那么,人们就有权毫不含糊地把**一切**起作用的力量界定为**权力意志**。从内部来观看世界,依据其"智性特征"来定义和界定世界——世界将是"权力意志",而非其他。

"有权"——科学方法为之辩护,甚至还要求对这一假设进行最宽广的扩展:在成功解释了人类和有机物之后,人们有权得出最宽广的结论,即本体论的结论。尼采首先在1881年的笔记中获得这一结论;之后,在对这一结论的首次公开呈现中,尼采将之暗示为我与浪潮共享的秘密;在《扎拉图斯特拉如是说》中,则成为由扎拉图斯特拉与你们最智慧的人共享的秘密。

在《善恶的彼岸》中,尼采止步于此。他给出自己的论证,拥有自由心灵的你要思考这个结论是否能够使人信服和是否真实。尼采在格言36结尾放了一个破折号,这一小小的停顿记号表明格言36与短小的格言37有关联。正如施特劳斯注意到的,格言36和格言37在形式上类似于尼采置于中心的格言34和格言35,分别构成一对。尼采把格言36和格言37安排为一对,由此从哲学走向哲学之诗。

尼采从哲学走向哲学之诗:《善恶的彼岸》格言37

格言37是一个回应,是尼采的听众对尼采的结论——世界是权力意志,而非其他——的及时反应。在格言37中,尼采允许他那拥有自由心灵的真正听众大声发言,说出他们的想法,他们对刚刚听到的结论有什么感受:

"什么?用流行的方式讲,这不就意味着:上帝被驳倒而魔鬼却没有——?"

自由心灵受到震撼,他们证实了尼采在格言35中关于现代自由心灵的批评:他们并不完全自由,而是受制于他们认为真理与善相一致的观念。如果权力意志是真实的,那么他们所认为的善,即位于历史终末的永久和平,一个实现权利平等和苦难终结的天堂,就既不可获得也不真实。尼采说,他们以"流行的方式"讲话:他们采用了上帝和魔鬼的普通语言。但他们是自由心灵:他们不信仰上帝或魔鬼。他们以流行方式讲话,因为只有这种语言才能表达他们的极端感受。只有上帝和魔鬼这古老的极端才能表达出他们对尼采就权力意志推出的结论的恐惧。

用不那么神学的语言讲,他们的回应是说,如果世界是"权力意志而非其他",那么,他们奉为崇高、尊贵和善的一切就被他们认为低微、卑劣和恶的事物摧毁和取代。你的结论认为一切不过是一场追逐权力的争斗,而这一结论是一种令人恐惧、丑陋、邪恶的观点。这不是你的权力意志观点的意思吗?"恰恰相反!恰恰相反,我的朋友们!"尼采的回应与他们的回应一样掷地有声,只是需要解释,但他没有给出解释。你必须思考相反的情况,这很容易用自由心灵刚用过的流行语言来表达:魔鬼被驳倒而上帝却没有。施特劳斯曾五次说,尼采的观点是"对上帝的辩护"。

尼采说"恰恰相反!恰恰相反!",为他的朋友带来一个深刻的神学教诲。这些朋友是现代的自由心灵,他们已失去对神学的兴趣,对宗教的重要性毫无感知。尼采的"恰恰相反"说,你们对上帝和魔鬼的观念有严重错误。只要把他们颠转过来,你们就更接近真相了。这一颠转成功谴责了他们唯一能想象到的神学,基督教神学。"恰恰相反!恰恰相反!"意味着:你们的上帝观念(他们当然不信仰上帝)是超验的、超自然的存在,上帝创造世界、看管世界、审判世界——要把上帝看成魔鬼。你们的魔鬼观念(他们甚至更不信魔鬼)是世界之主,基督教神学称其为黑暗之王,并把整个世界看作堕落的、属于魔鬼的世界——要把魔鬼看成神。什么是神?——这是尼采让他的具有自由心灵的无神论朋友们要问的问题。

尼采最后的神学教导是:"至于魔鬼,谁强迫你用流行语说话!——""谁?"古老的上帝强迫他们,上帝已死却未离去,道德上帝的观念仍然统治着他们关于什么是神的观点。你们在神学上要多学习,尼采如此建议具有自由心灵的朋友们,建议我们这些现代无神论者。尼采问,谁强迫你谈论魔鬼?他没有问,谁强迫你谈论上帝。他没有问是因为谈论上帝正是他想要的:一种言说什么是神或什么是诸神的新方式。

《善恶的彼岸》中刚刚发生了什么?在论哲学的第二章"自由的心灵"中,尼采将他对权力意志的唯一一次哲学论证置于中心之后。这一论证具有"极不妥协的智识真诚",并导向一个关于诸存在的存在的全面结论。随即,他听到朋友们将这一哲学结论与宗教相联系:他唯一可能的听众以宗教语言作出回应。而尼采做了什么？他站在宗教这方,同时暗示他的哲学观点没有驳倒上帝,反而在为恰当理解的上帝作辩护。

在论宗教的那一章,尼采将会这样描述他具有现代自由心灵的听众:"他们甚至不再知道宗教有什么益处。"(《善恶的彼岸》格言58)尼采知道宗教有什么益处,并在论宗教的那一章的最后两节讨论了这个问题。这两节认为,宗教对任何社会秩序都是有益和必要的。如果把宗教教给年轻人,让年轻人摄入宗教,宗教就能指导他们区分好坏贵贱,分辨什么值得为之而活、什么必须排斥。这两节表明了宗教的用途:把统治者与被统治者连接起来,为其他人提供一条通向更高灵性的修炼之路,让普通人觉得生活可以忍受。尼采主张,为了确保宗教的健康,宗教必须以适宜的方式由智慧者,由哲人,由那些自身不受宗教指导的人来指导。哲学必须统治宗教,理性必须统治崇拜和膜拜的本能。

尼采视宗教为必需且可欲。不止于此,他讲到人类"造神的本能",还惊愕地说"将近两千年都没有一个新神!"(《敌基督者》19)其实他并不惊讶,因为他晓得个中缘由:西方过去的两千年一直由嫉妒的上帝、一神论的上帝统治。尼采拿上帝的嫉妒开了他最佳的玩笑:

> 诸神中的一位有一天说,"只有一个上帝,在我之前,你们不该有其他神"。其他所有的神——笑死了。因此,只有一位上帝。①

在论宗教的那章,尼采批评基督教,同时回顾了古希腊的多神宗教,荷马的宗教,赞扬后者"展现出浩荡无垠的感激"。问题不在于诸神本身,而在于启示的上帝,基督教的上帝。现代心灵从这位上帝那里解放了自己,在自由思考中收获颇丰。同时,这也是尼采这里的观点:这些收获付出了巨大代价,牺牲了诸神本身,现代心灵甚至不再知道宗教有何益处。

尼采知道宗教有何益处;哲人们知道宗教有何益处,正如在柏拉图的《王制》中,在荷马宗教濒死的时代,苏格拉底为有理智的年轻人修正或改

---

① 参见《扎拉图斯特拉如是说》第三卷"论背叛者"结尾。

革荷马宗教。只有宗教可以构建一种文化的日常生活。文化系于信仰和实践：人们自幼就从讲给小孩子的故事中摄入这些信仰，并在仪典、节庆和风俗中强化信仰，正是这些赋予日常生活意义和结构。为了让宗教切实可行，尼采似乎认为，必须要有诸神。我将讨论尼采稍后指出的现实的诸神。不过，我们已经从格言36、37看到宗教或哲学之诗如何自然地脱胎于尼采的哲学，所以我想首先简要考察尼采哲学之诗的另一层面，尼采将之首次置于《善恶的彼岸》之中，之后才在结尾讲到诸神。

哲学之诗（一）：永恒复返

在《善恶的彼岸》的宗教篇章，尼采没有以上帝或诸神作为主要论题，而大致以西方宗教即基督教的历史为主题。在这一章的中心，尼采谈到西方宗教的危机。这次危机是一场宗教灾难，包含两方面：上帝之死和他所称的谋杀古老的灵魂概念。在中心之后，尼采迈出完全在情理之中的一步，谈到最深的灾难：虚无主义，即现代自由心灵愈益感觉到没有什么真正有价值。在完成截至当前的完整历史描述之后，尼采设置了《善恶的彼岸》中讨论永恒复返的唯一一节。在格言56中，一位哲人把永恒复返的肯定视作未来走出虚无主义的可能性，而虚无主义源于上帝之死和谋杀古老的灵魂观念。我在第二讲提到施特劳斯使用了格言56，但是我在此想进一步考察，以此作为我论述尼采哲学之诗的首个要点。

尼采在论虚无主义一节的结尾说，"我们早就对此有所了解。——"末尾的破折号指向下一节的开头：

> 谁若像我一样，怀着某种谜一般的渴望，想要深透地思考悲观主义……谁若真正……观察、俯察一切可能的思考方式中最否定世界的那一种。

"像我一样"——整个格言将关乎迫切要深透思考现代悲观主义的思想者尼采。驱使他的"谜一般的渴望"只能是哲学；今天的哲人迫切要研究"一切可能的思考方式中最否定世界的那一种"。

尼采继续表明自己的身份：他站在"善恶的彼岸，不再……受制于道德的诱惑和欺骗"。由于从道德偏见中解放了自己，哲人尼采"无意之中或许就此大开眼界，看到了相反的理想：最有精神、最鲜活、最肯定世界的人类的理想"。思想者尼采从思考一个理想，即最否定世界的可能的思考方式，走向"相反的理想"，即最肯定世界的可能的思考方式。我想强调施特劳斯所强调的：尼采放在这里的插入语"无意之中"。这句话很重要，因为说到了尼采的意图：尼采进行他的研究不是为了发现一种新的理想。驱使他的并不是对一种新道德或新宗教的需要；驱使他的是"谜一般的渴望"，即理解的需要——他是哲人，而非道德家，亦非宗教人。

尼采无意之间瞥见的新理想，是"最有精神、最鲜活、最肯定世界的人类的理想……他们想要让曾是和今是之物永远重复下去，不满足地大叫'从头再来'"。那个最肯定世界的人想要世界永恒复返，想要它。永恒复返是他的理想，永恒复返是最肯定世界的人欲求之物。尼采随即阐明了这种渴望："不仅对他自己，也对整出戏和演出，而且不仅对一场演出，说到底也是对恰恰需要这场演出的人……"整场演出的肯定最终是观看演出者的自我肯定——这一肯定是对世界的肯定，因为世界让哲人成为可能，因为世界产生了一位观看者，他有理性，有自我意识，认识可认识的整体的残片。

《善恶的彼岸》就永恒复返所说的就是这些。但是对于一部意在作为"对现代性的批判"的作品来说，这些内容足矣。在对现代宗教的批判中，《善恶的彼岸》非常简要和精准地提供了一个指向，即指向对虚无主义可能的超越：在虚无主义之中，现代性对基督教的必要摧毁给受启蒙的现代西方人留下了作为一个整体的宗教。因此，永恒复返是尼采哲学之诗的一部分，是新的最高理想：它是理想必然之所是，即一个能评估价值的人对最高理想的设定。总结到此，我要转向尼采哲学之诗的第二个层面，在《善恶的彼岸》这部批判之作中，尼采仅仅再次一致地点出这一层面。

哲学之诗(二):诸神

施特劳斯讨论尼采《善恶的彼岸》的宗教篇章时,曾在某一点上说:

> 尼采的"神学"有一个重要的组成部分,甚至是其中枢,我未曾谈及,也不会谈及。

以这一突出而强烈的拒绝,施特劳斯避免谈论尼采神学的中枢,这一中枢似乎就是尼采对诸神的引入。施特劳斯曾经表明,尼采"怀疑是否可能存在一个不以上帝为中心的世界",此处的世界指文化的世界,有信仰的人类栖居的世界。施特劳斯是一位哲人,也是一个犹太人,终其一生都对20世纪犹太教的命运牵肠挂肚,他拒绝谈论尼采的神学-政治方案,尽管这一方案有可能是未来世界的中心。但尼采本人必须谈论,正因为不可能存在"一个不以上帝为中心的世界"。尼采知道,他要谈论诸神就面对着一个问题,因为他唯一可能的听众是拥有自由心灵的现代怀疑论者,他们"甚至不再知道宗教有何益处",对他们而言,唯一想象得到的上帝是一神教死去的上帝,而他们只乐意帮忙弑杀这个上帝。

尼采说"我难得像神学家那样说话",这不过是夸大其词。不管时代怎样违和,他不得不像神学家一样说话,以便引入一种关于神是什么的新观念,颁给那些已经摄入老旧的上帝观念的人。在《善恶的彼岸》格言37,他开始像神学家一样说话,他暗示恶魔被驳倒而上帝并没有。他还在该书恰当的地方表明,宗教和诸神不可或缺。但直到最后可能的时刻,他才亮出自己关于神是什么的真实观点:他首次将他有关诸神的新教诲显著地置于结尾,并在该书最华美的格言295中表达了自己的观点。在那里,尼采最终像神学家一样说话。

尼采一上来先说到他对诱惑神——施特劳斯称之为"一位超-苏格拉底"——的体验,对其作一长段又美妙的描述。尼采对诱惑神的描述令人难忘,引人入胜,却没有为之命名。当尼采终于准备命名诱惑神时,他说诱惑神"不是别的神,就是狄俄尼索斯神,我曾将……我的头生子献于这位伟大的模棱两可、长于诱惑的神"。尼采的头生子便是其处女作《悲剧的诞生》,他在其中将狄俄尼索斯描绘为希腊悲剧背后强有力、迷狂的神。

> 与此同时,我对这位神的哲学……有了更多了解……我是狄俄尼索斯神最后的门徒和弟子——我认为我也许总算可以开始给你们,我的朋友们,品尝一下这种哲学了……

自处女作以来,尼采对狄俄尼索斯了解了很多,他完全可以把自己看成这位神"最后的门徒和弟子"。他也对听众有了很多了解,他现在必须对他们谈论诸神。他说,他认为诸神搞哲学,这一观点将会冒犯哲人们,因为柏拉图和柏拉图的第俄提玛教导说,诸神不搞哲学,因为他们已经拥有智慧,自此以后哲人们全都在神学上的"同一条道路上"——哲人们将反对一位哲人引入一种关于诸神搞哲学的观念。那么尼采的朋友们呢?

> 在你们中间,我的朋友们,它看起来没那么冒犯,除非它来得太迟,不合时宜;因为今天,就像我已经听说的,你们不再愿意信仰上帝和诸神。也许我的讲述应该更加直言不讳,而非总是取悦于你们耳朵的挑剔习惯?

尼采就诸神所言同样会冒犯他的朋友们,只是冒犯的理由不同:对朋友们来说,此刻谈论诸神时机不当。他的朋友们还未准备好倾听任何有关诸神的讨论,因为他们刚从古老的上帝那里得到解放不久——尼采的朋友们,刚刚被解放的无神论者,不想听有关诸神的任何讨论,因为他们刚刚从僭主式的上帝那里得到释放。但尼采必须谈论诸神,且只能在当下谈论,不管当下如何仓促。

尼采大胆向朋友们讲授神学教诲,其中非常重要的一点属于尼采自《悲剧的诞生》以来所学到的诸多内容之一:狄俄尼索斯神总是有另一位神相伴,他所爱的阿里阿德涅(Ariadne)。狄俄尼索斯和阿里阿德涅,尼采引入的两位神。尼采知道诸神有何益处,他为什么引入这两位神且仅仅引入这两位神?他当然相信人性可以退回过去,并重建荷马的宗教——荷马最先提到这两位神的名字。究竟是什么使得两位神与众不同,值得在晚期现代被重新引入?

施特劳斯注意到,尼采认为人类有"造神的本能",这是我们身上的一种自然倾向,即把我们奉作至高的东西植入诸神。它属于我们进行神化的天性,即把任何我们最为尊崇的东西植入神圣的位格。如果我们欲求的是生命的永恒复返,那我们最尊崇或奉为至高的是什么?我们把生命自身奉为至高。生命是出生和死亡不断更新的循环,出生源于交配繁殖。狄俄尼索斯和阿里阿德涅是被造神本能提升至诸神的交配繁殖,是被神化的交配繁殖。狄俄尼索斯是雄性或男性神,阿里阿德涅是雌性或女性神。他们是一对,是生产、生成所有生命的一对。作为一对,他们各自不同,又相互属有。他们是两性之间的战争,也是两性之间的爱。这神圣的一对的特别之处和奇异之处就在于此。狄俄尼索斯和阿里阿德涅是大地上的生命,是生命的出生和死亡,他们被抬高到人可授予的最崇高地位。狄俄尼索斯和阿里阿德涅是代表大地上的繁衍的普世神,尽管他们被给予地方性或希腊的名字。他们远不止这些,我只想提另外一点:狄俄尼索斯是位搞哲学的神——他被驱使去理解。阿里阿德涅呢?她没有搞哲学;在某种更根本的意义上,她已经知道,她拥有领人走出位于迷宫核心的秘密的线团,正如关于阿里阿德涅的希腊神话认为的那样。

显然,尼采作为神学家挑出这两位神作为尘世宗教的神,与对生命的永恒复返的肯定密切相关。不过,我们由这些神立即看到,神学家尼采不能做神学家柏拉图在引入非荷马的新神时所能做的事:《王制》中的苏格拉底说,他可以将活动和仪典、歌舞留给既有的规制——这些已经建立或已被摄入的活动和仪典将适应于新的活动和仪典。尼采的问题部分在于,并没有敬拜狄俄尼索斯和阿里阿德涅的既有规制。尼采引进新神与引进新的至高理想遇到的问题一样:如何摄入一种关于神是什么的新意识,如何制造节庆、歌舞来庆祝新神。只有当诸神始终被信仰时,当他们是我们从小便知道的祖先的神时,当我们早已知道如何歌唱来赞颂他们、如何舞蹈来感激他们时,诸神才看起来是可信的。

我必须提到尼采自传中的一句话,"我与宗教的创立者毫不相干"(《瞧啊,这人》4.1)。哲人尼采引诱的是未来的认知者而非未来的信徒,无论认知者多么少,信徒多么多,无论认知者在多大程度上认识到只有围绕一位神一切才能转变为"世界"。关于诸神,似乎尼采对他的朋友们说:承认宗教的必要性;承认狄俄尼索斯和阿里阿德涅作为生命之神的普遍自然性,承认这一点,并将之交给造神的本能。对生命的爱将会行爱在人类中间所做之事,促使我们神圣化,把我们最爱的东西神圣化,把交配繁殖的生命神圣化。狄俄尼索斯和阿里阿德涅是爱生命的人类的自然之神,人类造神的自然本能将会确保诸神的重生。

尼采哲学之诗的第三个层面还未得到广泛认识,我想以之作结,因为我觉得这一层面尤其让人满怀希望。

哲学之诗(三):生态学,人类在大地上存在的方式

像永恒复返与狄俄尼索斯和阿里阿德涅两位神一样,第三个层面也源自尼采的哲学:他将人类理解为大地上生命的一种形式,联系着并依赖人类由之演进而来的整个生命网络。这一关于大地上的人类生命的哲学观点产生了人类行为的原则,这些原则的基本命令就是尼采的扎拉图斯特拉从山中返回时首先给出的命令:"要对大地真诚。"尼采是西方第一位教授一种全面的生态论哲学的哲人;他的教诲是一种全面的道德和政治教诲,根本上基于对大地的爱;而大地被理解为与某个彼岸世界相对的此在世界,与任何无时间的超越相对的时间性,与任何不死性相对的终有一死——大地是权力意志,而非其他。

尼采哲学之诗的第三个层面就是生态学,即对大地上生命的爱,它比前两个层面优越之处在于:它必须摄入一个至高理想和诸神;至高理想和诸神显得是可能的或有效的,只要它们已经被相信,已经成为传统。但

是，相反的理想和上帝现在已经被摄入，而且它们依然影响着那些逐渐怀疑或不相信它们的人。所以，我们几乎不能想象一个全然不同的理想或全然不同的诸神。最终，如我们这般的现代怀疑论者便对一切至高理想和诸神怀有偏见，这种偏见很可能成为运用至高理想和诸神的尼采之诗的最强大阻碍。

但是，尼采政治哲学的第三个层面，一种生态学或环保主义的伦理，更容易被当代的听众、被我们接受。我们不会厌恶它，反而从一开始就被它吸引。自我的第一本书《尼采的教诲》以来，这种看法就是我对尼采的哲学政治的理解的一部分。在我的第二本书《尼采与现时代》中，我将尼采描述为全面的生态论哲人。自撰写这些著作以来，我逐渐意识到施特劳斯多么有助于理解尼采政治哲学的这一观点。在第二讲中，我读到了施特劳斯有关尼采的论文第35段中的一句话，它表达了施特劳斯有关补充性的人的主要观点：

> 他的至高无上由以下事实得到展现：他解决最高、最困难的问题。

施特劳斯界定了这一问题："人正在征服自然，而且这种征服没有可规定的界限。"解决现时代的最高问题，就是找到给征服自然规定界限的好理由。在施特劳斯那里，我没有发现那种在如今变得流行且重要的一般的生态论或环保主义兴趣。施特劳斯所反对的征服自然是借助权利平等和终结苦难的现代理想来征服人的自然。对人的自然的现代征服意味着终结大地上的哲学，因为哲学依靠承认和支持一种等级秩序，也依靠苦难的持续，而这里的苦难应当被理解作人为获得至高之物尤其是知识的努力。由匮乏造成的认识上的苦难，只有通过牺牲性的努力——使所有冲动屈从于寻求知识的冲动——才可补救。施特劳斯以此作为他的尼采论文的顶点，至高的终点，最切题之处。尼采的神学-政治方案，他的侍养之诗，可以解决对人之伟大亦即哲学的现代威胁，因为它出于对自然的爱为现代的征服自然规定了界限，它对自然的爱体现在这一至高理想之中:自然的整全无数次如其所是地复返。

结束这一主题前,我想考察尼采本人何时首次想到最困难问题的解决方案,首次充分洞见到晚期现代这一最大的现实问题及其解决方案。我曾强调,尼采全面的哲学观点在1881年的笔记中首次一起出现、首次得到完成。在这部笔记中,日后成为权力意志的本体论和永恒复返的肯定都是首次出现。就我所知,这部笔记还包含尼采对其哲学之诗的生态论或环保主义的首次表述。请记住,这部笔记的写作是在《快乐的科学》第四部分"圣雅努斯"之前,在《扎拉图斯特拉如是说》之前,在《善恶的彼岸》之前。

我要讨论的笔记条目出现在这部笔记的早期。尼采是在完成《朝霞》后开始写作这部笔记,早期的条目大多延续了《朝霞》所思考的特定问题,继续反思道德,特别是阐发他的这一洞见,即自利与利他的道德区分掩盖了一项事实:人的一切行为从根本上是自利的或服务于我。这个条目同样以这一主题开始,它和其他条目一起将自利的领域扩展成"沉迷拥有",而尼采不久会将之扩展为一种本体论或对所有存在的自然的真实论述。

这条笔记在 Colli – Montinari 编的《考订版全集》(*Kritische Gesamtausgabe*)中编号为1881年初秋11[21]。它一开始便设定了任务:

> 描述我 – 感觉的历史:表明在利他之中这种想要占有才是本质所在。

所以,尼采"我 – 感觉的历史"以道德的根基为起点。想要占有,拥有的冲动,我 – 感觉的本质,是自利和利他的共同基础,对他人的感觉被误解为自利的对立面。这条笔记余下的内容描述了"我 – 感觉"的历史可能会成为什么;它走出自利的排他性,也走出利他的感觉,走向超越我和他者的宽广领域。这条笔记余下的内容像一本书的概要,论述尼采在笔记中发现并写下的"占有的冲动",即他首次发现的自利的真相。

这条笔记继续写到,

> 表明道德的首要进步并不在于"非我与我"的观念,而在于对他者、我和自然之中的真相更为锐利的理解。

因此,要害在于更为锐利地理解我和他者共同的真相——然后理解扩展至自然的真相。自然这个词尤为重要,因为它将更为锐利的理解扩展至自然自身,自然的自然,这一自然当然也呈现于他人和我身上。

更为锐利的理解允许认知者接下来这么做:

> 由此越来越多地将想要占有从占有的纯粹表象中解放出来,从虚构的占有中解放出来,由此净化我-感觉,摆脱自我欺骗。

虚构的或制作的德文是 erdichteten,字面上可理解为作诗的(poetized)。重要之处在于:道德上的首要进步就是要更为锐利地理解真正的占有冲动实际是什么;道德上的首要进步就是认识到占有冲动的真相,而且这一认识会净化我-感觉,将之从幻觉或自我欺骗中解放。

然后,尼采描述了对我、他人和自然的真相更为锐利的理解实际可能是什么,净化我-感觉、摆脱自我欺骗可能会带来什么:

> 或许会造成这一结果:不是我,而是我们认识到事物的关联性和敌对性。

一定要注意或许。尼采向前看,他惊奇于这一过程会在它实际结束的地方结束吗,即会在认识中结束吗?净化我、摆脱自我欺骗的努力的顶峰,或许在于认识到万物因其所是而相互关联,但这种关联性包含"敌对性"。这一努力或许结束于一种不可分的亲近和敌意,相像和争斗。在此,我们能听到权力意志观点的开端。

我的错误,我的自我欺骗,因此就在于我意识到自己全然不同于他人,而道德进步的动力就不在于"非我与我"的概念,因为这一概念具有欺骗性。这一概念掩盖了根本问题,模糊了非我和我的共同源头,即非个人的动态进程,这一进程既产生我-感觉,也产生我对他人的意识,利他的意识。这一进程是一种关联性和敌对性,超越我与非我,指向自然本身中的真相。

之后,论述我-感觉的这条笔记转向认识事物的关联性/敌对性的第一个后果:

> "不要为他人而活","只为真理而活!"

从这句话开始,连续十一句话都以感叹号结尾,有力地强调每句话的重要性。这第一句话说不要为他人而活,但基督教伦理及其后继者现代伦理都要求为他人而活:这句话预示了一种根本的转变,预示社会秩序要为真理而活。

> 为真理而活会重塑我-感觉! 削弱个人倾向! 让眼睛习惯于事物的实在。

这些短句都有感叹号,它们部分是为了阐明这样偏离主流伦理后会获得什么:对我-感觉的重塑将会削弱个人倾向,允许非个人主宰一切,并习惯于我、你和自然背后的事物的真正实在。命令式表示感到需要做所说的事情:重塑、削弱、习惯。我省略了下面的短句,每个短句都有感叹号,并引向同一类型的最后一个句子:

> 有新的东西要创造:不是我,也不是你,更不是所有人!

这个不是我、你或所有人的新东西将会看见我、你和所有人身上的"事物的关联性和敌对性"。以一种新方式观看我-感觉,将会导致用一种新方式观看你和整全,这一新方式标志着道德通过和真理的结合而取得的进步。

而这条笔记勾勒了我-感觉的历史未来的诸阶段,这些阶段引向最终的阶段,即看到有新东西要创造。孤独的思想者尼采期待这些阶段。哲人尼采在思想上的进步、他对这些阶段的理解引领他看到需要创造新东西,这新东西并非我之所是、你之所是或所有人之所是。如果这条笔记事实上是一本书的概要,那么这部书就旨在引导读者思考这些理解的阶段,并看到需要创造新东西。

这条笔记的前半部分就是这样。在进入后半部分之前,我想就前半部分做一些概括。不管关于"道德的进步"的这一论述是什么意思,尼采都不是空想家(utopian)。他没有梦想在我–感觉的历史终末会出现某种想象的完美结果,就像现代人一贯梦想的那样:历史的某种完美终结。尼采明确且理性地宣称自己不是空想家,不是梦想家,而且这本笔记清晰地说明尼采的宣称为什么正确:他已经理解使人类成为我们之所是的进程,即历史和文化的塑造性进程,这一进程基于构成我们的真实冲动。我们人类始终已经被造就,造就我们的是我们摄入的一种对诸冲动的特殊平衡,一种关于好和坏的特殊文化教诲,这一教诲组织诸冲动,评判它们的好和坏,并按等级秩序排列它们。这一摄入的文化平衡始终是一种张力,始终是一种对根本的动力和冲动的不安的等级式解决。人类始终会是一种不安的存在,经受着我们特殊的心灵等级秩序和社会等级秩序强加于我们的特殊形式的苦难。尼采的教诲所应许的不是某个乌托邦,而是走出道德时期终末的虚无主义和动荡,从而更好地重新组织诸种冲动——之所以更好,是因为这一教诲将培育出更强大、更高贵的人类样本,是因为这一教诲出于上一原因而更健康。道德行为的这一整体转变仅仅基于一样东西,那就是一个哲人对激情更好的理解和更好的处理,对我–感觉以及我–感觉与他人和自然共通的东西更好的理解和欣赏。

现在我们转向在此开始并结束那条笔记的段落。这一段落以"NB"开头——两个字母在拉丁文中表示"密切注意"(Note Well)。这个 NB 标记着一个极端重要的 NB:

> 密切注意。没有在年轻人中努力必得(müssen)或想要(wollen)的占有!同时也没有对他人发号施令的威望——这两个冲动根本没有生发出来!

在此，我完全按照字面意思把尼采的德文译为不太符合语法的笨拙英文，因为意思必须要准确。努力（erstreben）仅仅是给定的，是人就会这么做：努力是冲动的基础——冲动总是为某个东西努力。这一基础的努力可以发展成或被鼓励在这个方向上努力，而不是在那个方向上努力。这就是文化之化（enculturation）所做的，教育或摄入所做的：训练人朝某个特殊的方向努力。这就是尼采的 NB 的意思：他的新摄入方案旨在创造"某种新东西"——重新矫正努力的方向，以此培育和鼓励新的我－感觉，从而引向对你和所有人的新感觉。现在，尼采对我－感觉的历史的洞见将指导对年轻人最基础的训练。

新的训练的第一步是不训练什么：首先，不要训练任何占有——下面会解释尼采的意思。也不要训练对他人发号施令的威望。我将德文 Ansehen 译为 prestige[威望]，这里的意思是被看成特殊之物。所以，不要突出对他人发号施令的我。这是一位哲人在言说，一位孤独的思想者以最大的智识努力和精神努力获得了对我－感觉的新理解，现在他作为一位教育者在言说：如何能训练其他人接受他的新理解？这些人不是像他一样的少数人；他可以诱惑或教导那些少数人摆脱陈旧的理解方式去思考。他在此从整体上谈论社会中年轻人所受的教育或训练，因为所有年轻人总是会摄入某种总体的观点，所以尼采关注将被摄入的新观点。

讲过不训练年轻人什么后，NB 标记的段落开始讨论要教导年轻人什么。此处，我们遇到最重要的问题。注意新教育的积极内容，即它旨在训练的内容：

> 让我们被事物（而不是被人）和最大可能范围的真实事物占有。

尼采没有教年轻人努力想要占有，借此在他们心中扎下古老的我－感觉；也没有教年轻人感到对他人发号施令的威望。他教给年轻人的是哲人自己在第一段落中学到的东西。他已经学会挣脱虚假的我－感觉，挣脱一个分离的、孤立的、占有性的我，并且已获得自由去认识万物的关联。这一认识引领他体验想要被真实事物掌控的欲望，想要让真实事物在他身上成为它们之所是的欲望。哲学认知者在认识过程中的这种体验——这种体验在认识到什么是权力意志而非其他时达到顶峰——将他引向他的 NB,引向他在我-感觉的历史的新阶段教育年轻人的使命。他第一个体验到这一新阶段,在这一体验中,我-感觉就是要让事物成为它们所是的真实事物,想让自然事物成为其所是,保留它们持续的生成和朽坏、它们自然的等级秩序、它们自然属性的所有其他方面。这条笔记两个分开的段落表明,尼采重复了真正的哲人们的体验:先洞见到存在,继而洞见到为了这一洞见当下必须如何行动。因此,在这条笔记的后半部分,尼采转入侍养之诗,转入可以通过训练年轻人来重构社会秩序的教诲。尼采侍养之诗未来的内容由这里开始。它开始于摄入或训练接受新的、真实的、朝向真实事物的我-感觉。

尼采的我-感觉的历史还差最后一步。讲到被"最大可能范围的真实事物"占有后,尼采说:

> 从中生长出的东西在期待之中:我们变成事物的耕地。

尼采可以轻易预测从被真实事物占有所生长出的东西,因为他知道我们人类是什么样子:德文 Acerland 的意思是农场、耕地、具有生产能力的土地,在这样的土地上,特定的"植物"自然地生长和繁育。我们很容易知道被真实事物掌管之后会出现什么,因为即将出现的东西生长于我们之中,一如植物生长于肥沃的土地。我-感觉的历史的最后一步描述了这些"植物",它们自然地生长于那些已经摄入真实事物的人的肥沃土地:

> 生存的影像将会生长于我们之中:然后我们会成为这一沃土强迫我们成为的样子:我们的倾向/厌恶就是产出这类果实的耕地的倾向/厌恶。

让真实事物成为其所是,将使我们多产的土地产出新的生存影像,这些新影像依照我们的倾向和厌恶涌现为存在,这些存在的自然特质是能够产出影像,它们所学所摄入的特质现在是让所是在生成和消逝中成为它自然之所是。

"生存的影像"是尼采我-感觉的历史的最后一步。我们人类天生是制作性的存在,创造性的存在。此处我们再次遇到柏拉图,他能用希腊语轻易地表明这一点。在《会饮》中,柏拉图使用了 poiein,该词最宽泛的含义是制作:我们人类是制作性的存在。poiein 特殊的含义指作诗:我们人类是作诗的存在。人天生是作诗的制作性存在:词与歌源自我们的天性,产自我们肥沃的土地。因此,在生存的影像作为主题的地方,尼采与柏拉图以根本的方式统一起来。由于我们的倾向和厌恶、我们的爱与憎,在我们身上产生了我们赖以生活的生存影像,这些影像作为价值和无价值的化身或理念而成为我们的权威。人类产生的生存影像变成衡量如何存在和作为什么存在、努力争取什么和努力反对什么的标准。尼采的我-感觉的历史期待着新的生存影像,这一影像与现在所理解的真实事物相一致。尼采结束于一位哲人通常结束的地方,结束于人们赖以栖居于大地之上的哲学之诗。新的生存影像将大地概念化为人性的自然家园;生物科学研究星球上相互关联的生命网络;政治的和社会的运动以生态学作为做决断的核心考虑,或如施特劳斯所说,出于对自然之爱为征服自然规定界限。

尼采补充了最后一句话:

> 这些生存的影像是迄今为止最为重要的:它们将统治人类。

尼采结束于柏拉图结束的地方:哲人们逐渐认识到人类被影像统治,年轻人摄入这些影像并在成熟之后受其统治。哲人们认识到影像的统治,并为了哲学的利益被迫去统治,于是他们通过关于影像的立法来统治。柏拉图通过超验之物的影像统治,即通过理念、经过改造的荷马诸神、不朽的灵魂、进行奖惩的冥府统治。柏拉图的影像取得了成功,因为它们服务于构成人的深层次冲动。柏拉图的影像曾统治人类,但现今它们濒于死亡,而且应该死去。尼采新的生存影像旨在像柏拉图的影像一样统治人类,它们有望成功,因为它们也服务于构成人的深层次冲动,只不过尼采的影像服务于肯定性的冲动,而柏拉图的超验之物的影像服务于憎恨和复仇的否定性冲动,两种冲动相互冲突。

尼采新的生存影像是我们已经看到的尼采哲学之诗的关键元素:至高理想的影像。柏拉图将至高理想称为善,它具有超验的稳定性,像太阳一样统治万物———个纯属想象的太阳,永远同一,并将生存赋予永远同一的理念。尼采新的至高理想并非一种永恒的稳定,而是永远变化的生命如其所是地永恒复返。同时也是特殊的至高存在的影像,这些至高存在产生于制作性的存在的"造神的本能"。在柏拉图这里,至高存在倾向于善的一神论,而柏拉图式的诸神是道德的判官,他们在今生和来世奖惩我们。这些神如今不可信也无价值,他们可以被我们肥沃的土地的造神本能取代,被新的至高存在取代。(我想再次提起尼采谴责柏拉图背后的西方哲学的历史事件:柏拉图主义为基督教在罗马的统治做了准备;这一"民众的柏拉图主义"为现代反对基督教的必要战争做了准备;但是,欧洲的现代性延续了基督教美德的世俗版本,即终结苦难和权利平等的现代理想;尼采努力要取代的是这些柏拉图主义的晚近后果——尼采意义上的"使存在"[letting be]并没有暗示,应该允许非自然的理想是其所是;他的"使存在"知道,为它挑起的战争是必要的。)尼采赋予他的至高存在的影像以早已存在的希腊名号,即狄俄尼索斯和阿里阿德涅。这两位神并非我们的判官,他们并不奖惩我们,我们没有必要向他们卑躬屈膝或乞求恩惠。他们像我们一样,因为他们就像所有生命一样,是分雌雄、能生育、能繁殖的存在,但在阳刚和阴柔方面远远优越于我们。他们值得我们尽力膜拜和效仿。我们仰望他们,他们因其所是而提升我们。他们是我们最渴望成为的样子。

尼采的生存影像采用了至高理想和至高存在的这两个特殊形式。他还有其他的生存影像,例如一种能够凭靠自然的、肯定性的标准进行评判的新的好和坏,但是我们可以概括说,它们全都服务于根本的激情:吸引的激情,爱的激情。

尼采全部的故事就是这些,他最初把这个故事讲述为我-感觉的历史。他的故事结束于人类对自然存在的大地的爱和对自然存在的人类的爱,自然存在的人类能够超越生存影像的统治——这些影像教导报复生命本身的非自然理想。他的整个故事结束于生态学,结束于认识到大地上生命的相互关联,正是这种相互关联产生了人的命令:"要对大地真诚。"因此我认为,可以把尼采看作一位全面的生态学哲人。在我看来,尼采哲学之诗的这个层面是一种进入尼采的可行方式,即把他视为一场吸引着晚期现代人们的流行运动的奠基思考者。这场生态运动在西方的某些地方已经非常强劲,随着越来越不可否认的证据表明人类肇始的气候变化造成了环境灾难,这场运动必然越来越强劲。这类源自特殊关怀的运动,会在尼采那里发现它们的自然哲人。

对我而言,尼采哲学之诗的生态学层面自有一种优先地位,原因在于它与前两个层面的关系或可能的关系:尼采认为这个星球上的自然、生命和人的生命在生态上相互关联,新的生存影像从这一观点发端,最终通向对大地真诚的新神,并通向一个新的至高理想,即渴望大地上的事物整体如其所是地永恒复返。

最后我想回顾"苏格拉底如何成为苏格拉底"一讲的结尾。在《会饮》中,柏拉图展现了第俄提玛引领苏格拉底完成其哲学教育的最后阶段,即获得对作为本体论的爱欲的深层结构的洞见。在这次最深入的观看过后,柏拉图让第俄提玛就爱的阶梯发表长篇讲辞;她说,发生在顶峰的是一种观看与一种行动。爬至顶峰的人注视或观看完满的美,并且在美的面前孕生或参与到一种制作或创制中。尼采"我-感觉的历史"的结尾,标志着尼采成为尼采的首次完成,而且尼采的语词与柏拉图相似。在尼采这里,问题同样是注视与生产,或观看与制作。观看就是让真实的存在占有我们,它导向一种制作,亦即统治人类的"新的生存影像"的涌现。

在柏拉图和尼采这里,哲学都产生了哲学之诗。

讲座结束之际,我们回到施特劳斯。他在致克莱因的一封信中说,当柏拉图被视为显白的作家时，属于"那种特有的柏拉图式哲学"的柏拉图就能与"最切近我内心的"柏拉图区分开来。最切近施特劳斯内心的是真正的柏拉图，是隐微的柏拉图，这位柏拉图展现了苏格拉底成为苏格拉底，获得他全面的理解，即把存在理解为生成，理解为爱欲。就我来说，这是施特劳斯提供给我们的最大帮助：他向我们表明如何阅读哲人们，如何发现他们显白的教诲中暗含的隐微理解，他们有意将隐微理解留给那些与他们相似、被认识的激情驱动的少数人。然而，无论施特劳斯有多伟大，他的伟大与柏拉图和尼采的伟大不是一回事：他本人不是柏拉图和尼采所是的哲人和哲学诗人。施特劳斯向我们展现了如何同时阅读柏拉图和尼采，如何理解他们作为哲人的共通之处。在我看来，施特劳斯甚至不止揭示了两位哲人的亲缘关系：他还谨慎地鼓励我们把尼采当作我们时代的柏拉图式政治哲人。施特劳斯在他晚期的尼采论文中多次暗示这一点，以下是其中三处。

一、在《柏拉图式政治哲学研究》中，施特劳斯打破时间顺序，将这篇尼采论文置于中心，与论文"耶路撒冷与雅典"形成一对。通过这一设计，施特劳斯说：在我们的时代，柏拉图式政治哲学研究的核心是研究耶路撒冷和雅典以及尼采。

二、在这篇文章中，施特劳斯帮助我们理解尼采何以是一位柏拉图式哲人。施特劳斯说，哲人尼采的结论是，存在就是作为权力意志存在，权力意志"取代了*爱欲*……在柏拉图思想中占据的地位"。权力意志和爱欲是本体论的学说；尼采像苏格拉底一样，专擅关于爱欲事物的知识。施特劳斯还帮助我们理解尼采何以是一位柏拉图式的政治哲人；尼采发展出一套哲学之诗，施特劳斯称之为"重新堕入柏拉图主义"，因为柏拉图主义的这一面相完全属于处在与城邦/属人共同体的关系中的哲学。

三、这篇文章的结尾是 Die vornehme Natur ersetzt die göttliche Natur[高贵的自然取代神圣的自然]，与《城邦与人》的结尾一样。施特劳斯在结尾不想直接宣告，而是想让你发问和好奇。对我来说，好奇引向了这一点："高贵的自然取代神圣的自然"意味着尼采教授的自然取代了柏拉图教授的自然。

施特劳斯论尼采的文章出现在他最后一书的中心位置，并表明权力意志取代了爱欲占据的位置，末尾的德文引领我得出的结论重述了我此次讲座的标题"施特劳斯－柏拉图－尼采"：施特劳斯宣布，尼采在我们时代取代了柏拉图。

时代在变。诸神已死。变化的时代要求新哲人提供新的生存影像。对我来说，这就是尼采对我们时代的意义。

PHILOSOPHY AND PHILOSOPHIC POETRY:
STRAUSS, PLATO, NIETZSCHE

LAURENCE LAMPERT

Acknowledgement

I want to begin by thanking Professor Liu Xiaofeng for inviting me to give these lectures in China, in Renmin University. It is an honor to be invited and I am very grateful to Professor Liu. His invitation has given me the occasion to reflect on the work I have done for the past forty years and to summarize some of its main points.

Preface

My titles describe my lectures. Two will be on Leo Strauss; two will be on Plato; and two will be on Friedrich Nietzsche. And all six will be about philosophy and its poetry. Another way of saying that is that my lectures will be about *esotericism* and *exotericism* as the art of writing practiced by philosophers. It is an art that allows the philosopher to convey what he *thinks*—the esoteric part—through what he *says*—the exoteric part—without saying directly or simply putting it into words what he thinks. It is an art of writing that is both a showing and a hiding: the artfulness of the showing consists in the shown leading to the not – shown, to the hidden. And the hidden is always what matters most—what *you*, if you're interested but only if you're interested, can find out on your own. And finding it out, you will treasure it all the more because you found it out on your own. So the philosopher's art is a kind of temptation, a seduction of *you*, meant to win you to him and his thinking. The esoteric content that his art conveys to you he offers as a gift to you, his special reader. And it ties you to him. And you're grateful. And you live a life of gratitude to him and what he's given you. You're *caught*. All my writings are fishhooks, said Friedrich Nietzsche.

My first two lectures will be on Leo Strauss. Strauss rediscovered the philosophic art of writing and then wrote about it or disclosed it as no previous philosopher ever had. But even though Strauss made it a public topic he too practiced it. He was true to the philosophic art that he rediscovered and he conveyed what he really thought only indirectly.

My second set of two lectures will be on Plato, the ancient Greek philosopher who stands as the model for philosophic writing in the whole of the Western philosophic tradition. But Plato's writings display *his* model, the philosopher Socrates who was his teacher and who never wrote anything, but who spoke and in his speaking practiced the art that Plato found a way of writing. Plato's writing put Socrates's speaking into a more permanent form that generated a whole philosophic tradition: Western philosophy. Since Plato, western philosophy is exoteric and esoteric, or, it is political philosophy and philosophy. In words that make political philosophy more explicit, it is a theological – political program and it is philosophy. My titles call the theological – political program *philosophic poetry*, a term that goes back to Plato himself. And with respect to the history of Western philosophy as a whole, Nietzsche said that since Plato all theologians and philosophers have been on the same track.

Until him, that is, until Nietzsche. And my third set of two lectures will be on Friedrich Nietzsche, the German philosopher who aimed to put philosophy on a different track. *Different*, but Nietzsche's track too distinguishes between esoteric and exoteric, philosophy and philosophic poetry, or in the words that Nietzsche used, Truth and Art.

As for me, I am a scholar of philosophy, a reader, an interpreter of texts. In Nietzsche's good phrases, I am a *philosophic laborer* whereas he is a *genuine philosopher*. As a philosophic laborer, I judge Nietzsche to be the philosopher of our time, the philosopher to whom we have to pay the closest attention because he came to understand the whole sweep of Western philosophy since the early Greeks and therefore to understand *our time* with a clarity and depth exceeding anyone else's. For me, Nietzsche is the philosopher from whom we should *differ* only with the greatest caution.

LECTURE 1

Strauss Recovers the Tradition of Philosophic Poetry

I begin with Leo Strauss, the philosopher who rediscovered exotericism/esotericism and publicized it, choosing to make the distinction well known after a century and half of Western philosophy during which it had been almost forgotten. In my two lectures on Strauss I will deal first with his rediscovery of exotericism. And *exotericism* is the word I will consistently use in these lectures to name the whole practice of the philosophers. Others call it *esotericism* but Strauss himself called it *exotericism* because it more literally describes what the writings are: *exoteric*. After discussing Strauss's rediscovery of exotericism, I will deal with something that is still disputed by some of Strauss's followers: that Strauss himself practiced exotericism. I will show *that* he did and *how* he did it, by looking at things he said about Plato and then about Nietzsche.

Strauss's rediscovery of exotericism: his letters to Klein

Strauss left a record of his rediscovery of exotericism in letters that he wrote to his best friend, Jacob Klein, in 1938 – 1939 when he was 39 and 40 years old.

These letters deserve to become famous. They were written in German and have been translated into Chinese so you can read them. But they have not yet been translated into English so many of Strauss's English – speaking followers do not know them or know them well. Those who have not would be shocked to read them because Strauss is completely open here. The letters differ from all his publications in that openness. They deserve to become famous because they are so open and so radical. There has even been a debate in American Strauss circles whether they should have been published by Heinrich Meier at all in his edition of Strauss's works.

They are of course *private*; Strauss wrote them to his best friend who also spent his life studying the philosophers. But Strauss must have known that they would become known because he knew that his writings would make him famous and that those that he attracted would want to read everything he had written, including his letters. After all, Strauss himself paid close attention to Plato's letters, Machiavelli's letters, Nietzsche's letters. And he could very easily have destroyed them—he could have asked his best friend to burn them. He did not do that. We must read them.

The letters cover about 44 pages in Meier's edition and what I will do is read selections from them in chronological order from January, 1938 to October, 1939, and then make comments on the selections I have chosen. I'll skip some letters entirely and I'll read only parts of the others. If you read everything in the letters of these nearly two years, you get a good picture of Strauss in a time of real stress and worry about his family, his not having a job, the dangerous situation in Germany shortly before the Second World War— writing privately to his best friend Strauss expresses his deep concerns. But even those concerns cannot detract from the primary mood and feeling in the letters—extreme excitement and joy at discovering what the philosophers had written as if it were just for him, which in a way it *was*, and excitement at what he would have to report to a world that had become ignorant of what the philosophers really wrote and therefore ignorant of what philosophy is. The selections I have picked out concern only his rediscovery of exotericism.

The letters begin with *Maimonides* whom Strauss had already studied for years as the most important philosopher in the Jewish tradition and who lived in the 12th Century of Western time calculation (c. 1135 – 1204), more than 700 years before Strauss studied him. In his first book, *Spinoza's Critique of Religion*, which had already been published in 1928, Strauss said of Maimonides that he was "a believing Jew." Now, 10 years later he said this:

Lecture 1 Strauss Recovers the Tradition of Philosophic Poetry **149**

The Letter of January 20, 1938:
[Maimonides] was a truly free mind⋯ The crucial question for him was *not* world – creation or world – eternity (for he was persuaded of world – eternity), instead, it was whether the ideal lawgiver must be a prophet.

Maimonides was persuaded of the eternity of the world: that was the position of *philosophy*, not the position of the *Bible* and so not the position of a believing Jew. Strauss now saw that Maimonides rejected the Bible's view, the Jewish view, of the creation of the world. The question for him had become "must the ideal lawgiver be a prophet?" Judaism is a tradition of *law* and the Jewish lawgiver was Moses, the most important figure in the Jewish Bible. In Plato the *philosopher* is the ideal lawgiver. So the question as Strauss now saw it was this: Must the philosopher – lawgiver also be sent from God? That is, be seen as sent from God, present himself as sent from God?

It's very difficult to prove that because he discusses the question in an exegetical form.

For those who read Strauss today, this is *funny*: the exegetical form is the form of a commentator, and a commentator can hide his own view of what he is commenting on; he can appear to be merely reporting. Maimonides did that and made it hard to prove what he himself thought. And *Strauss* did that—he chose to write as a commentator. So it is very difficult to prove what Strauss thinks because he, like Maimonides, chose an exegetical form of writing.

February 16:
You can't imagine with what infinite refinement and irony Maimonides handles 'religion.' ⋯ If in a few years I explode this bomb (in case I live so long), a great battle will be kindled.

It is completely clear to Strauss what the implications are of revealing what he is discovering in Maimonides: he holds a *bomb* in his hand, a bomb that will explode the whole tradition of understanding Maimonides. The explosion will be deeply destructive because Maimonides is the greatest teacher of Judaism, its most respected and authoritative teacher.

> This will yield the interesting result that a simply historical determination—the determination that Maimonides in his beliefs was *absolutely no Jew*—is of considerable present-day significance: the incompatibility in principle of philosophy and Judaism would be demonstrated to the eye.

The "historical determination" is what a reader of the writings can learn, an historian like Strauss, reading them as an exoteric writing hiding an esoteric meaning for *you*, Maimonides' special audience whom he educates in the forbidden things because *you*, his special reader, are like him. So Strauss says that the science of history that is aware of the art of writing can show that Maimonides was *absolutely no Jew*. To be a philosopher, to depend wholly on *reason*, absolutely rules out being a Jew, which depends on *faith*, on what is written in the sacred book that the Jewish tradition holds is a *revelation* directly from God. Being a Jew depends on *obedience* to the laws given in that Revelation. Strauss maintained this major point throughout his life: the radical incompatibility of Revelation and Philosophy. Revelation establishes a tradition of *obedience*. Philosophy attempts to gain a *free mind* that can accept as true only what reason can demonstrate.

> An essential point in Maim.'s technique is *of course* that he says *everything* completely openly, if in the places where an idiot doesn't look.

You have to be careful here: An *idiot* is almost every reader. It's me; it's you. And *completely openly* means open only to the one whose skeptical free mind knows how to look for what almost every other reader does not look for. This is a most important point: the esoteric is not hidden somewhere beneath the surface or above the surface: it's *on* the surface but still hidden, hidden in plain view if you know how to look. One of Strauss's best sentences says this: "The problem inherent in the surface of things, and only in the surface of things, is the heart of things."

There's an aphorism in N. : when I hold the truth in my fist, dare I open my fist?

"N." is Nietzsche. N. is enough. Both know that N. can only be Nietzsche. (I've been informed that the Chinese translator did not know the N. was Nietzsche; he wrote simply "somebody.") In 1935, three years earlier, Strauss had said in a letter that "Nietzsche so dominated and charmed" him between his "22nd and 30th year (1921 – 1929)" "that I literally believed everything I understood of him" (letter to Löwith June 23, 1935). I haven't been able to find those exact words about holding "truth in my fist" in N. But the thought is certainly his. He spoke of three basic matters that were "true but deadly": "the sovereignty of becoming, the fluidity of all concepts, types and kinds; and the lack of any cardinal difference between man and the animals." And Nietzsche constantly faced the question that the philosopher faces—"dare I open my fist" on the deadly truths? I'll talk about that in my Nietzsche lectures but it is important to recognize from the start that the "deadly truth" is not deadly to *him*; he lives easily with it; he celebrates it because he seeks the truth and loves the truth. But he knows that it is deadly to society, deadly to the beliefs on which society depends for its health.

July 23:
I could actually be a bit proud that I've solved this riddle. But maybe my nerves aren't strong enough—or I lack '*scientia*'—or both are the case. In short, at times I shudder in the face of what I may cause by my interpretation. The upshot will be that I, poor devil, have to spoon up the soup in which this diabolical sorcerer of the twelfth century landed me.

I quote this personal remark by Strauss partly because it shows that he has a clear sense of where he stands: he knows how monumental his discoveries in Maimonides are. But I quote it mostly because it says something I don't hear in any of his publications: *doubt* about whether he can do it. Are his nerves strong enough? Can he bear the strain of this radical, even destructive unorthodoxy? Does he lack the knowledge or the nerve? Here he asks himself if he is strong enough in his *intellect* and his *will* to bear the burden of really learning what the philosophers know and of making it known to others.

Up to this point in the letters, Strauss's radical discoveries are confined to Maimonides. In his 1935 book, *Philosophy and Law*, Strauss had dealt with Maimonides and his *predecessors*; but there his predecessors were the Islamic philosophers, philosophers also raised in a tradition based on Revelation, on a book to which the believer had to submit, to surrender his intellect. But the Islamic philosophers pointed to *their* predecessors, the Greeks, to *pagans*, thinkers raised outside the tradition of obedience to Revelation.

It is at this point in his letters that Strauss turns back to those Greeks. That means that his letters to Klein do not discuss the exotericism of the Islamic philosophers who influenced Maimonides.

October 15:
I'm now reading Herodotus, who—I swear it as a Catholic Christian—is also an esoteric writer and one in perfection. In short, it's happening again.

"Catholic Christian" is a nice little joke by Strauss. So the first Greek Strauss turns to is the "historian" Herodotus. And not a so–called philosopher. (As a student at a classical *Gymnasium* in Germany, Strauss learned Greek and Latin, and read the classics. And he kept reading them. But just why he turned to Herodotus as the first Greek after his discoveries in Maimonides he does not say.)

October 20:
I'm really stunned, and prostrate myself before such artistry (= capability). My lucky star wants it that his work is really the single model for Plato known to me.

Lecture 1 Strauss Recovers the Tradition of Philosophic Poetry

Strauss bows down on the ground as before some god, honoring Herodotus for his mastery as an exoteric writer. But it's not Herodotus who is of the highest interest to him, it's *Plato*—and when he reads Herodotus he thinks of Plato as following the model not just of Socrates but of the writer Herodotus.

I can therefore show that what is nearest my heart about Plato is independent of the specifically Platonic philosophy.

This is a genuine *bomb*. He splits Plato in two: "the specifically Platonic philosophy" would be what we can call the *exoteric* Plato, the *teaching* Plato taught. And *that* is separate from what is nearest Strauss's heart—the esoteric Plato about which Strauss would have heard nothing from the scholars of Plato who had for a century abandoned the idea of an esoteric Plato. Strauss can *show* that distinction—he can interpret Plato's text as he can interpret Herodotus's text. The bomb is that Strauss can show that Plato himself did not *hold* what he *teaches*. And it's that hidden Plato that Strauss loves.

And with that we're at *the basic matter*. Plato is the teacher of Maimonides and Maimonides' Islamic predecessors—and he was a teacher of the necessity of exotericism even though he was not raised in a tradition of Revelation as were Maimonides and his Islamic predecessors.

November 2:
I find myself in a state of frenzy that's consuming me: after Herodotus now Thucydides too!

I include this state of frenzy because of the next letter:

November 27:
Herodotus, Thucydides, and Xenophon are *no* historians—of course not—but authors of exoteric ··· writings.

All three great ancient Greek historians wrote exoterically. This is the *first reference to Xenophon* in Strauss's letters on discovering exotericism.

Xenophon's *The Education of Cyrus* is

> a wholly great book of sublime irony, what Socrates is is shown through his caricature of Cyrus. Only through that medium does Xenophon show the true, hidden Socrates whereas he shows the manifest Socrates in his *Memorabilia*. His Socrates – image is therefore *not fundamentally* different from that of Plato.

Strauss moves very rapidly: just a few weeks after discovering *Thucydides'* exotericism, he can already say what *Xenophon's* writing strategy is: *Xenophon* shows the truth about the most important of all persons for him, Socrates, through a caricature of a *king or ruler*, a figure most people will think is more important than a mere philosopher: Cyrus is the founder of the Persian Empire, a *ruler* who *founds a whole empire*, a ruler who is a *practical* and not a *theoretical* man. What Strauss sees is radical: the true, hidden Socrates is in his very different way, a kind of *ruler* and a kind of *founder*. Through Socrates, a theoretical man, a *philosopher*, a new kind of empire comes into existence, the empire of a philosophic ruler. And Xenophon, a student of Socrates, shows that in his artful writing.

In the Western classical tradition Plato has almost always been held to be more important than Xenophon as a guide to Socrates. But traditionally Xenophon was given a very high place right next to Plato. In Strauss's time, however, more than a century of modern scholarship had completely destroyed Xenophon's reputation as great. And the reason was that the classical scholars had completely abandoned the tradition of exoteric reading. One of Strauss's greatest achievements is his recovery of Xenophon, the genuine Xenophon, the philosopher. Strauss's first published essay on the ancient Greeks was on Xenophon; it was published in 1939 while he was making these discoveries in exotericism. And Strauss's first book on the Greeks, *On Tyranny*, was on Xenophon's *Hiero*. And the two books that Strauss said were his best books were his two late commentaries on Xenophon.

There is another crucial point in the letter I just read: Xenophon's Socrates is "*not fundamentally*" different from Plato's. That is completely against the view of all other scholars when Strauss wrote it. And it is a major insight: Socrates, the fundamental teacher, can be understood through Plato and through Xenophon: both allow the esoteric Socrates to be seen, one can help illuminate the other because the two Socrateses are not fundamentally different.

December 2:
I'm curious about what is hidden in Sophocles who, according to tradition, was a friend of Herodotus—I'm afraid that here too it's philosophy and *not* the *city and the ancestors*.

I include this remark in order to show the *scope* of Strauss's recovery of the Greek writers: *Sophocles* is one of the three great writers of tragedies in classical Athens. Strauss himself never published anything that demonstrated his suspicion here but his most outstanding follower, Seth Benardete, did.

February 16, 1939:
Xenophon is my special favorite because he had the courage to clothe himself as an idiot and go through the millennia that way—he's the greatest trickster I know. I believe that he does in his writings exactly what Socrates did in his life. In any case with [Xenophon] too morality is purely exoteric, and just about every second word has a double meaning.

Xenophon dared to clothe himself as an idiot—and the whole of modern scholarship believed he *was* an idiot. A "trickster" is a swindler, a cool confident person who wins your trust in order to cheat you, to steal from you.

And if Xenophon does what Socrates did *Socrates is a trickster, a swindler*. This is very serious—it's the ultimate bomb about Socrates. Socrates is taken to be—and is—the greatest philosophic teacher of morality; he is the heroic model of the teacher of morality, but the morality he teaches is wholly exoteric. Strauss proves that he is right about this bomb:

Kalokagathia was, in the Socratic circle, a swear – word, something like "philistine" or "*bourgeois*" in the 19th century.

Kalokagathia is two Greek words taken together in order to describe the Greek gentleman, the pillar of civic life in the Greek civil order. The two words are *noble* and *good*. And what did that word for the *gentleman*, the noble and good man mean inside the Socratic circle? It was a word of *ridicule* used to diminish and mock. But we cannot forget that Socrates is the teacher of virtue to the young Greek gentlemen with whom he conversed. Socrates is the teacher who gives these young gentlemen good reasons for continuing to follow the virtue of their fathers and fore – fathers. What Strauss says is that that teaching is *exoteric* and the exoteric masks a genuine understanding that sees the true grounds and limits of the gentleman's virtue. Both matters are important: Socrates' exoteric moral teaching is a teaching of virtue for the young gentlemen; his true understanding of the virtues is to be learned by the very few like himself. Socrates' speech about morality has two meanings, one for each of his two audiences.

And *sôphrosunê* is essentially self – control in the expression of opinions.

Sôphrosunê is the Greek word for *moderation* or *self – control*, one of the four classical virtues with courage, justice, and wisdom. What does Strauss discover *self – control* to really mean within the Socratic circle? Self – control in speaking, *moderation* means *exotericism*; it means *controlling and guarding* what you say or write. So the philosopher reinterprets the virtues of the gentleman to have a different sense for *him* and his kind. *Philosophic* moderation means in part continued use of *the old moral words* but understanding them in a radically different way. The philosopher's moderate, moral *speech* shelters his radical *thinking*.

—in short, there's a whole system of secret words here exactly as in Maimonides, therefore a found feast for me.

You have to be careful with "*secret words*"—they are the common words like the words for the virtues. They are *secret* only in meaning something unspoken and different for the thinker.

July 25:
The identity of Xenophon's and Plato's Socrates is beyond doubt, it's the same Socrates – Odysseus in both, the *teaching* too. The problem of the *Memorabilia* is identical to that of the *Republic*: the problematic relation between justice and truth, or between the practical and theoretical life.

Xenophon's *Memorabilia* and Plato's *Republic* treat the same issue: the problematic or questionable relation between the *practical* and the *theoretical* life. Only in his published writings does Strauss spell out that "*problematic relation.*" The practical life is based on *loyalty* to common values or moral virtues that society holds to be true; the theoretical life is based on a *passion to know* and it comes to know that the virtues to which all are loyal are in the fundamental sense not true but only necessary. There is no need for Strauss to explain to Klein what the problem in the problematic relation is, because Klein already knows. Put briefly that problem is this: what the *philosopher*, the one who lives the theoretical life, comes to know can destroy the foundation of the society of which he is a part. And if the *society* comes to learn what the philosopher thinks, it can destroy him—it will see him as an enemy and could do to him what the Athenians did to Socrates, kill him. The problematic relation of the practical and the theoretical life leads the philosopher to exotericism. Exotericism protects society from philosophy and protects the philosopher from society. There are other reasons for exotericism besides this problematic relation and I have already touched on the main one: it is a temptation, a seduction to the philosopher's young kin.

Notice that in this letter Strauss calls Socrates, " *Socrates – Odysseus.* " Odysseus is the wisest man in Homer and in his poem, *The Odyssey*, wise Odysseus becomes a *philosopher*. But Strauss's main point here depends on Odysseus's reputation for being *wily*, being a trickster, a liar who cannot be fooled. I mention that because Odysseus will appear in my first Plato lecture as the model for Socrates.

October 10:
[Hesiod's *Theogeny* is] an answer to the question of what the first, the unborn things are; further, an illumination of the Olympian through this question; and finally, an enlightenment of what this question and answer mean, that is, what wisdom means. The first things are not the gods but such things as earth, sky, stars, ocean which at one place are expressly distinguished from the gods simply.

I include this mostly because it extends the great fact of exotericism back to the founding Greek poets, Hesiod and Homer. Their poetry is exoteric. Hesiod's *Theogeny* is his poem of the birth of the gods; it is authoritative for everyone, but the way it is written allows a few to learn "*What the unborn things are*"—the things that always are, the natural things, the things more important than the gods to one who seeks understanding. Learning what the unborn things are illuminates what "*the Olympians*" are; it shows what the gods who care about the human things are: the inventions of wise poets like Hesiod. And this enlightenment shows what wisdom is: wisdom is knowledge of nature and human nature; and knowledge of what a god is. What Strauss is discovering in these letters are the very matters that will occupy him for his whole life.

I'm convinced it's not different in Homer.

Strauss moves from Hesiod to Homer, the most important of poets, the one Plato calls "the educator of Greece." Strauss believes that "*it's not different in Homer*" than in Hesiod but he does not develop this insight either in his letter or in publications. But Seth Benardete did: *The Bow and the Lyre* on Homer's *Odyssey* demonstrates that the founding *poet* of Greece is also its founding *philosopher*.

October 25:
I've now understood [Plato's] *Symposium* in principle: it's the 'authentic' enlightenment about the profaning of the mysteries by Alcibiades; not Alcibiades but Socrates blabbed the secret of the mys-

teries. It's a case of the famous fact that the actual 'accuser' of Socrates is Plato.

This is the last of Strauss's letters to Klein that I will mention. I include it because it singles out Plato's *Symposium*. In a lecture course at the University of Chicago from 1959, twenty years later, Strauss showed why he regarded the *Symposium* as the most important of Plato's dialogues because it reveals the real secret of the mysteries. I will talk about this in my second Plato lecture because what happens in the *Symposium* is of the greatest importance. For now, I want to mention only one thing from the letter. Socrates "*blabbed*" the secret of the mysteries—to *blab* means to *say too much*, to *say what you shouldn't say*. The "*mysteries*" were the core of Athenian religion and Athenians were initiated into that religion through special secret rituals and rites. Once initiated, the initiates were strictly forbidden to say what the rites were—they were the *mysteries* and they were to be kept secret. But the mysteries Socrates *blabbed* in the *Symposium* are the secret truths about *philosophy* and the *philosopher*. Those truths will be the most important things I will have to say about Socrates becoming Socrates in my second Plato lecture.

And with that I end my report on Strauss's letters to Klein, the letters in which he reported his recovery of philosophic exotericism on the very days he was making his discoveries. Strauss's letters to Klein are unlike anything Strauss ever published, because in the letters he opens his fist on the bomb, first about Maimonides but then about Socrates and Plato and Xenophon. The letters to Klein give the readers of Strauss's other writings direct access to what he learned about exoteric writing in the very months in which he was learning it. And they give direct access to what Strauss thought. The letters help settle any argument about Strauss's real views.

But after Strauss made the discoveries recorded in these letters, how *did* he explode all those bombs he held in his hand about the philosophic tradition? He very soon developed a strategy for presenting his discoveries in a way that made sure that they did not explode immediately and obviously. His strategy was itself indirect. We could say that he provided his bombs with a long *wick*, a long string that he lit in you the reader, a string that would burn in you and lead you slowly, through your own discovery of what he is really saying; the bomb would explode for *you* and only after long work. Strauss's strategy taught you to read at the same time that it was teaching you what was really there in a philosophic author.

So Strauss developed his own manner of exoteric writing which was much more open than the traditional manners and which would eventually establish a tradition of reading that would make the philosophers' *esoteric* understanding more generally available. And he spent much of the rest of his working life writing about the great philosophers of the tradition—and doing it successfully as the global spread of his writings, and the global character of his readership demonstrates.

But the 1938 – 39 letters to Klein give clear access to what is of enduring importance in Leo Strauss: studying the letters can anchor the way we read Strauss and help us in reading the philosophers generally, reading them with constant attention to the two – fold character of their writings: what they teach on the surface and what they lead or tempt a reader to infer from the surface.

For the rest of my lectures on Strauss I'm going to talk only about his studies in the history of philosophy, and only about his studies of Plato and Nietzsche. That means I am going to *ignore* the other great topics to which Strauss devoted himself, including his very important work analyzing present day philosophy with a view to understanding why it had lost or forgotten the exoteric tradition, a loss that threatened to become permanent because current philosophic trends argued powerfully for the impossibility of philosophy, the impossibility of understanding the truth of things.

For Strauss on Plato and Nietzsche I will discuss two texts only, one on Plato and one on Nietzsche. Both deal with *philosophy* in a way that is intended to show that *philosophy* generates or gives birth to *philosophic poetry*. Both the Plato text and the Nietzsche text are short, but they are taken out of longer texts and their meaning in part depends on their setting within those longer texts. I will look closely at the words of the short texts and occasionally appeal to the setting in the larger texts. What I have to say will make clear that Strauss gave us, *his* readers, the same difficulty Maimonides gave his reader: like Maimonides, Strauss discusses philosophy and philosophic poetry in an exegetical form which makes his own view available only to inference.

The point of my discussing these texts is partly to show that Strauss wrote exoterically, but more importantly to show that Strauss made it possible for us to see the exoteric character of Plato's and Nietzsche's writing. I begin with Plato, with Strauss's most important statement on Plato: the central essay of *The City and Man*, "On Plato's Republic." I discussed this essay in detail in *The Enduring Importance of Leo Strauss*.

Strauss's essay on Plato's *Republic* in *The City and Man*

Strauss's essay "On Plato's Republic" has two parts separated by a little mark of punctuation: a dash at the end of paragraph 13. The first 13 paragraphs are on how to read a Platonic dialogue. Then comes the dash. Then the rest of the essay, an interpretation of the *Republic*, 65 paragraphs that can be considered as one separate, complete unit. The central paragraph of the 65 paragraphs is the 33rd and it deals with the central matter. That paragraph has 38 sentences. Its center, the 19th and 20th sentences, are two questions. I will focus on those two questions. I have to say two things about what I'm doing here.

First: Strauss taught that all the greatest writers *hid* the central matter in the central place. He called that "*the least exposed place*" compared to the most exposed beginning and end. But Strauss's emphasis on centers made the center the most exposed place. Did Strauss himself follow the greatest writers in this technique of writing? Of course he did. All his writings show this art of centering.

Second: You can't just look at centers. To understand the center you have to earn it, you have to work to see what prepares the center and what follows from the center. And you have to think about what all that means. What I'm going to say now is a kind of *cheating* or a kind of *crime*. It's never enough just to look at the center but that's what I'm going to do.

Strauss's central paragraph begins on education in Plato's *Republic*, children's education through stories and songs. It is education through poetry, a most important word. Those stories and songs are typically about gods and heroes, figures whose actions are to be admired and mimicked by children. Plato's emphasis is on the right kind of stories that teach the right kind of behavior and warn against the wrong kinds of behavior. "To indicate the right kind," Strauss says, "Socrates lays down two laws" for the gods. Socrates presents a theology that in part consists of untrue stories about the gods.

Notice: Strauss quietly says that Socrates is a *legislator*, a person who lays down laws, and Socrates lays down laws for the gods. And, very importantly, new laws for the gods. The untrue stories are for little children but Strauss says they are also "for the grown up citizens of the good city." The untrue stories that the citizens absorbed as children are what the grown up citizens believe: what is taken in during one's childhood is what one continues to believe and act on as an adult.

Socrates controls the conversation in the *Republic* and as Strauss says, Socrates makes the conversation *shift* almost unnoticeably "from the demand for noble lies about the gods to the demand for the truth about the gods." And now I'm at the part of the central paragraph that I want to read. I'll read Strauss's sentences and make comments on them.

> The speakers start from the implicit premise that there are gods, or that there is a god and that they know what a god is. The difficulty can be illustrated by an example.

It's not clear from the grammar of the sentence what the difficulty refers to but it becomes clear: the difficulty is *knowing what a god is*.

> Socrates asks Adeimantus whether the god would lie or say the untruth because of his ignorance of ancient things and Adeimantus replies that this would be ridiculous (382d6 – 8). But why is it ridiculous in Adeimantus' view? Because the gods must know best their own affairs, as Timaeus suggests (*Timaeus* 40d3 – 41a5)?

These two questions stand at the center of Strauss's central paragraph. What Strauss placed at the center of his central paragraph on Plato's *Republic* is two questions about whether the god would lie because of his ignorance of ancient things.

First question: The first question is about *Adeimantus*'s view of the gods. Adeimantus is one of the two young men who talk most with Socrates that night. He is a young man, noble and good in the way of a young gentleman, and his view of the gods would be the view he absorbed as an Athenian boy, the view passed down in the stories of Homer and Hesiod.

Now I have to pause here to say a little more about Adeimantus because it matters for what is happening here at the center. We know Adeimantus best from the long speech he had made earlier, a speech that helped force Socrates to take up the main question of the book: a defense of justice that was meant to persuade Adeimantus and the other young men that justice is better than injustice, being decent or moral is better than being immoral. In his long speech Adeimantus had expressed the beginnings of a moral rejection of the stories about the gods that he had been raised with, Homer's and Hesiod's stories about the gods. Adeimantus is a young man who has begun to lose his confidence in the stories about the gods that he had absorbed as a child.

To simplify and put that in a language familiar to us, young Adeimantus was beginning to experience a death of the gods. The Homeric gods, the old gods, the only gods he knew, were dying for him and he had good reason to be deeply shaken by that: if the gods were *immoral* as the stories seemed to imply, if the gods could be *bought*, if the gods even supported the *wicked*, then there seemed to be no good reason to be just—and Adeimantus, decent and noble young gentleman, dearly wants to continue being decent and noble, to continue being just, but if the gods themselves are *unjust* why should *he* take that hard and difficult way himself? This is a most important point because it helps define the times in which Plato acts. Plato is careful to define those times through the speeches of Adeimantus and his brother Glaucon: it is a time of the death of the gods for decent young men who have been brought into touch with the Greek enlightenment.

Second question: The other question at the center is about Timaeus's view of the gods. Timaeus is a philosopher, though Strauss does not mention that here. He is the philosopher Socrates will listen to in Plato's dialogue *Timaeus* as he lays out a whole cosmology, an account of the world as a whole. As a philosopher who shares the central place in Strauss's central paragraph with Adeimantus, Timaeus brings out what Adeimantus is not: Adeimantus is not a philosopher nor is he a potential philosopher. His interests lie elsewhere, with the poetry he learned as a boy and still loves and with the justice and decency that befits a young gentleman.

> It is true that Timaeus makes a distinction between the visible gods who revolve manifestly and those gods who manifest themselves so far as they choose, between the cosmic gods and the Olympian gods, and that no such distinction is made in the theology of the *Republic* where only the Olympian gods are identified.

The philosopher Timaeus makes a distinction with respect to the gods; he divides them into two categories of *cosmic* and *Olympian*, gods that are natural forces or entities like the sun and moon, and gods that are persons and who reveal themselves to humans. Strauss points this out because he wants to make the following point:

> But precisely this fact shows the "mythical" character of the theology or the gravity of the failure to raise and answer the question "what is a god?" or "who are the gods?"

So there is a *grave failure* in the discussion about the gods in the *Republic*, the failure to raise and answer the question "What is a god?" To understand that grave failure, I want to read something else. If you have studied Strauss's *The City and Man* you know how it ends. It ends with sentences I want to read now. So I interrupt our passage briefly to look to the end of Strauss's essay:

> ⋯ the pre–philosophic ⋯ city sees itself as subject and subservient to the divine in the ordinary understanding of the divine or looks up to it. Only by beginning at this point will we be open to the full impact of the all – important question which is coeval with philosophy although the philosophers do not frequently pronounce it—the question *quid sit deus*.

Notice that here at the very end of his book Strauss himself does not actually *pronounce* the question that the philosophers do not frequently pronounce: *What is a god? Or What might a god be?* Instead of pronouncing the question, he puts it in Latin. But in the central paragraph of his essay on Plato's *Republic* Strauss does pronounce it. He speaks of "the gravity of the failure" of Socrates and Adeimantus to raise and answer the question "what is a god?" or "who are the gods?"

Whose fault is that? Is it Adeimantus's? Adeimantus shows himself in the *Republic* not to be a philosopher or a potential philosopher. Why did Adeimantus not raise the question? Because Adeimantus *has no question*. Adeimantus *knows* what a god is. A god is what Homer and Hesiod said a god is. Adeimantus's question is not *what is a god?* his question is why the gods aren't more just than they are, more moral than they are, more worthy of being trusted than they are.

Not raising the question is Socrates' fault. Like the philosopher Timaeus the philosopher Socrates will have raised and answered the question of what a god is. But having raised and answered that question, a philosopher knows that it is *unwise* to frequently pronounce that question. And he does not pronounce it with Adeimantus.

Back in his central paragraph, after pronouncing the question himself, Strauss goes on:

> Other Socratic utterances might enable one to ascertain Socrates' answer, but they are of no use for ascertaining Adeimantus' answer and therewith for gauging how deep the agreement is which Socrates and Adeimantus achieve.

So Strauss points to Socrates' answer but does not give it. He leaves it to you to pursue that question, because he goes on here to what Socrates and Adeimantus agree on. There are various ways to pursue Socrates' answer. The easiest is to follow Strauss: he gives references for two such utterances in his Nietzsche essay. You can look them up to get a start on Socrates' answer: *Sophist* 216b5 – 6 refers to "a kind of refutative god" (the Stranger), and *Theaetetus* 151d1 – 2 says "They are far from knowing that no god is ill – disposed to human beings. " Both references suggest something remarkable: *philosophers* are gods; and the context in Strauss's

Nietzsche essay suggests just what that means as we will see in my Nietzsche lectures.

But the important thing for us at the center of Strauss's essay on the *Republic* is this: Why does Socrates fail to pronounce that question in the *Republic* or give his answer? The reason is that Socrates has a different purpose in speaking with young Adeimantus. He has no intention of raising the question of *what a god is* because in the *Republic* he is doing what Strauss said he was doing: laying down laws for the gods. Socrates is legislating what a god is for tortured Adeimantus, a young man who thinks he knows what a god is but is critical of the *actions* of the gods in the stories he was raised to believe and is tempted not to believe them or not to trust the gods. What Socrates does is alter or modify the gods Adeimantus thinks he knows in order to make them more moral, make them more worthy of Adeimantus's respect and honor.

If we look away from Strauss's central paragraph to the paragraph just before the central paragraph, we see that Strauss spoke there of how the *philosopher* was first introduced into the *Republic*. He was introduced in a way that corrected Socrates' earlier view of the arts—of the doing and making that humans engage in. In the corrected view of the arts, there is a hierarchy of arts where "the highest art, the art directing all the other arts ... will prove to be philosophy." So Strauss introduced that directing action of philosophy in the paragraph before his central paragraph. As an art, as a doing or making, philosophy is the highest or directing art; philosophy is the ruling art.

Plato himself put Socrates' famous statement that *the philosopher must rule* only later in his *Republic*. In fact Plato put that statement at the very center of the *Republic*. So what Strauss has done is move *Plato's* central statement to just before *his own* center. And it is very easy to see why Strauss did that: at the center of his essay on Plato's *Republic* Strauss shows just how what Plato put at the center of his *Republic* actually came about. At the center of his essay on the *Republic* Strauss shows how Socrates the philosopher actually ruled: a philosopher rules by laying down new laws for the gods; a philosopher rules by ruling the view of the gods that will rule the minds of the young men. If we look specifically to Adeimantus we can say that the philosopher rules by ruling the minds of young men like him who will welcome Socrates' reform of Homer's gods. Adeimantus stands for all noble young men rising to maturity in the crisis time in Athenian history when the very gods are mistrusted or doubted.

And Socrates' success in coming to rule the mind of Adeimantus and other young men like him points to Socrates' ultimate success: through Adeimantus and his like, Socrates' new legislation for the gods will rule the minds of all the boys and girls of the coming generations who will be raised in the views of their parents and who will continue to hold those views as grown – up citizens of the city. How the philosopher Socrates ruled—that is what Strauss put at the center of his essay on the *Republic*.

I turn now to general lessons from this central point.

Viewed *historically*—that is, looking at this event in the *Republic* against the background of the Greek past—we can say this: Homer and Hesiod, the founding Greek poets, the educators of Greece, were in their poetic way philosophic rulers through their gods and their heroes. But at the time of Plato's *Republic*, Homer's and Hesiod's gods were in crisis. Socrates in the *Republic* sets out to become a *philosophic ruler* during the crisis time of Homeric religion when Homer's gods were dying. That will be a theme of my first Plato lecture.

And viewed *historically* by looking backward from *Nietzsche's* perspective, we can say this: Socrates succeeded. Socrates became, as Nietzsche said, "the one turning point and vortex of so – called world history" (BT 15). That will be a theme of my Nietzsche lectures.

So, returning to Strauss's essay on Plato's *Republic*, we can see that at its center Strauss shows Socrates putting in place his *theological – political program*. And to quote Nietzsche again: since Plato, "all theologians and philosophers are on the same track" (BGE 191)

Now, in summary, I can say that this is part of what my coming five lectures will be about: the *theological – political programs* of the philosophers Plato and Nietzsche, what I call in my titles, their *philosophic poetry*. But of course there is something of even greater importance than philosophic poetry and my lectures will be about that as well. That more important matter is the *philosophy* that lies behind the theological – political programs, the understanding of *being* or *nature* that lies behind them or that generates them.

One way of looking at *philosophy itself* is this. In his final sentence of *The City and Man*, Strauss speaks of "the all – important question that is coeval with philosophy," the question, what is a god? That question is "*coeval*" with philosophy because it arises whenever and wherever philosophy arises. The reason it arises is that the question, What is a god?, is an *ontological* question, a question about *being*. It asks, what is the *highest possible being*? So while the question "What is a god?" has a practical dimension as it has in Socrates' discussion with Adeimantus, for a philosopher the essential dimension of the question is ontological; it is *theoretical* and not *practical*. It is a specific ontological question within the comprehensive ontological question; the comprehensive question asks, *What is the being of beings*?; a specific question within that question asks, *What is the highest being*?

So the two themes of the rest of my lectures are *philosophy* and *philosophic poetry* in Plato and Nietzsche. And my approach will be the approach of a reader: How does the distinction between the *exoteric* and the *esoteric* lead us to a proper understanding of *philosophy* and *philosophic poetry* in Plato and Nietzsche?

I want to end this first Strauss lecture on a point about Strauss. I focused on the central sentences of the central paragraph of his essay on the *Republic* not in order to demonstrate that Strauss too wrote exoterically. Of course he wrote exoterically. Instead, I focused on the central sentences of the central paragraph in order to show that what Strauss chose to treat at the center, *what a god is*, is not only an ontological question but becomes a part of a philosopher's legislation. We see from Strauss's central treatment of what a god is that legislating what a god is is in part an instrument in a philosopher's rule. Strauss shows that it is so with Plato, and it is also so with Nietzsche.

Plato himself returned to the issue of *what a god is* in the last book of the *Republic*, Book 10, in which Socrates forces a return to the topic of poetry and a resolution of the "*ancient quarrel between philosophy and poetry*"

Lecture 1   Strauss Recovers the Tradition of Philosophic Poetry

(607b). The resolution of the quarrel is based on the natural superiority of the wise, that is, the naturally legitimate rule of the philosopher. As the natural ruler, the philosopher employs poetry. And Book 10 shows that the most striking aspect of that poetry is the philosopher's new teaching on the gods and on the soul. The teaching that Socrates puts forward in Book 10 continues his legislation about the gods and the soul: he makes the gods the moral judges of human behavior and he makes the soul immortal, living out its next life in reward and punishment for its actions in this life.

Part of the long story of Western philosophy must include a large chapter on how *disastrous* this new teaching by Platonic philosophers turned out to be in opening the way for Revelation or Christianity. I will say more on that in later lectures but to end this lecture I will ignore that in order to end on a very fine phrase by Strauss describing this new Socratic legislation on the gods and the soul. He calls it *"ministerial poetry"* and both words are important. It is *poetry*, something made and made by human invention, human imagination. And that's where my titles on *"philosophic poetry"* come from. In its origins this use of the word *poetry* is Plato's use, and I'll deal with that in my Plato lectures. But here Strauss makes it his own by adding the word *ministerial* as an adjective to modify *poetry*. It is the *perfect word* because it has a double sense, *political* and *social*, and both senses apply.

Strauss emphasizes the political: *ministerial* in this sense means in the service of the ruler or government, for instance, the *Minister* of Finance serves the ruling government. Plato's new ministerial poetry of gods and the soul is in the service of the new king, the philosopher ruler; the new ministerial poetry serves the interests of philosophy and that is its ultimate reason for existence. But the exclusivity of that first sense is modified and beautified by the second sense that Strauss does not mention.

The verb *minister* carries a secondary sense in English, a *social* or *therapeutic* sense of giving aid or service to those in need of it; one *ministers* to the sick or the wounded in order to ease their distress. And that too is what philosophic ministerial poetry does: the Socratic poetry of moral gods and immortal souls gives aid and comfort to those like Adeimantus who suffer spiritually from the loss of their beliefs in justice and in the gods. And Adeimantus stands for a whole generation that will be ministered to by the new Socratic poetry.

That's why I use the phrase *philosophic poetry* in my titles: *philosophy*, the drive to understand, comes to understand; and out of that understanding it generates or gives birth to a poetry that *ministers* to *its* interests while ministering as well to the larger civil community within which alone philosophy can prosper. So my lectures are about "Philosophy and Its Poetry." They are about the *philosophy* of Plato and of Nietzsche, and I'll say right now and try to demonstrate in my lectures, the *philosophy* of Plato and Nietzsche seems to me to *converge* or to *share essentials* when Plato and Nietzsche are read as Strauss showed us how to read them. And my lectures are about the *philosophic poetry* of Plato and of Nietzsche and that poetry *diverges* radically or stands in warlike opposition, one against the other. And the divergence has reasons as good as the reason for the convergence regarding philosophy itself.

And finally my lectures are also about the *good reasons* for Nietzsche's opposition to Plato's philosophic poetry and why those reasons naturally turn *us* toward Nietzsche's philosophic poetry.

LECTURE 2

Strauss, Nietzsche and the Philosophic Poetry of the Future

In my first lecture, I looked at Strauss's recovery of exoteric writing in his letters to Klein and then at a text by Strauss that showed how he too wrote exoterically and, more importantly, how he led his reader to the esoteric heart of Plato's exoteric book, the *Republic*.

In today's lecture, I look at a text by Strauss that shows that he wrote exoterically about Nietzsche too, and, more importantly, led his reader to the esoteric heart of Nietzsche's exoteric book, *Beyond Good and Evil*. Today's lecture is a commentary on parts of Strauss's late essay, "Note on the Plan of Nietzsche's *Beyond Good and Evil*." It was written from March, 1972 to February, 1973; Strauss died seven months later, in September, 1973. Strauss arranged what he knew would be his last book, *Studies in Platonic Political Philosophy*, so that this essay on Nietzsche would occupy a special place in it. The book has a roughly chronological order from ancients through moderns but Strauss planned that his Nietzsche essay would be placed out of order at the center, paired with "Jerusalem and Athens" which it follows. This is a *structurally* significant move for a thinker who took centering to be part of a careful author's art, and who himself constantly practiced the art of centering in beautiful ways. It is an even more significant *thematic* move: after the long, historically defining conflict of Jerusalem and Athens comes Nietzsche.

Strauss's lifelong study following his discovery of the exotericism of the philosophers was Platonic political philosophy. Nietzsche had been the philosopher who so dominated and charmed him from his 22nd through his 30th year that he literally believed everything he understood of him. Although he ceased being simply dominated and charmed by Nietzsche in his 30th year, 1929, Strauss continued studying Nietzsche all his life. By putting his Nietzsche essay out of chronological order at the center of his last book, Strauss seems to be saying quietly: in the study of Platonic political philosophy, Nietzsche now occupies the central place, just after Jerusalem and Athens.

The opening of Strauss's essay: Nietzsche and Plato

Strauss opens his Nietzsche essay by singling out *Beyond Good and Evil* as Nietzsche's "most beautiful" book and to clarify what he means he moves in his very first paragraph to Plato and Plato's books. From the very beginning then, Strauss puts Nietzsche and Plato together. And he will put them together constantly throughout his essay including at the very end.

In his 3rd paragraph, Strauss notes that Nietzsche "presents himself as the antagonist of Plato" and he summarizes what he had said in his 2nd paragraph about Nietzsche and his most beautiful book by again referring to Plato: he says *Beyond Good and Evil* is the book in which Nietzsche "'platonizes' as regards the 'form' more than anywhere else." Nietzsche's way of presenting his thoughts in this book *platonizes*— Nietzsche's way resembles Plato's way of presenting *his* thoughts. Plato and Nietzsche are both exoteric writers who beautify their thoughts through what Strauss calls a "graceful subtlety as regards form, as regards intention, as regards the art of silence," crucial elements of the exoteric art: *form*, *intention*, and *an art of silence*.

Immediately after saying that, Strauss turns in his 4th paragraph to Nietzsche's preface to *Beyond Good and Evil*, specifically to Nietzsche the *antagonist* of Plato: "Plato's fundamental error was his invention of the pure mind and of the good in itself." Strauss then brings in Plato himself in order to make a very important point about *Plato's* artfulness in his invention of pure mind:

> From this premise one can easily be led to Diotima's conclusion that no human being is wise, but only the god is; human beings can only

strive for wisdom or philosophize; gods do not philosophize.

Strauss thus moves from Nietzsche's *opposition* to Plato's invention of the pure mind and the good in itself to a *defense* of Plato that brings in the gods from a dialogue by Plato. That dialogue moves the pure mind out of human beings and locates it only in the gods. Plato is subtle: his "fundamental error" seems not to be a statement about human minds but only about the gods' minds—and what could *that* mean?

Strauss's defense of Plato through Plato's subtlety then leads him to jump from the preface of Nietzsche's book to its very end:

> In the penultimate aphorism of *Beyond Good and Evil* in which Nietzsche delineates "the genius of the heart"—a super – Socrates who is in fact the god Dionysos—Nietzsche divulges after the proper preparation the novelty, suspect perhaps especially among philosophers, that gods too philosophize.

So is Plato *wrong* about the gods and their pure minds? Do the gods too philosophize as Nietzsche *divulges*? To divulge is to *reveal a secret*, perhaps a dangerous secret. If it is especially suspected among philosophers that gods philosophize, what about wise Diotima, Socrates' teacher in the *Symposium* who said they do not philosophize?

Strauss then does something he had learned to do very early as a careful reader: separate an author's *character*, a figure in a dialogue, from the author himself—he separates *Diotima* from *Plato* in order to make a most remarkable suggestion: "Plato could well have thought that gods philosophize (cf. *Sophist* 216b5 – 6, *Theaetetus* 151d1 – 2)." If you look up those two references you find that they suggest that the gods *do* philosophize—and more than that, they suggest that the gods who philosophize are the *philosophers themselves*.

So Strauss suggests that *Plato* held a different view from what he had his *Diotima* teach. But more importantly than that for us, Strauss, at the beginning of his Nietzsche essay, arranges or engineers a contrast between Nietzsche and his apparent *antagonist* Plato that forces us to think about whether Plato himself really held what Nietzsche said was his "fundamental error." Did Plato the philosopher make that error in his own thinking? Or did Plato the philosopher find it desirable to have his Diotima, Socrates' teacher, *teach* that view?

By setting up the contrast and then simply giving two references Strauss suggests to a reader who is paying attention that Plato *thought* what Nietzsche thought but found it desirable to *teach* something different through Diotima. And that suggests that Strauss thought that Nietzsche and his antagonist Plato really thought the same thing about the gods and philosophy, the difference being that Nietzsche divulged the secret about the gods philosophizing by introducing the philosophizing god Dionysos.

But Nietzsche himself suggested that "this novelty" was not entirely a novelty because it was "suspect perhaps especially among philosophers." Nietzsche may well know that the novelty he introduces is no novelty at all but a thing long known to philosophers, though covered up by philosophers like his antagonist Plato who had his Diotima teach the opposite. So Nietzsche's platonizing, his "graceful subtlety as regards form ··· intention ··· [and] the art of silence," includes divulging about the gods what Plato also thought but did not divulge, or divulged only to a reader like Strauss who looks away from what Diotima taught to other passages in Plato to discover what Plato really thought.

So in his Nietzsche essay, Strauss almost begins—not by *divulging* secretive Plato's secret view but by subtlety indicating that Plato knew the same truth Nietzsche knew but kept it secret while Nietzsche divulged it. By pointing to Plato's secret, Strauss points to a feature of Plato's own platonizing in a context where he is examining Nietzsche's platonizing. And by pointing to Plato's secret, Strauss suggests that Diotima tells a *noble lie* about the gods that serves Plato's political purpose for philosophy. And Nietzsche, Strauss may also suggest, divulged that secret in order to serve *his* political purpose for philosophy.

And here I draw a conclusion that only the rest of my lectures can show to be valid: Plato and Nietzsche platonize for the same reason, the well – being of philosophy; they platonize in the service of philosophy. Their difference in keeping secret and divulging—on the matter of the gods and philosophy! —can be traced to the same reason: each interpreted the spiritual situation of their times and each taught what the times required for the well-being of philosophy.

Strauss contrasts Nietzsche and Plato throughout his essay but because we don't have time to consider all of those occasions, I jump to the very end of Strauss's essay with *its* contrast of Nietzsche and Plato. The issue is no longer the gods but the virtues, a crucial matter of morality, one of the themes of the second main part of Nietzsche's book. The specific issue is the virtues as part of "the philosophy of the future" to which, Nietzsche said, *Beyond Good and Evil* is a "prelude." In particular, the issue is "the virtues of the philosopher of the future." Strauss brings in Plato by saying that those virtues "differ from the Platonic virtues." In Strauss's example two of the Platonic virtues are replaced by two modern virtues. And the last sentences of his essay say: "This is one illustration among many of what [Nietzsche] means by characterizing nature by its 'Vornehmheit' (aph. 188). *Die vornehme Natur ersetzt die göttliche Natur.*"

And that's the end. Strauss ends his English essay with a German sentence. He hides his meaning in a foreign language, Nietzsche's language. The sentence says "*Noble nature replaces divine nature.*" That is, nature as Nietzsche taught it, noble nature, replaces nature as Plato taught it, nature and the super-natural that transcends it. Does Strauss mean to *endorse* that replacement? Does Strauss's essay-long contrast between Nietzsche and Plato end on his own veiled recommendation of Nietzsche's teaching on nature as replacing Plato's teaching on nature? Strauss left it veiled. So for now at least we can leave it veiled.

I want to end this first part of this lecture on another aspect of Strauss's contrast between Plato and Nietzsche on *platonizing*. Toward the beginning of his essay, Strauss calls attention to the over-all structure Nietzsche gave his book, its "plan" as divided into nine chapters. Strauss emphasizes that Chapters 1 and 2 are on philosophy and Chapter 3 is on religion and that these three chapters are separated from the later chapters by a chapter of "about 123 'Sayings and Interludes.'" This separating chapter divides the book into 2 main parts. Strauss's conclusion about this form Nietzsche gave his book is that "Philosophy and religion, it seems, belong together." Part of Nietzsche's platonizing as regards form puts philosophy and religion together and separates them from morals and politics; Nietzsche separates the two most important things from the also important things. Now I can turn to just *how* philosophy and religion belong together for Nietzsche.

Nietzsche's philosophy chapters

Chapter One of *Beyond Good and Evil* is "On the Prejudices of the Philosophers": it criticizes those prejudices in order to free the mind from them. Chapter Two, "The Free Mind," is also on philosophy and it sets out what a free mind can attain, what Nietzsche's free mind has already attained. Part of the platonizing form of Chapter Two is that Nietzsche gave it a meaningful center.

Strauss begins his first paragraph on the philosophy chapters with this sentence: "Nietzsche says very little about religion in the first two chapters." Of course he does: these are the chapters on *philosophy*. Strauss's sentence makes it clear that his interest here is *religion*, religion's presence in the philosophy chapters. Strauss's ultimate interest is of course philosophy. But this is a writing by Strauss and *its* chief interest is religion in the philosopher Nietzsche, Nietzsche's theological – political program or his *philosophic poetry* in its aspect as religion. Strauss's next sentences say:

> One could say that he speaks there on religion only in a single aphorism which happens to be the shortest (37). That aphorism is a kind of corollary to the immediately preceding one in which he sets forth in the most straightforward and unambiguous manner that is compatible with his intention, the particular character of his fundamental proposition according to which life is will to power or seen from within the world is will to power and nothing else.

Notice: Strauss says "a single aphorism" on religion and that single aphorism is "a kind of corollary" or consequence of the preceding aphorism which contains Nietzsche's *fundamental proposition*. Notice too that Strauss suggests that Nietzsche "sets forth" his "fundamental proposition" in a manner that is not completely straightforward or unambiguous: Nietzsche is not

Lecture 2 Strauss, Nietzsche and the Philosophic Poetry of the Future

completely open with his fundamental proposition; he has a particular intention in the way he sets it out. But Strauss's main point is at the end: Nietzsche's "fundamental proposition" concerns *life* in Nietzsche's sense and life in that sense is simply "the world," the whole of things. We would say, in the language of philosophy that Nietzsche refuses to use, that his fundamental proposition concerns *being as such*; it is an *ontology*, a statement about the nature or character of beings as a whole: "seen from within," seen the way we can never actually see it, "the world is will to power and nothing else." Strauss is clear: *will to power* is Nietzsche's name for the being of beings, the nature of nature.

Strauss then connects Nietzsche's ontology with Plato's ontology:

> The will to power takes the place which the *eros*—the striving for "the good in itself"—occupies in Plato's thought.

Strauss's definition of *eros* here, *the good in itself*, is part of what he had said was Nietzsche's view of Plato's fundamental error. For me that shows Strauss's intention: he has no intention of setting out the relation between Nietzsche's ontology and Plato's ontology in a completely straightforward or unambiguous manner; he keeps that relation somewhat more ambiguous than it actually is.

Strauss goes on in the paragraph to touch on an issue that lies behind the whole history of exoteric teachings in philosophy, the recognition by philosophers that the truths they discover are dangerous, and Strauss uses Nietzsche's word for that, "*deadly*." Both will to power and *eros* give expression to a truth about reality that is *deadly*. As Seth Benardete said, to begin his account of *eros* in Plato's *Symposium*: "The truth about Eros is terrifying." What does Nietzsche do with the fundamental truth that he regarded as deadly? Strauss says this:

> Nietzsche's statements or suggestions are deliberately enigmatic (aph. 40). By suggesting or saying that the truth is deadly, he does his best to break the power of deadly truth; he suggests that the most important, the most comprehensive truth—the truth regarding all truths—is life – giving.

"*Deliberately enigmatic*" : Nietzsche is obscure on purpose, obscure in order to suggest something; "*aph.* 40" speaks about the necessity of masks for everything "profound. " What is *deliberately enigmatic* about saying that "the most comprehensive truth" is *deadly*? Strauss says that it is Nietzsche's way of beginning to *break* its deadly power. This is crucial. The comprehensive truth at first *looks* deadly, but it is actually *life – giving*. Seen correctly what looks deadly is life – giving. And Strauss will show that Nietzsche does exactly that in the passage that will say it only once : Nietzsche shows how what appears deadly is in fact the opposite. That is coming as the main point of my lecture.

To get to that point, Strauss treats another aspect of Nietzsche's platonizing as regards form : the *structure* he gave to his series of aphorisms. Nietzsche arranged the series with great care, as Strauss shows by calling attention to the central aphorisms of this chapter on the free mind :

> The connection between aphorism 34 and 35 is a particularly striking example of the lucid, if somewhat hidden, order governing the sequence of aphorisms : the desultory character of Nietzsche's argument is more pretended than real.

What looks *desultory*, or seems to lack a definite plan or purpose, is in fact *lucid* or clear if *somewhat hidden*. Why pretend there is no plan or purpose when there is a plan or purpose? Strauss does not say but it's obvious and frequent in Nietzsche : pretending there is no plan or purpose allows you to *notice* a plan and then to work to discover the *purpose* of the plan. *You* discover it, *you* make it your own : you realize Nietzsche is teaching you.

Strauss's next paragraph begins with this : "We can now turn to the two aphorisms in BGE I – II that can be said to be devoted to religion (36 – 37). " We can now turn to what Strauss had said was *one paragraph* devoted to religion but now says is *two paragraphs* devoted to religion. He will correct himself by returning to one paragraph but to say *two* makes you look for a reason to say it and the reason seems to be the connection between the religion aphorism and the one just before it, a connection that reflects the connection between 34 and 35 and is of high importance: "Aphorism 36 presents the reasoning in support of the doctrine of the will to power."

Aphorism 36 is *reasoning*; it is philosophy. Aphorism 37 is only *a kind of corollary* because it follows the reasoning with something that is not reasoning but that belongs to religion. Strauss does not repeat the reasoning of section 36. Instead, he judges it, assigning it very high praise indeed: it combines "what is at the same time the most intransigent intellectual probity and the most bewitching playfulness." The reasoning combines the strictest philosophical logical seriousness and play. The intellectual probity of the reasoning of section 36 pursues strictly logical inference about what the mind can know of the self, the other and the world as a whole. The reasoning of section 36 draws the conclusion that the world, the totality, seen from inside, would be will to power and nothing else. The most bewitching playfulness follows in section 37 where the reasoning triggers horror in Nietzsche's "friends" and indispensable help that Nietzsche offers his friends. The reasoning and the play are a pinnacle of philosophic communication on the fundamental matters.

I will look at the reasoning in my last Nietzsche lecture. Here I want to call attention only to Strauss's emphasis that aphorism 36 is philosophic method applied to nature as a whole. In his philosophy chapters, Nietzsche leads his reader to a comprehensive rational conclusion about the nature of nature, about what philosophy ultimately seeks. Strauss sets that out even more briefly than Nietzsche did because he has already told us that his essay is concerned with *religion* in *Beyond Good and Evil*. Religion cannot be more important than philosophy but Strauss chose to focus on religion, that is, on philosophic poetry. After the reasoning comes the kind of corollary or inference. Strauss shows that that corollary is what the reasoning draws out of the audience that hears it, draws out of the free minds that Nietzsche is training. The free minds respond to the reasoning but not with more reasoning, not with *philosophy*, but with a deeply human reaction to philosophy's rational conclusion, the response Nietzsche anticipates even from his best prepared, free – minded friends.

So we move to paragraph 9, to the "kind of corollary," to Nietzsche's "fundamental proposition:" "After having tempted some of his readers (cf. aph. 30) with the doctrine of the will to power Nietzsche makes them raise the question as to whether that doctrine does not assert, to speak popularly, that God is refuted but the devil is not."

Which readers does Nietzsche tempt by forcing them to raise that question? Strauss quotes Nietzsche's answer next; it is addressed to "my friends"—Nietzsche tempts his "friends," the free minds, those he makes his friends by what he teaches them. But here they face a serious problem. By saying "(cf. aph. 30)," Strauss suggests that we should think of Nietzsche's readers with the distinction in mind that Nietzsche made in aphorism 30, his only explicit reference to the exoteric and the esoteric. If you do what Strauss says and read aph. 30 you see that Nietzsche says that the philosopher's "highest insights" will sound foolish and sometimes like crimes when they come to the ears of "those who are not the kind for them." In section 37 Nietzsche suggests that even his potential friends, those who *are* the kind for it, will hear the highest insight of his reasoning in the way aphorism 30 says: they will judge, that's *madness*; that's *criminal*. Nietzsche says that his friends *speak popularly* in speaking of God and the devil. But his friends are the free minds; they do not believe in God or the devil. But as modern free minds they no longer have a language that can state strongly enough just how *criminal* they find Nietzsche's conclusion. So they adopt the old language, the popular language for a moment and use *its* extremes, God and devil, to express their shock at his crime.

Having only paraphrased what Nietzsche's friends say, Strauss *quotes* what Nietzsche himself says: "He replies 'On the contrary! On the contrary, my friends! And, to the devil, what forces you to speak popularly?'"

Nietzsche is emphatic, repeating "On the contrary!" But he does not explain what the "contrary" is, nor does Strauss. So the reader has to think it out for himself. It's not hard. The contrary to "God is refuted" is "the devil is refuted." The transcendent God of Christian theology is what Nietzsche's friends think of as God; they are post-Christian atheists whose only concept of God is the Christian God. And if it's true that the totality of the world is will to power and nothing else, there is nothing beyond the world different from the world. Nietzsche's reasoning refutes a transcendent God. But the transcendent God of Christianity had condemned the world as the kingdom of darkness, as the place of the devil from which he would redeem us. So the contrary that Nietzsche's friends must think is that *that* God, the refuted God, is the *devil*, the refuted devil. Nietzsche invites his friends to think the greatest blasphemy. When they do what Nietzsche suggests and think the contrary, they think on their own the great blasphemy that Nietzsche himself does not pronounce. Strauss noted a similar technique in Machiavelli and gave the reason for it: it forces the reader to become Machiavelli's *accomplice*, the reader thinks the shocking thought.

The other half of Nietzsche's "On the contrary!" is the great lesson in theology that Nietzsche teaches his Christian – atheist, free – minded friends: the contrary to "the devil is not [refuted]," is "God is not." Nietzsche thus suggests that his will to power view has a place for God, or for *gods* as we will see. Nietzsche's friends must broaden their thinking about God or gods.

After we think through the two contraries as both Nietzsche and Strauss silently invite us to do, we come in Strauss's translation to: "And to the devil, what forces you to speak popularly?" Nietzsche's German word that Strauss translates "what" is *wer* or *who*: Nietzsche asks "*who* forces you?" That's important because there is an implied answer to *who* forces you: Nietzsche's friends do not believe in God or the devil. So the *who* forcing them to "speak popularly" of God and the devil must be *the dead God* himself. The transcendent God is dead but not *gone*. The dead God still defines even for Nietzsche's free – minded friends *what a God is*. The two thousand years old tradition is still powerful in its late atheists— when they think of "God" they think only of *that* God, the dead God, still powerful as their only idea of God. If the will to power view does *not refute God*, then Nietzsche's friends are going to have to start thinking differently about what a god is.

So the combination of reasoning and play in aphorisms 36 and 37 allows Strauss to end this key little paragraph saying, "The doctrine of the will to power—the whole doctrine of *Beyond Good and Evil*—is in a manner a vindication of God. " Nietzsche's ontology, his view of the world seen from the inside, *vindicates God*, as Strauss says and says five times. Nietzsche's ontology introduces a new way to think about divinity, about what a god is. Strauss has led his reader into the heart of this *temptation* by Nietzsche. The philosopher Nietzsche, having thought about what a god is, will offer a new teaching on the gods. That new teaching may not be all that new: at the beginning of his Nietzsche essay, Strauss had suggested that Nietzsche and Plato may not differ on what a god is, that the "super – Socrates," the philosophizing god Dionysos, may represent a shared view of what a god is. We can leave that issue for a moment and ask instead:

Why would Nietzsche *vindicate* God, why would he free God from blame or justify God? Even if "God" now means something entirely different from the transcendent God, why not just be atheist? Strauss answers that question without ever asking it directly: he ends his paragraph saying: "(Cf. aph. 150 and 295, as well as *Genealogy of Morals*, Preface Nr. 7.)"

Strauss refers to aphorism 150 later to suggest that for Nietzsche there can be no livable "world" for humans without gods. Nietzsche seems to agree with Plato and the philosophic tradition that gods are necessary for a healthy social order. As for "aph. 295," it is the long aphorism that Strauss had already quoted on the "super – Socrates" who is in fact the god Dionysos. And Strauss's other reference, "*Genealogy of Morals* Pref. No. 7," speaks of a new complication and possibility for "the Dionysian drama of the ' Destiny of the Soul' " and of Dionysos himself as taking advantage of that new possibility, he, "the great old eternal comic poet of our existence!" In keeping with that reference, Strauss opens his account of the religion chapter as Nietzsche opened that chapter, on "the whole history of the soul hitherto"—for Nietzsche, the history of religion offers a history of the human soul at the point of a new complication and possibility for the human soul perhaps in some way connected to the super – Socrates Dionysos.

Strauss ends his account of the philosophy chapters in *Beyond Good and Evil* on the one aphorism on religion in those chapters. He ends his treatment of philosophy with Nietzsche's invitation to his philosophically inclined friends to think differently about what a god is, to think about divinity free of Biblical transcendence, to think of divinity in connection with the fundamental proposition, to think of the implications of the will to power ontology for God or gods. More specifically, Strauss ends his account of philosophy saying that the ultimate conclusion of philosophy's reasoning, the world is will to power and nothing else, is a vindication of God and he adds three references to help you think about a new view of the gods. Perhaps Nietzsche's *philosophy* can generate a new view of the gods, a new poetry of divinity for humans whose world can turn only around a god. After suggesting that promise of Nietzsche's *philosophy* for religion, Strauss moves directly to Nietzsche's chapter on religion.

Nietzsche's religion chapter

Strauss first lays out *the plan* of the religion chapter: it deals with religion up till now and the religion of the future and religion as a whole. Strauss treats in greatest detail the series of aphorisms that deal with religion today and in the future. Nietzsche treats religion today in aphorisms 53 and 54, the central two of his chapter; one is on *atheism* today, the other is on *the assassination of the soul* today. Contemporary thought rejects these two central Christian teachings on God and the soul. The next aphorism, 55, deals with the consequence of today's atheism and soul – assassination as something far worse even than Christianity: modern nihilism, though neither Nietzsche nor Strauss uses the word *nihilism*. Strauss treats the step after nihilism in a separate paragraph.

"Nietzsche does not mean to sacrifice God for the sake of the Nothing, for while recognizing the deadly truth that God died he aims at transforming it into a life – inspiring one or rather to discover in the depth of the deadly truth its opposite." Strauss says "*aims at transforming it*"—but he knows that's wrong, that's not what Nietzsche did and he corrects himself: "or rather" Nietzsche *discovers* the opposite, discovers an unexpected fact—nothing needs to be transformed; instead, Nietzsche discovers the opposite to deadly truth. So the movement here is similar to what Strauss had said earlier about Nietzsche's "deliberately enigmatic" statements:

what first appears deadly is in truth "life – giving." Strauss then turns to aphorism 56, the one directly after the nihilism aphorism. He paraphrases, quotes, and comments on this most important aphorism in the religion chapter, the single aphorism on eternal return.

"But Nietzsche, prompted by 'some enigmatic desire,' has tried for a long time to penetrate pessimism to its depth ···. He thus has grasped a more world – denying way of thinking than that of any previous pessimist." The "enigmatic desire" can only be *the passion to know* that has driven Nietzsche in his inquiry. Penetrating pessimism to its depth, Nietzsche arrives at what seems to be the most world – denying way of thinking, the way of thinking that views the world as will to power and nothing else—to which his friends first reacted as horrifyingly world denying.

"Yet a man who has taken this road has perhaps without intending to do this opened his eyes to the opposite ideal—to the ideal belonging to the religion of the future." That's exactly what Nietzsche says: "opened his eyes to the opposite ideal." That ideal is the eternal return of everything that is, and it is important that both Nietzsche and Strauss call it an *ideal*. But why add that ambiguous "*perhaps*" that could mean *perhaps without intending to do so*? Strauss's next sentence explains the *perhaps* as Nietzsche did not:

"It goes without saying that what in some other men was 'perhaps' the case was a fact in Nietzsche's thought and life." No, it does not "go without saying," it has to be said and Strauss has to say it because some of his followers maintained that Nietzsche was fundamentally *looking for* a new ideal, that Nietzsche was most basically a religious teacher in search of a new ideal to counter the absence of ideals in our now nihilistic culture. Strauss says with this clarification of *perhaps* what Nietzsche himself said: he did not *mean* to discover a new ideal, he discovered it "without actually meaning to do so."

So again Strauss corrects himself, as he did with *transform* and *discover*, and both corrections say the same thing: Nietzsche is a *philosopher*, not a *religious thinker*. Nietzsche's thought and life intended one thing: to discover the true. He did not *intend* to find a new ideal; instead, he found a new ideal as a consequence of his passion for the truth, as a consequence of his discovery that the world is will to power and nothing else.

That discovery had as an unintended consequence his glimpsing a new ideal. This is the important sequence that allowed Nietzsche to move from philosophy to religion: his discovery of the truth opened his eyes on a new ideal; philosophy led to philosophic poetry.

"The adoration of the Nothing proves to be the indispensable transition from every kind of world – denial to the most unbounded Yes: the eternal Yes – saying to everything that was and is." The unexpected insight of the truth – seeker who thinks nihilism to its depth is the new ideal that the world as it is returns *just as it is* an infinite number of times. Strauss goes on in his paragraph to make some interesting comments about that ideal that I have omitted; he then quotes the end of the aphorism:

"'And this,' Nietzsche concludes his suggestion regarding eternal repetition of what was and is, 'would not be *circulus vitiosus deus*?'" The Latin phrase is ambiguous as Strauss notes: A vicious circle made god? God is a vicious circle? Strauss makes two important comments. First, "[Nietzsche's] atheism is not unambiguous, for he had doubts whether there can be a world, any world whose center is not God (aph. 150)." There it is again, aph. 150, which Nietzsche seems to have made the central aphorism of *Beyond Good and Evil*. It suggests, Strauss indicates, that only around a god can things become a world; the human world, the *lived world*, the cultural world as a place of meaning and significance, is possible only with god or gods. Nietzsche's atheism is ambiguous because he suggests that gods are necessary, socially necessary, necessary for there to be a cultural world.

Second, "The conclusion of the present aphorism [56] reminds us, through its form, of the theological aphorism occurring in the first two chapters (37) where Nietzsche brings out the fact that in a manner the doctrine of the will to power is a vindication of God, if a decidedly non – theistic vindication of God." (Note incidentally that Strauss returns to his true judgment: *the* theological aphorism in the philosophy chapters, *the one*, is 37, his friends' mistaken reaction to his will to power view that God is refuted but the devil is not.) Strauss restated the end of aphorism 56: would eternal return "not be *circulus vitiosus deus*?" If that "reminds us" of aphorism 37 then *we* have to add something: we have to say what

Nietzsche said in 37: "On the contrary! On the contrary, my friends."
The contrary here is that eternal return is not a *vicious* circle but, on the
contrary, the *virtuous* circle of life made eternal, made god in some sense.
Eternal return is the making divine of the whole natural cycle of things. E-
ternal return is a non – theistic vindication of God.

So Strauss leads his reader to see that in aphorism 56 Nietzsche shows
his friends the *genuine response* to understanding the world as will to power
and nothing else. The will to power view does not *refute* God but instead
leads to a new ideal, even to a new conception of divinity.

I said in my 1996 book, *Leo Strauss and Nietzsche*, that this insight into the connection between will to power and eternal return, between philosophy and religion, is Strauss's greatest contribution to Nietzsche studies. It is an *exegetical* contribution, the contribution of a most exceptional
reader with lifelong experience in reading Platonic political philosophers.
Strauss shows that *he* is the reader Nietzsche wants; *he* gives the proper interpretation to the two most important conclusions in *Beyond Good and E-
vil*. First comes *philosophy*'s deepest insight: to be is to be will to power
and nothing else. Second comes its corollary for *religion*: the new view of
what is leads to a new highest ideal, the affirmation of the world as it is,
and it leads to a vindication of god, of what alone can make a world possible for humans.

Strauss saw the inner coherence of Nietzsche's thinking as Nietzsche
laid it out in the first three chapters of *Beyond Good and Evil*. That inner
coherence is the deepest *platonizing* in Nietzsche: that is, in Nietzsche as
in Plato, philosophy at its deepest *generates* or *gives birth to* a political philosophy or philosophic poetry in the form of a theological – political program. This is the ultimate way that Nietzsche is a *Platonic political philosopher*, a philosopher who succeeded in doing what Plato did. First comes
the *esoteric insight* into the world reserved for the philosopher, wholly a
matter for the intellect. Then comes *an exoteric teaching* for all, a teaching
founded on the human passions that makes a mere totality into a world, a
livable world for human communities.

My Plato lectures will treat both these matters in Plato: Plato's account of *philosophy's deepest insight* into *eros*, and Plato's account of *philosophic poetry*, the *platonism* that was the result of Plato's understanding

of the spiritual situation of his time, the platonism that came to dominate Western philosophy. And my Nietzsche lectures will treat both these matters in Nietzsche: Nietzsche's *philosophic insight* into will to power as the fundamental fact; and Nietzsche's *philosophic poetry* as reasoned opposition to Plato's platonism that was the result of Nietzsche's understanding of the spiritual situation of our time.

I want to quote one last statement from Strauss's account of Nietzsche's religion chapter: "There is an important ingredient, not to say the nerve, of Nietzsche's 'theology' of which I have not spoken and shall not speak since I have no access to it."

This is emphatic. This is vehement. This is Strauss's adamant refusal to speak. I want to speak about that but I will wait until my Nietzsche lectures to speak about *the nerve* of Nietzsche's theology as his actual reintroduction of gods, of what he seems to regard as necessary to make a world. But now, to end my Strauss lectures, I want to move to the most important point in his treatment of Nietzsche's chapters on morals and politics.

Nietzsche's chapters on morals and politics

Strauss has shown that in Nietzsche philosophy generates a new highest ideal as philosophic poetry. But Strauss also shows that in Nietzsche philosophy generates a program for *morality*, a new good and bad that is fundamentally different from the good and evil of Platonism. Here, I will deal with only one point in Strauss's treatment of morals and politics. It arises at the end of his account of the chapter, "Our Virtues" where he shows how a new teaching on human virtue arises out of Nietzsche's new understanding of nature. Strauss emphasizes that Nietzsche the philosopher aimed to see again "the terrible basic text of homo natura," of human nature, the "eternal basic text," as Nietzsche called it. And Nietzsche went beyond *seeing* human nature, to *act* on what he *saw*. His action concerns how "man is to be 'retranslated into nature,'" how man can be "made natural" after thousands of years of moral thinking according to which humanity is in some way both subnatural and supernatural.

So we get to Strauss's paragraph 35, the most important paragraph of this part of Strauss's essay, where he speaks of "···an order of rank of the natures; at the summit of the hierarchy is the complementary man." Nietzsche says *complementary man* once in *Beyond Good and Evil*. Strauss says it five times. It is Nietzsche's name for *the philosopher* at this point in human history, the philosopher as thinker and actor. Strauss has some remarkable things to say about the complementary man that I have to omit. But the following sentence may be Strauss's most thought – provoking sentence in the essay: "His supremacy [the supremacy of the complementary man] is shown by the fact that he solves the highest, the most difficult problem."

Strauss is very careful with his words. He does not say, *aims* to solve the highest, the most difficult problem or *tries* to solve it. He says *solves* it. What is that problem? Strauss states it as *the problem of late modern times*, the problem facing a philosopher who lives in the maturity of modern times when *the ideal* that rules modern times has itself become the problem.

I have to say one thing about modern times that my six lectures do not give me space to enlarge in detail. *Modern times* are the times of the *technological mastery of nature* based on the *scientific understanding of nature*. That revolutionary way of thinking and acting did not just happen; it was the result of concerted work by *philosophers* who judged it to be necessary—this is one of the most important events in Western history and in global history. It is an amazing chapter in the history of Western philosophy when the foundation of modern times is laid by philosophers of whom the most important seem to me to be Francis Bacon and René Descartes. They judged it necessary to launch the view whose problematic outcome is what Strauss here addresses. I will expand a bit on that at the end of this lecture.

Strauss defines the problem in his next two sentences: "As we have observed, for Nietzsche nature has become a problem and yet he cannot do without nature. Nature, we may say, has become a problem owing to the fact that man is conquering nature and there are no assignable limits to that conquest."

Our common understanding of the problem of the conquest of nature is the problem of modern technological science in its effort to master nature:

the ecological disasters that the attempted mastery of nature can generate. But here, Strauss follows Nietzsche in identifying the problem differently. The problem of "no assignable limits" to the conquest of nature is the problem of the conquest of *human nature*, a conquest that is the direct result of *modern virtue*.

Strauss identifies the problem: "As a consequence, people have come to think of abolishing suffering and inequality."

These are the two chief features of modern virtue according to Nietzsche: the *abolition of suffering* and *equality of rights*. As Nietzsche showed, they are the modern, secular version of Christian virtue. They pose the fundamental problem for Nietzsche for one reason only, the reason Strauss identifies: "Yet suffering and inequality are the prerequisites of human greatness (aph. 239 and 257)." The greatness that matters most is the greatest human greatness, philosophy itself, the attainment of insight by the highest human spirituality, and the necessary action that that insight alone can see to be necessary. Strauss's point is Nietzsche's point: the limitless conquest of nature threatens to bring about the *end of philosophy*.

Strauss then turns to *Thus Spoke Zarathustra* to build on what he had said earlier. I have to omit that because I haven't discussed the earlier points. But for us it is enough to read the end of the paragraph. Strauss's last sentence says this: "Nature, the eternity of nature, owes its being to a postulation, to an act of the will to power on the part of the highest nature." Strauss's wording ties Nietzsche's act of solving the highest, the most difficult problem to similar acts by the great philosophers across the history of philosophy. The key word is *postulation*—it means to *posit something as true* or to *claim that something is true*. To *postulate* something as true is what all the great legislative philosophers have done. The actions of the highest natures, the history-making philosophers, postulate as true what they see as beneficial to philosophy and humanity in their times. What begin as a philosopher's legislative postulations come to be lived as true by the social order that gradually embraces them. Such postulations by the philosophers are all what Strauss says Nietzsche's postulation is: acts of the will to power on the part of the highest natures.

Strauss says Nietzsche's act of *postulation* concerns the eternity of nature, the eternal return of nature. He does not say at the end what he had already said at the start: Nietzsche's postulation of eternal return solves the highest, most difficult problem of the conquest of nature that knows no assignable limits. *Just how* does Nietzsche's postulation solve that problem? Strauss does not say directly but the whole drift of what his essay has been saying provides the answer, Nietzsche's answer. The doctrine of eternal return solves the highest problem because it is a *preservative* teaching, the ultimate *conservatism*, as Strauss says somewhat ironically.

Eternal return is not fundamentally a cosmological proposition; it is not fundamentally a *description* of the way the world is, although it may be lived that way by most people. Instead, all of Nietzsche's accounts of eternal return agree that it a statement of *desire*, the desire of a lover: the lover says to *the world as it is*, the totality as it naturally is, *that's* what I want and I want it an infinite number of times just as it is. It may be trivializing to say it, but it is the love of that lover that assigns limits to the conquest of nature, *beloved* nature. Beloved nature, beginning with beloved human nature is not to be conquered through alteration but celebrated as it is. That trivial – sounding solution is in fact profound and wholly non – Romantic, based as it is on Nietzsche's analysis of the human passions and in particular on his analysis of the passion for *revenge* and the ways in which that passion has won historical supremacy and grounded our view of good and bad.

Strauss's essay on Nietzsche almost ends on the argument he makes that the complementary man solves the highest, most difficult problem. I take this to be one of Strauss's most important insights into Nietzsche. It is an insight into an aspect of Nietzsche's thinking that I have spelled out in my books on Nietzsche. From my first book on I have argued that Nietzsche's philosophy is *the first comprehensive ecological philosophy*, the philosophy whose moral imperative is the one that Nietzsche's Zarathustra announced at his beginning: "Be true to the earth!" or "Be loyal to the earth!"

That's almost where Strauss ends his essay, and that is where I end my Strauss lectures. The complementary man *solves* the highest, the most difficult problem. I find that breathtaking. For me, there is no stronger *endorsement* of Nietzsche than that. Nietzsche *solves* the highest, most difficult problem of late modern times, the problem of assigning limits to the conquest of nature. Of all the things I find wonderful in Strauss, I find nothing more wonderful than that.

That ends my Strauss lectures but Strauss will continue to be present throughout the rest of my lectures. The distinction between the *exoteric* and the *esoteric* that Strauss recovered in the history of philosophy will be present in my lectures on Plato and Nietzsche as the distinction both drew between *philosophy* and its *poetry*.

With Plato, Strauss showed how to read Plato in a new way that is actually the old way, the classical way. That way of reading recovers the genuine Plato, the Plato that Strauss said was "nearest my heart." I will use Strauss in aid of my main topic in Plato, a theme that Strauss noticed but did not develop himself: *How Socrates became Socrates*, the double story of how Socrates became the philosopher and political philosopher who Nietzsche said was the one turning point and vortex of so – called world history.

With Nietzsche, I will use Strauss more directly but my main point will be one that Strauss did not develop: *How Nietzsche became Nietzsche*, the story of Nietzsche's becoming himself that he thought it was necessary for him to tell. I will use Nietzsche's autobiographical remarks to trace his becoming, but mostly I will look closely at a private notebook in which Nietzsche's becoming is displayed involuntarily in the chronological order of his notebook entries.

So my Plato and Nietzsche lectures look to the beginning of the *ancient* or *classical* tradition and to the other extreme, the end of the *modern* tradition in our time. And Strauss, I will show, provides indispensable aid for those extremes in what I called in my second book, *Nietzsche and Modern Times*, "the new history of philosophy made possible by Friedrich Nietzsche." That new history, aided by Strauss, can show that philosophy took a new turn with Plato or Socrates, a turn that ended with Nietzsche's conscious, anti – platonic turn to a new way. That new history of philosophy necessarily highlights a transition point between the two extremes of Plato and Nietzsche that I will not be able to treat in any detail in these lectures. That turning point is the founding of the modern world by philosophers fully aware of what they were doing and why they were doing it. I will say only a few words about it here.

The Founding of the Modern World

The founding of the modern world in Western Europe is the great event in philosophy and philosophy's poetry that still surrounds us, the wave that still "bears us today" as Strauss said. That European event has become a global event as its founders knew it would. It was a *philosophic* event in which the greatest philosophers of the time united to defeat the common enemy and to secure rule for philosophy. Strauss showed that Machiavelli is the initial great founder of modern philosophy and his book *Thoughts on Machiavelli* is probably his greatest book.

I don't dispute the singular importance of Machiavelli, but for me, the modern founding is most associated with Francis Bacon and René Descartes, two philosophic followers of Machiavelli. They are the masters whose exoteric writings led to the establishment and advancement of the scientific and technological view of nature. Like the philosophers before them to whom they pay credit, Machiavelli and Montaigne, and the philosophers after them who learned from them, Hobbes and Spinoza and the rest, they fought what Strauss too called "*the kingdom of darkness*," Christianity. And they succeeded in taming it. In my view, Bacon and Descartes tamed Christianity with their philosophic poetry, their modification of Christianity's *otherworldly* promises into *worldly* promises promising a paradise at the end of history through a scientific technology applied to nature. Their conscious secularization of the Christian dream gradually re-focused European dreaming on worldly rather than heavenly ends; they succeeded thereby in *taming* Christianity, a ruling religion whose warring fanaticism in their time cost Europe the Renaissance; their philosophic founding launched the modern view of nature and of human goals. It is a complex and wonderful story and I tried to do justice to Bacon's and Descartes's part in it in my book, *Nietzsche and Modern Times*, a book that also argued that Nietzsche embraced the *scientific* aspects of the modern revolution while modifying or assigning limits to its *technological* aspects.

The exoteric, public teaching of Bacon and Descartes still stamps our time, a time now defined by the conquest of nature and what Strauss identified as the highest, most difficult problem, that man is conquering nature and there are no assignable limits to that conquest. A full assessment of Nietzsche's political program for philosophy would require a detailed study of the early modern philosophic founding and how it responded to religious rule over philosophy made possible in the West by Platonism made actual by Christianity.

I will say one thing more about that great modern turning point. Descartes long contemplated just how he could best *mount the stage*, as he said, how he could best begin his part in the great modern fight to reestablish philosophy against ruling religion. He experimented with many different ways of mounting the stage and finally chose one way, the way he took in his first book, published when he was 40 years old and already well known across Europe as a mathematical and scientific genius. His book begins with a six – part *autobiography*, his *Discourse on the Method* which he calls a *"history"* of his becoming himself that he invites you to think of as a *fable*. In that *fabulous history*, Descartes shows himself *becoming a philosopher* and then necessarily becoming a *philosophic poet* whose poetry, whose permission for dreaming, would advance Francis Bacon's poetry on behalf of science and technology.

I learned from Descartes as I had learned from Nietzsche the rhetorical benefit of a philosopher telling the story of how he *became* himself. With Nietzsche and Descartes as examples, I was prepared to pay attention when Plato too in his different way put special emphasis on telling the tale of a philosopher *becoming* himself. Plato chose to make available to readers who studied the structures of his dialogues the story of how *Socrates became Socrates*. While omitting the philosophic establishment of modern times, my lectures on Plato and Nietzsche look to the origins of the great tradition of Western philosophy and to its late modern stage as represented by Nietzsche. And with both Plato and Nietzsche I will use their stories of a *philosopher becoming himself* as guidance into their main themes of philosophy and philosophic poetry.

LECTURE 3

Socrates' Philosophic Poetry

Leo Strauss made the difference between the *exoteric* and the *esoteric* in the writings of the philosophers more clear than any previous writer had. Plato was the absolute master of that philosophic art of writing: what you meet first in his dialogues is an exoteric teaching by Socrates that is easily known; careful study of the dialogues, and there are 35 of them, leads you to suspect a much less well known set of conclusions that can be seen only after careful study. Plato's writings make it clear that Socrates is his special teacher. And Plato's writings make many of his readers think of Socrates as *their* special teacher. And for those readers devoted to Socrates, a natural question arises: how did this teacher I so admire *become* himself? Plato has something special to say to such a reader that he makes visible only through a careful study of the dialogues.

Most of Plato's dialogues make it clear *with whom* Socrates is talking and also just *when* and *where* each particular dialogue is taking place. And it is these details of place and time and audience that Plato used to answer the question these readers will have about *how Socrates became Socrates*. And that is the topic shared by both of my Plato lectures.

Plato showed Socrates becoming Socrates in two different respects: *first*, Plato showed how Socrates *the philosopher* came to understand the fundamental truths of being and knowing; he shows the stages of Socrates' development as a thinker about nature and human nature. And *second*, Plato showed how Socrates the philosopher came to understand what was necessary for a philosopher to *do* in his time and place. Plato shows Socrates' development as a *political philosopher*, as a teacher of a theological –

political view, or of what I have called in my titles *philosophic poetry*, for good platonic reasons.

Today I will deal with the second aspect, how Socrates became the *political philosopher* he became. I follow this order for a good platonic reason: Plato leads his reader to Socrates the philosopher through Socrates the political philosopher; he leads to the esoteric or hidden Socrates through the exoteric or evident Socrates.

I begin with Leo Strauss. Strauss began his Plato essay in *The City and Man* by classifying all 35 of Plato's dialogues. He treats them as one giant written work of art: each single dialogue belongs within the construct of all the dialogues. Strauss's classification is actually Plato's: it follows a distinction Plato built in to his dialogues. 9 of the 35 dialogues are *narrated* or *reported*. That is, we read a text in which some single person speaks or reports the whole dialogue that he witnessed and that the reporter reports to some listener or listeners in the dialogue. And we listen in as the reporter reports. I'll call these the *reported dialogues*. The other 26 dialogues are *performed* like a *drama or play*. We read a text presented to us like a play in which each of the characters just speaks his part; the speakers perform their speeches before us. My Plato lectures will leave all 26 performed dialogues aside except for occasional reference.

Plato's 9 reported dialogues can be further subdivided. In 6 *Socrates* is the reporter. And in the 3 others *someone else* is the reporter, in each case a named person. Today, I will deal with 3 of the 6 dialogues reported by Socrates. They are connected to one another initially by another feature that Plato built in to his dialogues, their *dramatic date*, that is, the time or the year in which the dialogue took place, a time in the history of Socrates' life *and* the corresponding time in the history of Athens, Socrates' home. For Plato constructed his dialogues to have a *date*, a discoverable date that often requires his reader to think, *When did this happen?*, and to find the answer that Plato made it possible to find while making the date seem relevant or worth your while to think about.

A different sort of dating has occupied the Plato scholars: not the time in Socrates' life in which Plato *set* them, but the time in Plato's life in which he supposedly *wrote* them. Dating of this sort, the so-called *composition date*, is always only a scholar's theory and we can do what Strauss did: ignore it entirely in favor of what is not a theory, the dates on which Plato set them.

On each of the dramatic dates, Socrates was a certain number of years old and *Athens* was at a certain point in its history. Athens was the leading city of Greece in both economic and military power, the center of an empire held together by its ships, merchant ships and war ships. And Athens had become the leading city of the Greek enlightenment and Plato often showed Socrates in conversation with leading figures of the Greek enlightenment who had come to the imperial city on diplomatic missions or seeking to attract students. Strauss paid close attention to all the details of the dialogues but he left some very important features of the dramatic dates either not observed or not commented on.

As Strauss said, "The problem inherent in the surface of things, and only in the surface of things, is the heart of things." The surface of things in a Platonic dialogue is a very complex set of details. *Only* a close study of the details can lead the reader to the heart of things, to the most important conclusions. I therefore have to mention a lot of details about the dialogues and only then draw the conclusions. The three dialogues I will deal with today are the *Protagoras*, the *Charmides*, and the *Republic*. Socrates is the reporter in each of these three dialogues. These are the three I spent 400 pages on in my book, *How Philosophy Became Socratic*, so I have to be selective.

Strauss's first observation about the *Republic* in his *City and Man* essay is this: "While the place of the conversation is made quite clear to us, the time, i. e. the year, is not" (62). But that's *wrong*. Plato made *both* the place and the time, the year, clear in his very first sentence. That sentence runs,

> Down I went yesterday to Piraeus with Glaucon, son of Ariston, to offer prayers to the goddess; and, at the same time, I wanted to observe how they would put on the festival since they were now holding it for the first time.

Plato set the *Republic* on the day the Athenians held the festival of "the goddess" for the first time. A question is built in to this sentence: *which goddess would have had her festival for the first time during Socrates' lifetime*? *So there is some uncertainty* about the date from the first sentence taken by itself. Later in the dialogue, Plato has Thrasymachus refer to the feast of the *Bendideia*; so Plato tells his reader that it is the festival of *Bendis*, a Thracian goddess, a *foreign* god, whose festival was held for the first time in Athens last night in the Piraeus—*last night* because today, Socrates is reporting it in Athens.

So Plato made the date of his *Republic* clear and prominent by putting it in his first sentence and by building in a little uncertainty that he settles later in the dialogue. And *that* day was of course a famous day, a momentous day, on which Athens, pious Athens, did something totally new in the experience of any Athenian alive at that time: *introduce a foreign god* into the gods honored by the city. Pious Athens did not ordinarily invite foreign gods into the gods it honored—and it did so here and now only under great stress.

Plato obviously *wanted* the date of the *Republic* to be known by anyone who gave the question some attention. And every Athenian who did so would know exactly when that was because it was such an important and unprecedented event. What day was that? For us, almost two and half thousand years later, it is hard to learn exactly what day that was. But a student of mine, *Christopher Planeaux*, with 10 years of intense single-minded work, made himself a master of all the issues of dramatic dating in Plato's dialogues and assigned each of them their dramatic date. Planeaux settled the date of the *Republic* with some certainty: it was *early June*, 429 BCE.

We can know a lot about that summer because the events that took place then are described by Thucydides, the historian whose book he said was "a possession for all time" (1.22). Many of Plato's dialogues, themselves written as possessions for all time, can be assigned their exact dramatic dates because Plato connected them to Thucydides' possession for all time. From Thucydides we can know that 429 is the third year of the great war between Athens and Sparta. And it is the second summer of the great plague that devastated Athens, and Thucydides describes it in horrifying detail. Bendis the Thracian goddess was introduced in early

June, 429, partly for war – related strategic reasons, but she was introduced especially because she brought her male consort, a healing god: a hope for healing Athens in the depth of the plague.

So Plato set his *Republic* in a time of extreme Athenian crisis. And the dialogue makes clear that there is another, even more important aspect of that crisis, a *spiritual crisis* that Thucydides describes and that Plato emphasizes, the deepest possible spiritual crisis for a society. So the time, the year of the *Republic* turns out to be very important. And Plato made its importance even greater by the dramatic date he gave to the *Charmides*.

The first sentence of the *Charmides* runs:

We came on the day before in the evening, from Potidaea, from the army camp, and because I had arrived after some time away, I gladly went around to the places where I usually spend my time.

The first sentence of the *Charmides* also states the day on which it happened, the day after Socrates' return from Potidaea. When was that? With the *Charmides* too, Plato made the exact day a little uncertain in its first sentence because the Athenian army had been at Potidaea for a long time and Socrates, a regular soldier called a *hoplite*, could possibly have returned at some earlier time even though the army as a whole remained away for some three years. So a little later in the dialogue Socrates says to the person he's reporting it to: "Just before we departed, a battle had occurred at Potidaea which those here had just been learning about." From that comment we learn the exact date of the *Charmides*: it was the day after Socrates returned from the great Athenian defeat at Potidaea when the whole army returned in disarray. Socrates was among the first to return and those present at the gymnasium where the conversation takes place are eager to hear what happened, who survived and who was killed. And here again, every Athenian who was interested would know *that* date too.

For us, that's 2½ thousand years ago. But Christopher Planeaux determined that date exactly too, partly from Thucydides who reports in detail on the Athenian army's actions in that first campaign of the war and on the great defeat Athens suffered in that battle. As Platonic scholars now recognize: the *Charmides* is set in late May, 429.

And the *Charmides* has Socrates say something remarkable: not only has he been away from Athens for some time, two and half to three years, but remarkably, he says he comes back *different*, comes back having learned new things from someone he calls "a doctor of Zalmoxis."

So now we see just what Plato did for his interested reader: he set the *Charmides* in late May, 429, and he put that date in the first sentence and made it exact a little later in the dialogue. And he has Socrates say in the *Charmides* that he came back different. And Plato set the *Republic* in early June, 429, a week or two after the *Charmides*, and he put its date in the first sentence and made it exact a little later in the dialogue. And he has Socrates in the *Republic* set out his teaching on justice with all the elaborations that that huge work gives. Strauss shows his reader that there is nothing accidental in Plato's artful dialogues: the close proximity in time that Plato gave to the *Republic* and the *Charmides* forces their interested reader to ask, Why did Plato lead me to wonder why the *Republic* closely follows the *Charmides* in time? How might the *Charmides prepare* me for the *Republic*, the second dialogue of Socrates' return, especially given the arresting fact that Socrates says he returned different?

Once the dramatic date of the *Charmides* and the *Republic* are linked and the Socrates in these dialogues is seen to be a returning Socrates returning different, then the question must arise about Socrates *before* his return. Are there dialogues that Plato set *earlier* than 429 BCE? It turns out that the *Protagoras* has a dramatic date that makes it *the first* of the dialogues by dramatic date. Plato made it easy to learn that the *Protagoras* happened before the war, with the great city of Athens at the very height of its power and glory: it is the Athens of Pericles, the Athens of the classical age, when the great marble temples on top of the Acropolis were built. Plato set his *Protagoras* about 433 when the most commanding of all those temples, the Parthenon, was having its decoration completed. Plato set his *Protagoras* before the war broke out, the war that lasted 28 years and left Athens defeated. It is the *chronologically* first of the dialogues, the earliest of them all. (There are other pre-war dialogues with the *Alcibiades* dialogues being especially relevant to the *Protagoras*, but I must leave them undiscussed here.)

The *Protagoras* is the chronologically first of the dialogues but there is a noteworthy fact about three other narrated dialogues that Plato set much later in Socrates's life, one at the time of his trial and death, and two after his death. Each of these three dialogues, the *Phaedo*, the *Parmenides*, and the *Symposium*, contains a section, in one of them a very large section, that takes their reader back to a still earlier time in Socrates's life, a time *before* he appears in the *Protagoras* in 433. So each of these three dialogues shows a Socrates *younger* than that Socrates of 433 and what matters most about Plato's three accounts of this younger Socrates is that each of them shows a young Socrates at a *turning point* in his philosophic life. That is something truly special that Plato reserves for his most interested reader: in these three dialogues Plato gives his reader a chance to think about how Socrates became the philosopher he became. These three dialogues show Socrates completing his philosophic education *before* 433, before all the dialogues begin and Socrates mounts the public stage with the *Protagoras* in 433. That will be my topic for my other Plato lecture: *how Socrates became Socrates* (and the topic for my second book on Plato that I am planning to write).

Protagoras

For the rest of today's lecture on the *Protagoras*, the *Charmides*, and the *Republic*, I begin with Socrates in the *Protagoras* in 433. My single, simple question is, Who is the Socrates of the *Protagoras*, a pre–war dialogue? The question matters because in the *Charmides*, the dialogue of Socrates' return from the siege of Potidaea, Socrates says he comes back *different*, having learned something in his absence.

Plato shows that Socrates had two great aims in the *Protagoras* and both aims can be seen to belong to philosophy's politics:

One: Socrates arranges a contest in argument with the much older Protagoras, "the wisest man in Greece," the founder of the Greek enlightenment, deservedly famous everywhere in Greece. Socrates, about 36 years old, steps forward in order to *restrain* and *redirect* the great Protagoras who is about 65 years old and has never in his life been defeated in argument. One learns from a careful study of the dialogue that Socrates challenges Protagoras because he judges Protagoras to be *too outspoken*; he puts Greek wisdom, Greek philosophy, at risk. Protagoras is *not cautious enough*. Plato himself must be very cautious about this in order to keep philosophy's exoteric practice somewhat veiled, so it is *only* by careful study that one learns that Protagoras too knows the difference between the exoteric and the esoteric. Protagoras *respects* that distinction, but Socrates shows him in a veiled way that his exotericism is much too open and threatens the whole tradition of Greek wisdom. So who is the Socrates of Plato's *Protagoras*? Socrates is a man of the enlightenment who judges that the *founder* of the enlightenment puts the whole enlightenment at risk with his inadequate exotericism. In the *Protagoras* young Socrates warns old and famous Protagoras that he has to be more cautious with the truth.

Two: Plato shows that Socrates' second aim in the *Protagoras* is to attract and win as his own student the young Alcibiades who is not yet 20 years old. This is also a political aim because Alcibiades is the *most promising* young Athenian of all those who aspire to political glory and greatness. Thucydides shows Alcibiades to be the great hope of Athens in its war with Sparta. But Alcibiades is attracted by Protagoras, as are other promising Greek young men. Socrates recognizes in Alcibiades a young *political genius* who aspires to rule Greece and is likely to do so. And Socrates aims to *win* Alcibiades to himself, to win over the coming political leader of Athens in part to save the Greek enlightenment. Socrates does not aim to persuade Alcibiades to become a philosopher but to maintain in Athens a public spirit friendly to philosophy.

When the *Protagoras*, the most important pre-war dialogue, is understood this way, this *political* way, a question is opened about the *Charmides* and the *Republic*, the two dialogues set just after Socrates returns from a long absence with the army, the two dialogues that Plato set together as the dialogues of a *returning* Socrates who says he comes back *different*, having learned something important while he was away. The question is: *Who is the returning Socrates?* How is he different from the Socrates before the war, the Socrates of the *Protagoras*?

Notice: these questions do not arise from *external* considerations about the dialogues: they arise from problems that Plato built into the surface of the dialogues and that compel their student to raise questions. Only by pursuing the questions inherent in the problems of the surface of the dialogues can the heart of the dialogues be discovered.

Charmides

Plato's *Charmides* answers some of the questions it raises by referring to Homer. All of Plato's contemporary readers knew Homer, the founding poet of Greek civilization revered by all Greeks as the wisest and most authoritative of teachers and memorized by young men inclined to learning. Homer's two epic poems are the *Iliad* on the ten – year war the Greeks fought generations earlier with Troy, and the *Odyssey* on the ten – year return from Troy by Odysseus after the war. Odysseus was the king of Ithaca and the wisest of the Greeks at Troy. Plato quotes or refers to Homer hundreds of times in his dialogues and his quotations and near – quotations from this founding poet of Greek religion and Greek wisdom are always worth very close attention.

Plato made four references to the *Odyssey* in the *Charmides* and the four are crucial because in the *Odyssey* wise Homer shows the *return* of the wise king Odysseus after twenty years away. As Seth Benardete argues in *The Bow and the Lyre*, Homer's *Odyssey* shows Odysseus's odyssey to be his gradual learning of the wisdom that is *philosophy* and the wisdom that is *political philosophy*. Benardete makes it possible for us to see that Odysseus, Homer's wise king, is Homer's *philosopher king*. In the *Odyssey* that wise king returns after a long absence to set things right in his kingdom. He returns *masked* as a beggar, returns *hidden* because he has a great task to perform and cannot risk being recognized as himself. In the *Odyssey*, Homer has Odysseus reveal himself in a series of *recognition scenes* to win his necessary allies to accomplish his goal.

With that background we can understand an important feature of the surface of Plato's *Charmides*: its four references to the *Odyssey* are *all* to *recognition scenes*, scenes in which the returning hidden wise king reveals himself to select followers to show them what he must do and to gain their help. Plato put all four references to the *Odyssey* in the proper order, matching the sequence in the *Odyssey*; he made his *Charmides*, his dialogue of Socrates' return from a long absence, match Homer's *Odyssey* in this important way. So *who is* the Socrates returning to Athens in the *Charmides after his long absence*? *He is a new returning Odysseus*, a returning wise king, openly returning but returning hiddenly as a wise man with a political project through which he will rule.

Odysseus's political project in the *Odyssey* is a deed of founding that had two dimensions, the first is a new *political order* that will not be dependent on a rare wise man like himself to rule it: he returns looking to the *succession* of wise rule without wise rulers. The second dimension is to establish a new *teaching on the gods*: Odysseus's purely *political* founding requires a *religious* founding, a wise ruler's alteration of the gods to aid in the succession of wise rule. So the Plato who invites his reader to think of his returning Socrates as Socrates/Odysseus invites him to think of Socrates as returning with a founding deed that is a *theological – political* program.

As Plato arranges things in the *Charmides*, Socrates is introduced to Charmides as a *doctor* who has a drug that might be able to cure Charmides' illness, an illness possibly related to the plague. Forced to play a doctor Socrates first says he has a certain healing leaf but for the leaf to be effective certain "*incantations*," magic words or formulas, must be spoken, and the healing *words* gradually replace the leaf in the *Charmides*. Socrates says he learned those incantations while he was away from his teacher who was a doctor of *Zalmoxis*. Zalmoxis is a god who teaches that to cure the body the soul must also be treated and that the soul can be treated only with incantations which are "beautiful speeches." Socrates adds that the doctors of Zalmoxis, "even *immortalize* people"—the doctors of Zalmoxis teach that the soul is immortal.

By bringing in Zalmoxis Plato refers to *Herodotus*, the Greek historian, without mentioning his name. Plato's reader can learn more about Zalmoxis from Herodotus who shows that the people who believe in Zalmoxis believe they are *immortal* and that their god is *the only God*. And Herodotus adds that the people who believe this, the Getae, are *the most courageous and most just* of peoples, the only people to effectively resist the Persian invaders—he thus implies that belief in one God and in the immortal soul made the believers courageous and just, made them virtuous. By referring to Zalmoxis and thereby to Herodotus, Plato tells us more about the Socrates returning to Athens after a long absence. This new Odysseus, this wise king returning to establish a new regime and to bring a new teaching about the gods, returns having learned beautiful healing speeches that teach that there is only one God and that the soul is immortal—the doctor of Zalmoxis taught Socrates the teaching of the *Republic*. By placing his *Charmides* a few weeks before his *Republic* and by having it announce a new teaching it does not elaborate, Plato forces his careful reader to conclude that Socrates' teaching on the gods and the soul in the *Republic* is the new *political* project of a Socrates returning hiddenly as Socrates/Odysseus.

The *Charmides* is a short dialogue and after the things I just mentioned it deals mostly with the topic of *moderation*. Socrates discusses moderation with Critias, the most brilliant of his students before he left with the army. The dialogue intimates that Critias had learned from Socrates a view that would eventually turn him into a notorious Athenian criminal, a most immoderate sophist and tyrant in the Athenian civil war. In the *Charmides* Socrates learns that he had corrupted Critias—another powerful reason for altering his teaching. I must omit this important topic, the most prominent topic of the *Charmides*, because it would take us away from my main point here.

I can end that main point about Socrates as a returning Odysseus with this: Plato ends the *Charmides* with Socrates having taught *none of the healing words* he says he brought back and a reader paying close attention will see that fact about the *Charmides*. But by ending his *Charmides* this way and placing it just before his *Republic* Plato allows that reader and only that reader to draw the conclusion Plato hid just for him: the teaching of the *Republic* is the teaching of a Socrates/Odysseus who returns different from a long absence and aims to found a new political order based on a foreign, non – Homeric teaching about the gods and the soul.

And with that I can turn to the Socrates of the *Republic* and begin to justify my title for today's lecture: *Socrates' Philosophic Poetry*. I can begin to show the way in which Socrates' *philosophic poetry* is what Strauss said it was, *ministerial*, in the service of philosophy and aiding or caring for the sick and wounded.

Republic

The returning Socrates as Odysseus

Plato names Odysseus in the *Republic* only twice, once near the beginning and once at the end. And he *avoids* the name Odysseus elsewhere, speaking instead of "the wisest man at Troy." Socrates speaks the name Odysseus to end the very first argument of the *Republic* where he also names Homer for the first time. He says: "The just person, it seems, has come to light as a kind of thief, and I'm afraid you learned this from Homer. For he admires Autolycus, Odysseus's grandfather on his mother's side who surpassed all men 'in stealing and in swearing oaths.'"

Autolycus means Wolf Himself and *swearing oaths* means tying your actions to the gods: it is *an act of piety*: Autolycus combines stealing and piety. Autolycus gave Odysseus the name *Odysseus*: giving his grandson that name is symbolic of this wise grandfather *passing on his wisdom* to his grandson. And Socrates adds: "Justice, it seems, according to you and Homer ··· is a certain art of stealing, for the benefit of friends." Polemarchus, the young man Socrates is talking with, of course did *not* mean that and if the definition of justice that he offered implies that, then he believes that he had to be *wrong*. But Socrates *did* mean that: the practical wisdom of the wise man is a certain art of stealing in which the pious – looking wise man steals sons away from their fathers by making those sons his own followers, to their great benefit—and that is what Socrates the teacher will do with the young men he speaks to in the *Republic*.

So at the opening of the *Republic* stands this identification of Odysseus as having his grandfather's characteristics. The only other time the *Republic* names Odysseus is at the end of its closing myth, the last lesson of the *Republic*. That famous myth pictures the immortal souls choosing their next life after their long period of reward or punishment in Hades. The souls typically make hasty and foolish choices. But the last soul to make its choice is different:

> And by chance Odysseus's soul had drawn the last lot of all and went to choose; from memory of its former labors it had recovered from love

of honor; it went around for a long time looking for the life of a private man who minds his own business; and with effort it found one lying somewhere neglected by others.

The *Republic* ends suggesting that the soul of Odysseus chooses *the life of Socrates*, the life of a private man who minds his own business, the business of philosophy and everything it entails to protect itself and advance itself. Notice: It is the *soul of Odysseus* that makes that choice. It is not *Odysseus* himself but the soul that in a way he got from Autolycus, his grandfather on his mother's side who gave him his name.

So Plato's *Republic* never really names Odysseus himself. Instead, it refers first to one of Odysseus's *forefathers*, a *wise man prior* to Odysseus. And it refers last to Odysseus's *successor*, *the wise man after* Homer's Odysseus, Socrates himself. Plato in the *Republic* makes the returned Socrates of the *Charmides* the thinker who recognized in himself the soul of Odysseus. Socrates, Plato suggests, carries on and advances the tradition of Greek wisdom that began before wise Odysseus, before Homer, and was passed on after improvements by Homer, and is passed on to Socrates, that "son" of Homer who improves Homeric wisdom and passes it on to his "sons" after him.

"*Improves*" may be the wrong word: what Plato seems to suggest in the *Republic* is that Socrates *adapts or adjusts* Greek wisdom to the new conditions introduced into Greece by the passage of time, one condition in particular being the most important, as we will see. Plato's suggestion seems to be this: a wise man knows *who he is* and he knows *where he is* and he learns what *he must do* because of who he is and where he is.

That's the first of the two things that Plato shows his reader by putting the *Charmides* just before the *Republic* in time. Thinking about that arrangement of the two dialogues, the reader can think of Socrates' innovations or novel teachings in the *Republic* as the work of a wise returning Odysseus.

The returning Socrates as a student of Zalmoxis

In the *Charmides* Socrates says he came back different. To return different is to return different from what Plato had shown Socrates to be before, that is, in his *Protagoras*. The *Charmides* suggests that Socrates came back as a kind of doctor who had learned a curing art while he was away. He came back having learned certain *incantations* or magic words that can cure sick souls, and he learned those curing words from the follower of a foreign god.

Socrates does not speak one word of his healing incantations in the *Charmides*. But a few weeks later, on *the perfect occasion*, Socrates introduces a new teaching into Athens. In the *Republic* the returning Odysseus, Socrates, teaches the incantations he learned while he was away. And the occasion is perfect because while Socrates is introducing *his* teachings from the foreign god Zalmoxis, outside the house in the port of Piraeus, on that very night, the Athenians were themselves importing a foreign god, Bendis.

In the *Charmides* the healing words were supposed to heal Charmides' sickness in the head. And in the *Republic*? While it takes place in the Athens suffering from the plague, it shows that there is another form of sickness in Athens, a sickness more important and more disastrous than even the plague.

The main conversation of the *Republic*, between Socrates and the two brothers Adeimantus and Glaucon, takes place only after the brothers have made long speeches (Book 2). Those speeches show that these two talented young men have been exposed to the Greek enlightenment and learned the teaching of teachers like Protagoras, teachings that seem to them to destroy the reasons for living a moral life, a life of justice. They are young gentlemen of genuine decency and they want to live decent lives but they have been seriously shaken by the teaching of Protagoras and others. They *demand* of Socrates that he prove to them that the just life is better than the unjust life.

From their two speeches Plato's reader learns just what the deepest crisis is that grips the Athens to which the new Odysseus returns: it is not only the war and the plague but the greatest possible crisis, a spiritual and moral crisis that I think we can call *the crisis of the death of the gods*, Homer's gods. Adeimantus and Glaucon speak for all decent young Athenians caught up in the war and the plague and exposed to the enlightenment brought by teachers like Protagoras. Protagoras's insufficient exotericism, his failure to hide adequately his own skeptical views, has led the younger generation to mistrust their gods.

So the Socrates who returns different returns to a *different Athens*, an Athens in which the war, the plague, and the enlightenment have made doubt about morality and the gods a crisis of civilized life, a crisis that is the greatest of all emergencies, a crisis similar to what Nietzsche would call *nihilism*.

Reading Plato's *Republic* with Plato's *Charmides* in mind, as Plato invited us to do by setting them a few weeks apart, we learn how the returning Odysseus, Socrates, responds to the spiritual crisis faced in particular by the decent young men who have learned some of the thinking of the all – too – rash wise, the incautious wise like Protagoras.

And here Plato's chronological arrangement of the three dialogues, *Protagoras*, *Charmides*, *Republic*, allows us to compare the political philosopher Socrates before the war to the political philosopher Socrates who returned different to a different Athens. By making such a comparison possible Plato allows his devoted reader to see Socrates *becoming* Socrates, becoming in 429, at about age 40, the mature political philosopher that he would remain all his life. His concerns remain what they were in *Protagoras*, the Greek enlightenment and the Athenian young, but his way of dealing with each has changed.

First, with respect to Socrates' aim to moderate the Greek enlightenment, to teach Protagoras and the followers of this founder of the Greek enlightenment to practice a more effective exotericism. In the *Republic* Thrasymachus is the representative teacher of the Greek enlightenment; as a leading figure of the next generation of sophists he is much less restrained or moderate than Protagoras was. He is much more open about expressing the real and radical position of enlightenment teachers, less concerned with giving his teaching an exoteric shelter—although we must remember that in the *Republic* Thrasymachus is speaking in private to a select audience.

Leo Strauss showed beautifully that in the *Republic*, Socrates makes a special effort to win Thrasymachus as his *friend*. At an important point near the middle of the dialogue Socrates even says that he and Thrasymachus have *just become friends without having been enemies before* —although Thrasymachus began, near the beginning of the dialogue, by acting as if *they were* enemies in order to gain an advantage over Socrates with the young men. Socrates' strategic aim in the *Republic* is to persuade Thrasymachus that he can best serve his own advantage by adopting Socrates' strategy for philosophy. Speaking to the young men, his prospective customers and clients, as a friend of Socrates would entail that Thrasymachus *adopt a version* of Socrates' moderate strategy for philosophy.

With respect to the Greek enlightenment then, the Socrates of the *Republic* has learned a new strategy that may succeed with its enlightened teacher, Thrasymachus, as Socrates' pre – war strategy did not succeed with Protagoras, the founding teacher of the Greek enlightenment.

Second, with respect to Socrates' aim to attract and direct the Athenian young. The *Republic* shows that Socrates has learned a moderate strategy for the public presentation of philosophy that could make him more successful with the young men than he was with Alcibiades. For Socrates learned before the war that he had failed with Alcibiades, as Plato allows us to learn from Alcibiades himself in the *Symposium*. Of course there is no Alcibiades among the young men with whom Socrates speaks on his return from Potidaea. Alcibiades is an incomparable political genius, one of a kind. Instead, Socrates speaks with Adeimantus and Glaucon, and with Polemarchus and other young men more typical of the talented politically ambitious young men who can be effective leaders in a democratic order like Athens. They are young, spirited gentlemen who aspire to fulfill the role of the gentleman in Athens, a public – spirited political and military role.

For this second way in which Plato showed Socrates *becoming* himself with respect to political philosophy, the *Charmides* is crucial because in the *Republic* we hear what the returning Odysseus of the *Charmides* actually returns to *teach*. In the *Republic* we hear the promised healing incantations that are the "beautiful speeches;" we hear what Socrates as a follower of Zalmoxis is prepared to teach. With the preparation Plato gave his reader in the *Charmides* we can understand the meaning of the main teachings of the *Republic*, teachings on *the soul*, on the *knowledge of reality*, and on *the gods*. Socrates' new teachings are all anti – Homeric teachings foreign to the Greek tradition, teachings meant to persuade and cure young men like Adeimantus and Glaucon. I will summarize these three teachings very briefly with what is necessarily a very simplified summary.

First, the returned Socrates teaches a new anti – Homeric view of *the soul*:

Socrates teaches Adeimantus and Glaucon that the soul has a three part structure and that the *thumotic or spirited part* must be ruled by the *rational part*. The spirited part dominated Greek souls raised on Homer: the young men all desire to be like Achilles, the greatest warrior at Troy. Or even to outdo Achilles for the Homeric ideal is *competitive*: all the heroes at Troy aim to outdo the others in the virtue of the warrior. Socrates' new teaching on the soul takes the virtue of the spirited part, *courage*, which Socrates calls "*political* courage," and places it under the rule of the rational part.

Socrates adds a new element to his teaching on the soul with his argument in Book 10: he proves to his young listeners that the soul is *immortal*. This foreign, non – Homeric view of the soul includes Socrates' non – Homeric teaching on *Hades* or the afterlife. Homer treated Hades as the place that all the shades of humans descend to after death; it is a place Achilles hates. Socrates makes Hades the place of reward or punishment that souls go to after they die, with rewards in Hades for the good and just and punishment in Hades for the bad and unjust. The returned Socrates's teaching on the soul's afterlife is most clearly a teaching that he learned while he was away from the doctor of Zalmoxis—or, Plato suggests, perhaps from Herodotus, the Greek historian who reports the teachings of Zalmoxis and their salutary or beneficial effects, and who says that the people of Zalmoxis are most courageous and most just.

Second, the returned Socrates brings a new teaching on *knowing and being*:

This is the famous teaching on the *ideas* in the *Republic*. On this topic, Leo Strauss is almost outspoken. He says in his essay on the *Republic* that "no one has ever succeeded in giving a satisfactory or clear account of this doctrine of ideas." Strauss gives a satisfactory and clear account: he shows that the doctrine is an exoteric teaching that can easily persuade non – philosophers who have been raised to believe in glorious gods like Nike and Dike, the gods of victory and justice. Dike, the goddess of justice is a singular, self – standing, immortal being, the glorious cause of every human just act. The *idea* of justice is similar to the goddess, it is the permanent, unchanging, glorious reality in which every just act participates. Part of Socrates' effort to persuade sophist – influenced young Athenians that justice is better than injustice is to persuade them that justice has a permanent, independent reality that can be known by humans. The young men's learned skepticism about Homer's gods leaves them with a concept of what a god is that prepares them for Socrates' teaching on the ideas. Strauss says, that for us, "to begin with," the doctrine of the ideas "is utterly incredible, not to say that it appears to be fantastic." Those famous words by Strauss prepare his demonstration that the doctrine of ideas is *not* to begin with utterly incredible to Glaucon but in fact easily credible because of what he knows a god is from Homer.

Strauss makes it easy for his readers to understand that Socrates' teaching on the eternal, transcendent ideas is a teaching consciously tied to its time, the time of the death of the Homeric gods; it *is exoteric*; it is *philosophic poetry*; it is not part of the Plato nearest to Strauss's heart. (Of course, there is much more to be learned from the ideas about Socrates' genuine insight into human perception and cognition, or sensing and understanding—but that is a different issue entirely, and not one that would be of interest to Glaucon.)

Third, the returned Socrates brings a new teaching on *the gods* that reforms Homer's gods in a moral way:

This is what Strauss chose to place at the center of his account of the *Republic* in *The City and Man* and that I dealt with in my first lecture. Socrates the legislator lays down two new laws for the gods. The first is that they are the cause only of the good. Here Socrates is explicitly anti – Homer: he quotes Homer who says that Zeus metes out both good and bad to human beings. The second is that the gods do not change their shape or lie. This too is a view of the gods contrary to Homer and Strauss stresses that Socrates must argue Adeimantus out of the view he inherited from Homer that of course the gods lie. I think it is proper to say that Socrates teaches Adeimantus the lie, the noble lie, that the gods do not lie. It is proper to say that because of *what a god is* in Socrates' view—and with that we touch an issue on which Strauss was very careful but on which he nevertheless made himself clear: he indicated that in Plato's view as in

Nietzsche's view gods philosophize or the gods are the philosophers. I will deal with this further in later lectures.

A crucial part of making the gods more moral than Homer had made them is what Socrates adds in Book 10: he makes the gods ultimately responsible for punishing or rewarding the soul after death in Hades.

Socrates teaches an additional new thing about the gods: through his teaching on the ideas and the idea of ideas, the idea of the good, Socrates' moves toward the *monotheism* of Zalmoxis. Plato was certainly read that way by the monotheists who were Christians, like Saint Augustine. And this openness to monotheism is an important part of what Nietzsche and other modern philosophers before him regarded as the disastrous consequence of Plato's teaching: it opened the way in the West for the successful introduction of Christianity. I'll say more about this great event too in later lectures.

That is a summary of the new teaching that the returning Socrates brought back from Potidaea. His new teaching is his new *philosophic poetry*, his *ministerial poetry*, as Strauss calls it, his poetry to serve philosophy while ministering to the spiritual needs of the young men like Adeimantus and Glaucon. And this new teaching introduced by Socrates in the summer of 429, is the teaching that remains his mature political philosophy to the end. And Plato means *to the very end*, to 399, because Plato has Socrates repeat in his *Phaedo*, on his last day and with the last argument of his life, the teaching on the ideas that he introduced in 429, thirty years earlier, and he has Socrates tell new stories that teach lessons on the immortal soul and on the gods that are similar to the stories he first told in 429 when he returned from Potidaea.

So paying attention to what Strauss said was not given in the *Republic*, its time, its year, allows us to learn a great deal that helps us understand the *Republic*. Learning that the returning Socrates of the *Charmides* and the *Republic* is returning in the late spring and early summer of 429 allows us to reflect on the sublime setting, the poetically beautiful and fitting setting that Plato gave to "the most famous political *work* of all times." On the very day on which numberless Athenians streamed back up to Athens to report on the all-night spectacle of the introduction of the new goddess,

Socrates came back up to Athens to report on what he introduced privately on the same night in the same place and now introduces to whoever wants to hear it in Athens, for Socrates reports the whole *Republic* in Athens to an unidentified audience, to anyone and everyone.

The Athenian introduction of Bendis failed to do anything to change the ultimate fate of Athens. Socrates' introduction of his new teachings succeeded in changing the fate of philosophy in Athens and, ultimately, in changing the fate of Western civilization. Socrates is what Nietzsche says he was, "the one vortex and turning point of so – called world history."

I want to end this lecture by discussing Plato and Homer and Nietzsche.

The Socrates who returned from Potidaea brought anti – Homer teachings. In Book 10 of the *Republic* Socrates makes his criticism of Homer more explicit and more complete. His criticism is meant to break the hold that Homer had on the minds of the young; his criticism helps Socrates replace Homer's teaching and put his own new teaching in place. In a dramatic way, by breaking the power of Homer's influence, Socrates *kills off* Homer and rises to replace him.

But Socrates also honors Homer. As the returning Odysseus, Socrates learned from Homer what Odysseus had to do to be successful. And one of the things that Socrates learned from Homer gave Socrates a kind of permission to kill Homer by supplanting Homer or taking Homer's place as the ultimate authority. In his *Odyssey* Homer emphasizes that the returning Odysseus must kill all 108 suitors of his wife, Penelope. The suitors compete to marry Odysseus's wife because her husband the king has been gone for 20 years and can reasonably be presumed dead. The suitor who is successful in his suit would marry Odysseus' supposed widow and become king of Ithaca himself. The 108 suitors represents the old order that will continue in the old way with Odysseus gone and a new rightful king in his place.

The returning Odysseus is Odysseus the king but Odysseus returns as the *wise* king who knows that he must establish a new order politically and religiously. Politically that means establishing a new order to be ruled by his son, Telemachus, a fine young man but of course not that great rarity that his father is, a wise ruler. Wise Odysseus must see to the succession by establishing a more democratic order to be ruled by Telemachus and his associates like Eumaeus, the loyal pig farmer. But for that new order to succeed all 108 suitors must die—the new order can be well established only if the old order is wiped out. So of course all the suitors must die.

But right establishment of the new requires that the suitors must not only die: they must seem to *deserve it*, they must be judged wicked, memory of them must be memory of their wickedness. So Homer paints them wicked. Homer makes the memory of them the memory of the wicked suitors that righteous Odysseus brought to justice with the help of Athena herself. Homer does what Machiavelli, more than two thousand years later, explicitly says must be done.

And Socrates? Socrates knows from Homer that he can establish the new order only by killing off the old order. Socrates learns from Homer that he must kill Homer. And Socrates knows from Homer that he must make Homer seem to deserve it. So Socrates teaches that Homer deserves to die, to be supplanted as the ultimate authority because Homer made Zeus responsible for human evil and Homer was ignorant of the ideas and Homer was ignorant of the soul's immortal destiny. Socrates exoterically and actually killed off Homer, replacing Homer as the ultimate authority and replacing Homer's teaching with his own teaching. But esoterically Socrates honors Homer as his own teacher, as the now passing authority who must give way to his successor, as Autolycus gave way to Odysseus.

And Homer expected to be killed off, he *taught* that he must be killed off by the coming wise man whoever he was, whenever he came, whatever he brought. That coming wise man learned from Homer that all 108 suitors must die, that Homer well knew that he must die for the necessary new wise teaching to take root.

Times change, gods die, and politic wisdom must change with the times by teaching new gods.

And for me, there is no better way to begin Nietzsche than that: Nietzsche made every effort to *kill off Plato*, the philosopher who had "the greatest strength any philosopher has so far had at his disposal" (BGE 191). But Nietzsche kills off Plato with Plato's permission, he kills the

Plato who killed Homer with Homer's permission, he kills the exoteric Plato whose teaching ultimately led to a cultural disaster.

But Nietzsche *honors* Plato as Plato honored Homer. Plato remains what he was, "the most beautiful growth of antiquity" (BGE Preface), and the most beautiful growth of antiquity is immortal, living on forever in the underworld of the wise as the wise man he esoterically was. But historically there is no going backward, antiquity itself must be supplanted by the late modern as it was first supplanted by the modern. Plato must be supplanted by Nietzsche.

LECTURE 4

Socrates Becomes Socrates

My first Plato lecture dealt with the dialogues that I treated in my published Plato book. Today's Plato lecture is on the Plato book that I have not yet written but that I want to write next, after I finish my new Nietzsche book.

Today's Plato lecture is also on three dialogues, the three narrated or reported dialogues that Plato made unique by making them the only dialogues that are reported by someone other than Socrates, the *Phaedo* reported by Phaedo, the *Parmenides* reported by Cephalus, and the *Symposium* reported by Apollodoros. This lecture too makes use of the dramatic dates that Plato gave his dialogues, the dates on which Plato set the conversations. And these three dialogues have another feature that makes them unique: within each of these dialogues, after the dialogue has started, Plato takes the reader back to an earlier time in Socrates' life and each of those times comes to light as very significant because in each of them Socrates is at a different stage of his philosophic life and in each of them he learns something crucial for his advancement in philosophic understanding.

If you as a reader think about those three events, think about each in relation to the others, you can very easily put them in the right order and you have to think that Plato *intended* you to do this work. Plato scattered these three events on purpose putting them in three different dialogues to which he gave the formal similarity that they are the only ones reported by someone else. Plato's intentional complication has the effect of really getting your attention. It makes you think, there must be more to this, more to learn. Plato must be trying to *teach* me something.

The order that Plato invites you to see is a sequence in time that is a logical sequence in which the *Phaedo* comes first, then the *Parmenides*, and finally the *Symposium*. That logical sequence is Socrates' progress in thought. It begins with Socrates' earliest beginnings as a philosopher in the *Phaedo* including a step he made wholly on his own, a new step in Greek philosophy. Then comes the step in the *Parmenides*: Parmenides, great Parmenides, shows Socrates that that new view of his is logically inadequate, no, logically impossible, and even if it was possible, we could never know that it was. Learning *that* about his proud invention, Socrates is led to the ultimate step, the point of deepest insight that a philosopher can attain and he learns that in the *Symposium*.

With these three linked dialogues, linked *formally* as the only dialogues reported by someone other than Socrates, linked *logically* by Socrates' movement from his earliest stages through to his ultimate insight, Plato teaches you, you the really interested, really working at it, how *Socrates became Socrates*, how the philosopher who is Plato's model, the philosopher Nietzsche said is "the one vortex and turning point of so - called world history," how *that* philosopher became himself. Another way of saying this is that Plato's calculated presentation of the exoteric Socrates is intended to lead his most interested reader to the esoteric Socrates.

There is something else that Plato intentionally built in to this arrangement of three dialogues. Once you see the proper sequence of Socrates' learning and put the steps in the chronological order that Plato intended, you also see that Plato made it possible to date those steps in the life of Socrates against the background of the life of Athens. One important fact about the actual dates that Plato makes it easy to discover is that they all fall before the *Protagoras*. That is, Plato shows that Socrates' private development as a philosopher was in a sense complete before Plato had Socrates first mount the stage as a public teacher in the *Protagoras*.

It is important to see that these details are not some *theory* about the dialogues; they do not *bring* to the text some fixed set of ideas about texts; they are instead features that Plato built into these dialogues without calling undue attention to them. Their presence in the text can be explained only as Plato's intention; he put them in the surface of the text to be noticed by readers who pay close attention and who read with the aim of learning what

Plato had to teach and who have already seen that Plato is a master of artful writing who teaches in the way Socrates taught, that is, without saying everything.

Leo Strauss noticed the chronological arrangement of the three dialogues that show Socrates becoming a philosopher. So did Seth Benardete who called them the "three stages in Socrates' philosophic education." But neither Strauss nor Benardete worked out those stages by linking in detail the three events that Plato arranged. That's what I want to do here and do in much more detail in my next book on Plato.

There is one last complication I have to mention: Plato gave another account of a younger Socrates in his *Apology of Socrates*. There, in his defense speech, Socrates made his famous statement that *the god at Delphi* told his friend Chaerephon that no one was wiser than Socrates. Socrates reports that when he heard what the god said, he *turned* to the way he practiced philosophy ever since. Socrates tells this story to the "*men of Athens*," to all his fellow citizens present at his trial. In his only public speech to all of Athens, his defense speech or his speech of self – explanation, Socrates tells all his fellow citizens a story of how he became himself.

Socrates' speech to the public must be interpreted as a *politic* speech. Socrates says to all his fellow citizens: think of me this way, think that what I do as a philosopher I do in obedience to the god. That is, Socrates tells the men of Athens, I do what I do in obedience to the highest authority that all of you know, the god at Delphi. Socrates' public account of himself is a *mythically* true account of how he became himself: he became himself in obedience to the highest authority. But how is *highest authority* to be understood? Socrates knows that authority to be *reason*, his fellow citizens know that authority to be *the god at Delphi*. The account of Socrates becoming Socrates that Plato spread across three different dialogues, *Phaedo, Parmenides, Symposium*, for *you* to discover, is the *non – mythic* account of how Socrates became himself, the account of what his reasoning led him to discover, the account *you* will very much want to learn and will work to learn. That account is the esoteric presentation of the exoteric story Socrates told of his becoming, told everyone, in the *Apology*.

Given these two different accounts in the dialogues, we could ask,

When did that Delphi event with the god, *that* turn in Socrates' life, occur in the life – sequence of events that Plato made it possible to discover from the dialogues as a whole? That seems to me to be the wrong question for a mythic story. It misunderstands a mythic account by treating it as an historical account. The historical account Plato scattered in the three unique dialogues.

With that preparation, we can begin the substance of what I want to say today. I will follow the logical development that the three dialogues, the *Phaedo*, *Parmenides* and *Symposium*, show Socrates following in becoming himself.

Phaedo

The *Phaedo* is reported by Phaedo who was one of the frequent visitors to Socrates in his prison cell and who was present on the last day when Socrates talked with his friends and then drank the poison and died. Phaedo reports his story of Socrates' last day to a group of *Pythagoreans* in Phlia, a city in the Peloponnese far from Athens. The Pythagoreans were a school of Greek philosophers whose teaching had some influence on Socrates. And the Pythagoreans at Phlia were interested in Socrates. So Plato could perhaps be suggesting that the already existing Pythagorean schools could be one possible means of carrying forward the memory of Socrates and what he taught.

Phaedo reports for the Pythagoreans what happened on Socrates' last day and what Socrates said on his last day. On the day he was to die by drinking the poison when the sun went down, most of what Socrates said was about what happened to the soul at death, and Pythagoreans already believed that the soul was immortal. Two young Pythagoreans had also been regular visitors to Socrates' cell, but these two young men had doubts; they wondered if what they had been taught about their immortal souls was really *true*. So most of the conversation that day was Socrates presenting arguments to these two young Pythagorean doubters in order to persuade them by arguments that their souls were in fact immortal.

Phaedo's report leads finally to one last reason to doubt stated by one of the young men, *Kebes*. Socrates pauses before he answers. He pauses before his final argument that day, the argument he knows will be *the last argument of his life* because the sun is sinking and he has to drink the poison at sundown. He pauses, he says, because the objection Kebes raised requires that he consider "the cause concerning generation and destruction as a whole." Kebes' question concerns the comprehensive topic of philosophy, the *cause* at work in the whole of nature, the whole of becoming. To deal with that great topic of the cause of coming into being and passing out of being, Socrates offers to "go through my own experiences about them." And then Socrates goes back to the very first philosophical reflections of his life.

So Plato has arranged *something remarkable*: before the *last argument of his life*, Socrates goes back to his *first philosophic experiences* in order to tell the story of his becoming a philosopher from its very beginning.

Socrates says that "as a young man I was wondrously desirous of that wisdom they call 'inquiry into nature.'" The youngest Socrates we ever see in Plato was a young man with a passionate desire to understand nature as a whole, a young man who was what the Western tradition of philosophy came to call a "pre-Socratic philosopher." As Socrates reports it on his last day, he came to see problems in the way the early Greek philosophers of nature explained cause in terms of natural causes at work in nature. While investigating those problems of cause he found no way out of the problems until he heard about a philosopher who explained change in nature as caused by Mind as the ordering cause. According to this explanation of cause, everything in nature is what it is because it was *for the best* that it be that way as judged by mind. All events of coming into being and passing out of being could be explained *teleologically*: everything that happened happened because of the *goal* or *end* intended for it by ruling Mind. When Strauss deals with this view in *Xenophon's Socratic Discourse*, he calls it Socrates' *teleotheology*, a word invented by Strauss to express the view that the gods rule the world by causing each event to be directed toward the best end.

But Socrates reports in Plato's *Phaedo* that when he read the books of this teacher of teleology, Anaxagoras, he found that the teacher himself did not use that form of explanation, he did not show how this thing or that thing is what it is because it is best that it be that way. Instead, even

Anaxagoras looked to *natural causes* and not to Mind. (This may be an indication of Anaxagoras's own use of exoteric and salutary teaching to cover his own esoteric naturalism.)

Socrates goes on to say on his death day that natural causes alone cannot explain human things like what caused him to be sitting in prison waiting to drink the poison. The *true causes* of that fact cannot be explained by the actions of his "bones and sinews" but have to be explained by human opinion, what human beings judge is for the best, what Athenians judge is best for them, that Socrates die, and what Socrates judges is best for him—that he drink the poison that Athenians say he deserves. So natural causes are not enough to explain all events, in particular human events; and an all - governing Mind seems also not to be an adequate explanation; what *is* the cause of generation and destruction as a whole?

And here, before the last argument of his life, Socrates says that very early in his life he devised his *own way* and he asks the young Pythagorean, Kebes: "···do you want me to make a display ··· of the way by which I've busied myself with the second sailing in search of the cause?" A "second sailing" is a metaphor from the Greek experience with ships: when the wind does not blow and fill the sails, the traveller has to use another means, he has to use *the oars*, he has *to row*. Socrates explains his philosophical "second sailing" as a turn away from the things to be explained and a turn toward the speeches or accounts that human beings use to talk and think about the things: perhaps in the speeches, in the *logoi*, he will find the proper cause for the things. In Socrates's words for this turn to the speeches he says this: "I'm going to try to show you the form (*eidos*, idea) of the cause with which I've busied myself." And that, he says, was the way he began with the *ideas* or *forms* that he has been talking about ever since.

The particular ideas he talks about in the *Phaedo* are the idea of the *Beautiful*, the idea of the *Good*, the idea of *Bigness*. And the basic thought is that every beautiful thing is beautiful because it *participates* in the Beautiful itself— the Beautiful, the idea of the beautiful never changes but each beautiful thing does: it becomes beautiful and then ceases to be beautiful: it comes to participate in the beautiful and then ceases to participate in the beautiful. It's not important now to understand more of Socrates' "theory of ideas"—as Strauss says, "for us, to begin with it is utterly incredible, not to say that it appears to be fantastic." All that matters for us is that *this* is what Socrates, the young philosopher passionate about the explanation of cause in the events in nature, *turned to* when he was dissatisfied with what his predecessors in Greek philosophy had said about the cause of all generation and destruction as a whole.

And he says on his last day that he is still using this way of talking about the ideas to explain cause. And in the last argument of his life that he now begins, Socrates uses the ideas to prove that the soul is immortal. And young Kebes finds it completely persuasive; now he knows by argument that his soul is immortal. Now he can let Socrates die because Socrates cured his doubt—one more reason to owe a cock to Asclepius for a healing.

Socrates was about 70 years old when he made this last argument of his life and then drank the poison. How old was Socrates when he made that turn to the ideas that he has been talking about ever since? How old was he when he made these first steps in his philosophic life, starting with the Greek philosophers of nature and his turn to the ideas? He does not say, but Plato lets his readers know in the *Parmenides*. So we can now look at the *Parmenides* in order to get clearer about this first stage of Socrates becoming Socrates.

Parmenides

Plato set the conversation reported in the *Parmenides* at a famous moment in the philosophic history of Athens, a moment that all Athenians with an interest in intellectual things would know: it was the famous visit of the great philosophers *Parmenides* and *Zeno* to Athens. That visit occurred in 450 BCE at an Athenian festival, the great Panathenaia that Plato refers to. The Socrates who speaks to Parmenides and Zeno is a "very young" man, says a speaker in the *Parmenides*, but he has already developed his view of the ideas, because he uses the ideas to challenge the old philosopher Parmenides and his younger follower, Zeno, challenge them and win a great victory for himself.

That means that Socrates' turn to the ideas that he reports in the

Phaedo came earlier than this 450 conversation. In 450 Socrates was about 19 *years old*. So Socrates' passionate engagement with natural philosophy, and then his insights into the problems with natural cause, and then his enthusiasm for teleology and his recognition of *its* limits as an explanation of cause, and finally even his *turn* to the speeches and to the *ideas* as cause all came before or when he was about 19. So Plato shows something remarkable about Socrates: he was a *philosophic prodigy*, a *young genius in philosophy* who by age 19 had thought through the whole history of Greek philosophy before him and arrived at his own novel solution to the problem of cause, his view of the ideas.

The setting of the *Parmenides*

The setting that Plato gave his *Parmenides* tells us why there still exists a record of the conversation that the 19 years old Socrates had with two mature, famous philosophers, 65 years old Parmenides and his 40 years old disciple, Zeno. It is a complicated but very important setting for anyone who is interested in how Socrates became Socrates.

The narrator or reporter of the *Parmenides* is a man named *Cephalus*; he is one of the "men of Clazomenae," a Greek city in Asia Minor, who sailed across the Aegean sea to Athens to find out if *the one person* who *might have memory* of that conversation is still able to remember what was said about 60 years ago—the "frame" of the *Parmenides* having been set by Plato about 394 BCE (as the fixing of the dramatic dates by Christopher Planeaux shows). The men of Clazomenae had heard that that man had been taught when he was young to memorize everything that was said that day by a man who had actually been present in 450 and heard it all and memorized it himself. It is far too late to ask Socrates or any other participant about it; they are all dead.

When the men of Clazomenae arrive in Athens Plato has them run into Adeimantus and Glaucon in the marketplace, the two main characters from the *Republic*, and it is their half – brother, Antiphon, that they are looking for. Together, they all go to Antiphon to learn if he can still remember the speeches he had memorized years ago. Antiphon does still remember what he memorized but he does not want to go through the hard work of saying it all again. He has lost all interest in it but the men of Clazomenae persuade him to work at recalling it all anyway.

The 450 conversation

In the first stages of the conversation that Antiphon reports to the men of Clazomenae, the young Socrates presents his view of the ideas as something he himself devised; and he presents in the way a 19 years old philosophic innovator would present it: he is proud, competitive, victory – loving; he is eager to prove that these two famous philosophers are *wrong* and that he, only he, solved their great problem, the problem of cause. It's all a contest and the 19 years old just knows that he will be the victor.

The man who was present in 450, Pythodorus, was sure that Parmenides and Zeno would be *angry* at being treated that way. But no, they *admired* Socrates for what he said. That is, they saw in the young Socrates a man of their own kind, a great rarity of the kind a philosopher always seeks.

After Socrates made his proud speech refuting them, Parmenides raised a first logical difficulty with Socrates' view of transcendent, fixed ideas. Socrates has no answer to that difficulty so Parmenides says to him:

> Well, you're still young, Socrates, and philosophy has not yet taken hold of you as it will, in my opinion ⋯ As for now, you still look to the opinions of men, because of your age.

Parmenides thus suggests to the young thinker Socrates that there is way too much love of victory driving him, the "opinions of men" still matter far too much to him, but Parmenides believes there is great promise in Socrates.

Parmenides then raises deeper and even more serious arguments against the possibility of the view that Socrates thought would bring him victory. Socrates has no argument that can defend transcendent ideas against Parmenides' arguments. At the end of these unanswerable arguments Parmenides says to Socrates:

> Only a *naturally gifted man* could learn that there is a certain kind and beinghood in itself for each thing; and only a *still more wondrous person* will discover all these things and be able to teach someone else

to be able to judge them clearly and sufficiently for himself."

Could *Socrates* be that "naturally gifted man" who can learn that there is a certain kind and beinghood in itself for each thing? Parmenides is challenging young Socrates. It seems that Socrates has made the fundamental step of philosophy and learned for himself that things have *natures*, that each thing belongs to a *kind*, a natural kind; that is what the "idea" of a thing means. But in the competitive battle that this conversation is, the older philosopher challenges young Socrates even further: could *you* be that "still more wondrous person" who will be able to discover all these things and also "be able to teach someone else to be able to judge them clearly and sufficiently for himself."

Fine old Parmenides brings his challenge to an end by telling the young Socrates why it is necessary for him to push forward in thinking about the ideas and not to take his defeat as a refutation of the very notion of the ideas:

> "And yet," said Parmenides, "if someone, in turn, Socrates, after focusing on all these problems and others still, shall *deny* that there are ideas of the beings and will not distinguish a certain idea of each single thing, wherever he turns he'll understand nothing, since he does not allow that there is an ever – same idea for each of the beings. And so he will entirely destroy the power of dialogue or dialectics. But you seem to me only too aware of this."

The very possibility of understanding is at stake in the ideas. If things are to be understood at all, then each thing must have its idea, must be an instance of its own kind. It must have a nature. And furthermore, that nature must in some sense be knowable. For *philosophy* to be possible at all, things must have natures or be of a kind, and these kinds must in some sense be knowable. Do you have it in you, Socrates, to move beyond your refuted view of the ideas? Are you one of *that* kind, *our* kind, Zeno and me? Does your natural genius extend so far that you will be able to discover and to show others the grounds of the possibility of philosophy? Socrates of course knows that Parmenides' arguments have proven that his view of the ideas is rationally indefensible. It is *wrong*. But will he be able to meet Parmenides' challenge? Is he of the same kind as the great Parmenides, whom he thought he could refute with his now refuted view?

What a story *that* is. Cephalus had identified the men of Clazomenae as "quite the philosophers." And hearing that story, they must have rejoiced at their decision to sail across the sea in the mere hope of hearing a story about a young Socrates conversing with Zeno and Parmenides.

The implications of the setting and the conversation

Pythodorus was there in 450 and heard everything. It was at his house that Parmenides and Zeno were staying while they were in Athens. *He*, the host of these great philosophers, knew the importance of what he was hearing with the young Socrates and he memorized it. Then, much later, concerned that what he had heard and memorized be preserved, he passed on what he had memorized to his young friend, Antiphon, and helped *him* to memorize it. But Antiphon lost interest in it; he failed to see why it had to be passed on, and he does not want to go to all the trouble of trying to remember it. The story would have died with him except for the men of Clazomenae.

And what about Adeimantus and Glaucon, the young men taught by Socrates in the *Republic* in 429, 36 years ago now? —394 being the time in which Plato set the *Parmenides*. Plato has made it clear that Adeimantus and Glaucon had no real interest in this story of the young Socrates: in all those years they never bothered to ask their brother to tell them the story of the young Socrates. For all *they* cared, the story would have died with their brother.

And that seems to me perfectly right and instructive: they heard what Socrates had to teach them as young men after Socrates himself had learned his proper poetry, his proper exoteric teaching. And that was enough for them. With that they learned all the lessons of the *Republic*, all the main lessons of Socrates' public teaching, and they were fully satisfied with that. For them, Socrates is the teacher of the view that they are now fully content to *believe* as the grounds of their lives of justice and decency. Socrates taught them how to get over the doubts caused by the Greek enlightenment and he taught them the nature of their souls, and the fixed permanence of the ideas, and of moral gods who will reward their justice in Hades.

But the men of Clazomenae? They are different from Antiphon and Adeimantus and Glaucon in the essential way: they have to know what the young Socrates said to or learned from the great Parmenides and Zeno. They have already learned enough about Socrates to know that they must hear this story of his early thinking. In the language I'm using here, they want to learn how Socrates *became* Socrates, how Socrates became the philosopher that they so admire, admire so much that they are willing to cross the sea on the basis of a mere rumor that that story of the young Socrates might still be heard.

So this is what Plato seems to be saying by setting up the *Parmenides* this way: The only ones who can really care about hearing this important event in the young Socrates' life are nameless latecomers from abroad, some few willing to sail across the sea in the mere hope of learning what a young Socrates and an old Parmenides said to one another. Plato seems to be saying that what he, Plato, preserves in this dialogue is only for the passionately interested few, nameless future travelers from afar, potential philosophers willing to expend a lot of time and effort to learn what even close associates of Socrates do not need to know.

It seems that this is how Plato thinks the tradition of philosophy works, how Socratic philosophy will be passed down: the essential esoteric Socrates is embedded in the preserved conversations of the exoteric Socrates. Those conversations can continue to train the Adeimantuses and Glaucons in the edifying, moral teaching with which philosophy will be identified and which they will believe. But there will be those few, those who correspond to the nameless men of Clazomenae in being driven to inquire further, driven to investigate the Socratic speeches in order to understand what is esoterically sheltered in them: they will not simply believe what Socrates tells them, they will work to understand what Socrates is also implying and they will test that and judge that for themselves.

The men of Clazomenae learn what Socrates learned at 19. They learn that the doctrine of transcendent fixed ideas, the doctrine Adeimantus and Glaucon trust, is impossible. That's their reward for their needing to know what old Parmenides said to young Socrates. And after learning that, they know that their travels must continue, they must follow Socrates' learning further. To what? We can assume that Plato left that question open in order to have it be pursued in the way that he himself arranged.

For Plato, the author of all these stories, *records* this great event in Socrates' past, this turning point in the process of Socrates becoming Socrates, the event that forced Socrates to abandon transcendent ideas as an adequate understanding of cause. And Plato shows a lot more by the chronological sequence he gave these two dialogues. Clearly, Plato's *Parmenides* shows the Socrates who had already made the first step in philosophy that Plato showed in the *Phaedo*. The *Parmenides* shows the second step in the philosophic education of Socrates. But by *linking* the *Phaedo* and the *Parmenides* this way, Plato forces his reader to confront a very big problem: On the last day of his life, at age 70, in the last argument of his life, Socrates teaches young Pythagoreans the very view of the ideas that he himself, 50 years earlier, learned from Parmenides was rationally indefensible. And Socrates says on his last day that this is what he always brings in, the ideas as cause. Of course Socrates never forgot what Parmenides did with this view of the ideas. So why is he still teaching, on the last day of his life, and why has he always been teaching, the view that he learned was rationally indefensible when he was 19?

The *Phaedo* itself indicates why without saying why: in the *Phaedo* Socrates repeatedly calls his last argument using the ideas, *the safe view*, the view his young audience can *trust*; it is the view he encourages them even *to shout* whenever anyone argues for a contrary view. And they do trust it; they do believe it; and we can imagine them shouting it. Believing the ideas this way, they will not be victims of the doubts and fears that they express in the *Phaedo*. And that's enough for them, just as the *Republic* was enough for Adeimantus and Glaucon. They do not go on to question Socrates' last argument, as Socrates himself suggests that even the last argument of his life, the argument based on the ideas, might be questioned—and in fact is questioned, by someone, "I don't remember who," Phaedo says. By not questioning the argument from the ideas, by just believing it, the two young men prove one thing: they are not of Socrates' kind. They would never sail across the sea in hopes of hearing a story of Socrates' origins.

The *Phaedo* and the account of the young Socrates in *Parmenides* are separated by 50 years. By linking the last day of Socrates' life to the day he learned that the ideas are not an adequate explanation of cause, Plato shows that that view of the ideas in the *Republic* and the *Phaedo* belongs to political philosophy as a safe view that makes philosophy publicly defensible as morally trustworthy. It is a part of philosophic poetry, part of what Strauss called ministerial poetry. But we are still left with the serious philosophical problem that Socrates already had at age 19, the problem of understanding nature, understanding cause. And with that as the problem we can move directly to the third and last stage of Socrates' philosophic education in the *Symposium*.

Symposium

Leo Strauss gave two reasons for holding that the *Symposium* is Plato's most important dialogue: it is the only dialogue whose topic is *praise of a god*, Eros or Love. And it is the only dialogue named for its occasion, the event at which it happened: a *drinking party* at which wine loosens tongues and things are said that might otherwise not be said. From these two visible points, Strauss moves to a hidden feature of the *Symposium* suggested by its dramatic dates: this dialogue *profanes the mysteries*, it tells what it is a crime to tell, a secret about the gods and what they know.

Important guidance to the *Symposium* is also supplied by Seth Benardete. What I have to say about the *Symposium* makes use of both Strauss and Benardete, especially Benardete.

In the *Phaedo*, Phaedo tells the story of Socrates' last day at which he was present; but within the story he tells, Socrates himself reports his earliest beginning in the philosophic life. In the *Parmenides*, two memorized recollections take the reader back to the actual conversation in which the 19 years old Socrates speaks. And again in the *Symposium*, two memorized recollections take the reader back to the actual conversation reported, and there it is again Socrates who tells the story of this last stage of his becoming himself, a story he wants to tell of his much younger self—and he knows a devoted follower is listening to everything because he invited that follower to the party.

The *Symposium* has a complicated chronology. It opens at a time when two different groups of Athenians have a great interest in hearing about a drinking party at Agathon's house at which Socrates and Alcibiades and others made speeches about Eros. Christopher Planeaux shows that that frame for the dialogue is set in 399 just before the trial of Socrates: that's the reason for all that interest in Socrates and Alcibiades.

Why is 399 significant?

First, it is significant because it is the time of Socrates' trial. Part of the charge against him originated in the suspicion that he corrupted Alcibiades—and many Athenians regarded Alcibiades as a great criminal partly or even mostly because he was suspected of profaning the mysteries in 416. The *Symposium* demonstrates that Socrates is innocent of the charge that he corrupted Alcibiades; the two supplied audiences for the reporting of the *Symposium* can therefore judge Socrates innocent of that charge. Another trial in Athens in 399, the "trial of Andokides," likely just before Socrates' trial, showed that the 416 crimes were a pressing, much talked about issue because Andokides was tried for being involved. This trial, like Socrates' trial, was an event in the purification of the city of Athens after the war with Sparta ended in 404 and after the civil war against the 30 Tyrants who were led in part by *Critias*, the other great Athenian who was thought to have been corrupted by Socrates. 399 was a time of fervent religious purification to which Socrates fell victim.

There's a second reason that 399 is important: in his defense speech at his trial, Socrates told the story that became famous: the god at Delphi said that no one was wiser than he was and that made him turn to what became his customary practice in service to the god, testing what the god said. This story, as I said, we can regard as mythically true. But in the *Symposium*, also set in 399 when Socrates told that story about himself, we hear the deeper truth about how Socrates became himself—in the *Symposium* we hear Socrates tell the genuine origin story of his wisdom.

The 399 reporter is Apollodoros who says that he got the story from Aristodemos who was there because Socrates invited him. The party was held the second night after Agathon, the host, won the tragedy contest. As the writer of a prize-winning tragedy, Agathon was famous; all Athenians would know that his victory occurred in 416.

Why is 416 significant?

Everyone knows that the shocking crime of profaning the mysteries happened in 416, the crime of revealing the secret core of Athenian religion. Alcibiades was widely thought to be guilty of that crime, of having ridiculed and exposed the most sacred secrets. Studying the *Symposium* with that crime of revealing secrets in mind leads the reader to see what Strauss emphasizes: a profaning of different mysteries, the mysteries of what a philosopher is and what a philosopher can know. Socrates' speech at the drinking party, that setting for loosened tongues, opens for inspection the most hidden truths about philosophy that Plato will ever reveal, an unveiling of the mystery of Socrates' being as a philosopher that is at the same time an unveiling of the mystery of being itself. The crime of profaning the mysteries of Athenian religion violates Athenian law. But the mystery Socrates in some sense reveals is the genuine mystery of nature. Its being secret does not depend on some convention that makes it unlawful to speak about. Instead, the genuine mystery of nature always withdraws from articulation, resists being put into words. *Nature loves to hide*, Heraclitus said. But the *Symposium* suggests that to a degree, or in a way, that mystery can be divined—but it suggests that in a way that is itself mysterious, true to the hidden ways of nature.

A third event in time complicates the chronology of the *Symposium*. In his speech at the party, Socrates takes his audience back to an earlier event in his life: he reports that he learned something of primary importance when he was younger, around 440 it seems, when he was about 30 years old.

Why is 440 significant?

What Socrates says about this event of learning shows that it must have occurred after 450 when Parmenides refuted Socrates' view of transcendent ideas. What Socrates here reports learning can be seen as a solution to the problem he was left with by Parmenides' refutation. Because the story Socrates that tells about the event of 440 comes after Parmenides' refutation of the ideas, it completes the three stages of Socrates' philosophic education.

That fact of completion in 440 tells us something else that is important: Socrates had already completed his philosophic education *before* the *Protagoras* in 433 in which Plato shows Socrates first mounting the public stage. Socrates's *philosophic* education came before his education in *political philosophy* that Plato set out in the three dialogues I discussed in the previous lecture, dialogues set in 433 and 429.

Back in 416 at the drinking party, Socrates says something very important for his coming speech after they have decided on the topic for their speeches: "I claim to have expert knowledge of nothing but erotics" (177d). *Erotics* are the things of eros, experienced first as a profound human passion of love or attraction that the Greeks elevated to a god. All the speeches of the *Symposium* are offered in praise of Eros, but Socrates' speech is the speech of a self-proclaimed knower, the speech of an already famous and celebrated philosopher who claims that this is the single thing of which he has expert knowledge. Socrates is famous for claiming ignorance but in the *Symposium* he introduces himself as a knower with expert knowledge of what all the others are also going to make speeches about. Those others make up a very special group: they are among the most sophisticated knowers in highly sophisticated Athens, they are a special intellectual/spiritual few and each will speak as an expert. This is the most distinguished audience that Plato will ever show us for a speech by Socrates.

So the drinking party in 416 is a private gathering of special men, all in their way, men of the Greek enlightenment. Instead of drinking they spend the party making speeches about the god Eros—and they dismiss the flute girls. It's just them, for private speeches among the enlightened few. In 416 Socrates is about 53 years old, fully mature. He speaks sixth or last, and only *after* that speech does Alcibiades *arrive*, late and drunk, and he makes a speech in praise of Socrates. Alcibiades is absent for the greatest of all speeches by Socrates.

Socrates starts his speech speaking as he usually does; he examines and refutes the view of Eros that Agathon, their host, just gave. Socrates brings Agathon to a point of perplexity, of admitting that he does not know what he thought he knew and had talked about so beautifully. That is,

Socrates does young Agathon *the favor* of showing him his actual ignorance, his need for knowledge where he wrongly believed he already had it. Then he does Agathon another great favor: he says that he too was once put in that same state of neediness by a wise teacher who then led him, with the help of his own persistent questioning, to genuine knowledge of eros. Socrates' speech to everyone present is especially for one person, that brilliant young writer of tragedy who had just won the prize for tragedy. Socrates suggests to him that there's more than prize – winning; it's possible to grasp, on his own, the true understanding of eros that he wrongly thought he already had, but achieving that *more* depends on him, depends on him questioning as Socrates questioned.

Socrates tells Agathon that his teacher was a wise woman named Diotima and that when she led him to perplexity, he then questioned her and she taught him the essential lessons about Eros—and Socrates reports some of his conversations with Diotima.

What Socrates learned in 440

The first thing Diotima does with Socrates is refute his view, a view that was also Agathon's, that Eros is beautiful and good and wise. But Eros is not ugly or bad or ignorant. Instead, Diotima teaches Socrates that there is a *between* between the extremes of beautiful and ugly, and good and bad, and wisdom and ignorance. By beginning with what lies between wisdom and ignorance, Diotima begins her account of eros where the philosopher always begins. She first speaks of this between as "correct opinion"—that is the common way of occupying the *between* between wisdom and ignorance. Philosophy too occupies that between but occupies it differently. Neither wise nor ignorant, the philosopher experiences the passion for wisdom. He is *driven* to remedy his lack of wisdom. He occupies the between *erotically*. He is passionate to have what he knows he lacks.

Socrates' speech in the *Symposium* thus begins with *extremes* as he had begun in the *Parmenides* where the extremes were the ideas and the particulars, or we could say, pure permanence and pure flow. The *Symposium* goes on to show how philosophy, driven erotically, can best think the reality that lies between those abstractions of permanence and flow, the reality that the philosopher in fact *is* as erotic, *is* as one particular in the totality of particulars. The philosopher can come to know by knowing himself.

Diotima then teaches Socrates that Eros is not a god but something between a god and a mortal. Taught to get over his shock at Eros not being a god, Socrates asks Diotima what such a between can *be* and what kind of *power* eros has. The power of *ferrying* Diotima replies, the power of mediating or carrying things between the immortals and the mortal. This representation seems to imply that the power of eros is constantly generating mortal approximations of immortality. Diotima here seems to be in the realm of *the mythic*, in a kind of *theology* by means of which the fundamental condition or the fundamental human condition is represented by myths that account for that condition. Certainly what Socrates asks next leads Diotima to a most illuminating *mythic* picture of eros. Who is his father? And who is his mother? Socrates asks. That is, what are the origins of eros?

Diotima answers with a myth about the birth of Eros. A myth can only suggest or point to things to be thought about rationally. Myth must be followed by reasoning about what the myth suggests, and Diotima does go on to supply that reasoning. I will deal most extensively with the myth and then take up one feature only of her reasoning.

According to Diotima's myth, on the day Aphrodite, the goddess of sexual love, was born, the gods held a feast. Present at the feast was *Poros* or *Resource*, the son of Intelligence. And Penia, *Poverty*, came to the feast to beg. Resource got drunk and laid down in the Garden of Zeus. Poverty was plotting to have a child by Resource because she lacked resources, and she laid down beside him in the garden and conceived Eros. Strauss draws his main conclusion about the myth, or about the *Symposium* as a whole, from Poverty's *plotting*, her planning, her calculating. Plotting Poverty shows that she cannot be simply ignorant: she knew what she lacked and she wanted to have it and she acted to get it. Poverty, that is, is *resourceful*; she does not lack intelligence. Strauss says: "Eros, I conclude, resembles only his mother"—because eros too is resourceful poverty. Eros and his mother have the same essential quality of resourceful poverty. That is, the myth suggests that the parent of *eros* is eros. As Francis Bacon concluded on this very point, *Eros has no parents*—and that is the greatest thing, Bacon says. And Plato too seems to be saying that: it is the greatest thing that eros has no parents and that we can know that eros has no parents. Eros springs from eros and eros results in eros.

George Dunn has a nice word for that: he says that eros is *auto – poietic*, self – making in Greek, self – generating—eros as self – generating never simply *is* but is always coming into being as a result of its own activity and always slipping out of being as a result of its self – expenditure, its dying away in its expressing itself.

Seth Benardete makes the same point about eros and he adds a helpful generalization about Platonic myth: myth splits into *two* what is actually *one*, and that splitting displays the complex structure of the one so that we can, after learning from the splitting, go back to the one now knowing the internal structure of the one. Eros is one and has a complex structure. In Benardete's words, Eros is need and neediness (awareness of need); Eros is "self – aware desire." And Benardete emphasizes a second, indispensable matter: the deep structure of eros always disappears into the concrete experience that it enables: that always present disappearing is what makes eros essentially elusive; eros is in principle elusive because the deep structure of eros is always masked in the particular that it always disappears into.

So that's the primary conclusion about the always masked: Eros is desire or drive with an internal structure. The myth suggests that the structure of eros is to have a direction or impetus built into it as what it is: in being what it is, it is dynamic and directed out beyond itself toward that for which it is eros. The myth therefore suggests that the conclusion be expanded in a way that Benardete suggests: in its dynamic structure eros is always in a relation, always related to something outside it, as Penia desires to mate with Resource in order to produce offspring.

And the myth suggests yet another conclusion: its dynamic of always being in a relation gives it an always temporal aspect, it is always stretched out in time toward some future having. We can bundle all three aspects of this conclusion and say that the myth suggests that the internal structure of desire makes it always *dynamic*, *relational*, and *temporal*.

By splitting the mother of Eros from Eros and giving them the same quality, the myth suggests that the origin of desire is desire, and that the outcome of desire is desire. Backward toward its origins and forward toward its outcomes, eros is always desire directed by its very nature to fulfillment or satisfaction, and its fulfillment always drains away and revives seeking fulfillment.

I have to add a word about *fulfillment*. And that means reaching outside the myth to touch the main point of Diotima's reasoning after she tells the myth. The first stage of her argument considers eros as desire for the beautiful but Socrates can't answer her question about what the fulfillment of that would mean. So she moves to consider eros as desire for the good and the fulfillment of *that* Socrates can answer in a series of steps: ultimately, desire for the good is fulfilled in the happiness of the good's being one's own forever. But the difficulty of the *forever* leads Diotima to her final formulation of the fulfillment of eros: "begetting in the beautiful." (206b) Begetting in the beautiful is the *Symposium*'s ultimate definition of the fulfillment of eros. But Diotima makes it clear that this fulfillment always wanes or dies away while eros always renews itself. With respect to the origins of eros I used George Dunn's word *auto – poietic* or self – generating. With the fulfillment of eros, its end or goal, I can use his word *auto – telic*, or having its goal, its *telos*, in itself as begetting or giving birth. So the myth suggests that the origin of eros is eros. And the reasoning suggests that the end or fulfillment of eros is eros.

Putting all this together, we can see that wise Diotima taught Socrates the ultimate philosophic lesson, a lesson that begins in a philosopher's self – knowledge as an erotic and extends out to the whole of what is as erotic. When Socrates says that he has "expert knowledge of nothing but erotics," he seems to make a modest or moderate knowledge claim; but in fact he makes a giant knowledge claim, the largest of all possible knowledge claims: he has expert knowledge of the character or way of all that is. Strauss states this comprehensive conclusion this way: "Eros, we can say, is the heart of coming into being and perishing. Eros, we can say, is the nature of nature."

What Diotima leads Socrates to is the intelligible character of the whole of what is. She leads Socrates to an *ontology*, a reasoned conclusion about beings as a whole: to be is to be eros and nothing else. The ontology Diotima suggests is therefore an ontology of "the sovereignty of becoming," to use Nietzsche's words, where becoming has the intelligible character of eros. It is a thing worthy of wonder and of gratitude that the totality has an intelligible structure that can be known by humans existing within it.

If we step back and interpret this lesson in the *Symposium* as one part of what Plato presents as Socrates becoming Socrates, we can see the coherence of the story Plato tells, or rather, intentionally *obscures* by scattering it across three dialogues. When the three stages are put together, the meaning of the *Symposium*'s final stage becomes clear as the completion of the first two stages. Plato put the first stage in the *Phaedo* where he has Socrates on his last day tell the story of his beginnings in philosophy: he began where the Greek philosophers before him began, with the question of *cause* concerning generation and destruction as a whole. The *range* of Socrates' concern did not shrink to the human things alone when he struck out on his own with his turn to the speeches or accounts. Instead, that second sailing provided him with the route that took him first to transcendent ideas as the cause of all generation and decay. But Plato showed in the second stage, the *Parmenides* stage, that this first solution to the problem of cause by the 19 years old Socrates fell victim early to Parmenides' proof of the rational impossibility of transcendent ideas. The third or *Symposium* stage of Socrates' philosophic education solves the problem of cause by resolving the problem set by Parmenides. What Socrates chose to present as what he learned from Diotima was the proper way to understand cause: what *is* lies in a *between* between pure flow and the pure fixity or permanence of the ideas; everything that *is* has the dynamic, relational, temporal character of *eros*. Socrates' expert knowledge of the erotic things is ultimately knowledge of the cause concerning generation and destruction as a whole. The *Symposium* completes Plato's story of Socrates' becoming Socrates because it shows his solution to the problem of cause with which he began. That solution answers philosophy's ultimate question, the question of the being of beings or the nature of nature.

The route to this knowledge passes through the self – knowledge of the philosopher, he lives erotically or passionately in the *between* between wisdom and ignorance. That the erotic *between* of the philosopher can ultimately be seen as a guide to the erotic between – ness of all things helps us understand what Socrates said so often: *Know thyself*. That command, put up at Delphi as the god's command, has a special meaning for the philosopher: through knowing himself as erotic he gets his clearest, nearest glimpse of what is true of all things: all beings exist in a way that is similar to the way that the highest, the most intellectual/spiritual being exists. Self – knowledge and then knowledge of the human as such is the route to the knowledge of the beings.

Now let's think again about the chronology that Plato built in to the *Symposium*. It begins in 399 just before Socrates' trial and it takes us back to 416 when Socrates tells the tale of his ultimate learning which occurred around 440. 416 is the time of the great Athenian crime of the profaning of the mysteries of Athenian religion. Could Plato be suggesting that Socrates committed the crime of *profaning* the genuine mysteries, the highest secrets of the philosophers and the secret of the being of beings? No, because Plato wrote the *Symposium*: if Socrates is a criminal for saying it, Plato is a worse criminal for writing it. No, Plato suggests something else by his complicated chronology of linking the time of discovering the truth of the ultimate mysteries, the time of the crime of profaning the religious mysteries, and the time of Socrates' trial. Plato suggests that Socrates, discoverer of the genuine mysteries, treated those mysteries, the mysteries hardest to know but knowable, in the way appropriate to them. And if *we* put Socrates on trial and test what he is saying then we too can discover that Socrates—and Plato—treated the genuine mysteries in the proper way, a way that is itself hard to know but knowable. Unlike those criminals who profaned the religious mysteries, criminals that may include Alcibiades, Socrates treated the genuine mysteries appropriately: Socrates provided a way to be *initiated* into the mysteries, a way that initiates into the true secrets of nature those who pay him the closest attention. That initiation is suggested by what Socrates did first when it came time for him to speak: he refuted Agathon or led Agathon to perplexity: he gave Agathon the gift of knowing that if he was ever to know what eros is he had to begin again.

And the way for him to begin is the way Socrates began by asking Diotima. Can Agathon do that? Can he think through the stages that Diotima took the questioning Socrates through? —Socrates who seems to have been about Agathon's age when he began questioning Diotima. Only if he does that, only if Socrates becomes *his* Diotima, can he come to know what Socrates knows. And he will know *that* because he has in a way learned it on his own. In Plato's *Symposium* Socrates does not betray the mysteries but prepares an initiation into them. And by writing the *Symposium* Plato makes Socrates, the instrument of Agathon's possible initiation, available for all future Agathons, for you and me. For our initiation.

There's one last thing that Diotima says in the *Symposium* that I want to be the last thing I say about Socrates becoming Socrates. Diotima has led Socrates to the ontological insight that is the final stage of philosophy, to be is to be eros. After leading Socrates to this insight, she makes a very long speech that is the last thing she says. Her long speech describes a ladder whose rungs or steps she climbs upward until she reaches the highest peak. She describes what happens at that peak as both *a seeing* and *a doing*. The one who has climbed to the peak *beholds* or *sees* perfect beauty and that one *gives birth* or engages in a kind of *making* or *poetizing* in the presence of the beautiful. *Two* things happen at the peak, a beholding and an engendering or giving birth, a seeing and a making. And I end my lecture "Socrates Becomes Socrates" on *that* because in the last stage of Nietzsche's becoming Nietzsche something remarkably similar happens. He too will describe a beholding or seeing and he too will speak of an engendering or making that is its natural consequence. In both Plato and Nietzsche *philosophy*, seeing, leads to *philosophic poetry*, making.

And Strauss understood that: he says in his Nietzsche essay that Nietzsche's "fundamental proposition" is that "life is will to power or seen from within the world is will to power and nothing else," and he says next: "The will to power takes the place which the *eros* ··· occupies in Plato's thought." And Strauss shows how Nietzsche's philosophic insight into that fundamental or ontological matter led in Nietzsche's religion chapter to an engendering, a making or a poetizing of the new highest ideal.

Plato and Nietzsche belong together: in becoming themselves philosophers become akin; they are of one kind; they see what is and what they see is of course similar or shared *because* it is a seeing of what is.

And each philosopher generates a teaching out of what he sees being to be. And the teaching each generates is *different* because a teaching must fit its times, must be ministerial in an effective way that depends on a true understanding of the times. Because times change the teachings of the philosophers differ. The teachings of the philosophic kin Plato and Nietzsche differ radically, they stand in warring opposition to one another. That is as it must be: for the new to be established, all 108 suitors must die.

LECTURE 5

Nietzsche Becomes Nietzsche

Nietzsche is the subject of my last two lectures and with Nietzsche I'm on home territory. It was from Nietzsche, not from Strauss, that I first learned what a philosopher is and what a philosopher can know. Those events of learning came with my study of *Thus Spoke Zarathustra*, particularly of "The Dance Song." There I first learned that Nietzsche laid claim to an ontology, an understanding of the being of beings, and that first learning was confirmed by my further study of Nietzsche's works, beginning with the chapter of *Zarathustra* called "On Self – Overcoming" in which Zarathustra reports his discovery in the Dance Song to one audience only, "you wisest." What I learned from Nietzsche was confirmed by my later study of Strauss who also points to Nietzsche's ontology, and by my later study of Plato and of Bacon and Descartes. My Nietzsche lectures reflect my debt to Nietzsche and my alignment with Nietzsche, and the way that both Strauss and Plato further that alignment.

When the master author Plato constructs his dialogues in a way that allows you to discover that Socrates *becoming* Socrates is a theme that Plato himself wants his dedicated reader to pay attention to, *you pay attention.* My Plato lectures were meant to show that Plato structured his dialogues very artfully to allow you to discover the two basic aspects of Socrates' becoming: his becoming a *philosopher* and his becoming a *philosophic poet.*

My Nietzsche lectures are concerned with Nietzsche becoming Nietzsche. At an important point in his philosophic life, Nietzsche made his own becoming a theme for his reader. That is, he saw that he had to explain his becoming, he had to turn *autobiographical* and write about "Herr Nietzsche," "Mr. Nietzsche," even though, as a philosopher, he was naturally solitary, naturally a hermit whose private thinking was what mattered most. So in emphasizing Nietzsche's becoming, I'm following what Nietzsche himself encouraged his reader to do.

Nietzsche began to make his becoming public only at a certain point in his philosophic life. After finishing the two greatest books of his maturity, *Thus Spoke Zarathustra* and *Beyond Good and Evil*, he spent the second half of the year 1886 writing new *Forewords* to his previous books. He intended those Forewords to show how those books trace the progress of his thinking until he gained his mature thought in *The Gay Science*, his 1882 book just before *Zarathustra*. Then, two years after these autobiographical Forewords, late in 1888 as he was planning to publish his new major work, he published a whole book, *Ecce Homo*, *Behold the Man*, that was autobiographical. It was intended to show that he had won the right to publish the decisive, history – making book that would come next and that he never got to finish.

And there is another fact that points to the importance of Nietzsche's becoming: he thought of *Thus Spoke Zarathustra* as his most important published book, and that book was written to show Zarathustra's becoming, the stages of thought that he moved through to reach his mature position. And Zarathustra's becoming is a poetized version of Nietzsche's becoming: *Thus Spoke Zarathustra* is itself a version of Nietzsche's autobiography.

Before getting to Nietzsche's becoming, I want to say something about his relation to his philosophic predecessors, about whom he is *very critical*, singling out for special criticism, the ancient philosopher Plato and the modern philosopher Rousseau, the two philosophers he held most responsible for what Western philosophy and Western culture had become in his own time. At the very end of what he originally intended to be the second and final volume of *Human All Too Human* he placed a very special section, number 408 of *Assorted Opinions and Maxims* (*Vermischte Meinungen und Sprüche*) :

I too have been to the underworld, like Odysseus, and will be there many times again ··· There have been four pairs who do not refuse themselves to me ··· Epicurus and Montaigne, Goethe and Spinoza, Plato and Rousseau, Pascal and Schopenhauer ···. Whatever I say, decide, think through for myself and others, upon these eight I fix my eyes and find theirs fixed on me.

In this amazing reflection, Nietzsche shows that *this* is who he is, *this* is where he belongs, among the thinkers of the highest rank. He visits these eight thinkers in the underworld; they are all dead but live on, alive in their works. What Nietzsche pictures himself doing is what Homer's Odysseus did, descending to the underworld where the first figure he met was the wise man *Teiresias*—and Odysseus learned from Teiresias his own task as a wise ruler. In the underworld of the wise to which Nietzsche descends, his special eight are his Teiresiases. And they include Plato and Rousseau, the two philosophers he most criticizes. What he says about his eight is that whatever he *says*, *decides*, *thinks through for himself and others* "upon these eight I fix my eyes and find theirs fixed on me." Nietzsche put this statement at the very end of *Human All Too Human*, the book that began his attempt to win complete freedom for his mind. And those three verbs, *saying*, *deciding*, and *thinking through for himself and others*, do not say that he takes his *thinking* from them. His thinking is different from his *thinking through for myself and others* (in German, his *denken* is different from his *andenken für mich und andere*). Nietzsche's *thinking* is wholly his own. Working to become *wholly free in his thinking*, he takes his *standard of action* from the history of great thinkers and actors who have determined the spiritual and intellectual course of the West.

Nietzsche lives and acts in the presence of the greatest thinkers. They are the standard by which he determines his own doings and he knows that their doings determined the history of the West. Nietzsche lives and acts as the latest one of those and measures himself by them and sees them measuring him.

Nietzsche thought very highly of himself. And he had every right to do so. He knew himself.

I want to make a second general point about Nietzsche and his books: In his autobiography, *Ecce Homo*, he called all his books from *Beyond Good and Evil* on, "*fishhooks.*" He explained his use of *fishhook* in letters: his books were intended to *catch* those readers he really wants, the few "who are related" to him. They would be drawn to him for further instruction in a philosophical school that would be like the ancient Greek schools of philosophy. He imagined establishing such a school while he was writing *Human All Too Human* in 1876 – 8. His reason was that not everything can be said in books; and training in philosophy could be conducted best in a small school of the like – minded. Nietzsche never got to establish such a school so the books have to stand by themselves. Still, even as fishhooks Nietzsche wrote his books to be a schooling, to teach his reader how to read and how to think.

That Nietzsche thought of his books as fishhooks already indicates the presence of the *exoteric/esoteric distinction* in his work. Nietzsche spoke of that distinction most explicitly in *Beyond Good and Evil*. It comes early in the second chapter, "The Free Mind," just after he has said that there are *exceptions* to the rule that everyone is satisfied with the "simplifications and falsifications" with which almost all people live. There are exceptions to that rule who want to know the truth. But not only that, there are *exceptions among the exceptions* who want to know exactly how they differ from everyone else in their thinking: they "go down" to examine others and they "go inside" to know themselves. They do what Socrates did. To readers prepared in this way by the first sections of The Free Mind, he then speaks of the exoteric and the esoteric in *Beyond Good and Evil* #30:

> Our highest insights must—and should! —sound like follies, possibly like crimes, when they come without permission to the ears of those who are not the kind for them, not predestined for them.

Our highest insights, that is, the insights of the exception among the exceptions, the philosopher, whose drive it is to know and to know himself. Non – philosophers will judge the philosopher to be a madman or a criminal if *his* insights come to *their* ears, the ears of those who are not the kind for them—Socrates had said the exact same thing in Plato's *Repub-*

lic. Nietzsche then says that this is an old and well-known view:

> The difference between the exoteric and the esoteric as one formerly among philosophers distinguished them among the Indians as among the Greeks, Persians, and Muslims⋯.

Nietzsche's good friend, the scholar of Sanskrit philosophy, Paul Deussen, introduced Eastern philosophy to Germany. He answered Nietzsche's questions about Indian philosophy, and may have later informed him about *Chinese philosophy* but Nietzsche knew very little about it.

Nietzsche's sentence on exotericism goes on to say what the distinction between exoteric and esoteric does *not* mean: It is not a distinction between the outside and inside as if you could pass from outside to inside just by being told something or whispered something. Instead, he says,

> the much more essential is that [the exoteric approach] views things from below and the esoteric *down from above.*

The exception among exceptions looks down from a very high height—from a perspective that you have to *work* to achieve. The exception among exceptions has won a privileged viewpoint that you cannot share unless you climb to that height yourself. Still, Nietzsche can *report* what he sees from there:

> There are heights of the soul where, to look out from which, tragedy itself ceases to have a tragic effect, and taking all the woe of the world together, who may dare to decide whether its sight *necessarily* seduces and compels precisely to pity and thus to doubling the woe?

Nietzsche's report from above simply *says* that the exception among exceptions, the philosopher, looking down from above on tragedy does not feel the standard effects of tragedy which are pity and fear. Tragedy remains tragedy; life is not transformed in the view from above. The *effect* of tragedy is different.

The second part of what I just read expands tragedy to *the whole of human suffering* and asks: who may dare to decide that the view from above necessarily leads to *pity* for the human, that is, to the great modern virtue, pity? *Who* may dare? The answer must be the exception among the exceptions, the philosopher, *now* dares that. Because he has the privileged viewpoint, down from above, Nietzsche faces the profound question of whether to take pity on suffering humanity, to view humanity's tragic fate, and consequently—although Nietzsche does not say this here—feel the responsibility to offer humanity some *deliverance*, some *redemption* or other. That is what the fact of the exoteric/esoteric distinction results in for Nietzsche—will the philosopher *today* generate a teaching that will cover over the tragedy, the totality of suffering, and make it seem bearable because there is some deliverance, as philosophers in the Platonic tradition have taught till now? Or does the philosopher now judge that the time has come for a new response to the view from above, down on human suffering? Is it time for a new teaching that does not lie about suffering by inventing or endorsing some comedy of a purpose to existence that gives suffering meaning? Nietzsche's answer is that, yes, the time has come for such a new teaching. A notebook entry from 1888, two years later, puts one aspect of that conclusion in a way that condemns all of the platonic teachers:

> We're proud not to have to be liars any more, or slanderers, or discreditors of life.

The philosophic tradition of exoteric noble lying comes to a self – conscious end with Nietzsche. He's proud not to have to be a liar. It's easy for me to imagine that right here Nietzsche felt the eyes of his underworld judges on him for not continuing what Plato called the "noble" lie. And Nietzsche knows how extremely dangerous that is, because it opens up exposure to fundamental truths that he himself called "true but deadly" (the sovereignty of becoming, the fluidity of all concepts, types, and kinds, the lack of any cardinal difference between man and the animals). It is worthwhile to note again that the "deadly" truths are not deadly to Nietzsche; he judges them deadly to society based on a belief in a purpose of existence for human beings.

As I will emphasize, the Nietzsche who is proud not to have to be a liar any more, *does* have an exoteric teaching. The exoteric/esoteric distinction still means for Nietzsche what it meant for Plato in this sense: in Nietzsche too genuine philosophy generates philosophic poetry; in Nietzsche's language, philosophy generates *art*. And the poetry or art that philosophy generates in Nietzsche can be given a label that derives from Leo Strauss: the ultimate art in Nietzsche is a theological – political teaching—philosophic poetry.

So those are the themes of the rest of my Nietzsche lectures: Nietzsche is a genuine philosopher who lives on in the underworld with the other great philosophers; and Nietzsche the philosopher continues the exoteric/esoteric tradition of philosophy but in a new way.

I'm now writing a new book on Nietzsche, on how Nietzsche *became* Nietzsche. The topic of Nietzsche's becoming has not been adequately treated in Nietzsche studies partly because Strauss's recovery of the exoteric/esoteric distinction has not been applied to Nietzsche. My new book does apply that distinction and aims to set out Nietzsche's genuine becoming. For the rest of this lecture I will give an outline of Nietzsche's becoming and then a more detailed outline of what he actually became.

Nietzsche's 1876 turn

In his first five books (1882 – 1886) Nietzsche put himself in the service of others, of Schopenhauer and Wagner; those books are *pre – Nietzschean* books although they contain a great deal that is important for really knowing Nietzsche. Then, in the summer of 1876, Nietzsche made a decisive *turn*; he turned away from the perspective of his first five books to take his own path in philosophy, the path to achieve a free mind as he called it. Freeing the mind has one aim above all others, to discover the truth; the way to the truth passes through an understanding of the ways in which the mind is unfree or "prejudiced." In the very first book of what became a series of books on freeing the mind, Nietzsche quoted Descartes "In Place of a Foreword" and what he quoted was Descartes's own statement on his turn to the philosophic life. Nietzsche's 1876 turn can be regarded as his *turn to the philosophic life*.

Freeing the mind meant for Nietzsche studying the *human soul* with knowledge of his own soul, *self – knowledge*, as a crucial component: how do the drives and passions of the soul influence or prejudice human understanding? It also meant studying *human culture* in its history from human beginnings through the high culture of the Greeks in which he had his professional training: how did culture build bias and prejudice into human understanding? It also meant studying the *history of philosophy*, studying his great predecessors to see how their teachings influenced the particular perspectives or prejudices of western culture; in particular, it meant studying Kant and his followers in order to understand how the faculties of perception and cognition place essential limits on the capacity of the human mind to know the world.

And crucially for him in the second half of the 19th Century in Europe, it meant using all the resources of *modern science* which had been advancing knowledge and publicizing it since the beginnings of the Enlightenment almost three centuries earlier, and which had made solid progress with strict methods of gaining and communicating knowledge: modern science with its dependable findings was a now indispensable part of freeing the mind. Nietzsche strongly criticized the education he had gotten because it had not given him a grounding in the sciences of physics and chemistry and anthropology. (After completing *Thus Spoke Zarathustra* Nietzsche planned to go to a University to study *physics* for five years.)

So there was a lot for Nietzsche to do after his decisive turn in 1876 to *gain* a free mind and at the same time to *teach the ideal* of the free mind— to win other talented minds for this project of understanding.

Nietzsche continued to publish books while following his path to a free mind. The first of those books, *Human All Too Human* in 1878, he subtitled *A Book for Free Minds*. Then he published a separate book with the same title but as an *Appendix* or *Addition* in 1879; and in 1880 he published *The Wanderer and His Shadow*, a book with the same aim. Then his project of freeing the mind took the focus that he would maintain to the end, the focus first gained in the book *Daybreak* in 1881. He viewed that book as a new beginning for him, what he called his "campaign against morality." Having come to understand the power of morality and its dangerous and negative effects, his study of morality extended to a war against it.

After he finished *Daybreak*, he started again as he always did, with a *new notebook* in which he wrote entries intended for his next book. He thought that the entries would prepare a second book called *Daybreak*, chapters 6 through 10. But when he finally published that new book it had only four chapters and had the title, *The Gay Science*. In the fourth chapter of that book he reported his decisive breakthrough that he had first written out in his notebook. I take this breakthrough on the path of freeing his mind to be Nietzsche's decisive step into his maturity. With book 4 of *The Gay Science*, Nietzsche became Nietzsche.

The 1881 turn

Nietzsche gave a sign of his breakthrough in a Notice that he put on the back cover of the first edition of *The Gay Science* when it appeared in the summer of 1882. That notice says:

With this book a series of writings by Friedrich Nietzsche comes to its end, the writings whose common goal it is to erect a new image and ideal of the free mind.

And then he listed the books in this series from *Human All Too Human* to *The Gay Science*. So the great project of Nietzsche's 1876 turn, to erect a new image and ideal of the free mind, is *over* in 1882; he *completed it* successfully. That is, Nietzsche's free mind had reached the goal that the whole free mind project existed to reach: the truth, fundamental truth that freeing his mind had aimed at from the start. So erecting the ideal of the free mind could no longer be his highest ideal any more. Now his books could have a different aim: *showing what the free mind can come to know*, showing the truth that the freed mind can rightly *tie* itself to, rightly *bind* itself to—*because* it's the truth. And that's what Nietzsche's next books do: *Thus Spoke Zarathustra* and *Beyond Good and Evil* lead the reader into the truth Nietzsche discovered.

So this turn, the 1881 turn that Nietzsche first made public in book 4 of *The Gay Science* is the decisive turn in his life. What had Nietzsche discovered, what truths had he gained, that made this turn possible? That's what both my Nietzsche lectures are about: what Nietzsche's free mind discovered and what his books from then on were written to introduce.

The notebook with the new discoveries

To show what Nietzsche discovered it seems best to me to go back to the writing in which Nietzsche first wrote out those discoveries. That writing is the new notebook he began in March, 1881, just after completing *Daybreak*; he filled that notebook with entries from the spring of 1881, through the summer and into the fall. Then he composed much of *The Gay Science* from entries in that notebook. *The Gay Science* contains the new discoveries *in the form* Nietzsche wanted them to have in their first public presentation. He never intended that anyone ever read the notebook in which he first wrote them out; that was private, for him alone. Luckily for us, however, Nietzsche's sister Elisabeth preserved that notebook and every other scrap of writing by her brother, and she established the Nietzsche Archive to make them permanently available to scholars. And she began the project of publishing those private notes.

Before looking into that 1881 notebook I want to say something about Nietzsche's notebooks generally. They are like the notebooks of no one else for this reason: Nietzsche suffered from very bad eyesight from birth that included extreme near-sightedness. While he was composing *Human All Too Human* in 1876 and 1877, one aspect of his bad eyesight got much worse: his eyes became even more sensitive to light with the result that he could read or write for only about $1\frac{1}{2}$ hours each day before it caused extreme headaches. That is a disaster for a thinker whose thinking life is furthered by reading and writing. In order to save the one thing he lived for, Nietzsche devised a practice that he followed for the rest of his writing life. He described it in a letter to his best friend.

For 6 to 8 hours every day he would take long walks. On those walks he composed his thoughts, and his arguments, and his images, composed them into sentences and paragraphs while he was walking. After his 6 to 8 hours of walking, he returned to his room, usually a single room he rented in some rooming house. There he wrote out his already composed paragraphs in the large notebook that he kept in his room. Except for the ones from near the end of his writing life, these notebooks are very orderly, written in steady handwriting on almost every line of the lined pages. The entries are not random; they are not scattered thoughts hurriedly written down; they are already polished paragraphs, long and short, that he had composed while walking. Then, in the later stages of composing a book from his notebook entries, Nietzsche would organize and assemble these already coherent paragraphs into ordered themes and chapters, editing and rewriting the entries, adding and subtracting, until he had arranged the entries into whole chapters. Especially in the later books, each chapter is a disciplined sequence with a beginning, middle and end.

The 1881 notebook that he began just after *Daybreak* and filled with material for *The Gay Science* seems to me the most important of all the notebooks. Its entries show Nietzsche in the process of discovering the two most important insights of his mature philosophy. And that's what the rest of my Nietzsche lectures will be about: the two discoveries that made it possible to end the free mind series of books and begin the books of his maturity.

The 1881 notebook and *ontology*

The 1881 notebook shows Nietzsche's thought advancing beyond his close focus on *morality* with its popular division of human actions into *egoistic* and *altruistic*. Egoistic actions serve the self or the "I," altruistic actions serve the other or others. The prevailing morality judged egoistic actions mostly bad and altruistic actions mostly good. Already in *Daybreak*, Nietzsche judged that *all* human actions including moral actions are based on drives or passions that are in principle egoistic or self – serving. Every seemingly altruistic action actually fulfilled a veiled or hidden egoistic drive.

Nietzsche's investigation of the drives behind human actions belongs to *psychology* or the study of the human soul. It is a study of the actions of others but it is also, as philosophers at least since Socrates emphasized, the study of one's own soul, *self* – study, leading to self – knowledge. Nietzsche's growing investigation of the human, self – knowledge and knowledge of others, led him to the conclusion that the drives are not only egoistic, but that they all share a fundamental characteristic, that they are all similar in one way and Nietzsche gave that way different names in the notebook. Listen to some of the words he used to describe this shared quality. My words are English translations of Nietzsche's German words, each is a compound word that the German language can build so easily into long single words:

> *Addiction to having. Wanting to have. Wanting to hold on to. Urge for property or ownership. Wanting to own. Drive for ownership. The passion to appropriate. The passion for power.*

These compound words try to name the drive itself: addiction, urge, wanting, passion. And they try to name *the object* of the drive: having, holding on to, owning, appropriating, making into my property. Nietzsche used these compound words *first* to describe human actions, to try to give the right name to the feature he found present in all human actions, even if those actions don't seem to be what is named. Another aspect of that common drive comes up often in Nietzsche's notes: *love*. Love is a passion to possess and to possess all of the desired object.

Another main feature in Nietzsche's entries in the notebook puts the drives into an *order of rank* from lowest and most common to highest and rarest. His usual phrase for the highest of the drives is *the passion for knowledge*, what he recognized as his own most powerful passion, a passion not categorically different from the other passions but the peak of the passions, the *geistigste*, the most intellectual/spiritual, the top of the rank order of the passions.

Another main feature of these entries is that within the individual soul the drives exist in a constant war with one another fo r*supremacy*, or for *rule*.

The most important development in this notebook shows Nietzsche's thinking about morality and the drives basic to it moving in the direction in which philosophy always moves: from an understanding of the particular toward the more comprehensive. And this notebook shows Nietzsche arriving at the most comprehensive possible application of these words for the common feature of the drives of the human soul; the words describe what is true of all human actions; but more than that, they are true of all actions of all living things; and then comes the most comprehensive judgment: they are true of all actions of all things.

So *psychology*, knowledge of the human soul including self – knowledge, expands to *biology*, knowledge of the organic, of all aliveness, and that expands to *physics*, knowledge of all beings and all actions: and in each of these fields, the same common property is the ultimate explanation of what is at work there. It is in this notebook that Nietzsche arrived at that ultimate expansion. He did not use philosophy's word for this, *ontology*, a word he avoided because of his suspicions about what he called "university philosophy." But we can use it as philosophy's word for the most comprehensive study, the study of *being* or of *the being of beings*, which is what the Greek word *ontology* literally means. Nietzsche arrived at his ontological conclusion in the 1881 notebook and named the drive present in all things the addiction to have, *Habsucht* in German, the most common word Nietzsche used for it in the notebook.

It is important to say that within a year Nietzsche gave a different name to the fundamental phenomenon, because he had come to understand it better, differently and far more subtly. So he replaced the term *Habsucht* with the new comprehensive term, *Wille zur Macht*. The "addiction to have" he replaced with "will to power." The reason for the change was Nietzsche's continued push to understand the fundamental force ever more adequately. It was *not* basically a desire to have, as if possession of what was out there was what drove it. Instead, Nietzsche saw that what was basic was a desire to overcome; it was a force that reaches beyond itself and encounters the other in the form of *resistance*, and drives to overcome that resistance. And that other is not other in its essence; it too is a desire to overcome. So what is ultimately at work in all things is *force* that always exists within a *field* of forces. And Nietzsche decided that it was best named *will to power* because what it is is its need to discharge its excess of force against resistance which is itself force. And that was the name Nietzsche then used in *Thus Spoke Zarathustra* and all of his books after that. But Nietzsche clearly recognized the inadequacy of even that label, *will to power*. He called a "weakening and limiting metaphor" (BGE 22), but no other term seemed to him to come as close to naming the fundamental phenomenon.

I want to be clear because I'm talking about *Nietzsche becoming Nietzsche*: I jumped from the ontology expressed in the 1881 notebook to the more adequate ontological insight and terminology that he first attained a year or so later. I did that to make clear from the start that he refined and improved the ontological insight of the 1881 notebook. But with that brief look at Nietzsche's ultimate ontological insight, I want to jump back to the 1881 notebook because it is there that he first made the ontological step into an understanding of being as such.

So the 1881 notebook shows Nietzsche arriving at his comprehensive application of his explanatory principle of the human drives. And this 1881 notebook also shows Nietzsche arriving at his second crucial discovery, the one for which the notebook is well known among Nietzsche scholars: it records Nietzsche's discovery of *eternal return*, the teaching for which Nietzsche wanted to be known. That's what makes this 1881 notebook, after *Daybreak*, before *The Gay Science*, the most important of them all: it contains both of Nietzsche's most crucial thoughts, the thoughts through which Nietzsche entered his maturity as a philosopher. Gaining these two thoughts, Nietzsche became Nietzsche, became who he was.

Now I want to look at what Nietzsche, the writer of books, *did* with his achievement of an ontology in his 1881 notebook. He reported it first in *The Gay Science*, the book that made public all his main insights from the notebook. The structure of *The Gay Science* is important. Its first three chapters are very much like *Daybreak* in their investigations of morality and art and science. Nietzsche seems to have composed those chapters in January, 1882. But then he wrote a very different fourth chapter that he decided would be the last chapter. It was different from the first three for one reason only: he wrote that last chapter *after* he had decided in that January of 1882 that he would write a book called *Thus Spoke Zarathustra* and *that book* would be a more complete report on the discoveries in his 1881 notebook. So before writing that most important book he would ever write, he finished *The Gay Science* by adding a last chapter very different from its first three. It is the only chapter with a title: "*Sanctus Januarius*" in Lat-

in, *Saint January* in English.

January is the first month of the new year; it is a time for looking back over the old year and forward to the new year; and it is a time for judging your life and making resolutions for a better life. *Saint January* opens a new year in Nietzsche's thought; he titled its first section "*To the new year*" and made it his new year's resolution. Then he structured his chapter around his two new thoughts. The single most important thought, *the drive to possess*, he placed carefully just after the center, well prepared by the actual center. The second most important thought, *eternal return*, he placed very carefully at the end.

How *Saint January* introduced Nietzsche's ontology

Nietzsche prepared his most important section beautifully with the two sections that precede it. Just before the center is a section titled "*The history of every day*" and it asks *you*, in the singular familiar, how you spend your every day—Like everyone else? With their everyday concerns of praise or blame or respectability? Or are you of a different sort driven to examine the inside of things and of yourself? With this *you* Nietzsche singles out his genuine reader, the only reader he really wants. Here, for you, he baits his fishhook for the ones related to him.

Next comes his central section called "*Out of the seventh solitude.*" Here, the "wanderer" who has overcome every obstacle faces an unexpected, final crisis—he stands in a garden but it is a garden with a temptation: in this garden the wanderer can finally rest and believe he has attained his goal. But Nietzsche calls it "*Armida's garden*," a literary reference that only a few will understand: *Armida's garden* is a temptation to *a man with a mission*, the great *Rinaldo* in the story; Rinaldo is tempted to stop just short of his ultimate achievement, conquest or capture of the Holy City. To achieve that most difficult final conquest *you* must tear yourself away from Armida's garden and strive for the truly ultimate gain. And when you see *that*, when you see what these two sections at the center do in singling *you* out and warning you of a last temptation, you know you're not making it up, you're finding what Nietzsche put there for you; you're not inventing some theory but are actually on your way to discovering the central matter.

After this careful preparation, Nietzsche placed the section he called, "*Will and wave.*" It begins with a poetic description of a wave, waves of the sort he often watched that winter of 1881 – 1882, the waves of the Mediterranean Sea near the Italian city of Genoa where he wrote *Saint January*:

> How greedily this wave comes in, as if it had to reach something! How it creeps with terrifying haste on into the inmost crevices of the rocky cliff! It seems that it wants to beat someone to it, that there is something hidden that has value, high value. —And now it comes back, somewhat slower, still completely white from excitement, —is it disappointed? Did it find what it sought? Is it feigning disappointment? —But already another wave nears, greedier and wilder still than the first, and its soul too appears to be full of secrets and of the passions of treasure – hunting.

So there is the whole activity, the passionate drive forcing itself into the most hidden. And it falls back white with excitement. In *disappointment*? Or could it be *faking* disappointment? If it is faking disappointment it *found what it sought*, it achieved its goal. Its achievement occurs in a *contest* of strivings for the hidden because the next wave is already coming.

And Nietzsche then wrote,

> ⋯ That is how the waves live – that is how we live, we who will! —

"*Will and wave*" is the title; we the willful wanderers are like the waves; the waves are an image for what we are. Then Nietzsche added a resolution or vow, followed by a speech addressed to the waves themselves in the plural familiar:

> —more I won't say. – So, you distrust me? You are angry with me, you beautiful monsters? Are you afraid I will divulge your entire secret? ⋯ For – hear this well! —I know you and your secret; I know your kind! —You and I, we have indeed One secret!

This is Nietzsche's report for *you* the singular reader whose everyday is like his. You might be able to gain the secret that the willful share with the waves, but only if you too are a wanderer like him who can push on beyond Armida's garden to the ultimate gain.

What is that secret? *Will and wave* does not say: the last words I read are the last words of the section. Nietzsche does not tell the secret he shares with the waves; he does not betray, does not profane, his secret and the secret of the waves. He leaves it to be wondered about and figured out by you.

"More I won't say," Nietzsche said. But in the draft he wrote of "*Will and wave*" he wrote words that he decided not to publish, words he struck out. And those word go a long way in betraying the secret of what he shares with the waves. It's cheating to look at them but here they are. After describing the *greediness* of the waves crashing into the rocky cliff and penetrating to the hidden, and then another wave coming, "greedier than the first and it too seems to be full of secrets and of the passions of treasure – hunting"—right after that Nietzsche spoke directly to the waves using two German words that I want to repeat in German:

Oh ihr Habsüchtigen, ihr Wissensgierigen.

Those German words,*Habsüchtigen* and *Wissensgierigen*, *name* the secret of the waves, the secret that is also *his* secret. The first word, *Habsüchtigen*, is the German word for *possession addicts*, you who are *driven to possess*, *driven to have*. The second word, *Wissensgierigen*, means you who are *greedy to know*. So Nietzsche says to the waves, "Oh you *possession – addicts*, you *knowledge – greedy.*" And he says *that* to the waves of the sea.

In the 1881 notebook,*possession – addiction* is Nietzsche's word for the quality or property that is present in all things or events—the word for the comprehensive or universal ontological drive. And *the greed to know* is a word for the passion for knowledge, the highest or supreme drive of the human way of being. So the two words name the drive of *all beings* and the drive of the *highest being*. In the published version of *Will and wave*, instead of saying to the waves, *Oh you possession – addicts*, *you knowledge –*

greedy, Nietzsche says what I read, "So you mistrust me? ⋯ Are you afraid I will divulge your entire secret?" The published version keeps the secret as the draft version did not. The published version leaves it to *you* to figure out the secret of what you in your knowledge – seeking share with the waves crashing into the cliff and trying to force their way into every crack and corner of the cliff. The published version keeps the secret by putting it only in the poetry of the likeness of waves and the knowledge – seeker.

We are considering *Nietzsche becoming Nietzsche* and this is the essential step in his becoming himself, his ontological insight. And *this* is how Nietzsche chose to make his first ever public indication that he had arrived at a conclusion about a comprehensive ontology, the hidden quality shared by all things from the waves of the sea to the driven inquirer. That is the beautiful form that Nietzsche chose for his first indication that he had arrived at the deepest insight a freed mind can gain. In publishing it this way Nietzsche took care to place it at the center of "*Saint January*"—the center contains the central matter and the central matter, the *ontology*, deserves to be treated in this indirect, secretive way. And remember, before Leo Strauss called everyone's attention to the center by insisting that that's where good writers hid their most important points, before Strauss made the center prominent, the center was the least prominent place in a writing, the place where one is most likely to have lost his focus in comparison with the attention he paid at the beginning and at the end. But *you*, the *you* Nietzsche actually spoke to in asking, How do *you* spend your everyday?, *you* paid attention at the center because Nietzsche spoke it to you.

The 1881 notebook and *eternal return*

Now I want to consider the second of Nietzsche's two most basic discoveries, eternal return, and the way he chose to first make *that* public. If you continue to read the entries in the 1881 notebook after the ones that first state the ontological conclusion about addiction to possession and the similar ontological terms, you come almost immediately to the famous entry that is Nietzsche's first ever account of eternal return. Nietzsche himself made that entry famous by referring to it in his autobiography seven years later and making that notebook entry the first thing he said about *Thus Spoke Zarathustra* and even mentioning that he wrote it in his notebook. In the notebook it is the first *dated* entry, "the beginning of August, 1881." By dating it Nietzsche indicated its importance to him.

After that first ever entry on eternal return every entry for many pages concerns the new thought and all of those, including the first, have one primary concern: *how to introduce* that thought. So it seems that Nietzsche first had the thought of eternal return on his walk and that it came as the overwhelming thought he reports it to be. But he didn't write down that experience itself in his notebook: the first entry is not about the overwhelming thought itself. Instead, it is a detailed, well-structured *book plan* that deals with the problem of how to introduce this thought to others.

The problem is this: eternal return appeared to Nietzsche as the new ideal, the opposite ideal to the one that shaped Western culture and all other cultures since the beginning of what he called the moral period. How can a new ideal be introduced? How can an ideal opposite to the prevailing ideal be introduced? Who would ever believe it or value it or even take it seriously when it is so contrary to what we already believe?

The book plan in the notebook with Nietzsche's first ever mention of eternal return plans five chapters with eternal return appearing only in the last chapter. The book plan is orderly and rich and sets out conclusions that Nietzsche had been working toward for years. We don't have time to look at the whole plan so I'll compress it all into the *one word* that is most important and that Nietzsche used constantly in connection with eternal return in the notebook. That word in English is *incorporation* and the German word, *Einverleibung*, is identical in its structure. The first part, the *in* of *in*corporation, stands for *taking in*, a taking in to the *corpus* or the *body*. To *incorporate* is to take into your body—like taking in food which becomes a part of the body, bone, flesh, blood. The body is *formed* and *sustained* by what it takes in: the body is a product of *incorporation*.

Nietzsche was interested in the *physiological* or bodily aspects of incorporation and he took them to be basic. But he was more interested in the *spiritual* aspects of incorporation where the same kind of operation is at work. Nietzsche's German word is better than *spiritual* because that word, *geistig*, includes spiritual and *intellectual* and with Nietzsche of course, the intellectual is what counts most. So Nietzsche's first four chapters set out his view that to be a mature human being is *always already to be formed or stamped* by the inescapable processes of incorporation that have made us. A philosopher, that is, a thinker who has worked to free his mind, frees his mind of incorporated views as far as that is possible: among other things his freed mind sees, his freed mind sees the necessary errors of *cultural* incorporation, all the *ideals* and *values* we have taken in and made our own in our education and training: those ideals and values have *made* us what we are. But the freed mind of the philosopher also sees that the errors of cultural incorporation are subject to alteration; they can be changed because they have all been taught and it is possible to teach different ideals and values, different from those already incorporated.

That's a summary of four/fifths of the book Nietzsche planned to write. My summary is meant to show the problem Nietzsche consciously faced in introducing his new ideal, his new highest value, as Strauss calls it. Because it's new it will necessarily sound strange and foreign and false to those who have already incorporated a different highest value; it will be unwelcome because it opposes what is already deeply incorporated as a way of thinking and believing. To be effective, a new ideal must *already* be incorporated, must be a part of what everyone *already* knows, what one has begun to know from the very beginning of one's conscious life. When the thought of eternal return first came to Nietzsche, he knew he faced the founder's abstract problem of introducing novelty into a culture that had already incorporated a different view.

Now, staying with the notebook, I move from the problem of incorporation to another important issue about eternal return. The first ever entry on eternal return *comes after* Nietzsche's comprehensive ontological conclusion. The chronological sequence in which Nietzsche wrote out the thoughts he arrived at on his walks shows that he *first* drew his ontological conclusion and *only then* did the ideal of eternal return come to him. And when you think about it, that is the only possible *rational sequence* for these two thoughts: *first* comes the comprehensive understanding of the way the world is, the way all beings are. *Only then* can the thought of eternal return arrive because that thought says to the world now known: *that's what I want*, I want *that world*, the world *as it is*, and I want it *again*, and I want it all *an infinite number of times* again exactly as it is—because I want my life just as it is again.

Strauss recognized this connection between Nietzsche's two main thoughts: he called will to power, "*the fundamental fact*," and he called eternal return "*the highest value.*" The relationship between the two is the relationship between *fact and value*. So of course, *first* comes the fact, *then* comes the affirmation of the fact, the *yes* to that fact. The connection between fact and value is the connection between *understanding* the world and *loving* the world understood. And Strauss gave that connection its proper name: he called it Nietzsche's "*relapse into Platonism*," a relapse that cannot be altogether avoided by the philosopher.

So that's what Nietzsche's 1881 notebook shows by the simple chronological sequence of its entries. It shows the philosopher Nietzsche coming to understand that to be is to be will to power and nothing else and then, only then, glimpsing the new ideal of wanting that world, the world understood, to be an infinite number of times.

How *Saint January* introduced eternal return

Now I want to look again at *Saint January*, the final chapter of *The Gay Science*, in order to see how Nietzsche chose to present his eternal return discovery publicly for the first time. His chosen way of publicizing *that* is just as illuminating as his chosen way of publicizing his ontological discovery: *that* discovery he placed at the center of the chapter as a secret, challenging *you* to discover what you share with the waves. Nietzsche hid his ontological discovery at the center of his chapter. But he put his second discovery, his discovery of eternal return, at the end of the chapter and he made it highly prominent, noticeable even by someone who leafed quickly to the end to see how this book would end.

At the end of *Saint January*, the end of *The Gay Science*, Nietzsche arranged a series of important sections; he ended in a *January* way, a way that fits a new year. First, he builds toward the end with a series of important sections that summarize his chief themes of morality and then, in the third section from the end, he speaks of what is ending, the core teaching of the old year. In a section called "*The dying Socrates*" he makes Socrates ultimately responsible for the teaching that came to dominate western civilization, the teaching that life can only be suffered and that humans need to be redeemed from a life of suffering by a healing god: Nietzsche interprets the last words of the dying Socrates—"I owe a cock to Asclepius"—as saying that for life to be over is a blessing. But now, as that old year passes, the dying Socrates is dying, his ideal, his anti – life teaching is dying.

The next section, the second last, promises what the new year will bring, the new teaching to replace the teaching of the dying Socrates. The title of that section is "*The heaviest weight*" and it announces the new teaching that will give things weight again, make things important again. And this section makes Nietzsche's *first ever* public announcement of eternal return. This section, the second from the end of Nietzsche's book, first introduces Nietzsche's new teaching for the new "year." That section again speaks to *you* and it makes you think of a demon whispering to you in your solitude, saying to you that you will experience your life exactly as it is again and again, with nothing changed, nothing different, nothing better. The whole question of the section is: what will your reaction be? Would you curse the demon for saying something horrifying? Or would you say to him, "You are a god and never have I heard anything so divine"?

Then the scene changes, the demon is gone, and "this thought has gained power over you." In his first public announcement of his thought, Nietzsche here shifts to what concerned him in his notebook. The sudden announcement by the demon is replaced by what would happen to you if you had had the thought of eternal return already incorporated into you by all your training and all you had ever heard from your parents and your teachers. As the already always present thought becomes more and more conscious for you as you mature and begin to think about it, *then* the thought "would transform you as you are and perhaps crush you." The thought of eternal return is a *selecting* thought, a *separating* thought depending on who you are. For some, the thought of eternal return transforms you, exalts you, gives you joy. For others, the thought of eternal return crushes you, depresses you, makes you despair. It all depends on what your disposition to life is; it depends on your love or hate of your own life.

That's all Nietzsche says about eternal return in this first public announcement of it in the second last section of *Saint January*. Then comes the last section of *Saint January*. It pictures someone called "Zarathustra" leaving his home, going into the mountains, spending ten years there, and now preparing to return, ripe with a new teaching he had discovered in his solitude. And that ends *Saint January* and ends his book: dramatically, oddly, in a way that no reader could possibly understand and that every reader would find surprising and questionable. A few well-informed readers might know that Zarathustra was the great Persian prophet who was the founding teacher of transcendence and of an afterlife of reward for the good and punishment for the evil, but even they would wonder why Nietzsche ended his book on Zarathustra returning. Only Nietzsche knew what his reader could come to know only later, for the last section of *The Gay Science* is the first section of the book he was now planning to write, *Thus Spoke Zarathustra*, and that book would describe this great founding teacher preparing to return to humanity and eventually teaching eternal return. *Thus Spoke Zarathustra* exists to present the teaching of eternal return.

So the two great discoveries that Nietzsche wrote out in that notebook in the summer of 1881 set his writing career for the next years. The difference between those two discoveries can already be seen in Nietzsche's first public treatment of them in *The Gay Science* where the ontology is a secret hidden at the center and eternal return is the prominent teaching announced at the end. And this way of presenting the two discoveries in *Saint January* set the pattern for how Nietzsche would treat them in *Thus Spoke Zarathustra* and in *Beyond Good and Evil*. *Saint January* set the pattern for understanding just what these two discoveries from Nietzsche's 1881 notebook are.

How the great books of Nietzsche's maturity treat his two great discoveries

In *Thus Spoke Zarathustra* the ontology of the drive to possess now bears the name will to power and of course it appears first. *Will to power* is used once in Part 1 but as the peak insight into what lies behind "the greatest power on earth," morality. Only in Part 2 is will to power explained but the explanation is for a limited and special audience only: those that he names "*you wisest.*" For them only, he names and explains will to power as the truth that lies behind their "will to truth." His explanation can come only after "The Dance Song," for there, in the poetry of that song, Zarathustra abandons his skeptical "Wild Wisdom" who had maintained that life or being is unfathomable and he embraces instead his true love, Life herself who suggests to him that she is *not unfathomable*. Life herself suggests to her lover Zarathustra that she can be *fathomed*, that she has a character or way that can be understood. Zarathustra then names and argues for "will to power" with "you wisest;"; at the end of his argument he says to them, "Let us *talk* of this together"—they alone need to discuss with him his newly discovered and expressed ontological view.

Then Zarathustra ends his speech to the wisest saying, "There is many a house yet to be built." Will to power is a truth that needs to be known only by those with the most powerful passion to know—and they, together with Zarathustra, will build the house yet to be built; they will construct the teachings that will house future human beings, or be incorporated into future human beings. Eternal return is the new teaching, the *teaching for all* that will house future humanity. *Thus Spoke Zarathustra* therefore has eternal return appear only after Zarathustra has argued for will to power with the wisest: that is the necessary order for an *insight* for a few and a *teaching* for all.

Beyond Good and Evil treats will to power and eternal return in the same way. Nietzsche uses the phrase *will to power* four times in the first chapter on philosophy; will to power is what ultimately drives the highest inquiry, *philosophy*, and will to power drives all the things studied by *biology*, living things, and all the things studied by *physics*, all things, and the thing studied by *psychology*, the human soul. In that first chapter on philosophy Nietzsche gives no explanation of this fundamental truth; instead, as Strauss said, these all appear as *dogmatic* claims about will to power. In the next chapter, "The Free Mind," Nietzsche *does* offer an argument on behalf of will to power as the comprehensive truth but his argument is only for his special audience of freed minds he has been educating. The ultimate step in their education is that well – prepared argument whose conclusion is that the world is will to power and nothing else. It's only for them, and we have already seen how even they react: "God is refuted but the devil is not." I will say more on that in my last lecture. As for eternal return, *Beyond Good and Evil* treats that in the *religion* chapter at just the right place in just the right way, as the public teaching for everyone that arises out of the nihilism caused by the death of the old public teaching, the old religion.

So that's my main point: in the 1881 notebook Nietzsche became Nietzsche. There, he arrived for the first time at the two chief conclusions of his mature philosophy, first, an insight into the world as it is, the kind of insight that can interest only those whose ruling passion is the passion to know. And second, an insight into eternal return as the highest ideal of those whose natural disposition is to love life and love their own life. The first insight belongs to philosophy proper and the second belongs to philosophic poetry. What Nietzsche arrived at in the 1881 notebook determined the rest of his lifework. From *Saint January* through *Thus Spoke Zarathustra* and *Beyond Good and Evil* and on to the next major work that Nietzsche was planning and even writing when his breakdown occurred. In that last planned work too the will to power would be a *truth* to be thought through by those driven to think whereas eternal return would be a *teaching* within which everyone could live their lives and celebrate their lives and celebrate the whole of life.

So the mature Nietzsche, the Nietzsche Nietzsche became, is a philosopher and a philosophic poet. In my final lecture I will say more about Nietzsche the philosophic poet. Here I want to end on one thing more about Nietzsche the philosopher: his relation to Plato. Nietzsche the philosopher achieves an ultimate ontological insight according to which to be is to be will to power and nothing else. Plato the philosopher achieves an ultimate ontological insight according to which to be is to be eros and nothing else. In my view these two insights are close kin; they are different ways of *wording* an insight that is similar. Here we are at the highest and hardest. Here the limitations of language and of thinking and of *my* thinking are most evident, but I want to try to summarize some of the aspects of the kinship of will to power and eros as ontologies.

Both assert the "*sovereignty of becoming.*" Both assert that *becoming* is a surging and satisfying and surging again. Both assert that in that *ever – self – renewing activity* there is an internal directionality that aims at a kind of self – satisfaction: it is *auto – telic*. Both assert that this *discharging of energy or force* is a reaching beyond itself that encounters the *other* as a discharging of force reaching beyond *itself*, encounters the other as *resistance*. Both assert that this process of *directional energy – or force – expression* is *relational*; the relations are individual relations whose occurring is part of a field of such relations where the total field of such relations is the *totality simply*, *all that is*.

Plato's language of *eros* is attractive and affirmative, expressing the process in human terms that make it easily lovable. Nietzsche's language of *will to power* is less attractive in keeping with his tough – minded resolve to avoid what he called "word – tinsel" or verbal beautification, in favor of wording that described the process more exactly though necessarily still inadequately, "as a weakening and limiting metaphor—as too human" (BGE 22). But those initial differences in the terms themselves mask what seems to me the fundamental kinship of understanding shared by Plato and Nietzsche.

Nietzsche became Nietzsche in a way similar to the way in which Socrates became Socrates. Genuine philosophers are genuine kin.

LECTURE 6

Nietzsche's Philosophic Poetry

I want to begin this last lecture with Strauss's formulation of proper method: *"The problem inherent in the surface of things and only in the surface of things is the heart of things."* The surface of things to which he paid the most careful attention was the surface of philosophers' texts. There, woven into the surface through their art of writing, was the heart of things, what the philosopher who composed that surface wanted *you* to follow into the heart of things. And the heart of things that Strauss discovered and wanted his careful readers to discover was what a philosopher always aims to discover, the truth, ultimately the truth of being or of what is, the ontological truth. We can discover that truth only with the most responsible and thorough skeptical method that tests what is mere belief in order to discover if anything can be known. And Strauss showed that with good method, exegetical method that learns the philosophers' art of writing, we can read our way into the genuine heart of the philosophers Plato and Nietzsche. That heart is an ontology: to be is to be eros and nothing else, to be is to be will to power and nothing else. This main point of all my lectures leads to the second main point: genuine philosophy *generates* philosophic poetry, a teaching that can be lived. As Diotima put it in her description of the peak, philosophic *seeing* results in an *engendering* that is the making of poetry.

With that I arrive at today's topic: Nietzsche's philosophic poetry. In his essay on Nietzsche, Strauss looked first at Nietzsche's philosophy even though the topic of his essay was religion in Nietzsche. In my second lecture we looked at what Strauss said about the most important section of

Beyond Good and Evil, section 36, which contains the only argument for will to power in the book. I want to consider that argument again in order to see how it initiates the move to Nietzsche's philosophic poetry.

Nietzsche's philosophy: *Beyond Good and Evil* #36

Section 36 comes just after the center of "The Free Mind" chapter. The free mind had been Nietzsche's primary topic since he broke with Wagner and the Wagnerian perspective of his early books in August, 1876. Now, 10 years later, the center of "The Free Mind" chapter deals with the conclusion that modern free minds have ultimately arrived at, "epistemological skepticism," skepticism that anything can really be *known*, the skepticism reinforced by Kant's account of knowing.

Nietzsche views this as the highest point reached by modern free minds, minds trained in their freedom partly by Nietzsche's books on the ideal of the free mind; these free minds represent his only possible audience, his "friends." In the long central section of the chapter, #34, Nietzsche aims to raise a question about the finality of skepticism, about whether skepticism is in fact the highest attainment of the human intellect. Connected to that long section is the very short section 35 in which Nietzsche raises a powerful question about a hidden *motive* behind modern skepticism. Section 35 in its totality says this:

> O Voltaire! O humaneness! O nonsense! There is something about "truth," about the *search* for truth; when a human being goes about it too humanely—"He seeks the true only to do the good"—I bet he finds nothing!

The French skeptic Voltaire had maintained that "*He seeks the true only to do the good*" (a statement Nietzsche wrote in French and that I translated into English). What is Nietzsche's point? It is an *accusation* against the skepticism of the free minds like Voltaire, who had been the hero of Nietzsche's first free mind book, *Human All Too Human*. Nietzsche accuses the *search for the true* of modern free – minded skeptics of being fatally limited by their belief that the true and the good must coincide;

their primary desire is to hold on to the modern *good*, to modern *virtue*, and that curbs their search for the true, making skepticism about knowledge an appealing fall back position protecting their view of the good. Skepticism about knowledge excuses continued *belief* in modern virtue, allowing their unfree minds to hold on to the modern virtues of *equality of rights* and the *end of suffering*. In the classical language of the Voltaire quotation, belief about the *good* still binds their unfree minds keeping them from the *true*. A search for the true as a support for their good is bound to fail: "I bet he finds nothing."

This lovely, humorous, profound accusation says that skepticism is attractive to modern, enlightened free minds because if you can't know the *true* then you can keep on believing in the *good*, the modern good. Skepticism gives permission to place morality above knowing. The epistemological skepticism of the *free minds* is really a sign of *bound minds*, minds that are merely moral.

So the two linked sections at the center of "The Free Mind" aim to provoke, to unsettle the free – minded reader in order to force a question on him about the actual freedom of his mind. And immediately after that challenge to his only possible audience, that invitation to perplexity, to doubt their doubt, Nietzsche makes his essential argument for what a truly free mind can know. It's clear: Nietzsche's careful placement of his only argument on behalf of the will to power view alerts his careful reader to the actual, historical setting for the ontological claim he is about to make: the times are unripe for such a claim but the philosopher must nevertheless speak; he must voice his argument.

Nietzsche does not assume that his argument will be persuasive, however complete and valid it is. As a valid argument what it does is *invite* the free minds to think about his argument, to question their skepticism and entertain the possibility of a fundamental truth that can be known. Nietzsche's strategy here is the same strategy his Zarathustra used: at the end of his only argument for will to power, Zarathustra says to his only audience "Let us *talk* of this, *you wisest*." The audience for the argument in both of Nietzsche's most important books is the most select audience: *you wisest* in Zarathustra, *you freest minds* in Beyond Good and Evil; in both cases, only *you* need to concern yourself with this. This is the esoteric core of Nietzsche's thought however much it lies open on the page.

Nietzsche's argument is subtle and has to be studied in all the steps he set out. Here I look only at the core of it, *look at it*, not explain its details or try to persuade you of anything. Remember though, that Strauss praised it as "the most intransigent intellectual probity."

To open his argument, Nietzsche emphasizes that scientific method requires economy of principles and therefore: "we have to make the experiment of positing the causality of the will hypothetically as the only one," the only kind of cause. "*Have to*" because of the two – fold demand of scientific method, *economy of principles* and that conclusions be drawn *hypothetically*. Therefore, "one has to risk the hypothesis ··· whether all mechanical occurrences are not, insofar as force is active in them, will force, effects of will." Wherever we recognize *cause* in nature we must suspend the view of classical modern physics (the physics of Descartes and Newton) that a *mechanics* of cause and effect is at work within a mechanistic world – whole. Instead we must view events in nature hypothetically as *will* events, events in which *will* is active.

Nietzsche then turns to *what* is to be investigated by this inquiry into cause. Having himself begun with what is given, *human passions and desires*, his subject for 10 years, he here begins with his postulated basis for the instincts driving them: "Suppose we succeeded in explaining our entire instinctive life as the development and ramification of *one* basic form of the will—namely, of the will to power as *my* proposition has it." A free mind does what Nietzsche did, investigate one's self and other human beings to understand what the roots of all our actions may be. Beginning with knowledge of the human soul, can we explain our instinctual life as Nietzsche explained it, first as different forms of *Habsucht*, the addiction to have, the drive that he later came to understand more deeply as *will to power*. Suppose you *could* do that; then, in accord with good method, you must experimentally expand your conclusion about the roots of human action to a broader field: "suppose all organic functions could be traced back to this will to power." You must move from what explains human actions to an explanation of the functioning of all organic things, all living things, everything studied by the science of biology, the unstated premise that needs to be proven experimentally being that human beings are not essentially different from other living beings.

Finally, assuming you succeed in applying the hypothesis of will to power to the whole realm of living things:

> then one would have gained the right to determine *all* efficient force univocally as—*will to power.* The world viewed from inside, the world defined and determined according to its "intelligible character"—it would be "will to power" and nothing else. —

"Gained the right"—scientific method justifies, it even requires this broadest of all hypothetical expansions: explanatory success attainted with the human and the organic gives one the right to draw the broadest conclusion, the ontological conclusion first arrived at in the 1881 notebook, then merely hinted at as the secret of what I share with the waves in Nietzsche's first ever public presentation of it, and what Zarathustra then shared with *you wisest* in *Thus Spoke Zarathustra.*

In *Beyond Good and Evil* Nietzsche leaves it at that. He stops there. He has made his argument and you, with your free mind, are to think whether the conclusion can be cogent and true or not. Nietzsche put a little dash at the end of this section 36 and this little punctuation mark suggests a connection with the very short section 37: as Strauss noted, sections 36 and 37 resemble in form the pair of sections Nietzsche placed at the center, 34 and 35. By making 36 and 37 a pair, Nietzsche moves from *philosophy* to *philosophic poetry.*

Nietzsche's move from philosophy to philosophic poetry: BGE #37

Section 37 is a *response*, an immediate reaction by Nietzsche's audience to his conclusion that the world is will to power and nothing else. In section 37 Nietzsche allows his true audience of free minds to speak up immediately and say what *they* think, how they *feel* about the conclusion they have just heard: "What? Doesn't this mean, to speak in the popular way: God is refuted but the devil is not—?" The free minds are *shocked:* they confirm what Nietzsche suggested of modern free minds in section 35: they are not fully free but are bound by their view of the coincidence of the true and the good: if will to power is true, their good of perpetual peace at the end of history in a paradise of equality of rights and the end of suffering is neither attainable nor true. Nietzsche says they speak in "the popular way:" they adopt the common language of God and devil. But they are the free minds: they don't believe in God or the devil. They speak in the popular way because only that language can express their extreme feeling. Only the old extremes of God and devil can express the horror they feel about his reasoned will to power conclusion.

Put into less theological language, their reaction says that if the world is "will to power and nothing else," then everything they hold high and noble and good is destroyed and replaced by what seems to them low and ignoble and evil. Your conclusion that everything is a conflict of drives for power is a horrifying, ugly, evil view. Isn't *that* what your will to power view means? "On the contrary! On the contrary, my friends!" Nietzsche's response is as emphatic as theirs but it needs an explanation he does not give. *You* have to think the contrary and it is easily stated in the popular language the free minds just used: *The devil is refuted but God is not.* As Strauss says five times Nietzsche's view is "a vindication of God."

Nietzsche's words, "On the contrary! On the contrary!," carry a deep theological lesson for his friends, modern free minds who have lost interest in theology and lost any sense of why religion is important. His contrary says: there is something seriously wrong with your concept of God and devil. Just reverse them and you get closer to the truth. And that reversal succeeds in denouncing the only theology they can imagine, Christian theology. "On the contrary! On the contrary!" implies this: Your concept of God (which of course they do not believe in), a transcendent, supernatural Being who created the world, watches the world, judges the world—think of that as the devil. And your concept of the devil (which they believe in even less), the Lord of this world, the *Prince of Darkness* as Christian theology calls him and takes the whole world as fallen, as belonging to the devil—think of *that* as divine. *What is a god?* —that is what Nietzsche makes his free-minded atheist friends ask.

Nietzsche has a final theological instruction: "And as to the devil, who forces you to speak in the popular way! —"*Who?* The old God forces them, the God who is dead but not gone, the moral God whose concept still rules their view of what a god is. You have a lot to learn theologically, Nietzsche suggests to his free minded friends, us modern atheists. Nietzsche asked, who forces you to speak of the devil? He did not ask, who forces you *to speak of God*. And he did not ask because speaking of God is what Nietzsche wants: a new way of saying what a god is or what the gods are.

So, what just happened in Nietzsche's book? Just after the center of his second chapter on philosophy, the chapter on "The Free Mind," Nietzsche placed his only philosophical argument for the will to power in *Beyond Good and Evil*. It is an argument of "the most intransigent intellectual probity" and leads to a comprehensive conclusion about the being of beings. Then, immediately, he hears his friends link that philosophical conclusion to religion: his only possible audience reacts in religious terms. And what does Nietzsche do? He *stays* with religion while suggesting that, no, his philosophic view does not refute God but vindicates God properly understood.

In his religion chapter Nietzsche will describe his audience of modern free minds this way: "they no longer even know what religions are good for" (BGE 58). Nietzsche knows what religions are good for and he deals with that in the final two sections of his religion chapter. Those sections argue that religions are good for, necessary for, any social order. Religion, taught to the young, *incorporated* into the young, gives guidance to what is good and bad, noble and base, what it is worth living for and what it is necessary to reject. These sections show the uses of religion in binding the rulers to the ruled, offering others a disciplined path to higher spirituality, and making life endurable for the common people. For religion to be *healthy*, Nietzsche argues in these sections, it must be guided in the appropriate way by wise men, by philosophers, by those not themselves guided by religion. Philosophy must rule religion; reason must rule the instinct to worship and adore.

Nietzsche views religion as necessary and desirable. More than that, he can speak of the "god – creating instinct" in human beings and say in amazement, "almost two thousand years and not a single new god!" (A 19). He is not really amazed because he knows the reason: the last two thousand years in the West have been ruled by the jealous God, the God of monotheism, the God whose jealousy gave Nietzsche his best joke: "One of the gods said one day, 'There is only one God, thou shalt have no other gods before me.' And all the other gods—died laughing. Thus there was only one God."

In his religion chapter, while criticizing Christianity, Nietzsche looked back to the polytheistic religion of the ancient Greeks, Homeric religion, and praised it for "the enormous abundance of gratitude it displays." The problem is not gods as such, the problem is the God of Revelation, the God of Christianity from whom modern minds have freed themselves, and made tremendous gains in free thinking. But also, and this is Nietzsche's point here, those gains have come at tremendous cost, the cost of gods as such, the cost of no longer even knowing what religions are good for.

Nietzsche knows what religions are good for; philosophers know what religions are good for, as Socrates showed in Plato's *Republic* when he altered or reformed Homeric religion in the time of its dying for intelligent young men. Only religion can structure the daily life of a culture; cultures live on beliefs and practices; on incorporated beliefs that one takes in from the earliest age in the stories told to little children and reinforces in the rituals and festivals and customs that give meaning and structure to ordinary daily life. And for religion to be viable, Nietzsche seems to think, there must be gods. I will speak about the actual gods to whom Nietzsche points later. But first, having seen from sections 36 and 37 how religion or philosophic poetry arises naturally out Nietzsche's philosophy, I want to look briefly at the aspect of Nietzsche's philosophic poetry that Nietzsche put first in *Beyond Good and Evil*, before speaking of gods at its very end.

Philosophic poetry 1: eternal return

Instead of making God or gods the main theme of his religion chapter in *Beyond Good and Evil*, Nietzsche made its theme roughly the history of Western religion, of Christianity. And he placed at the very center of his religion chapter the crisis of Western religion. That crisis is a religious catastrophe with two aspects: *the death of God* and what he calls *the assassi-*

nation *of the old soul concept*. Just after these central sections Nietzsche placed the completely understandable next step, the step into the deepest catastrophe: nihilism, the growing sense among modern free minds that nothing is truly of worth. Then, just after that, with his historical sketch complete into the present moment, Nietzsche put the only section in *Beyond Good and Evil* to deal with eternal return. In that section, 56, a philosopher sees the affirmation of eternal return arising as a future possibility out of the nihilism that results from the death of God and the assassination of the old soul concept. I touched on Strauss's use of section 56 in my second Strauss lecture but I want to look at it more closely here as my first main point on Nietzsche's philosophic poetry.

Nietzsche ended his section on nihilism saying, "We all already know something of this. —" That dash at the end of that statement leads to the next section which begins: "Whoever has endeavored with some enigmatic longing, as I have, to think pessimism to its depths···whoever has really··· looked into, down into the most world – denying of all possible ways of thinking." "*as I have*"—the whole section will be about Nietzsche the thinker driven to think modern pessimism to its depth. That "enigmatic longing" driving him can only be philosophy; the philosopher today is driven to investigate "the most world – denying of all possible ways of thinking."

Nietzsche goes on to identify himself further: he stands "beyond good and evil and no longer ··· under the spell and delusion of morality." Driven to free himself of the prejudices of morality, the philosopher Nietzsche "may just thereby, without really meaning to do so, have opened his eyes to the opposite ideal: the ideal of the most high – spirited, alive, world – affirming human being"

Nietzsche the thinker moves from thinking through one ideal, the most world – *denying* possible way of thinking, to "the opposite ideal" which is the most world – *affirming* possible way of thinking. I want to emphasize what Strauss emphasized: the little clause that Nietzsche put in here, "without really meaning to do so." Those words are important because of what they say about Nietzsche's intention: he did not undertake his investigation in order to discover a new ideal. He is not driven by a need for a new morality or a new religion; instead, he is driven by the "enigmatic longing" that is the need to understand—he is a philosopher and not a moralist and not a religious man.

The new ideal he glimpses without really meaning to do so is "the ideal of the most high – spirited, alive, world – affirming human being ⋯ who wants to have *what was and is* repeated into all eternity, shouting insatiably *da capo* (from the beginning)." That person, the most world – affirming human being, wants the eternal return of the world, *wants* it. Eternal return is his ideal, eternal return is what is desired by the most world – affirming human being. And Nietzsche clarifies that wanting immediately: "not only to himself but to the whole play and spectacle, and not only to a spectacle but at bottom to him who needs precisely this spectacle⋯." The affirmation of the whole spectacle is ultimately the self – affirmation of the human spectator on the spectacle—the affirmation is an affirmation of the world because the world makes the philosopher possible, because the world generated a spectator who is a rational, self – conscious, knowing fragment of the knowable whole.

That is all that *Beyond Good and Evil* says about eternal return. But it is enough for a book whose intention it is to be "a critique of modernity." In its critique of modern religion it provides, with great brevity and great precision, a pointer to what could lie beyond the nihilism in which modernity's needed demolition of Christianity left religion as a whole for enlightened Western moderns. Eternal return then, is part of Nietzsche's philosophic poetry, the new highest ideal; it is what ideals necessarily are, a positing by a human being, the valuing being, of the highest ideal. And with that summary, I move to a second aspect of Nietzsche's philosophic poetry that Nietzsche, again consistently, only pointed to in *Beyond Good and Evil*, that book of critique.

Philosophic poetry 2: gods

When Strauss discussed Nietzsche's religion chapter in *Beyond Good and Evil* he got to a certain point and said, "There is an important ingredient, not to say the nerve, of Nietzsche's 'theology' of which I have not spoken and shall not speak." With this emphatic, this vehement refusal Strauss avoids speaking about the *nerve* of Nietzsche's theology that seems to be his introduction of gods. Strauss had suggested that Nietzsche "had doubts whether there can be a world, any world whose center is not God," and *world* here means *cultural* world, the world inhabited by human beings, believing beings. Strauss, a philosopher who is a Jew and who had a lifelong sensitivity to the fate of Judaism in the 20th century, refuses to speak about the theological – political project that Nietzsche suggested could be the center of a future world. But Nietzsche himself *must* speak, precisely because there cannot be a "world whose center is not God. " And Nietzsche knew that he had a problem in speaking about gods because his only possible audience were the modern free – minded skeptics who "no longer even know what religions are good for" and for whom the only imaginable God was the dead God of monotheism they are only too happy to help kill off.

Nietzsche said "I rarely speak as a theologian" but he exaggerated. However unwelcoming the times were, he had to speak as a theologian in order to introduce a new concept of what a god is to those who had incorporated the old concept of God. He began to speak as a theologian in *Beyond Good and Evil* #37 when he suggested that the devil was refuted but God was not. And he suggested in the appropriate places in his book that religion and gods were indispensable. But he saved his actual view of what a god is until the last possible moment: he placed a first taste of his new teaching about the gods prominently, at the very end, and he expressed his view in the most beautiful section of the book, section 295. There, finally, Nietzsche spoke as a theologian.

He began with a long, lovely description of his experience with "the tempter god" that Strauss called "a super – Socrates. " Nietzsche describes him hauntingly, magnetically but does not name him. When he finally gets around to naming him, he says he is "no less a one than the god, Dionysos, that great ambiguous one and tempter god to whom I once offered ··· my first – born. " Nietzsche's "first – born" is his first book, *The Birth of Tragedy*, where Dionysos is described as the forceful, ecstatic god behind Greek tragedy. "Meanwhile I have learned much ··· more about the philosophy of this god ··· I the last disciple and initiate of the god Dionysos— and I suppose that I might begin at long last to offer you, my friends, a few tastes of this philosophy···. " Nietzsche has learned a lot about Dionysos since his first book, enough to think of himself as "the last disciple and initiate" of this god. He has also learned a lot about his audience, those to whom he must now speak about the gods. His view that the gods philosophize will offend philosophers, he says, because they have all been "on the same track" theologically since Plato and Plato's Diotima taught that the gods do not philosophize because they are already wise—the *philosophers* will oppose a philosopher introducing a concept of philosophizing gods. But what about his friends? "Among you, my friends, it will not seem so offensive, unless it comes too late and not at the right moment; for today, as I have been told, you no longer like to believe in God and gods. Perhaps I shall have to carry my frankness further in my tale than will always be pleasing to the strict habits of your ears?"

What Nietzsche has to say about gods will also offend his friends but offend them for a different reason: it comes *at the wrong time* for them. His friends are not yet ready to hear any talk of gods because it is too soon after their liberation from the old God—Nietzsche's friends, newly liberated atheists, do not want to hear anything about gods because of their recent release from the tyrannical God. But Nietzsche must speak of gods and can only speak in the present, however too soon the present is.

Among the theological lessons Nietzsche dares to speak to his friends is a very important one that belongs to the *much* that he has learned since *The Birth of Tragedy*: the god Dionysos is always accompanied by another god, his beloved, *Ariadne*. Dionysos and Ariadne. Those are the two gods Nietzsche introduces. Why does Nietzsche, who knows what gods are good for, introduce *these* two gods and *only* these two? Of course he does not believe that humanity could go backward and reestablish the religion of Homer who first named these two gods. What makes these two gods different and worthy of being reintroduced in late modern times?

As Strauss noted, Nietzsche thought that human beings had a "god – making instinct," a natural inclination in us to make into gods what we hold highest. It belongs to our nature to *divinize*, to make into divine persons whatever it is that we most honor. And what do we most honor or hold highest if what we desire is the eternal return of life? We hold life itself highest. And life is the constantly renewing cycle of being born and dying, being born through sexual reproduction and dying. Dionysos and Ariadne are sexual reproduction elevated by the god – making instinct into gods; they are sexual reproduction divinized. Dionysos is the god of *maleness or manliness*. Ariadne is the god of *femaleness or womanliness*. Dionysos and Ariadne are a *pair*, the productive, generative pair of all life. As a pair, they belong together in their difference; they are the war between the sexes and the love between the sexes. That is the specialness, the singularity of the divine pair; Dionysos and Ariadne are life on earth, its being born and dying, raised to the highest elevation of honor that humans can confer. Dionysos and Ariadne are the universal gods of earthly reproduction given local or Greek names. And they are so much more but I will mention only one other point: Dionysos is a philosophizing god—he is driven to understand. And Ariadne? She does not philosophize; in some more fundamental sense she already knows, *she* has the thread that leads out of the mystery at the heart of the labyrinth, as the Greek myth of Ariadne held.

So of course Nietzsche as a theologian singled out these two gods as the gods of the earthly religion intimately connected with the affirmation of the eternal return of life. But with these divinities we see immediately that Nietzsche the theologian could not do what Plato the theologian could do when *he* introduced new, non – Homeric gods: Socrates says in the *Republic* that he can leave the practices and rituals, the song and dance, to the already established institutions: these already established or incorporated practices and rituals will adapt to the new. Part of Nietzsche's problem is that there are no established institutions honoring Dionysos and Ariadne. Nietzsche's problem with introducing new godsis the same problem he had introducing a new highest ideal: How to *incorporate* a new sense of what a god is and how to generate the festivals, the song and dance, that celebrate new gods. Gods too seem believable only when they have always already been believed, when they are the gods of the ancestors that we have known since childhood, and when we already know how to sing their praises and how to dance our gratitude.

I must also note that Nietzsche said in his autobiography, "There is nothing in me of the founder of a religion" (EH. 4. 1). Nietzsche the philosopher tempts prospective knowers not prospective believers, however few the knowers are, however many the believers are, and however much the knowers know that only around a god can everything turn into "world". With respect to gods it seems that Nietzsche says this to his friends: *recognize* the necessity of religion; *recognize* the universal naturalness of Dionysos and Ariadne as the gods of life: *recognize* that and leave it to the god – making instinct. The love of life will do what love does in human beings, prompt us to divinize, to make divine what we most love, life as reproduced through sexuality. Dionysos and Ariadne are the natural gods of human beings in love with life and the natural human instinct to make gods will see to their rebirth.

There is a third aspect of Nietzsche's philosophic poetry that has not been widely recognized. And I want to end on that because it seems to me particularly promising.

Philosophic poetry 3: ecology; the human way of being on the earth

Like eternal return and the gods Dionysos and Ariadne, this third matter springs from Nietzsche's *philosophy*, his understanding of the human as a form of life on earth that is connected with and dependent upon the whole network of life that evolved it. This philosophic view of human life on earth generates principles of human action whose basic imperative is the one that Nietzsche's Zarathustra gave first when he returned from the mountains: "*Be true to the earth*!" Nietzsche is the first Western philosopher to teach a comprehensive ecological philosophy; his is a comprehensive moral and political teaching based fundamentally on love of the earth, where the earth is understood as the *this – worldly* as opposed to some beyond, as the *temporal* as opposed to any timeless transcendence, as the *always mortal* as opposed to any immortality—and as *will to power* and nothing else.

This third aspect of Nietzsche's philosophic poetry, ecology, love of life on earth, has an advantage over the first two aspects: both a highest ideal and gods must be *incorporated*; they seem to be possible or effective only if they are *already* believed, *already* tradition. But the contrary ideal and God are the now already incorporated and they still exercise power even over those who have come to doubt or disbelieve them. Consequently, we can hardly imagine a wholly different ideal or wholly different gods. Finally, skeptical modern doubters like ourselves have a *prejudice* against all high ideals and gods that may be the strongest resistance to a Nietzschean poetry that employs them.

But this third aspect of Nietzsche's political philosophy, an ethics of ecology or environmentalism is something that could be much more easily welcomed by a contemporary audience, by us. Instead of being repelled by it, we are drawn to it from the start. This has been part of my understanding of Nietzsche's philosophic politics since my first book, *Nietzsche's Teaching*. In my second book, *Nietzsche and Modern Times*, I described Nietzsche as the comprehensive ecological philosopher. Since writing those books I have come to see how very helpful Leo Strauss is on this point of Nietzsche's political philosophy. In my second Strauss lecture I read Strauss's words from paragraph 35 of his Nietzsche essay. They express Strauss's main point about the complementary man:

His supremacy is shown by the fact that he solves the highest, most difficult problem.

Strauss defines that problem: "man is conquering nature and there are no assignable limits to that conquest." To solve the highest problem of modern times is to find good grounds for assigning limits to the conquest of nature. I don't find in Strauss any general ecological or environmental interest of the sort that has by now become popular and significant. Instead, Strauss warns against the conquest of nature as the conquest of *human* nature through the modern ideals of equality of rights and the end of suffering. That modern conquest of human nature would mean the end of philosophy on earth because philosophy depends upon the recognition and encouragement of an order of rank and the continuation of suffering properly understood, understood as the human struggle to attain the high, most especially knowledge; *that* known suffering from a lack can be remedied only through sacrificial struggle—subordination of every drive to the drive for knowledge. Strauss made that the culmination of his Nietzsche essay, the high end – point, Strauss at his most relevant. The modern threat to the human greatness that is philosophy can be *solved* by Nietzsche's theological – political program, his ministerial poetry, because it assigns limits to the modern conquest of nature out of the love of nature, a love expressed in the highest ideal that the whole of nature return just as it is an infinite number of times.

I want to end my lectures on that theme by looking at Nietzsche's own first *coming to* that solution to the most difficult problem, Nietzsche's first full insight into this greatest of late – modern practical problems and its solution. I have emphasized that Nietzsche's comprehensive philosophic view first came together, first gained completeness in his 1881 notebook, the notebook in which both the ontology of what became will to power and the affirmation of eternal return appear for the first time. That notebook also contains what as far as I know is Nietzsche's first statement of this ecological or environmentalist aspect of his philosophic poetry. And remember, Nietzsche wrote the 1881 notebook before "*Saint January*," the fourth Part of *The Gay Science*, before *Thus Spoke Zarathustra*, and before *Beyond Good and Evil*.

The entry I want to discuss appears early in that notebook. Because of the specific problems that had occupied Nietzsche in the writing of *Daybreak*, this early entry in the notebook that he began after finishing *Daybreak* begins on the theme of most of the early entries, his on – going reflection on morality, more specifically on his insight that the moral distinction between egoism and altruism hides the fact that all human actions are fundamentally egoistic, or serve the *I*. This entry falls among the entries that expand the field of that egoism as *Habsucht*, the drive to possess, and that Nietzsche will soon expand to an ontology or a true account of the nature of all beings.

The entry (numbered 11 [21] Frühjahr – Herbst 1881 in the Colli – Montinari *Kritische Gesamtausgabe*) opens by setting out the task: "To describe the history of the *I – feeling*: and to show that in altruism too this wanting to possess is the essential matter." Nietzsche's "history of the I – feeling" therefore begins with what underlies morality. W*anting to possess*, the *drive to have*, the essential matter in the *I – feeling*, is basic to both egoism and altruism, the feeling for the other that has been misunderstood as the opposite of egoism. The rest of the entry describes what the *history* the I – feeling could become; it moves out beyond the exclusiveness of *egoism* and out beyond the feeling of *altruism* to broader fields beyond the I and the other. The rest of the entry looks like a sketch for a book about what Nietzsche is discovering and writing out in this notebook about the drive to possess first discovered as the truth about egoism.

The entry goes on: "To show how the chief progress in morality does not lie in the concept 'Not – I and I' but instead in the sharper understanding of the *true* in the other, in me, and in nature." So the issue is a sharper understanding of what is *true* of both the I and the other—and then that great expansion, to *nature*. That word is especially important because it extends the need for a sharper understanding to *nature itself*, to the *nature of nature*, the nature that is of course also present in the other [person] and in me.

What that sharper understanding allows the knower to do comes next: "thus to free *wanting to possess* more and more from the mere appearance of possession, from *fabricated* possession, and therefore to purify the I – feeling from self – deception." The German word for *fabricated* or *made* is *erdichteten*, which can be understood literally as *poetized*. But the important thing here is this: *the chief progress* in morality is to gain a sharper understanding of what the genuine drive to possession really is: the chief progress in morality is coming *to know* what is true about the drive to possess; and that knowing *purifies* the I – feeling, freeing it from illusion or self – deception.

Nietzsche then describes what that sharper understanding of the true in the I and the other and nature may actually be, what the purifying of the I – feeling from self – deception would make possible: "Perhaps it ends in this: that instead of the I, we recognize the relatedness and the enemy – ness of things." The *perhaps* must be noticed. Nietzsche is looking ahead *wondering*, will this process end where it actually did end, in the *knowing* in which it actually ended? Attempting to purify the I from self – deception may *culminate in recognizing* that all things are *related* in *what they are*, related but in a relatedness that includes "enemy – ness." It may end in a unitary *kinship* and *enmity*, likeness and strife. Here we can hear the beginning of the will to power view.

The error of the I, its self – deception, would thus be its sense of itself as something wholly distinct from the other and the engine of progress in morality could not lie in the concept "Not I and I" because that very concept is deceptive. It masks what is fundamental; it obscures the common source of the Not I and the I that lies in the dynamic impersonal process that generates both the *I – feeling* and its sense of the other, its altruistic sense. That process is a relatedness and enemy – ness which extends beyond the I and not – I to the *true* in *nature* itself.

The entry on the I – feeling then moves to what seems to be a first consequence of recognizing the relatedness/enemy – ness of things: "To live not 'for the sake of the other' but 'for the sake of the true!'" This sentence is the first of a sequence of eleven sentences each ending with an exclamation mark, a punctuation mark that heightens the importance of each statement with a sense of resolve. This first such sentence states what *not* to live for, *the other*, what both Christian ethics and its successor modern ethics demand; it seems to herald a fundamental shift in what the social order is to live for—for the sake of the true.

Living "for the sake of the true," Nietzsche says, would "Reshape the I – feeling! Weaken the personal tendency! Habituate the eye to the reality of things!" These short sentences, each with its exclamation mark, serve to partially define what this move away from the dominant ethics would gain: a reshaping of the I – feeling would weaken the personal tendency, allow the impersonal to dominate, and habituate to the genuine reality of things that underlies I, you, and nature. The imperatives point to the felt need to *do* the things said: *reshape*, *weaken*, *habituate*. The short sentences continue in sentences that I omit; each has its exclamation mark and all lead up to a last sentence of the same kind: "There's something new to create: not I, not you, and not all!" The new that is not I, you, or all would see the "relatedness and enemy – ness of the things" in the I, you, and all. Beginning with seeing the I – feeling in a new way would lead to seeing *you* and the *whole* in a new way that marks progress in morality by aligning it with the true.

So the entry gives a sketch of the future stages in the *history of the I – feeling* leading up to this final stage of seeing that there is something new to create. Nietzsche, the solitary thinker anticipates those stages. He is the philosopher whose progress in thinking, whose understanding of those stages led him to see the need to create something new that is not I as I was, or you as you were, nor the all as it was. And if it is in fact a sketch for a book then the purpose of the book would be to lead its reader to think those stages of understanding and to see this need to create something new.

This is half the notebook entry. I want to say something general about that first half before moving to the second half. Despite what might seem to be the case in this statement about "progress in morality," Nietzsche is not a utopian: he doesn't dream of some imaginary perfect outcome at the end of the history of the I – feeling, as moderns typically do: some perfect end of history. Nietzsche explicitly and reasonably claims not to be a utopian, not a dreamer, and the notebook makes clear why he is right in that claim: he has understood the process that made humans what we are, the molding process of history and culture that is based on the real drives that constitute us. We humans are always already made by our incorporation of a particular balance of the drives, our incorporation of a particular cultural teaching on good and bad that organizes the drives, judges their goodness and badness, and puts them into an order of rank. That incorporated cultural balance is always a tension, always an uneasy hierarchical resolution of the fundamental impulses and drives. Humans will always be *the uneasy beings*, living the particular forms of suffering that our particular psychic and social orders of rank impose on us. The promise of Nietzsche's teaching is not some utopia; instead, its promise is that out of the nihilism and turmoil at the end of the moral period can come a better reorganization of the drives, better because it fosters stronger and more noble specimens of the human species, better because healthier for that reason. And that whole shift in moral acting is based on one thing only, a philosopher's better understanding of the passions and a better disposition toward them, a better understanding and appreciation of the I – feeling and what it shares with the other and with nature.

Now we can turn to the new paragraph that begins here and ends the entry in the notebook. It is marked at the start by an "NB"—those two letters that in Latin stand for "Note Well." And this NB marks an *extremely* important NB: "NB. No *possession* in the young to strive *to must have* (*müssen*) *or to want* (*wollen*)!: as well as no *prestige* for command over others—these two drives are *not to be developed* at all!" I translate Nietzsche's German here completely literally into awkward English, not very grammatical English because it is necessary to be exact. *Striving* (*erstreben*) is simply given, it's what we do as humans: striving is basic to the drives—drives always strive for *something*. The basic striving can be developed or encouraged to strive in *this* direction and not to strive in *that* direction. That is what *enculturation* does, what education or incorporation does: train to strive in some particular direction. That's what Nietzsche's NB is for: his *new program of incorporation* aims to create "something new"—to redirect *striving* in order to foster and encourage the new I – feeling, leading to the new feeling for the *you* and for the *all*. The most basic training of the young is now to be informed by Nietzsche's insight into the history of the *I – feeling*.

The first step in that new training is what *not* to train for: first, *not* for any *possession*—just what that can mean Nietzsche will explain next. And *not* for the *prestige* of command over others. The German word I translate as *prestige* is Ansehen, which means here *to be seen as something special*. No *singling out* of the I then, in *command* over others. This is a philosopher speaking, a solitary thinker who with the greatest intellectual and spiritual effort arrived at a new understanding of the I – feeling and now he speaks as an educator: how can his new understanding be trained into others? These *others* are not the few like him: those few he can tempt or teach to think their way out of the old understanding. Instead, he here speaks of the education or training from youth up in society as a whole: because *some* total view is always incorporated into all the young, Nietzsche looks to the new view that is to be incorporated.

After what *not* to train into the young, the paragraph marked by NB treats what the young *are* to be taught. Here we come to the most important matter. NB the positive content of the new education, what it aims to train in: "*Letting* us *be possessed* by the things (not by persons) and by the largest possible range of *true things.*"

Instead of teaching the young to strive to want possession and thereby develop in them the old I – feeling; and instead of teaching the young to feel prestige by commanding others, teach the young what the philosopher himself had learned in the first paragraph. *He* had learned to free himself from the false I – feeling of a separated, isolated, possessive I and had won the freedom to know the relatedness of all things, and that *knowing* led him to experience the desire to be taken over by the true things, the desire to let the true things *be the things they are* in him too. That experience in knowing by the philosophic knower—an experience that culminated in knowing what is to be will to power and nothing else—led him to his NB, his task to educate the young in the new stage in the history of the I – feeling that he is the first to experience, the experience in which the *I – feeling* is to let things be the true things they are, to want the natural things to be what they are in their continuous becoming and decaying, in their natural order of rank, and in all the other facets of their naturalness. The two separate paragraphs of this notebook entry show Nietzsche repeating what genuine philosophers experience: their insight into *what is* is followed by insight into the action necessary in their present on behalf of that insight. In the second part of this notebook entry therefore, Nietzsche moves to ministerial poetry, to the teaching that can structure the social order anew by being trained into the young. Here are the beginnings of the future content of Nietzsche's ministerial poetry. And it begins with incorporation, training in the new, true, I – feeling in its exposure to the true things.

Nietzsche's history of the I – feeling needs one final step. Having just spoken of being possessed "by the largest possible range of *true things*," he says: "What *grows* out of that can be anticipated: we become *farm land* for the things." Nietzsche can easily predict what grows out of being possessed by the true things because he knows what we humans are: *Ackerland* in German, *farmland*, *arable soil*, *productive earth* out of which particular "plants" naturally grow and flourish. It's easy to know what comes after being taken over by the true things because it *grows* out of us as plants grow out of fruitful soil. The last step in the history of the I – feeling describes these "plants" that grow naturally out of the fruitful soil of those who have incorporated the true things:

> *Images of existence* will grow out of us: and we would then be as this fruitfulness compels us to be: our inclinations/disinclinations are those of the farmland that would bring forth such fruit.

Letting the true things be what they are generates from our productive soil *new* images of existence that spring forth in accord with our inclinations and disinclinations as beings whose *natural* character is to be generative, productive of images, and whose *learned* incorporated character it now is to let what is be what it naturally is in its coming to be and passing away.

"*Images of existence.*" That is the last step in Nietzsche's history of the I – feeling. We human beings are, by nature, *making* beings, *creating* beings. Here we touch Plato again, who could make this point easily with Greek vocabulary. In his *Symposium* Plato used the word *poiein* which means in its most general sense *to make*: we human beings are the making beings; and in a particular sense *poiein* means to make poetry: we human beings are the poetizing beings. Humans are the making beings making poetry by nature: words and songs spring out of us by nature, generated by our fruitful soil. So here, where *images of existence* are the subject, Nietzsche and Plato unite in the fundamental way. Generated in us by our inclinations and disinclinations, by our *loves* and *hates*, are the images of existence that we live by, images that come to have authority for us as pictures or ideas of the worthy and the unworthy. The images of existence that humans generate become the standards of *how to be* and *what to be*, what to strive for and what to strive against. Nietzsche's history of the I – feeling anticipates new images of existence that accord with the true things now understood. Nietzsche ends where a philosopher always ends, with philosophy's *poetry* within which humans will dwell on the earth. The new images of existence conceptualize the earth as the natural home of humanity; biological science studies the interconnected web of life on the planet; political and social movements make ecology central to decision – making or, as Strauss words it, assign limits to the conquest of nature out of love of nature.

Nietzsche adds one last sentence: "These images of existence are *the most important* that there have been till now: they will rule over humanity."

Nietzsche ends where Plato ends: Philosophers come to know that humanity is ruled by images, images incorporated into the young and exercising their rule over us in our maturity. Knowing the rule of images and compelled by the interests of philosophy to rule, philosophers rule by legislating the images. Plato ruled through images of transcendence: the ideas, the reformed Homeric gods, the immortal soul, a rewarding and punishing

Lecture 6   Nietzsche's Philosophic Poetry   **289**

Hades. Plato's images succeeded because they serve deep drives that are part of the human make-up. Nietzsche's new images of existence aim to rule over humanity as Plato's images ruled over humanity but are now dying and deserve to die. Nietzsche's images have a promise of success because they too serve deep drives that are part of the human make-up, affirmative drives in conflict with the drives that Nietzsche saw as the drives that Plato's images of transcendence came to serve, negating drives of hatred and vengeance.

Nietzsche's new images of existence are what we have already seen as key elements of Nietzsche's philosophic poetry: the image of the *highest ideal*, what Plato called the Good that rules over all things in its transcendent fixity like the sun—a wholly imaginary sun in Plato, forever the same and giving existence to the ideas that are forever the same. Nietzsche's new highest ideal is not an eternal fixity but the eternal return of ever-changing life just as it is. And the image of particular *highest beings*, beings that "the god-creating instinct" generates in the making beings. In Plato, the highest beings tend toward the monotheism of the Good, while the platonic gods are moral judges who reward and punish us now and in the afterlife. Those now unbelievable and unworthy gods can be replaced by the god-making instinct of our fruitful farmland by new highest beings. (And I want to mention again the historic events in Western philosophy that lie behind Nietzsche's *blame* of Plato: platonism prepared the way for the rule of Christianity in Rome; that "platonism for the people" prepared the necessary modern war against it; but European modernity carried forward secular versions of Christian virtues, the modern ideals of the end of suffering and equality of rights; and it is those late consequences of platonism that Nietzsche acts to supplant—"letting be" in Nietzsche's sense carries no suggestion that unnatural ideals should be allowed to be what they are; his "letting be" knows the necessity of warfare on its behalf.) Nietzsche gave his images of the highest beings the already existing Greek names of Dionysos and Ariadne. These gods are not our judges; they don't punish or reward us; we don't have to bow down to them or beg them for favors. Instead, they are like us in being like what all life is, male and female, sexual, generative beings far superior to us in their manliness and womanliness. They are worthy of being emulated or copied by us, as far as we are able. We look up to them, they lift us up by being what they are. They are what we would most dearly love to be like.

Nietzsche's images of existence take these two particular forms of a highest ideal and of the highest beings. He has other images of existence, a new good and bad for instance capable of judging by natural, affirmative standards, but we can summarize them all as in the service of the fundamental passion of attraction, the passion of love.

That's Nietzsche's whole story, told early as the history of the I – feeling. His story ends in the human love of the earth as it naturally is and a love of the human as it naturally is, or as it can be, beyond the rule of images of existence that teach unnatural ideals wreaking vengeance on life as it is. His whole story ends in *ecology*, in knowledge of the interconnectedness of life on earth that generates the human imperative to be true to the earth. That's why it makes sense to me to see Nietzsche as the first comprehensive ecological philosopher. And that aspect of Nietzsche's philosophic poetry seems to me to be a *promising way* of entering Nietzsche, by seeing him as the founding thinker of an already popular movement that appeals to late modern people. That ecological movement, already strong in certain parts of the West, is bound to get stronger as the evidence becomes ever more undeniable that environmental disasters are caused by human – initiated climate change. Such movements, springing up from particular concerns, find their natural philosopher in Nietzsche.

This ecological aspect of Nietzsche' philosophic poetry has a kind of priority for me because of how it stands or could stand to the first two aspects: the new images of existence, finding their start in Nietzsche's view of the ecological interrelatedness of nature, life, and human life on this planet, could eventually lead to new gods true to the earth and a new highest ideal of desiring that the totality of earthly things eternally return just as they are.

Here at the end I want to recall what I said at the end of my lecture on "Socrates Becomes Socrates." In the *Symposium*, Plato showed Diotima leading Socrates to the insight that is the last stage of his philosophic education, insight into the deep structure of eros as ontology. After this deepest seeing, Plato has Diotima make the long speech on the ladder of loves; what happens at the peak, she says, is both a seeing and a doing. The one who has climbed to the peak *beholds* or sees perfect beauty and that one *gives birth* or engages in a kind of making or poetizing in the presence of the beautiful. The end of Nietzsche's "History of the I – feeling" gives his first ever completed version of Nietzsche becoming Nietzsche, and his wording is similar to Plato's. There too, it is a matter of beholding and engendering or of seeing and making. The seeing that is a letting the true beings take possession of us leads to the making that is the springing up of "new images of existence" that will rule humanity.

In both Plato and Nietzsche *philosophy* generates *philosophic poetry*.

And here at the very end we come back to Strauss. He said in one of his letters to Klein that when Plato is seen as an exoteric writer, the Plato of "the specifically Platonic philosophy" can be separated from the Plato "nearest my heart." Nearest Strauss's heart is the genuine Plato, the esoteric Plato who showed Socrates becoming Socrates, gaining his comprehensive understanding of being as becoming, as *eros*. And for me, that is the greatest service Strauss performs for us: he shows us how to read the philosophers and to discover in their exoteric teaching the esoteric understanding it implies, the understanding they intended for those few who resemble them by being driven by the passion to know. For however great Strauss is, and he is great, he is not great in the way Plato and Nietzsche are great: he is not himself a philosopher and philosophic poet as Plato and Nietzsche are. Strauss shows us how to read Plato and Nietzsche together and to understand what they share as philosophers. And it seems to me that Strauss even went beyond that revelation of kinship between these two philosophers: he expressed cautious encouragement of reading Nietzsche as the platonic political philosopher of our time. He gave many indications of this in his late Nietzsche essay; here are three of them.

One: Strauss chose to place this essay out of chronological order at the center of the book he called *Studies in Platonic Political Philosophy*, paired there with "Jerusalem and Athens." With this little device Strauss says: At the center of the study of platonic political philosophy in our time is the study of Jerusalem and Athens and Nietzsche.

Two: Within this essay, Strauss helps us understand just how Nietzsche is a platonic *philosopher*. Strauss says, Nietzsche's conclusion as a philosopher that to be is to be will to power "takes the place which *eros* ··· occupies in Plato's thought." Will to power and eros are ontological doctrines; Nietzsche, like Socrates, has expert knowledge of the erotic things. And Strauss helps us understand how Nietzsche is a platonic *political* philosopher; Nietzsche develops a philosophic poetry that Strauss calls "a relapse into Platonism" because this aspect of Platonism simply belongs to philosophy in its relation to the city/the human community.

Three: As the last sentence of this essay Strauss wrote: *Die vornehme Natur ersetzt die göttliche Natur.* He ended his Nietzsche essay as he ended *The City and Man*, with something he did not want to *pronounce* directly but wanted you to *question* and *wonder about*. For me, that wondering leads to this: "*Noble nature replaces divine nature*" means that nature as Nietzsche teaches it replaces nature as Plato taught it.

Strauss's Nietzsche essay, out of place at the center of his last book, stating that will to power takes the place that eros occupies, with its German last sentence leads me to a conclusion that restates the title of my lectures, "Strauss Plato Nietzsche": Strauss intimates that Nietzsche replaces Plato in our time.

Times change. Gods die. Changed times require of the new philosopher new images of existence. For me, that's the meaning of Nietzsche for our time.

图书在版编目（CIP）数据

哲学与哲学之诗：施特劳斯、柏拉图、尼采／（加）朗佩特（Laurence Lampert）著；刘旭，吴一笛译．－－北京：华夏出版社有限公司，2021.7
（西方传统：经典与解释）
ISBN 978－7－5222－0096－5

Ⅰ.①哲… Ⅱ.①朗… ②刘… ③吴… Ⅲ.①施特劳斯（Strauss，Leo 1899－1973）－哲学思想－研究②柏拉图（Platon 前427－前347）－哲学思想－研究③尼采（Nietzsche，Friedrich Wilhelm 1844－1900）－哲学思想－研究 Ⅳ.①B712.59②B502.232③B516.47

中国版本图书馆CIP数据核字（2020）第262185号

哲学与哲学之诗：施特劳斯、柏拉图、尼采

作　　者	［加］朗佩特
译　　者	刘　旭　吴一笛
责任编辑	马涛红
特约编辑	朱绿和
责任印制	刘　洋
出版发行	华夏出版社有限公司
经　　销	新华书店
印　　刷	北京汇林印务有限公司
装　　订	北京汇林印务有限公司
版　　次	2021年7月北京第1版 2021年7月北京第1次印刷
开　　本	880×1230　1/32
印　　张	9.875
字　　数	291千字
定　　价	75.00元

华夏出版社有限公司 　地址：北京市东直门外香河园北里4号　邮编：100028
网址：www.hxph.com.cn　电话：（010）64663331（转）
若发现本版图书有印装质量问题，请与我社营销中心联系调换。

西方传统：经典与解释
Classici et Commentarii
HERMES
刘小枫◎主编

古今丛编

克尔凯郭尔　[美]江思图 著
货币哲学　[德]西美尔 著
孟德斯鸠的自由主义哲学　[美]潘戈 著
莫尔及其乌托邦　[德]考茨基 著
试论古今革命　[法]夏多布里昂 著
但丁：皈依的诗学　[美]弗里切罗 著
在西方的目光下　[英]康拉德 著
大学与博雅教育　董成龙 编
探究哲学与信仰　[美]郝岚 著
民主的本性　[法]马南 著
梅尔维尔的政治哲学　李小均 编/译
席勒美学的哲学背景　[美]维塞尔 著
果戈里与鬼　[俄]梅列日科夫斯基 著
自传性反思　[美]沃格林 著
黑格尔与普世秩序　[美]希克斯 等著
新的方式与制度　[美]曼斯菲尔德 著
科耶夫的新拉丁帝国　[法]科耶夫 等著
《利维坦》附录　[英]霍布斯 著
或此或彼（上、下）　[丹麦]基尔克果 著
海德格尔式的现代神学　刘小枫 选编
双重束缚　[法]基拉尔 著
古今之争中的核心问题　[德]迈尔 著
论永恒的智慧　[德]苏索 著
宗教经验种种　[美]詹姆斯 著
尼采反卢梭　[美]凯斯·安塞尔-皮尔逊 著
舍勒思想评述　[美]弗林斯 著
诗与哲学之争　[美]罗森 著
神圣与世俗　[罗]伊利亚德 著
但丁的圣约书　[美]霍金斯 著

古典学丛编

赫西俄德的宇宙　[美]珍妮·施特劳斯·克莱 著
论王政　[古罗马]金嘴狄翁 著
论希罗多德　[古罗马]卢里叶 著
探究希腊人的灵魂　[美]戴维斯 著
尤利安文选　马勇 编/译
论月面　[古罗马]普鲁塔克 著
雅典谐剧与逻各斯　[美]奥里根 著
菜园哲人伊壁鸠鲁　罗晓颖 选编
《劳作与时日》笺释　吴雅凌 撰
希腊古风时期的真理大师　[法]德蒂安 著
古罗马的教育　[英]葛怀恩 著
古典学与现代性　刘小枫 编
表演文化与雅典民主政制
[英]戈尔德希尔、奥斯本 编
西方古典文献学发凡　刘小枫 编
古典语文学常谈　[德]克拉夫特 著
古希腊文学常谈　[英]多佛 等著
撒路斯特与政治史学　刘小枫 编
希罗多德的王霸之辨　吴小锋 编/译
第二代智术师　[英]安德森 著
英雄诗系笺释　[古希腊]荷马 著
统治的热望　[美]福特 著
论埃及神学与哲学　[古希腊]普鲁塔克 著
凯撒的剑与笔　李世祥 编/译
伊壁鸠鲁主义的政治哲学
[意]詹姆斯·尼古拉斯 著
修昔底德笔下的人性　[美]欧文 著
修昔底德笔下的演说　[美]斯塔特 著
古希腊政治理论　[美]格雷纳 著
神谱笺释　吴雅凌 撰
赫西俄德：神话之艺
[法]居代·德拉孔波 编
赫拉克勒斯之盾笺释　罗逍然 译笺
《埃涅阿斯纪》章义　王承教 选编
维吉尔的帝国　[美]阿德勒 著
塔西佗的政治史学　曾维术 编

古希腊诗歌丛编
古希腊早期诉歌诗人 [英]鲍勒 著
诗歌与城邦 [美]费拉格、纳吉 主编
阿尔戈英雄纪（上、下）
[古希腊]阿波罗尼俄斯 著
俄耳甫斯教祷歌 吴雅凌 编译
俄耳甫斯教辑语 吴雅凌 编译

古希腊肃剧注疏集
希腊肃剧与政治哲学 [美]阿伦斯多夫 著

古希腊礼法研究
宙斯的正义 [英]劳埃德-琼斯 著
希腊人的正义观 [英]哈夫洛克 著

廊下派集
剑桥廊下派指南 [加]英伍德 编
廊下派的苏格拉底 程志敏 徐健 选编
廊下派的神和宇宙 [墨]里卡多·萨勒斯 编
廊下派的城邦观 [英]斯科菲尔德 著

希伯莱圣经历代注疏
希腊化世界中的犹太人 [英]威廉逊 著
第一亚当和第二亚当 [德]朋霍费尔 著

新约历代经解
属灵的寓意 [古罗马]俄里根 著

基督教与古典传统
保罗与马克安 [德]文森 著
加尔文与现代政治的基础 [美]汉考克 著
无执之道 [德]文森 著
恐惧与战栗 [丹麦]基尔克果 著
托尔斯泰与陀思妥耶夫斯基
[俄]梅列日科夫斯基 著
论宗教大法官的传说 [俄]罗赞诺夫 著
海德格尔与有限性思想（重订版）
刘小枫 选编
上帝国的信息 [德]拉加茨 著
基督教理论与现代 [德]特洛尔奇 著
亚历山大的克雷芒 [意]塞尔瓦托·利拉 著
中世纪的心灵之旅 [意]圣·波纳文图拉 著

德意志古典传统丛编
论荷尔德林 [德]沃尔夫冈·宾德尔 著
彭忒西勒亚 [德]克莱斯特 著
穆佐书简 [奥]里尔克 著
纪念苏格拉底——哈曼文选 刘新利 选编
夜颂中的革命和宗教 [德]诺瓦利斯 著
大革命与诗化小说 [德]诺瓦利斯 著
黑格尔的观念论 [美]皮平 著
浪漫派风格——施勒格尔批评文集 [德]施勒格尔 著

美国宪政与古典传统
美国1787年宪法讲疏 [美]阿纳斯塔普罗 著

启蒙研究丛编
浪漫的律令 [美]拜泽尔 著
现实与理性 [法]科维纲 著
论古人的智慧 [英]培根 著
托兰德与激进启蒙 刘小枫 编
图书馆里的古今之战 [英]斯威夫特 著

政治史学丛编
克服历史主义 [德]特洛尔奇 等著
胡克与英国保守主义 姚啸宇 编
古希腊传记的嬗变 [意]莫米利亚诺 著
伊丽莎白时代的世界图景 [英]蒂利亚德 著
西方古代的天下观 刘小枫 编
从普遍历史到历史主义 刘小枫 编
自然科学史与玫瑰 [法]雷比瑟 著

地缘政治学丛编
克劳塞维茨之谜 [英]赫伯格-罗特 著
太平洋地缘政治学 [德]卡尔·豪斯霍弗 著

荷马注疏集
不为人知的奥德修斯 [美]诺特维克 著
模仿荷马 [美]丹尼斯·麦克唐纳 著

品达注疏集
幽暗的诱惑 [美]汉密尔顿 著

欧里庇得斯集
自由与僭越 罗峰 编译

阿里斯托芬集
《阿卡奈人》笺释 [古希腊]阿里斯托芬 著

色诺芬注疏集
居鲁士的教育 [古希腊]色诺芬 著
色诺芬的《会饮》 [古希腊]色诺芬 著

柏拉图注疏集
挑战戈尔戈 李致远 选编
论柏拉图《高尔吉亚》的统一性 [美]斯托弗 著
立法与德性——柏拉图《法义》发微 林志猛 编
柏拉图的灵魂学 [加]罗宾逊 著
柏拉图书简 彭磊 译注
克力同章句 程志敏 郑兴凤 撰
哲学的奥德赛——《王制》引论 [美]郝兰 著
爱欲与启蒙的迷醉 [美]贝尔格 著
为哲学的写作技艺一辩 [美]伯格 著
柏拉图式的迷宫——《斐多》义疏 [美]伯格 著
哲学如何成为苏格拉底式的 [美]朗佩特 著
苏格拉底与希琵阿斯 王江涛 编译
理想国 [古希腊]柏拉图 著
谁来教育老师 刘小枫 编
立法者的神学 林志猛 编
柏拉图对话中的神 [法]薇依 著
尼庇诺米斯 [古希腊]柏拉图 著
智慧与幸福 程志敏 选编
论柏拉图对话 [德]施莱尔马赫 著
柏拉图《美诺》疏证 [美]克莱因 著
政治哲学的悖论 [美]郝岚 著
神话诗人柏拉图 张文涛 选编
阿尔喀比亚德 [古希腊]柏拉图 著
叙拉古的雅典异乡人 彭磊 选编
阿威罗伊论《王制》 [阿拉伯]阿威罗伊 著
《王制》要义 刘小枫 选编
柏拉图的《会饮》 [古希腊]柏拉图 等著
苏格拉底的申辩(修订版) [古希腊]柏拉图 著
苏格拉底与政治共同体 [美]尼柯尔斯 著

政制与美德——柏拉图《法义》疏解 [美]潘戈 著
《法义》导读 [法]卡斯代尔·布舒奇 著
论真理的本质 [德]海德格尔 著
哲人的无知 [德]费勃 著
米诺斯 [古希腊]柏拉图 著
情敌 [古希腊]柏拉图 著

亚里士多德注疏集
《诗术》译笺与通绎 陈明珠 撰
亚里士多德《政治学》中的教诲 [美]潘戈 著
品格的技艺 [美]加佛 著
亚里士多德哲学的基本概念 [德]海德格尔 著
《政治学》疏证 [意]托马斯·阿奎那 著
尼各马可伦理学义疏 [美]伯格 著
哲学之诗 [美]戴维斯 著
对亚里士多德的现象学解释 [德]海德格尔 著
城邦与自然——亚里士多德与现代性 刘小枫 编
论诗术中篇义疏 [阿拉伯]阿威罗伊 著
哲学的政治 [美]戴维斯 著

普鲁塔克集
普鲁塔克的《对比列传》 [英]达夫 著
普鲁塔克的实践伦理学 [比利时]胡芙 著

阿尔法拉比集
政治制度与政治箴言 阿尔法拉比 著

马基雅维利集
君主及其战争技艺 娄林 选编

莎士比亚绎读
莎士比亚的政治智慧 [美]伯恩斯 著
脱节的时代 [匈]阿格尼斯·赫勒 著
莎士比亚的历史剧 [英]蒂利亚德 著
莎士比亚戏剧与政治哲学 彭磊 选编
莎士比亚的政治盛典 [美]阿鲁里斯/苏利文 编
丹麦王子与马基雅维利 罗峰 选编

洛克集
上帝、洛克与平等 [美]沃尔德伦 著

卢梭集

- 论哲学生活的幸福 [德]迈尔 著
- 致博蒙书 [法]卢梭 著
- 政治制度论 [法]卢梭 著
- 哲学的自传 [美]戴维斯 著
- 文学与道德杂篇 [法]卢梭 著
- 设计论证 [美]吉尔丁 著
- 卢梭的自然状态 [美]普拉特纳 等著
- 卢梭的榜样人生 [美]凯利 著

莱辛注疏集

- 汉堡剧评 [德]莱辛 著
- 关于悲剧的通信 [德]莱辛 著
- 《智者纳坦》（研究版） [德]莱辛 等著
- 启蒙运动的内在问题 [美]维塞尔 著
- 莱辛剧作七种 [德]莱辛 著
- 历史与启示——莱辛神学文选 [德]莱辛 著
- 论人类的教育 [德]莱辛 著

尼采注疏集

- 何为尼采的扎拉图斯特拉 [德]迈尔 著
- 尼采引论 [德]施特格迈尔 著
- 尼采与基督教 刘小枫 编
- 尼采眼中的苏格拉底 [美]丹豪瑟 著
- 尼采的使命 [美]朗佩特 著
- 尼采与现时代 [美]朗佩特 著
- 动物与超人之间的绳索 [德]A.彼珀 著

施特劳斯集

- 苏格拉底与阿里斯托芬
- 论僭政（重订本） [美]施特劳斯 [法]科耶夫 著
- 苏格拉底问题与现代性（增订本）
- 犹太哲人与启蒙（增订本）
- 霍布斯的宗教批判
- 斯宾诺莎的宗教批判
- 门德尔松与莱辛
- 哲学与律法——论迈蒙尼德及其先驱
- 迫害与写作艺术
- 柏拉图式政治哲学研究
- 论柏拉图的《会饮》
- 柏拉图《法义》的论辩与情节
- 什么是政治哲学
- 古典政治理性主义的重生（重订本）
- 回归古典政治哲学——施特劳斯通信集

***

- 施特劳斯的持久重要性 [美]朗佩特 著
- 论源初遗忘 [美]维克利 著
- 政治哲学与启示宗教的挑战 [德]迈尔 著
- 阅读施特劳斯 [美]斯密什 著
- 施特劳斯与流亡政治学 [美]谢帕德 著
- 隐匿的对话 [德]迈尔 著
- 驯服欲望 [法]科耶夫 等著

施米特集

- 宪法专政 [美]罗斯托 著
- 施米特对自由主义的批判 [美]约翰·麦考米克 著

伯纳德特集

- 古典诗学之路（第二版） [美]伯格 编
- 弓与琴（重订本） [美]伯纳德特 著
- 神圣的罪业 [美]伯纳德特 著

布鲁姆集

- 巨人与侏儒（1960-1990）
- 人应该如何生活——柏拉图《王制》释义
- 爱的设计——卢梭与浪漫派
- 爱的戏剧——莎士比亚与自然
- 爱的阶梯——柏拉图的《会饮》
- 伊索克拉底的政治哲学

沃格林集

- 自传体反思录 [美]沃格林 著

大学素质教育读本

- 古典诗文绎读 西学卷·古代编（上、下）
- 古典诗文绎读 西学卷·现代编（上、下）

柏拉图读本（刘小枫 主编）

- 吕西斯 贺方婴 译
- 苏格拉底的申辩 程志敏 译

中国传统：经典与解释
Classici et Commentarii
家亚看鱼
刘小枫 陈少明 ◎ 主编

知圣篇 / 廖平 著
《孔丛子》训读及研究 / 雷欣翰 撰
论语说义 / [清]宋翔凤 撰
周易古经注解考辨 / 李炳海 著
图象几表 / [明]方以智 编
浮山文集 / [明]方以智 著
药地炮庄 / [明]方以智 著
药地炮庄笺释·总论篇 / [明]方以智 著
青原志略 / [明]方以智 编
冬灰录 / [明]方以智 著
冬炼三时传旧火 / 邢益海 编
《毛诗》郑王比义发微 / 史应勇 著
宋人经筵诗讲义四种 / [宋]张纲 等撰
道德真经取善集 / [金]李霖 编撰
道德真经藏室纂微篇 / [宋]陈景元 撰
道德真经四子古道集解 / [金]寇才质 撰
皇清经解提要 / [清]沈豫 撰
经学通论 / [清]皮锡瑞 著
松阳讲义 / [清]陆陇其 著
起凤书院答问 / [清]姚永朴 撰
周礼疑义辨证 / 陈衍 撰
《铎书》校注 / 孙尚扬 肖清和 等校注
韩愈志 / 钱基博 著
论语辑释 / 陈大齐 著
《庄子·天下篇》注疏四种 / 张丰乾 编
荀子的辩说 / 陈文洁 著
古学经子 / 王锦民 著
经学以自治 / 刘少虎 著
从公羊学论《春秋》的性质 / 阮芝生 撰

刘小枫集
城邦人的自由向往
民主与政治德性
昭告幽微
以美为鉴
古典学与古今之争 [增订本]
这一代人的怕和爱 [第三版]
沉重的肉身 [珍藏版]
圣灵降临的叙事 [增订本]
罪与欠
儒教与民族国家
拣尽寒枝
施特劳斯的路标
重启古典诗学
设计共和
现代人及其敌人
海德格尔与中国
共和与经纶
现代性与现代中国
现代性社会理论绪论
诗化哲学 [重订本]
拯救与逍遥 [修订本]
走向十字架上的真
西学断章

编修 [博雅读本]
凯若斯：古希腊语文读本 [全二册]
古希腊语文学述要
雅努斯：古典拉丁语文读本
古典拉丁语文学述要
危微精一：政治法学原理九讲
琴瑟友之：钢琴与古典乐色十讲

译著
普罗塔戈拉（详注本）
柏拉图四书

经典与解释辑刊

1. 柏拉图的哲学戏剧
2. 经典与解释的张力
3. 康德与启蒙
4. 荷尔德林的新神话
5. 古典传统与自由教育
6. 卢梭的苏格拉底主义
7. 赫尔墨斯的计谋
8. 苏格拉底问题
9. 美德可教吗
10. 马基雅维利的喜剧
11. 回想托克维尔
12. 阅读的德性
13. 色诺芬的品味
14. 政治哲学中的摩西
15. 诗学解诂
16. 柏拉图的真伪
17. 修昔底德的春秋笔法
18. 血气与政治
19. 索福克勒斯与雅典启蒙
20. 犹太教中的柏拉图门徒
21. 莎士比亚笔下的王者
22. 政治哲学中的莎士比亚
23. 政治生活的限度与满足
24. 雅典民主的谐剧
25. 维柯与古今之争
26. 霍布斯的修辞
27. 埃斯库罗斯的神义论
28. 施莱尔马赫的柏拉图
29. 奥林匹亚的荣耀
30. 笛卡尔的精灵
31. 柏拉图与天人政治
32. 海德格尔的政治时刻
33. 荷马笔下的伦理
34. 格劳秀斯与国际正义
35. 西塞罗的苏格拉底
36. 基尔克果的苏格拉底
37. 《理想国》的内与外
38. 诗艺与政治
39. 律法与政治哲学
40. 古今之间的但丁
41. 拉伯雷与赫尔墨斯秘学
42. 柏拉图与古典乐教
43. 孟德斯鸠论政制衰败
44. 博丹论主权
45. 道伯与比较古典学
46. 伊索寓言中的伦理
47. 斯威夫特与启蒙
48. 赫西俄德的世界
49. 洛克的自然法辩难
50. 斯宾格勒与西方的没落
51. 地缘政治学的历史片段
52. 施米特论战争与政治
53. 普鲁塔克与罗马政治
54. 罗马的建国叙述
55. 亚历山大与西方的大一统
56. 马西利乌斯的帝国
57. 全球化在东亚的开端
58. 弥尔顿与现代政治